- def of lscpe incl. "cultural" ref. p.6
- what is "locational analysis" p.10
- larger quote con abstract terms to evaluate a la Sitten - pro classification leading to theory. p.16
  - perception of lscpe not select an universally agreed emotional response as does other sights - SS? p.27
- "Explanation" of XVIIIc Eng lscpe movement p.32-39
- prospect - refuge theory of aethetic - p.73 - the desire to see without being seen - basic says J.A., definitions p.85 "hide and seek aesthetics" p.161.
- panorama vs vista vs peep hole 87-89
- straight lined forest edge is not "satisfying" because it is forbidding & seems less accessable to enter the forest & use it as a "refuge" p.105
- farmstead in shelter belt = strong "refuge" symb p.123 good lsp design involves balance of "refuge & prospect symb"
- "Edge of the woods"
- prospect - refuge theory result of evolution from prehistoric utilitarian need. - the need to see without being seen - p.169, 172
- recreation types as p/R theory in action skiing, deer hunting golf - p.177-191.
- Says Nottle & Cap Brown et all have same aethestic basis p.226.

*The Experience
of Landscape*

# The Experience of Landscape

JAY APPLETON

**JOHN WILEY & SONS**
London · New York · Sydney · Toronto

*Library of Congress Cataloging in Publication Data:*

Appleton, Jay.
The experience of landscape.

Bibliography: p.
1. Landscape in art.   I. Title.
N8213.A66      701      73–20899
ISBN 0 471 03256 5

Printed in Great Britain by William Clowes & Sons, Limited
London, Beccles and Colchester

*To Iris*

In gratitude
for the first thirty years

# Preface

One of the purposes of a preface is to warn the reader of the task he is letting himself in for if he embarks on reading the book which follows. I confess I should find it easier in this case to tell him what sort of a book this is not rather than what it is. It is not, for instance, a geography book, although it is true that, as a Reader in Geography in the University of Hull, I earn my living by teaching that subject. It is not a textbook, if by that one means a concise exposition of a field of study, prepared from a comprehensive reading of the relevant literature, in order to enable a student to acquire an understanding of it. But I think the prospective reader is entitled to expect at least a hint about what the book *is*, and therefore I will do my best to explain.

The book begins with the question 'What do we like about landscape and why do we like it?' and it is the concern of the first two chapters to take stock, very briefly, of some of the problems which inevitably follow from the nature of the question, and to summarize, even more briefly, some of the enquiries which have so far been made within this field and within those fields which most immediately impinge on it. These two chapters contain little if any information which has not been published elsewhere, but they bring together a number of ideas drawn from widely differing disciplines and they take the reader to the starting-point of the main argument. In particular, they establish the absence of any generally accepted theoretical basis for the aesthetics of landscape and they underline the lack of any adequate machinery for linking the predominantly abstract generalizations of the philosophers with the *details* of actual landscapes as observed by the ordinary traveller or studied more deeply by the field scientists.

Chapter 3 makes an excursion at the most elementary level into the field of animal behaviour in an effort to recover some clues from those relationships which we can observe between animals and their perceived environments. These clues lead to two hypotheses. The first, expressed in very general terms, seeks to relate pleasurable sensations in the experience of landscape to environmental conditions favourable to biological survival. This we call 'habitat theory'. It tells us little which has not already been fully discussed in print, but it is essential to the understanding of the second hypothesis which we call 'prospect–refuge theory' and which opens the way to the analysis of landscapes in terms of their strategic appraisal as potential habitats.

The bridge which spans the gap between the requirements necessary for biological survival and the pleasurable sensations derived from the contemplation of landscape is to be sought in symbolism. In Chapter 4 a system of symbolism is set up and in Chapter 5 some of its implications are worked out in relation to the dominant characteristics of landscape types.

viii

This view of landscape is based on the assumption that our aesthetic reactions to it are in part inborn, and that they can only be brought into operation if we provide them with sign-symbols of a kind which can be spontaneously apprehended by a mechanism attuned to the natural environment. This does not mean that we cannot admire and enjoy landscapes which have been altered by man, but that there are limits to the manner in which, and the extent to which, we can replace the natural by the artificial without destroying the aesthetic experience. But the behaviour-mechanisms which give rise to these sensations are only *in part* inborn. Their potential must be developed in each individual by practice and by environmental experience. It follows that, if he is to experience landscape aesthetically, an observer must seek to re-create something of that primitive relationship which links a creature with its habitat. He must become 'involved' and Chapter 6 discusses some of the implications of this involvement.

A theory of landscape aesthetics which places the principal emphasis on such matters as experience, behaviour and strategic relationships rather than on form, order, pattern, etc., must be valid for any experience of landscape, irrespective of the medium through which that experience is achieved. Nevertheless, each medium does have its own potentialities and its own limitations and Chapter 7 examines the operation of prospect–refuge theory in, for instance, architecture, landscape design, painting, photography and literature.

A common stumbling-block which lies in the path of all aestheticians is the problem of 'taste'. Broadly speaking, there is a range of opinion whose poles are represented by two schools of thought, the one arguing that taste is based on fixed principles, the other that it is not. In terms of landscape this finds expression, for instance, in the argument between those who believe in absolute standards of aesthetic excellence deriving from nature, which it is the business of the painters to discover, and those who think that the beauty which people find in nature is simply what the painters have taught them to believe is beautiful. The wide variation which can be observed in people's preferences for landscape could be particularly embarrassing to a theory which postulates that all such preferences derive from the same behavioural laws. It is this sort of problem which forms the subject of Chapter 8.

I have said that this is not a geography book, but in Chapter 9 I have allowed myself to explore some of the implications of prospect–refuge theory within this field in so far as different places seem to be endowed with different aesthetic potential, and in Chapter 10 I have taken a backward glance to see how the theory fits in to the main stream of landscape aesthetics.

To find out more about the purpose of this book the reader must, I fear, read it for himself. He will find in Chapter 1 some further explanation of how it came to be written by an amateur. Here let me say simply that in the second half of the twentieth century it could hardly be written by anyone else. There are, of course, professionals who study landscape painting, landscape architecture, landscape in literature, landscape as the product of physical processes or as the legacy of past societies and of the economic use they have made of their environment. But these scholars are professionals only within their own fields. To find an aesthetic philosophy which can not only be sustained theoretically in terms of generalizations and abstract concepts but can also be applied *practically* in the comparative study of real landscapes, we must invade many fields and, as soon as we stray from the discipline we profess, we become amateurs in somebody else's territory.

Even here the amateur may have one advantage over the professional. Extreme familiarity with any field of study tends to condition the mind in such a way that it places newly acquired information into an established framework of conceptual thought. It is my hope that the specialists will find the ideas set out in this book worthy of being tested eventually in terms of their own disciplines. My purpose here is simply to establish these ideas at a *prima facie* level. I seek to prove nothing—merely to suggest. In doing this I think it is a positive advantage not to be too much of a specialist. All disciplines are traversed by well-worn paths, which those who are familiar with them tend to follow. The explorer is more likely to make discoveries if his travels are not so rigidly channelled along established tracks, and the amateur has a sporting chance of wandering around a little longer before he finds himself slotted into the tramlines.

*Cottingham, Yorkshire* JAY APPLETON

# Acknowledgments

I have had to draw so heavily on the advice of colleagues that I am not able to record more than a few of the debts I owe. I am grateful to Professor H. R. Wilkinson of the University of Hull for making available to me facilities in the Department of Geography, to Mrs Jacquie Burgess, Miss Vida Chapman, Dr. J. R. Clammer, Dr. Ivan Hall, Mrs. Elisabeth Hall, Dr. J. A. Michie, Dr. Alistair F. Pitty, Dr. A. B. Rostron, Mr. J. W. F. Somerville and Dr. J. H. Sudd for listening with patience to my ideas and providing me with useful information and suggestions, to Mr. R. R. Dean, Mr. J. B. Fisher and Mr. S. Moran for advice and help in the preparation of illustrative matter, to Mr. Anthony I. Key who drew Figure 45, and to Mr. Keith R. Scurr who drew Figures 8, 10, 33, 48 and 49.

I should like to thank my numerous correspondents for their help and I trust they will forgive me if I do not name them. I must, however, mention Denis Cosgrove of Oxford, whose criticism of my first draft has been the biggest single factor in enabling me to improve on it. I must also thank Dr. David A. Lanegran, of Macalester College, St. Paul, Minnesota, for bringing to my attention the work of A. E. Rölvaag, which I have drawn on in Chapter 5 and with which I was previously unfamiliar. I must also thank the Editor of *Country Life* for help in providing photographs for Figure 36, and Geoffrey Broadbent and Laurie Fricker of Portsmouth Polytechnic for helpful comments on my manuscript.

I owe debts also of particular kinds to Dr. Malcolm Easton, Reader in the History of Art in the University of Hull, who first awakened in me a serious interest in his subject, and to Jill Williams and Jane Gear, who taught me the practical rudiments of landscape painting. I am grateful to my wife for help in compiling the manuscript, and to her and my sons, Richard, Charles and Mark, for the contributions they have made to this book, sometimes unwittingly, by allowing their aesthetic reactions to landscape to be subjected to examination on innumerable occasions and for helping in many other ways. With a less tolerant family I think it unlikely that I should have brought the project to fruition.

Where authors, private owners, publishers or institutions have kindly granted permission for me to reproduce illustrative material, acknowledgment is made in the legend of the figure concerned. In addition the following have kindly granted me permission to quote from published works:

W. & R. Chambers, Ltd., from *Habits & Characteristics of British Wild Animals* by H. Mortimer Batten;

Gerald Duckworth & Co. Ltd. and Elizabeth Goudge, from *Towers in the Mist* by Elizabeth Goudge;

W. H. Freeman & Co., from 'The Language of Birds' (October 1956) by W. H. Thorpe and 'The Behaviour of Lovebirds' (January 1962) by William

# Contents

# CHAPTER 1

# The Problem

## The Problem Introduced

What is it that we like about landscape, and why do we like it? It would be truer to say that this book pursues some of the implications of these questions than that it aspires to answer them. It may be, however, that in the course of this pursuit we shall advance a few steps along the path of comprehension of a subject which is as old as human experience.

Some of the earliest written accounts of man's exploits make reference to the environments within which they take place. By the time of Homer the association between story and landscape is already well established. By the time of Virgil and Horace we can identify types of landscape which are repetitively invoked to arouse sensations of pleasure or of fear. There is a timeless satisfaction to be found in Virgil's word pictures of the Campagna, that beneficent landscape which yielded to the Italians of two thousand years ago their daily bread.

'Hour by hour the plains shall grow more yellow with ripening corn, the blushing grape shall hang on the uncouth bramble, and the sturdy oaks drip with honey-dew.' (Virgil, *Eclogue IV*, lines 28–30, see Jackson, 1908)

If this friendly country deceives us into the belief that, in that golden age, man had no need to wrest a hard-won living from a treacherous environment, how willingly are we deceived!

The Greek and Roman poets felt a powerful attraction to nature, but to a nature whose subjection was symbolized in the tamed landscape of garden, field and vineyard or the bucolic pastures of Arcadia. Of her wilder manifestations they remained afraid.

'They shrank with dread or hatred from all the ruggedness of lower nature—from the wrinkled forest bark, the jagged hill-crest, and the irregular, inorganic storm of the sky; looking to these for the most part as adverse powers, and taking pleasure only in such portions of the lower world as were at once conducive to the rest and health of the human frame and in harmony with the laws of gentler beauty. Thus, as far as I recollect, without a single exception, every Homeric landscape, intended to be beautiful, is composed of a fountain, a meadow, and a shady grove . . .' (Ruskin, *Modern Painters*, see Cook and Wedderburn, 1903–1912, vol. V, p. 234)

This is all very well, but what are these 'laws of gentler beauty' and by whose authority are they determined? And when Phyllis and Corydon were at pains to prevent their sheep from straying into the untamed world of nature which lay around their grazing grounds, how can we be sure that the glances which they cast from time to time into the encircling woods were entirely devoid of aesthetic enjoyment, whatever that may mean?

Even if we can answer these questions to our satisfaction our problems have only just begun. We have still to account for the fact that thousands today incur much trouble and expense in seeking out those very types of landscape which the ancients shunned. We should not, of course, be pursuing these questions for the first time; we shall find a host of footsteps to be followed. Whether these footsteps would reveal a helpful pattern is another matter. But even if we find them leading in many diverse directions—even if they seem to go round in circles, like those of the Woozle which guided Pooh and Piglet so fruitlessly round the spinney—at least we ought to have a look at them to see what they have to teach us before we begin blazing our own independent trail. But where to find them? Here is our next problem.

Landscape is a kind of backcloth to the whole stage of human activity. Consequently we find it entering into the experience of many kinds of observer as it is encountered in many kinds of context. For some the chief interest lies in the explanation and interpretation of the landscape itself, natural or man-made; for others in the way we look at it. For some it is more meaningful when perceived through the medium of painting; for others it must be experienced directly. For some it is a proper subject for scientific study; for others it belongs to the arts and this, perhaps, has proved one of the most difficult stumbling-blocks of all.

Even as late as the eighteenth, or at least the seventeenth century, the distinction between the arts and the sciences was ill-defined, if recognized at all. It is sometimes suggested that the foundation of the Royal Society in 1660 is a mile-stone which marks the formal recognition of science as something different from the arts. One could find evidence to suggest that, even since then, the dichotomy has been known to be false, but far more evidence that it has been tacitly accepted in practice as fundamental to academic research. Unfortunately this dichotomy lies at the root of many of our problems in enquiring into the basis of the attraction which landscape exercises over people in so many different ways. Any approach made through the arts is likely to arouse the deepest suspicions of the scientists. It will be 'woolly', imprecise, subjective, in short indigestible in the scientist's system. On the other hand, the artist or man of letters may be equally contemptuous of the scientific approach which, he will say, involves merely a superficial examination of nature and natural processes from which the aesthetic considerations necessary to give them deeper meaning have been excluded by the scientist's terms of reference.

There is, alas, a grain of truth in this, but the dichotomy is one which both sides have set up to protect themselves against the intrusion of ideas that their own systems are not competent to handle. It is a common barrier maintained by mutual consent and neither side is more to blame than the other. Unfortunately, the longer barriers remain in position, the more we tend to adjust ourselves towards them and thereby to establish them.

If we are to obtain an overall view of landscape and our experience of it, some kind of rapprochement between the arts and the sciences is essential. J. K. Wright, in a presidential address to the Association of American Geographers said:

'Unfortunately this deep-seated distrust of our artistic and poetic impulses too often causes us to repress them and cover them over with incrustations of prosaic matter . . .' (Wright, 1947, p. 7)

and from the viewpoint of a landscape architect Brenda Colvin has put it very directly:

'. . . the study of landscape design must now bridge the chasm between art and science. It is becoming ever more necessary for science and art to come to terms—their isolation and separate development is a danger to society. In spite of the continuing trend towards specialization, leaders in both fields are aware of the need for wider understanding, and perhaps they can come together most easily through the mutual appreciation of landscape.' (Colvin, 1970, p. xxii)·

One of the principal reasons why both sides are reluctant to come together in a common venture is the recognition that the arts and the sciences each have their own modus operandi, and that any attempt to mix them may result in the worst of both worlds. One can indeed conjure up a picture of the most prodigious chaos resulting from such a union if it is not accompanied by a recognition that every method, not only as between the arts and the sciences, but even within each of them, has its limitations and can only be employed to achieve an end which is consistent with itself.

We would do well also to remember that this building of bridges between the arts and the sciences cannot be achieved by pretending that there are no divisions within the whole field of knowledge. Whatever the virtues of 'breadth' in academic learning, we *do* live in a world of specialists, and we have to recognize that they are masters in their own chosen spheres. To take an analogy from medicine, what is needed is a kind of general practitioner who can refer to the specialist for advice on a particular problem without, however, abandoning the overall view which the specialist, from his particular viewpoint, does not have. The metaphor which is habitually used to describe the common consequences of overspecialization is itself drawn from the landscape; it is 'not being able to see the wood for the trees'.

At the same time as academic enquiry finds itself fragmented into separate disciplines, public awareness of the importance of environment in everyday life has been dramatically aroused by the discovery that we are polluting it at such a rate that the survival of some species is already in doubt, and that we ourselves could be numbered among such species in the not-so-distant future. Paradoxically enough the conservation movement has not proved as powerful a stimulus to *aesthetic* enquiry as might have been expected. The sheer urgency of the problems of control over detrimental practices has created an impression that there is no time to pause and reflect on the *reasons* why we value our environment at all, apart from the fact that we may destroy ourselves if we carry on in our present way. I am not against a sense of urgency. Would that it had come earlier! But it does mean that the interest of the public in its environment tends to be 'problem-oriented'. We rarely get down to asking what exactly it is that we enjoy in landscape and why we enjoy it. This is confirmed by the strength of conviction with which we hold conflicting aesthetic opinions. In Britain, for instance, the policy of the Forestry Commission in planting conifers is vigorously attacked by a well-organized lobby, and every attempt to build a reservoir has rallied a band of vocal opponents. Sometimes the opposition may have political, economic or social undertones, as when sheep farmers are put out of business to make way for a forest, or when Welsh Nationalists resent the stealing of water by the English. But always these campaigns have an aesthetic wing. Sooner or later one hears the phrase 'desecration of the countryside'. Yet it is usually only a few years before the coniferous forests show signs of overcrowding by the sight-seeing public at fine weekends and enterprising coach proprietors run day-tours to the artificial lakes. Places which are fortunate enough to have been desecrated by both the forester and the water engineer, such as Thirlmere, Lake Vyrnwy and the Elan Valley, top the list of attractions in the tourist offices.

If we do try to analyse our feelings for these surroundings, more often than not we come up with an argument which merely raises another question. The anti-conifer argument, for instance, is often explained by the incongruity of these trees in an area whose natural vegetation is deciduous hardwood. But how can we say that the intruders are incongruous if there is no 'natural' vegetation left with which to compare them? Justification by rational association is a highly dangerous device and would, incidentally, rule out many species of tree known to have been introduced by human agency quite recently, such as, in Britain, the Lombardy poplar (*Populus italica*) and even the London plane (*Platanus acerifolia*). It is much more honest to say that one does not want to see conifers planted because one does not like them, and to write off the ignorant who deign to take their pleasure among them as merely wanting in good taste. What, then, are the criteria by which this taste may be judged, and where do they come from? This problem will be pursued more closely in Chapter 8, but for the present let us keep to the question before us in the broader form in which we originally posed it; what is it that we like about landscape and why do we like it?

### A Diversity of Disciplines

It is first necessary to ask what landscape means to those people who, as professionals or amateurs, encounter it in their daily lives. Who are these people? To begin with there are a few whose jobs involve them almost exclusively with landscape. These are the landscape architects. But there are in addition a host of other categories of persons—conservationists, architects, art historians, journalists, naturalists, novelists, poets and many, many others, whose work touches marginally on some aspect of the subject. Indeed, we are all to some extent concerned. We encounter landscape more or less incidentally; it is there as a background to what we do. For much of the time we are barely conscious of it. In our urban society 'natural landscape', in the traditional sense, is often out of sight. Every now and then it impinges on our conscious mind, but few of us have occasion to stop and ask serious, fundamental questions about it.

The interesting thing about this casual, peripheral view of landscape is that everyone's viewpoint is individual and not surprisingly, therefore, we all perceive different things. If only we could consolidate this feast of experience, drawing on the perception and sensitivity of all who have touched on the subject from different backgrounds and varying artistic and technological viewpoints, we might perhaps find new ways of understanding our visible environment, and bring about the cross-fertilization of ideas to stimulate us to further enquiry within our own fields and disciplines. This exercise could act as a kind of catalyst which could reinvigorate the pursuit of old lines of enquiry and accelerate the invention of new ones.

Unfortunately we have little hope of finding anyone in our world of specialists sufficiently well qualified in all the relevant fields of knowledge to undertake this task with real authority. Perhaps we could find a group of experts to prepare a *symposium*, but this would be predisposed to set out specialist arguments in parallel, whereas what we need is someone to trace the threads which run across the boundaries of the various disciplines, connecting geology with aesthetics and animal behaviour with the history of art. Such a person must be prepared to invade territory with which he is not altogether familiar and to make at least tentative statements which he may not be able adequately to support. This sort of undertaking is not any more likely to commend itself to an established scientist anxious to preserve an academic reputation then to an up-and-coming arts man still seeking to establish one. Perhaps this is one reason why the challenge has not proved more attractive.

The Jack-of-all-trades who attempts this task should therefore be a person with modest professional aspirations which, preferably, he has already achieved. For the limitations of his knowledge of subjects other than his own, compensation must be provided by an interest in, even a love of, landscape in the widest possible sense. If he does not know at what pH value acidity begins to limit the growth of the beech, what, if anything, the eighteenth-century fashion for curved carriage-drives had to do with Hogarth, or why Breughel imported impossible mountains into otherwise authentic Flemish scenes, he must at least be aware that this is the sort of question to which somebody at some time has given thought and perhaps even come up with a plausible answer. He must be an optimist and he must accept the stark implication of rushing in where angels fear to tread. If he happens to be a geographer he will at least have had experience of trespassing in other people's territory without apology or even an honest blush, and if he is immodest enough to go into print, his arrogance must at least stop short of deceiving him into the belief that he is doing anything more ambitious than thinking aloud.

If my assessment of the situation is correct, and if the study of landscape has

6

figured in so many disciplines, it would seem sensible to review this field further in two stages. In this chapter we shall look briefly at some of these disciplines to see whether there is anything in their approach which makes them more or less efficient as channels of enquiry or which colours their attitude to landscape in any way; whether, in short, they have distinctive views and, if so, what is distinctive about them. This done, we can in the next chapter summarize some of the principal contributions so far made in preparing a meeting-ground for landscape and aesthetics. It may be appropriate for me to begin with my own subject first.

## The Environmental Sciences

The theme of landscape may seem at first sight to be more central to the discipline of geography than to most others, but this is only partly true. Since geography became established as a modern university discipline geographers have displayed an almost neurotic concern to find their own identity and recent changes in the subject, which have proved highly beneficial in some ways, have on the whole done little to strengthen the position of landscape in the curriculum of the subject. The British experience has been somewhat different from that of North America and continental Europe but will serve well enough to illustrate the limitations of academic geography in its approach to the visible environment.

Apart from a handful of earlier appointments, the introduction of teaching posts in geography in English universities dates from about fifty years ago (Steel, 1967). The first occupants of these posts could not, therefore, hold degrees in geography. They came into a new subject from outside, bringing with them the techniques of geology, botany, history and many other subjects. They had practically no literature which they could call their own except that of their overseas colleagues who had made an earlier start, and who not unnaturally influenced their attitudes. School textbooks there were, but these tended to embody a view of geography which suggested to them what needed to be changed rather than adopted. What they had was a large and almost untapped reservoir of raw material available in the landscape, and to this they assiduously turned. While some of them, particularly those who came from scientific disciplines, found themselves more interested in the physical environment and others, especially those with a historical training, concentrated on the man-made landscape, they were forced without exception to direct their enquiries as well as their teaching to the whole range of landscape, emphasizing particularly the interaction of its various components. They borrowed from the Germans the phrase 'Cultural Landscape' by which they meant 'the natural landscape as modified by man' (Bryan, 1933, p. v). Through the 'twenties and 'thirties most of the work produced by academic geographers tended to lay emphasis on the visible landscape as the source of geographical knowledge. Field work became the slogan of the dedicated; muddy boots the symbol of authority. Just as a threadbare and tattered gown was prized as a mark of experience and maturity in preference to the shining robes of the novice, so an Ordnance Survey map, dog-eared, half-pulped by regular soakings and annotated to the point of illegibility was proudly pulled out to show that its possessor had really made contact with his subject. The academic geographer of the inter-war years must have cut a novel figure in the senior common rooms—half don, half boy scout. No wonder his arrival was not universally relished!

Under these circumstances much was achieved in understanding and explaining the landscape, and for a time geographers managed to consolidate something like a tenable position from which they could wander freely through the terrain of other disciplines without giving up the option of returning to their seat on the fence between the sciences and the humanities. Such a seat, however, was inevitably precarious, and the very privilege which enabled geographers to appropriate everything within their field denied them the clearly defined standing of subjects like chemistry, economics and music whose fields of activity were more precisely demarcated.

In other countries geography has had its own distinctive characteristics and problems. The French tradition, for instance, laid emphasis on the 'personality' of the region. This was not defined exclusively in terms of its visible attributes, but still the recognition of areas which *looked* similar was fundamental to French geographical thinking and writing. Up to a point the same tendency can be discerned in Germany; indeed the nearest German equivalent to the word 'region' is Landschaft, 'landscape'. American geography differed again from the British pattern, for instance in so far as geomorphology was largely studied in departments of geology rather than geography. But everywhere there were problems of demarcation between geography and cognate subjects and some measure of controversy about the role of geography vis-à-vis its near relations.

In the post-war era great changes have taken place in the techniques of geography, but with one important exception these changes have not led to advances in the study of landscape comparable with those which have revolutionized other branches of the discipline.

In this period of change three main trends may be distinguished. The first has been the inevitable increase in specialization which has affected every academic discipline. As the field of knowledge grows, it becomes less and less possible for any individual to expand his own knowledge proportionately. Never before has the Jack-of-all-trades had poorer prospects of becoming master of any. To achieve any new discovery it has been necessary to work on an increasingly narrow front. In an age when the glamour is reserved for the specialist, the general practitioner is likely to appear as an inferior being. Unable to make the top grade he must content himself with the hack-work. It is ironical to find this attitude towards, for instance, the medical profession, subscribed to without qualification by people who owe their lives to the hacks. But such is the particular character of geography as a discipline that this trend finds expression in a centrifugal movement towards the periphery followed by a firm attachment to some subject cognate to the field of specialization.

The trend can be illustrated in terms of geography and botany. The first stage for the geographer may well be an interest in landscape and the recognition that vegetation is one of the most important of its components. This recognition leads logically to further enquiry into the rules which govern the distribution of plants. While the geographer is engaged on this safari along a particular part of the boundary of his own subject, a botanist, conscious that one of the most important aspects of that science concerns the conditions in which plants live, embarks on a pursuit of the study of their habitats. This path leads via 'ecology' towards that part of the boundary of botany which is contiguous with that of geography. As both explorers press on into the bush there comes the inevitable moment when the foliage is pushed aside and they stand face to face. If romance follows, it may, as has happened in several universities, be solemnized in something like matrimony—a semi-permanent, contractual association blessed with an issue of biogeographers, geo-ecologists, environmental scientists and holders of Joint Degrees. I make no complaint whatever about this. The liaison was long overdue. But the trouble about the matrimonial analogy is that it may carry with it a vow of renunciation of all other objects of interest and affection and, where this happens, its implication for landscape study is to direct the attention away from the whole towards the various parts.

What has happened in biogeography has happened also in other fields. The attractions of geology, history, economics, sociology and other disciplines have all proved highly stimulating and indeed fruitful to geographers, but they have tended to result in kinds of specialization which on the whole have been inimical to the *general* study of landscape; such contributions as they have made have been of a more particular kind.

This leads to the second trend in post-war academic geography. As these diversities of interest develop they have succeeded in prising open the crack which has always been apparent in the subject, dividing it into two principal compartments, generally labelled 'physical' and 'human' geography respectively. Of course one recognizes that this cleavage is to some extent a *de facto* situation, but to give it *de jure* recognition by the setting up of separate Chairs in Physical and Human Geography, as is being done in Britain and elsewhere, however much it may facilitate administration and research, cannot prove conducive to the study of *landscape* which, except in wholly unpopulated areas, is the product of the interaction of physical and human processes.

In terms of landscape study the situation which we are now asked to accept is one in which Professor A is interested in a landscape in so far as its character is related to the underlying rocks and the processes which shaped them, in so far as the rain falls on it to the tune of so many millimetres per annum and in so far as it is covered by vegetation, provided this is of natural occurrence and is not artificially introduced. In the latter eventuality it becomes part of the field of interest of Professor B, together with fences, footpaths, chimney-pots and large lumps of stone: always assuming they were put there by Neolithic Man and not by ice.

This dichotomy of interest is not new; the separation of physical and human geography is only setting the seal on a division which has always to some extent existed. Thus in Britain the word 'scenery' has tended to be pre-empted by writers on the physical properties of 'landscape', a term which is reserved for a more general connotation. Sir Archibald Geikie's *The Scenery of Scotland* (Geikie, 1865) and Lord Avebury's *The Scenery of England* (Avebury, 1902), both confined themselves to the physical aspects with, in both cases, rudimentary sections near the end referring to non-physical features. Later, A. E. Trueman (Trueman, 1938) again employed the word 'scenery' in the same sense as also did Dudley Stamp (Stamp, 1946). This restricted sense is still in fashion (e.g. Sissons, 1967), though there is no absolute uniformity of practice, and back in the 'thirties Vaughan Cornish was using the word as more or less synonymous with landscape (Cornish, 1932). On the other side of the coin we find the word 'landscape' used with reference principally to man-made features, for instance, by W. G. Hoskins in *The Making of the English Landscape* (Hoskins, 1955). This is not surprising, as Hoskins is an economic historian who probably knows more than anyone about how the artificial elements in the English landscape came into being, but even where, in the companion volumes, he calls on geographers, even geographers like W. G. V. Balchin (Balchin, 1954), with well-known interests in the physical field, the commission is clearly to use no more space on the physical evolution of the landscape than is necessary to introduce the real subject of the book. 'Landscape' in this sense, means what people have made of their environment after nature has handed it over to them.

The work which has been done since the war on physical and man-made landscape has enormously increased our knowledge of both, but it is *our* job to put the pieces together. We do not often find the authors doing it for us, and one of the reasons for this is to be sought in the third of these post-war trends.

The old techniques of landscape description have, on the whole, not proved equal to what geographers, particularly the younger geographers, have aimed to achieve. They found themselves not only not stimulated but frankly bored with methods which were too imprecise to yield satisfying scientific results. The remedy, they discovered, lay in mathematics and statistics. So effectively have these methods caught on that one cannot now raise the slightest misgivings about their use without stirring up suspicions that one has finally lost touch. Let me therefore make my own position very clear. Nothing in the history of academic geography has so extended its potentialities as the application of these techniques. But, in the present context, it is pertinent to note that, with the exception of their application in geomorphology, they have tended to lend themselves more effectively to the processing of data of a non-visual kind. It is not so easy to tie together quantitatively the visual components of a landscape as it is to analyse the location or distribution pattern of items which, in the process of analysis, are abstracted from it. So stimulating, even exciting, have researchers found these techniques, that they have tended to address themselves to the study of the kind of problems in which they can most easily be employed, and this has proved much less beneficial to the study of *landscape* than to that of other branches of the subject. Indeed one can go further and say that these quantitative techniques have provided at least a partial solution to the problem of the geographer's search for identity; they have led to the discovery of 'locational analysis', the scientific study of spatial relationships calculated mathematically. Landscape has not been ousted by these developments from the field of geography, but it is further than ever from assuming a central role.

When we turn to those other sciences concerned with the study of environmental phenomena, we find that they are even more limited in their approach than geography. Not only do they share many of the limitations of that subject,

FIGURE 1. NIAGARA
To the geomorphologist the observation of landscape is the starting point of his discipline and, although recent developments in the subject have tended to shift the emphasis from the morphology of landforms to the formative processes which have produced them, his ultimate objective remains unchanged—the understanding of the evolution of the landsurface, the infrastructure of landscape. Photograph by the author

in that the visible attributes of their subject-matter are only a part of what they study, but that subject-matter is itself only a part of the landscape. For both of these reasons we can deal with them more briefly. Geomorphology, for instance, is increasingly concerned with emphasizing the study of the *processes* which shape landforms, as any modern textbook on geomorphology will show (Figure 1). It may offer a more satisfying explanation of the genesis of landforms but it does not pretend to attempt a comprehensive analysis of the landscape *in toto*.

In geology the theme of landscape is even more peripheral. Much descriptive and explanatory work in petrology and palaeontology, for instance, has only a very indirect bearing on what the landscape looks like, and even those aspects of the subject which are more directly relevant, such as stratigraphy and physical geology, comprise only one component, albeit a very important one, of the whole environment with its cover of 'natural' and 'artificial' vegetation and its architectural appendages, which no plausible definition could possibly place within the discipline of geology.

It might well be argued that vegetation is the most important single element in the landscape. Certainly in the planning of a contrived landscape its manipulation can yield the most conspicuous results. It has been estimated by the Forestry Commission that, once the ground has been prepared, one man can plant a thousand trees in a day. What other human activity can produce such a massive long-term change in the visible landscape for so little effort? Yet the landscape of vegetation is far from being the exclusive or even the principal concern of the botanist. Plant physiology, for instance, though it clearly has a bearing on trees' growth and may help to explain why certain varieties establish themselves in one place and not in another, is far from being synonymous with the study of landscape. Even ecology, which is the most promising link between botany and landscape, shares something of the same limitations. Most of the questions which the ecologist asks are not concerned directly with the sensory impressions made on the eye by entire plant associations as they are directly observed.

When we come to those other sciences, such as meteorology, hydrology and the physics of light, which are very closely involved in the study of landscape, we do no more than trespass into these fields in pursuit of the answers to particular questions. We do not expect to find in them a ready-made theatre for the examination of landscape itself.

The natural sciences may be able to explain elements in the landscape as the product of *physical* processes if those physical processes are known. But much of the surface of the land has been so altered by human intervention that often its most conspicuous features are not natural at all but man-made. They are the product of *economic* processes and they may be similarly susceptible to explanation if we know what these economic processes are. There being no agreed frontiers within the field of knowledge, this material has been worked over by geographers interested in explaining patterns and distributions in terms of their economic antecedents, and by economic historians interested in the practices of agriculture, mining or whatever it may be, which have found expression in these forms.

The participation of economic historians in the study of landscape depends, therefore, on the fact that when a piece of land is used for some distinctive purpose, that use frequently alters the appearance of the land (Figure 2), sometimes temporarily, as when a field is ploughed, sometimes for a very much longer time. In an old settled country like Italy many features of the landscape are of great antiquity. Not only towns and roads, but even fields may owe their present distribution and configuration to very old economic systems. In the North Italian Plain, for instance, the Roman phenomenon of 'centuriation' has resulted in the farms, fields and road patterns assuming a marked rectilinear character reminiscent on the map, if not on the ground, of parts of the American

12

FIGURE 2. NUN MONKTON, YORKSHIRE

To the economic historian landscape is a palimpsest and he can read it like a document. His interest in it arises from the fact that the use of land frequently changes its appearance; the surviving landscape provides a record of the practices of the societies who have successively occupied it. This photograph by J. K. S. St. Joseph (Cambridge University Collection: copyright reserved), appeared as Figure 1A in Beresford & St. Joseph (1958) and is reproduced by permission of Dr. St. Joseph and the Committee for Aerial Photography, University of Cambridge

Middle West. The economic objectives which lay behind this kind of land division in both areas were basically similar, namely to parcel out productive farm land in a simple and convenient way; the periods involved were widely separated. In either case any detailed study of the resultant shapes would necessitate an enquiry into the social organization and practices of the communities concerned, into their economic objectives and into the technological facilities at their disposal. Many scholarly interpretations of particular landscape features along these lines have been made by economic historians, but they usually tend to be restricted to elements in the landscape rather than to landscapes in their entirety, and these visible manifestations of former economic activity form only quite a small part of the field of interest of the discipline as a whole.

The same concern with functional interpretation can be attributed to architecture and architectural history in so far as buildings reflect the needs and activities of the individuals or communities for which they were provided. But whereas all the disciplines so far mentioned concentrate primarily on interpretations which seek to relate causes, whether 'natural' or human, to effects, architecture impinges in addition much more closely on the approach and methodology of those disciplines which are associated first, with aesthetics, and secondly with 'problem-orientation'. That is to say, architecture is concerned with giving aesthetic pleasure as well as with *planning* for the provision of shelter and with arranging for the organization of enclosed, or even unenclosed space. It is not concerned merely with interpreting the functions of buildings.

When we further recollect that, especially in recent years, architects have been increasingly concerned with the environment of buildings and not merely the buildings themselves, it is not surprising that we should find in the literature of architecture many ideas which come close to the nature of the question we are pursuing. That is to say the 'discipline' of architecture has made far more progress than most in bridging, in Brenda Colvin's phrase, 'the chasm between art and science'. Indeed it might well provide the most fruitful country for our further quest were it not that its subject matter is still too limited; its real concern is with artificial structures, even if, in putting them into appropriate settings, it stretches its field of interest at least to glance at what lies around and beyond them.

I have left to the last, before turning to those disciplines concerned primarily with the study of how we experience landscape rather than with landscape itself, what is sometimes called 'landscape architecture', 'landscape gardening' or 'landscape design', because we are now in a better position to see its true role in the field of our enquiry. It has so much in common with the methodology of architecture that one is tempted to see it simply as an extension of architectural principles and practices into landscape. This, however, is something of an oversimplification. To quote Brenda Colvin again:

'Landscape architecture, like architecture itself, is concerned with the design of human environment. The two forms of design have much in common but differ profoundly in that architecture deals with the man-made, roofed-in structures of static material, while landscape architecture deals with the open-air, outdoor surroundings of human life, and with ever-changing materials. They differ, too, in other important ways, particularly in their scale.' (Colvin, 1970, p. 113)

The literature of landscape architecture falls into two main categories. First, there are those works which relate to the landscape architects of the past, whether contemporary writings by practitioners like Repton (Repton, 1803) or modern descriptive and analytical studies of their work. Second, there are publications aimed primarily at the instruction and guidance of persons concerned with present-day problems of landscape design. In both cases the emphasis tends to be on the techniques basic to a professional training. The approach of the landscape architect shares the limitations of the approaches of all professionals in any branch of planning. That is to say, the field of enquiry is ultimately circumscribed by what is practically attainable.

A clear impression of this can be obtained from the reference lists issued to postgraduate students in the courses in landscape design which are now available in several British universities. Certainly these encourage wide reading on the aesthetic side and on the general historical background. But they leave one in no doubt that all this is preparatory to the acquisition of a professional skill—indeed a professional qualification—in which any attitude other than a realistic recognition of practical limitations would be self-defeating. It is for this reason only that, as an outsider, I am not deterred from pursuing the present enquiry into what is perhaps the legitimate field of the landscape architects. If anyone can lay claim to a special relationship with such a promiscuous subject as landscape it is probably they. But one does not expect the custodians of a professional reputation to risk the kind of speculation which I have suggested is desirable, and indeed necessary, if we are to make a significant advance in the search for common, interrelated themes. Professionals cannot afford publicly to indulge in unsubstantiated flights of fancy, and we have as yet no grounds for claiming that the present exercise is anything more than that.

## Perception and the Arts

It is now time to turn from those disciplines which have concerned themselves principally with the content of landscape to those which study its perception. Here again we impinge upon a number of generally recognized disciplines which are involved in various ways. The one which faces most directly the question of how and why we derive pleasure from perception is that branch of philosophy known as aesthetics.

The history of aesthetics goes back at least to the ancient Greeks, and the literature on it is far too voluminous to be even summarized here (see Beardsley, 1966 and Stolnitz, 1960). But just as all the physical sciences which have concerned themselves with landscape have limitations which are inherent in their own methodology and point of view so, in their approach to the aesthetics of landscape, the aestheticians are encumbered by a number of restraints. These restraints are no doubt very necessary in so far as they help to guide them in the pursuit of their proper objectives, and here again the problems arise because those objectives are only related to, and are not synonymous with, our own. If their understandable reluctance to bend their own rules has saved the aestheticians from making fallacious interpretations of aesthetic experience, it has also discouraged them from straying into certain forbidden pastures where they might have found some promising clues.

This point can perhaps best be illustrated by taking a little further the principal discrepancy between their objectives and ours. Traditionally the aestheticians have been concerned with finding an explanation of 'beauty'. Any definition or any interpretation, if it is to satisfy them, must encompass beauty wherever it is to be found, and this necessarily involves a much wider field than mere landscape. Indeed, looking at the whole field of aesthetic enquiry from Plato to the present, one is struck by the reluctance until comparatively recent times to look for explanatory relationships on anything less than a comprehensive scale. One does not have to be a philosopher to see the reason for this. As soon as one determines that the object of one's enquiry is 'beauty', anything to which the designation 'beautiful' is attached is brought within that field of enquiry. This presupposes that beauty *is* a common attribute of all things which we call beautiful and automatically precludes any definition of beauty which excludes any object so designated.

If, for instance, we say that a cloud, a piece of music and a movement of the human body are all beautiful, then beauty must be a common property of them all. This begs a very important question, namely that there is in all these things a common 'something', beauty, and that it is the same 'something' in whichever of these manifestations it is found. As we shall see, developments in the twentieth century have shifted the emphasis of aesthetic enquiry in a direction which frees us at least partially from this limitation and allows us to make investigations at a lower level of generalization. As long as we have to ask 'what is beauty in landscape?' there is a presupposition that it must be the same as beauty in sculpture or in dancing, otherwise we should not describe it by the same word. But as soon as we re-phrase the question as 'What is the source of that pleasure which we derive from the contemplation of landscape?' we are perfectly free to postulate that it may be different from the source of pleasure to be derived from any other experience. It raises other philosophical questions, of course, such as 'What is pleasure?', but it does not impose the same limitations as that which for centuries so shackled the aestheticians as to render them impotent to give a generally acceptable answer to the simple questions 'What do we enjoy about landscape and why?'.

This, I believe, is the principal reason why the layman, seeking an understanding of the landscape as a source of aesthetic satisfaction, experiences a sense of disappointment in the works of most of the aestheticians. They seem to him to press their insistence on procedural rules to the point of perversity, yet at the same time they make assertions (and I am now thinking of earlier generations of aestheticians), which they 'support' with evidence of a kind that would not be acceptable to any modern scientist. Perhaps this is one reason why not many scientists trouble to read aesthetics. When they do find an author with an idea which they can understand, he does not present them with satisfactory grounds for believing it. This is in a way unfortunate, because many of the older ideas lack clarity and hence conviction for want of the kind of evidence which subsequently became available.

Consider, for instance, the idea that beauty is some sort of a reflection, or imitation, of an underlying 'order' which cannot be perceived except in so far as it is manifest in perceptible things. This idea appears in a great variety of guises from Plato onwards. A whole literature based on it had appeared before the time of Newton and Linnaeus. The kind of orderly arrangement at which Aristotle guessed may well have been something very like the kind of arrangement which Darwin subsequently disclosed. It would be going too far to describe the modern science of geomorphology as Latter Day Platonism, but the order which the geomorphologists have demonstrated as residing in the processes which lie behind the shaping of the earth's surface could hardly have failed to be seized upon by Plato as evidence fundamentally consistent with his beliefs.

Among the other difficulties which we find in marrying aesthetics with the environmental sciences problems of terminology may be mentioned. Semantic discussion permeates the literature of aesthetics, and it is not unusual to find one author taking a word in the same sense as that in which a previous author had used it, but adding by assertion some nuance of his own. This happens also, of course, in science, but usually in a context in which different shades of meaning can be made more explicit by concrete examples.

This leads to the next point. It is not uncommon for an aesthetic argument to be conducted solely in abstract terms for page after page. This is perhaps more noticeable in earlier works but is by no means confined to them. Words like 'concord', 'harmony', 'taste' are difficult enough to handle even if one knows exactly what they mean but, unless they are from time to time clearly exemplified, the difficulties of comprehending them may be, at least for the layman, insurmountable. Needless to say, a particular problem confronts the layman when he finds abstract nouns, the precise interpretation of which is dubious, employed in the *premises* of an argument, because the process of comprehension is then still-born. Yet there seems to be a common tendency for aesthetic arguments to be of this kind. Modern philosophers themselves are well aware of this problem as the following passage shows:

> 'The immediate effect of this principle [that philosophy deals with general notions] is to make people start their researches with attention to generalities: beauty, value, culture, and so forth. Such concepts, however, have no systematic virtue; they are not terms of description, as scientific concepts, e.g. mass, time, location, etc., are. They have no unit, and cannot be combined in definite proportions. They are

"abstract qualities" like the elementary notions of Greek nature philosophy–wetness and dryness, heat and cold, lightness and heaviness. And just as no physics ever resulted from the classification of things by those attributes, so no art theory emerges from the contemplation of "aesthetic values".' (Langer, 1953, p. 5)

In addition to these problems the philosophy of aesthetics exhibits in its own particular form a weakness which we have already found in all the other disciplines. It touches on landscape as only a part of its field of enquiry, and the particular form in which this weakness appears is the secondary role assigned by most aestheticians to nature as compared with art. In the words of Hepburn, 'contemporary writings on aesthetics attend almost exclusively to the arts and very rarely to natural beauty'. (Hepburn, 1968, p. 49)

Other complications arise from time to time. At various stages it has been regarded as essential to introduce moral arguments. Ethics as well as metaphysics become indissolubly involved, and the mere scientist sighs for the relative simplicity of a straightforward laboratory experiment. I am not asserting that there is no connection between aesthetics and ethics but merely that it is not helpful to base one's argument on the assumption that it *must* culminate in the demonstration of such a connection.

If I have painted a somewhat disparaging picture of the role of aesthetics in all this, let me hasten to add two or three points. I have been writing essentially of the older kind of aesthetics in which it was fashionable to look for some all-embracing 'system' which would account for the experience of beauty wherever it was found. It is precisely because so many of these ideas remained viable for so long that they have still to be reckoned with in philosophical discussion; they have become ingrained in the subject. The discipline itself has now turned its back on many of them (Tatarkiewicz, 1972), but even this is not entirely helpful, because among those which would receive little recognition from aestheticians at the present time are to be found some which, for our purposes, we can by no means afford to overlook. I refer in particular to those eighteenth-century efforts to explain the aesthetic enjoyment of landscape, efforts which will be more fully discussed in the next chapter. No doubt the contempt with which they are treated by some aestheticians today is the reward of their crudeness of concept, pomposity of expression, paucity of evidential support and, particularly, choice of what we should regard as relatively unimportant objectives (such as distinguishing between the Beautiful and the Sublime), but they contain the germs of ideas which virtually by-pass the nineteenth century and which could never begin to re-establish their relevance and credibility until aesthetics itself had changed its approach. They were, if you like, waiting for Dewey,[1] and in my view even he never fully recognized them because they were too heavily disguised in eighteenth-century dress.

From aesthetics the path of enquiry logically leads in two directions. First there are those disciplines which deal more specifically with the analysis of such art forms as are concerned with landscape. Architecture we have already touched on because its subject matter is an actual component of the landscape, but painting falls properly among those subjects which deal with the perceptual approach. Indeed it raises the question of perception at two stages. There is on the one hand the perception of the landscape by the artist and on the other the perception of the painting or drawing by the viewer, a point which has not escaped the aesthetic theoreticians. The first stage can be regarded as a particular form of comment on the 'real' landscape, whether the artist aims at achieving an exact reproduction of what he sees or whether his work is imitative only in the loosest sense, recasting what he has sensed in the environment into a very dissimilar arrangement. What he produces becomes the object of study at the second stage, taking the same name as the original subject—'a landscape'. The process of study of this work is the task of the art historian and art critic. It is clearly related to the approach of the aesthetician, though it is not the same. Munro says:

'Workers in the fields vaguely designated as "experimental aesthetics" or "the psychology of art" have rarely undertaken detailed studies of the various types of form in art, their cultural genesis, or their connections with personality traits. The direct, intensive study of works of art has been left on the whole to art critics and historians.' (Munro, 1956, p. 181)

Here again we find that the approach of the art critic and art historian is not aimed directly at our problem. We find, for instance, much attention paid by the critics to the actual techniques of painting, the use of materials, the style of brushwork, the structure of composition in the two-dimensional plane of the canvas (Figure 3), rather than to the objects portrayed in their three-dimensional arrangement on the ground.

Again we encounter the problem which arises because landscape is only a part and not the whole of the subject; more than that, the literature rarely follows a classification system which recognizes landscape as a discrete part of the art of picture-making. It is usual to make a division according to individual painters, schools, periods or media, and the work discussed may include portraits, still-life paintings, interiors, etc., as well as landscape. It is true that there are plenty of books on Constable or Canaletto, in whose work landscape predominated, but it is the painter, not his subject, that is the unifying theme. Such books on landscape painting as there are tend to lay stress on the technique rather than the intepretation of painting,[2] and, while they contain much interesting material, it is not quite what we are looking for in the present enquiry. An important exception is a small book by Kenneth Clark (Clark, 1949)[3] which is invaluable as an introduction to the subject and on which I shall draw frequently in the following pages. Another is Stechow's book on Dutch landscape painting of the seventeenth century (Stechow, 1966),[4] in part of which, at least, landscape features form the basis of the arrangement of the material. Thus there are sections on 'dunes and country roads', 'rivers and canals', 'woods', 'the beach', 'the sea', 'towns' and particular conditions of landscape suggested by the point of view, ('panoramas') by the season, ('winter') or by the geographical location of the subject ('Tyrol and Scandinavia', 'the Italian scene').

But perhaps the most intractable problems which confront those art critics who seek to interpret landscape painting are to do with the inadequacies of the tools at their disposal. There are, I think, two kinds of inadequacy. The first is

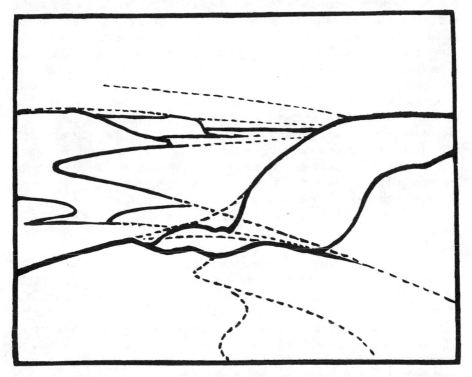

FIGURE 3. ANALYTICAL DIAGRAM OF AN ESTUARINE LANDSCAPE

The continuous lines represent edges (horizons or lines of contact between land and water) as they appear on the painting. Intermittent lines are inserted to show how the construction of the composition is based on the geometrical relationships between the various coloured shapes. Except for the uppermost, which represents a weak sky dado, they do not correspond with lines visible in the painting. The emphasis is strongly two-dimensional like the plane surface of the picture. Note how the landscape features in the foreground and in the distance are linked by the same structural lines. Analytical diagram of Plate XXXV, 'The Estuary, Barmouth, North Wales', in oils, by Leonard Richmond; from Richmond (1928), p. 96. Reproduced by permission of Pitman Publishing Ltd., London

one of language. The critics constantly find themselves in difficulty because they have to use two separate sets of words, the one relating to feeling or emotion ('passion', 'anger', 'grief', etc.), the other relating to the paraphernalia of landscape. To bridge the gap between them it is necessary either to invent new words, such as *Topophilia* (Yi-Fu Tuan, 1961), or to project established words metaphorically from one side to the other. When the critics speak of 'feeling' in a painting, this is no mere affectation, and in certain kinds of painting we have no difficulty in accepting their language or in understanding what it means. In portraiture it is easy enough to see a connection between 'feeling' and facial expression. In 'genre' painting there may well seem to be some emotional significance in the attitudes of figures or in the events or situations which are portrayed. We do not need to be told what 'emotion' lies behind the tears of a Madonna at the foot of the cross or the bouncing antics of Breughel's dancing peasants. The expression is so immediate that we can instantly connect 'form' with 'feeling'. The reaction of any mother to the death of a son is predictable and poles away from the toothless grins of the merry-making Flemings. The relationship between 'internal' emotion and 'external' expression is based on a well-understood and universally accepted system of cause and effect. In fact we know very well that pain and pleasure are *not* discrete categories of opposites which invariably produce tears and smiles respectively and also that no two people will either feel or express the same emotions in the same way when confronted with a common stimulus, but at least we are working in a field where the mechanism linking emotion and expression is intelligible because we have a familiar framework of stimulus and response. We can therefore employ the language of emotion, (using words like 'grief' or 'ecstasy') to describe what is actually represented. The language of 'feeling' can be effectively applied to 'form'.

When, however, we come to *landscape* painting, we find that explanations of 'feeling' tend to be less convincing, and this would seem to be partly due to the lack of a language appropriate to the purpose. I believe, however, that the language problem is only part of the difficulty and that we have also to face the second of the two inadequacies to which I referred. This is a lack of any universally accepted general theory by which landscape and emotion may be connected, and until we have found this the problem of language is bound to be even more acute. We are in fact trying to use a second-hand terminology to describe a relationship which we do not properly understand.

Let us take a simple example to illustrate both of these problems. If the word 'poignant' were used of a painting of the *Mater Dolorosa* we should understand very well what it meant, because the relationship between death and grief lies within our common experience and we do not feel it necessary to offer any further explanation. Indeed if we went on to say 'it is poignant because mothers are unhappy when their sons are killed' we should at best have added nothing to what we understand already and at worst have reached such a depth of trite banality as to distract the reader with comic relief.

If, however, we use the word 'poignant' of the light of sunrise and sunset, we might very well feel that some further explanation is required. Kenneth Clark does use the word in precisely this connection. Of Bellini he writes:

> 'In his early work he had loved the poignant light of sunrise and sunset, and these moments of heightened emotion he continued to portray when they could intensify the meaning of his subjects as in the *Resurrection* in the Berlin Gallery.' (Clark, 1949, p. 24)

Up to a point we know exactly what he means, especially when he goes on to draw a contrast:

> 'But as he grew older he became more in love with the full light of day in which all things can expand and be completely themselves.' (Clark, 1949, p. 24)

as in the *St. Francis* in the Frick Collection, which Clark then describes.

If in this context someone were to ask 'why should the light of sunrise and sunset be more poignant than that of the noon?' it would be anything but a silly question and very different from 'Why should a mother be unhappy if her son is killed?'. In fact, on a literal interpretation one could well argue that 'poignant' (i.e. sharp, pricking) would be more appropriately used of the bright light of noon rather than the subdued light of sunrise and sunset. We must, of course, allow that Kenneth Clark is using the word in a metaphorical sense, at least one step removed from its literal definition, and that the sharpness refers to an emotional rather than a physical sensation. But my point is that there is no universally understood reason why the light of sunrise and sunset should be more 'poignant' than that of mid-day, why those times of the day should be 'moments of heightened emotion' and why they should possess the power to 'intensify the meaning of Bellini's subjects'. All this we have to take on trust, because, I suggest, we do not have the same understanding of those emotional reactions which arise from our experience of our inanimate environment as we have of grief, anger, joy, etc., resulting from our relations with other people.

In the exploration of that 'no-man's-land' which lies between the physical world of our environment, with its sunlight and space-relationships of perceived objects, and the emotional reactions which we display in response to it, we have very little in the way of general theory to guide us. There are certain empirical assumptions which we can make from common experience, such as that moonlight is 'romantic' or that our spirits tend to be elated in the sunshine and depressed by rain. We lend credence to these assumptions by borrowing meteorological terms to describe our moods and dispositions. We say that somebody has 'a sunny disposition' or that 'his brow was clouded'. (The association of the word 'depression' with rainy weather and low spirits is fortuitous. Except, perhaps at very great elevations, where it can induce physiological changes, there is no evidence that low atmospheric pressure directly influences the mood. The Dutch are not the most ebullient and high-spirited of peoples, nor the Tibetans the most miserable!) Such axiomatic assertions do enable us to make interpretations of certain environmental associations. It *seems* appropriate that Beethoven should have died in a thunderstorm or that Macbeth's encounter with the witches should have taken place on a filthy night. But if we ask what the connection is between aesthetic satisfaction and the contemplation of distance, or why those North Italian valleys which contain lakes are more favourably regarded than those which do not, we should be hard pressed to base our answers on any assumptions as universally accepted as that which postulates a connection between a mother's grief and the death of her son.

One may, then, hope to be forgiven for seeing the art critics as anxious to cross from the field of aesthetics to that of the realities of landscape, but thwarted and frustrated by the absence, not only of a linguistic, but also of a conceptual bridge.

The phrase mentioned earlier, 'psychology of art' (p. 18, see Pickford 1972), points the way to the second path which leads forward from aesthetics. Psychology deals with the scientific investigation of the process of perception itself. It is an investigation carried out at two levels which we can call human and sub-human, the assumption being that there are enough similarities between the behaviour patterns of humans and animals to suggest that the investigation of one may well throw light on the other. The literature on this subject may therefore be found under 'psychology' or under that branch of zoology known as 'animal behaviour' or 'ethology'.

For our purposes the link between these two disciplines is important for a reason which will become apparent later. At the moment it will suffice to note two main points. One takes us back to my assertion that the post-war changes in the techniques of geography have, with one exception, not favoured advances in the study of landscape as much as that of other branches of the discipline (p. 7). That exception is the link-up between geography and psychology which has made possible what is generally known as 'environmental perception studies', of which more will be said in the next chapter.

The other point concerns the methodology of these sciences. Perception itself is a very difficult thing to measure. It cannot be directly observed; all that we can observe are the inferred consequences of perception. At the human level we can record symptoms; we can ask the subject to explain his reaction to stimuli. Many of the geographical perception studies referred to above are based heavily on this type of observation. The questionnaire provides the data for scientific analysis, but it has two serious limitations, quite apart from the fact that its use presupposes the readiness and competence of the participant to give correct answers. One is that it cannot be used in animal psychology, for obvious reasons. The other is that in human psychology, as in every other field of enquiry, its use is confined to the present, and in so far as there is ample evidence that taste tends to change from one period to another, perception studies based on questionnaire techniques may not provide a reliable means of assessing human reaction to environment except in terms of both the attitudes and the landscapes of the present. How fascinating to devise a questionnaire to measure sensitivity to environment and send copies to, say, Virgil and Capability Brown! Unfortunately the questionnaire cannot be used retrospectively, and it is certain that any inferences about 'taste', if drawn from questionnaires, must be massively loaded in favour of a particular, and possibly quite ephemeral, point of view. Within these limits, however, the questionnaire may be important.

There are, indeed, many other disciplines which touch less directly on our subject, and many other things which could be said about those we have so cursorily reviewed. But perhaps enough has been said to suggest one reason why more progress has not been made in the pursuit of our objective, and why the specialist in each discipline has felt himself deterred from a chase which takes him through so many unfamiliar fields. In each field sits an established occupier, secure in his title and able, no doubt, to put the imposter firmly in his place. I can only hope that he will be hospitable enough not to resent the present intrusion and charitable enough to reflect that not every aesthetician can tell a sedimentary from an igneous rock nor every psychologist recognize the handiwork of André le Nôtre, and that if, therefore, the alternatives are to trespass or to do nothing, trespassers will not be too severely prosecuted.

As long as men of taste scorn the Philistines of science, and as long as the scientists fear the verdict of guilt by association with such shady characters as art historians, so long shall we each feel obliged to opt either for studying the landscape as the subject of rational analysis or for enjoying it as the source of aesthetic satisfaction. Are these two kinds of experience really irreconcilable?

# CHAPTER 2

# The Quest

Although the task on which we have embarked touches on many disciplines, the ideas involved may, as we have seen, be grouped roughly into two categories, depending on whether they are concerned principally with the interpretation of the landscape or with our experience of it. In the former category we may include those attempts which have been made to explain the phenomena of our visible surroundings, how they originated and developed, how they are related to each other, how they differ individually and in association with each other from place to place. In the latter category our concern is with the observer, how he looks at his environment and how he seeks to explain the satisfaction which he derives from so doing.

We have seen, furthermore, how well established is the tendency for those who are academically interested in these two main fields of enquiry to keep strictly within those fields, even within their various subdivisions. But the isolation is not total. From time to time each party has thrown bridges across from one side to the other, flimsy structures, often enough, but capable of permitting sufficient movement of ideas to influence the further development of thought in either camp. Thus the way in which the landscape has been artificially contrived closely reflects certain tastes and fashions which have been based on changing philosophical concepts (e.g. see Lowenthal and Prince, 1965). At the same time these concepts have themselves been influenced by fresh scientific observations of the environment. The name of Immanuel Kant, for instance, will be found in every history of geographical thought as in every treatise on aesthetics, while a principal preoccupation of the eighteenth-century landscape gardeners was to reconcile changes in taste with the practicalities of gardening. Although, at that date, the study of landscape could hardly be described as a discipline in its own right, at least the great exponents of landscape gardening, such as Kent, Brown and Repton, were already being referred to, even if contemptuously, as 'the professors'. They were not 'professors' of botany, geology or any of the physical sciences, or of art or aesthetics, but of that field of practical activity in which all these were linked.

It would be quite impracticable in the present context to attempt a comprehensive survey of all those ideas in the history of aesthetics or in the study of landscape which are relevant to the question before us. There are, however, a number of such ideas which have so close a bearing on what we shall be considering later that I propose, in this chapter, to single out some of them without attempting to justify the basis of my selection beyond asserting that I wish the reader to be aware of them. The establishment of their relevance may come later.

## Some Eighteenth-century Milestones

For practical purposes we may take the eighteenth century as a suitable starting point for our further enquiries. Before that time significant steps had been taken both in the interpretation of landscape and in aesthetics, but in general neither side had approached close enough to the other to provide many points of fusion which we should regard as indispensable to our present enquiry. People had from time immemorial asked questions about the origins of land-forms. Some of the questions asked were extremely intelligent, but they were not accompanied by sufficiently accurate observation, and it is arguable that this, rather than a want of inspiration, was what so long prevented scientific enquiry from making progress. Strabo at the time of Christ discussed very sensibly the origin of the Mediterranean Sea (Jones, 1917, Bk. 1, pp. 182–193). Admittedly he was at his best when refuting the hypotheses of his predecessors, but at least the grounds of his refutations are clearly stated and undoubtedly correct. What he lacked was detailed observation over a wide enough field to enable him to propose a comprehensive hypothesis. It was for this reason that little real progress in geomorphological studies was possible until the late eighteenth century. During the sixteenth and seventeenth centuries there was no want of enquiry into the origin of landforms (Davies, 1966), but until the time of Hutton[5] and Playfair (1802) there was little attempt in Western thought to consider the observed evidence in isolation from a methodology inherited from the Book of Genesis. It was to the great credit of the early geologists, not that they rejected the Book of Genesis—after all a good proportion of them were clergymen—but that they began to look at the rocks in terms of what they saw in them rather than what they felt good Old Testament scholars ought to see.

Similarly the early enquiries in aesthetics were by their nature not suited to a scientific application to landscape. They usually proceeded deductively from abstract to concrete leaving a hiatus between the general concept and the details of the perceived environment. Many of the assertions of the philosophers about the nature of beauty did not obviously lend themselves to testing by direct observation: the generalization that metals expand when they are heated can be checked by experiments with physical objects. But how can one check experimentally the assertion that 'the beautiful is what is beneficial' or that 'the observation of nature is enjoyable because nature is imitative of more fundamental principles which underlie its apparent reality'? Try testing these hypotheses with two pine trees, a lake and the sunset. Is it not the same sort of exercise as trying to weigh the twenty-third Psalm? Even if one is not in a position to assert that a philosophical proposition is irrelevant, one cannot *use* it until its relevance becomes apparent.

One can very well understand why modern aestheticians have been so grudging in their recognition of the attempts of eighteenth-century philosophers to explain the source of man's enjoyment of landscape. Their workmanship was often crude and they allowed themselves to become mesmerized by terminology. Their arguments about the beautiful and the sublime became increasingly unconvincing in the detail of their logic as they grew more complex and less closely related to reality. Dewey says that they '. . . erected adjectives into nouns substantive, and then played dialectical tunes on the fixed concepts which emerge' (Dewey, 1958 edn., p. 223). This is very true, and to follow the development of the controversy through the various letters, pamphlets and other publications of the time is a tedious business. But underneath all the dialectic and all the semantics one encounters ideas which are more realistic than any which had preceded them, because they were assertions, not merely about the beautiful, the sublime and the picturesque, but about real landscape: trees, grass, rough and smooth water, light and shade and so on. And since, particularly in France and England, these philosophical arguments were more or less contemporaneous with a ubiquitous interest among the landed nobility and gentry in 'improving' the appearance of their estates, it is really at that moment that we find for the first time an explosion of enthusiasm resulting from the effective bringing together of these two main streams, philosophical thought and practical landscape experience.

That the times were propitious in other ways is also clear. Hussey attributes this English awakening of an appreciation of landscape to the fashion of the Grand Tour and the resulting contacts of the land-owning class of English nobility and gentry with the world of continental landscape painting and foreign, particularly Italian, landscape (Hussey, 1927, p. 12). Towards the end of the century also the idea of beauty being found not merely in the order of a tamed environment, but also in the wild places, was so much in tune with the onset of the Romantic Movement that it became the fashionable view. The achievement of this fashion, however, was neither realized at a single step nor by a single mind. It was a movement punctuated by a few outstanding milestones and dominated by a few outstanding figures.

Perhaps the first of these major milestones is to be found in the writings of Shaftesbury.[6] Shaftesbury took the idea of the 'Sublime', which up to this time had been a term used of literary style, and which had come much into vogue since 1674, when Boileau had translated into French the Greek text of Longinus *On the Sublime*. This is how Brett summarizes the role of Shaftesbury in changing the meaning and direction of the word:

'Shaftesbury's importance . . . does not lie in his discussion of style, but in the fact that he was influential in transforming the idea of sublimity from a rhetorical to an aesthetic one. It is not that he himself gave a new meaning to the word, so much as the fact that he drew attention to a realm of experience with which the word was to become increasingly associated. Before Shaftesbury the word "Sublime" was used almost always in connection with style; after the appearance of the *Characteristics*, it increasingly betokened a specific sort of feeling in the face of the awful and great.' (Brett, 1951, p. 146)

He goes on:

> 'In Longinus there had been the hint that sublimity is related to the
> kind of experience which comes to us when we contemplate the wonder-
> ful and tremendous in nature. With Longinus it had been no more than
> a hint, but with Shaftesbury it is a major and recurring theme . . .. But
> it is in his conception of the sublime as that experience which comes to
> us in contemplating natural phenomena that are too large to be com-
> prehended by the senses or the imagination, that Shaftesbury gives a
> newer and profounder content to the term. It is in the attempt to em-
> brace infinity that we experience sublimity.' (Brett, 1951, p. 149)

Shaftesbury's concept of sublimity was taken up by Addison and Kant and
became a central theme in eighteenth-century aesthetics. If we were principally
concerned with a study of philosophical aesthetics we should have to examine
the salient features of their thinking but, as we are not, it is Edmund Burke who
emerges as the next major milestone, unless we pause briefly to note the appearance of Hogarth's *Analysis of Beauty* in 1753 (Hogarth, 1753). Hogarth's
*Analysis*, however, displays that characteristic which we have already noted as a
source of difficulty in our enquiry, namely that his concern is with 'beauty' in
general and not in its particular application to landscape. It is furthermore
clearly influenced by Hogarth's own preoccupation as an engraver specializing
in 'genre' illustrations (with few exceptions landscape comes into his engraving,
if it comes in at all, only as a backcloth), and by an unhelpful methodological
approach. A mere recitation of the titles of his chapters suggests the method of a
pedantic drawing-master.

> 'I, of Fitness; II, of Variety; III, of Uniformity, Regularity or Sym-
> metry; IV, of Simplicity or Distinctness; V, of Intricacy; VI, of
> Quantity . . .' etc. (Hogarth, 1753, p. xxiii)

The preponderance of abstract terms sets a framework into which observed
features have to be fitted as best they can, while no opportunity is lost for elabo-
rating technical questions to do with Hogarth's own trade. Undoubtedly the
most influential idea to come out of the *Analysis* was that aesthetic properties
reside intrinsically in certain shapes of line—more especially the wavy line and
the serpentine line (that is a line which 'waves' in more than one plane). To these
two types he assigned the names 'the line of beauty' and 'the line of grace'.

Hogarth's aesthetics in fact had little to say directly about landscape. His
line of beauty he illustrated by chair-legs and ladies' corsets and his line of
grace by a bent horn. But in an age in which Kent and Capability Brown had
already banished the straight line from the park and replaced it with curvilinear
features, it was inevitable that some significance for the aesthetics of landscape
should be sought in Hogarth's lines.

But to return to Burke, his contribution was not only more strongly founded
and better argued but also more directly, though not exclusively, relevant to
landscape. *A Philosophical Enquiry into the Origin of Our Ideas of the Sublime*

*and the Beautiful* was published in 1757 though it had been written over a number of years. I intend only to single out certain ideas from the *Enquiry*, but the text taken as a whole may be said to have a more direct relevance to our subject than anything previously written. An excellent editorial introduction appears in Boulton's edition. (Boulton, 1958)

After an introductory Essay on 'taste', added for the Second Edition of 1759, Burke divides his *Enquiry* into five parts. The first puts his thesis in its philosophical context and establishes its principal assertion, which is that the Beautiful and the Sublime are to be explained in terms of what he calls 'the Passions'. These passions fall into two main categories depending on whether they belong to 'self-preservation' or to 'society', and it is the former category which is associated with what Burke means by 'The Sublime'.

> 'Most of the ideas which are capable of making a powerful impression on the mind, whether simply of Pain or Pleasure, or of the modifications of those, may be reduced very nearly to these two heads, *self-preservation* and *society*; to the ends of one or the other of which all our passions are calculated to answer. The passions which concern self-preservation, turn mostly on *pain* or *danger*. The ideas of *pain*, *sickness* and *death*, fill the mind with strong emotions of horror; but *life* and *health*, though they put us in a capacity of being affected with pleasure, they make no such impression by the simple enjoyment. The passions therefore which are conversant about the preservation of the individual turn chiefly on *pain* and *danger*, and they are the most powerful of all the passions.
>
> '... Whatever is fitted in any sort to excite the ideas of pain, and danger, that is to say, whatever is in any sort terrible, or is conversant about terrible objects, or operates in a manner analogous to terror, is a source of the *sublime*; that is, it is productive of the strongest emotion which the mind is capable of feeling.
>
> '... When danger or pain press too nearly, they are incapable of giving any delight, and are simply terrible; but at certain distances, and with certain modifications, they may be, and they are delightful, as we every day experience.' (Boulton, 1958, pp. 38–40)

Burke then turns to the passions which belong to society, distinguishing within this category those which pertain to 'generation', i.e. sexual passions, from those which pertain to 'general society', and in these passions, particularly those of a sexual kind, he seeks the origin of our ideas of the beautiful. (Boulton, 1958, pp. 40 *et seq.*)

In Parts II and III respectively Burke amplifies these ideas. First he deals with the Sublime. At the risk of gross oversimplification one may summarize as follows the attributes of the Sublime. 'Astonishment' is the most potent:

> 'Hence arises the great power of the sublime, that far from being produced by them, it anticipates our reasonings, and hurries us on by an irresistible force.' (Boulton, 1958, p. 57)

The 'inferior effects' are 'admiration', 'reverence' and 'respect'.

So he proceeds through 'terror', 'obscurity', 'power', 'privation', 'vastness' and 'infinity', to 'difficulty' and 'magnificence'. 'Light' and 'darkness' are both associated with the sublime when present in extreme forms and particularly when occurring in opposition or contrast.

'Mere light is too common a thing to make a strong impression on the mind, and without a strong impression nothing can be sublime. But such a light as that of the sun, immediately exerted, on the eye, as it overpowers the sense, is a very great idea.

'. . . A quick transition from light to darkness or from darkness to light, has yet a greater effect. But darkness is more productive of sublime ideas than light. . . . Extreme light, by overcoming the organs of sight, obliterates all objects, so as in its effect exactly to resemble darkness. After looking for some time at the sun, two black spots, the impression which it leaves, seem to dance before our eyes. Thus are two ideas as opposite as can be imagined reconciled in the extremes of both; and both in spite of their opposite nature brought to concur in producing the sublime. And this is not the only instance wherein the opposite extremes operate equally in favour of the sublime, which in all things abhors mediocrity.' (Boulton, 1958, pp. 80–81)

Referring then to 'colour', 'loudness' 'suddenness' and other attributes, he comes back to 'feeling' and 'pain'.

'Having thus run through the causes of the sublime with reference to all the senses, my first observation will be found very nearly true; that the sublime is an idea belonging to self-preservation . . .' (Boulton, 1958, p. 86)

In Part III Burke approaches Beauty along roughly similar lines, finding it necessary, however, to preface his review of 'beautiful' qualities with a number of warnings about what beauty is not. So he rejects 'proportion', 'fitness' and 'perfection' as the causes of beauty before considering what it is.

'Having endeavoured to show what beauty is not, it remains that we should examine, at least with equal attention, in what it really consists. Beauty is a thing much too affecting not to depend upon some positive qualities. And, since it is no creature of our reason, since it strikes us without any reference to use, and even where no use at all can be discerned, since the order and method of nature is generally very different from our measures and proportions, we must conclude that beauty is, for the greater part, some quality in bodies, acting mechanically upon the human mind by the intervention of the senses.' (Boulton, 1958, p. 112)

The properties of beautiful objects, he goes on, are 'smallness', 'smoothness', 'gradual variation', 'delicacy' and 'colour', provided it is of a particular kind, that is not '. . . dusky or muddy, but clean and fair', mild ('light greens; soft blues; weak whites; pink reds; and violets'), or, if not mild, at least 'variegated'. He goes on to consider beauty in the physiognomy, especially the eye, in 'grace', 'elegance and speciousness', in 'feeling' and in 'sounds', in 'taste' and in 'smell'. He then summarizes the comparison between the sublime and the beautiful as follows:

'. . . sublime objects are vast in their dimensions, beautiful ones comparatively small; beauty should be smooth and polished; the great rugged and negligent; beauty should shun the right line yet deviate from it insensibly; the great in many cases loves the right line, and when it deviates, it often makes a strong deviation; beauty should not be obscure; the great ought to be dark and gloomy; beauty should be light and delicate; the great ought to be solid, and even massive. They are indeed ideas of a very different nature, one being founded on pain, the other on pleasure; and however they may vary afterwards from the direct nature of their causes, yet these causes keep up an eternal distinction between them . . .' (Boulton, 1958, p. 124)

In Part IV Burke takes up a number of points previously raised in an effort to explain them further, and the Enquiry finishes (Part V) in a discussion of the use of words to convey the idea of the beautiful and the sublime.

In comparing Burke's *Enquiry* with Hogarth's *Analysis of Beauty* one will note certain superficial similarities. Burke, for instance, used as his headings the same sort of abstract nouns employed by Hogarth. It is in the direction in which he looks for his examples that he makes the exercise so relevant to the natural environment and hence to the landscape, whereas Hogarth constantly seeks to apply his abstract concepts to the social environment and the products of creative art.

Any philosophical exposition must necessarily be judged in terms of its own stated objectives. It is quite clear that Burke's objective was to demonstrate that the beautiful and the sublime were, as he conceived them, intrinsically different. The validity of any *explanation* of the difference can hardly be judged at all if the difference itself cannot be established, and since the whole concept of the dichotomy seems to us to be an artificial erection of eighteenth-century thought on dubious earlier foundations, by far the easiest way to deal with Burke's theory is to reject it, and this is what some modern aestheticians seem to have done. We shall find, however, among the débris a great deal of reusable material which is far too valuable to be despised merely because Burke built it into a structure which, in its totality, was generally judged to be a failure. Unfortunately the immediate successors of Burke were too enchanted by the questionable ingredients of the main argument to give due consideration to his subsidiary propositions, and they were dragged, to use the imagery of the sublime, into a kind of vortex of controversy in which ill-defined phrases spun round each other faster and faster until the whole misdirected effort spent itself and made way for the phraseology and concepts of the Romantic Movement.

The aftermath itself, however, the cult of 'the Picturesque', contained some ideas which are by no means the mere archaic curiosities they are sometimes made out to be.

Christopher Hussey describes the picturesque as an 'interregnum between classic and romantic art'.

> 'It occurred at the point when an art shifted its appeal from the reason to the imagination' (Hussey, 1927, p. 4), he says, and it '. . . provided the earliest means for perceiving visual qualities in nature. It consists in the education of the eye to recognize qualities that painters had previously isolated . . . Each art passed through a phase of imitating painting before developing into the romantic phase that came after, when the eye and the imagination had learnt to work for themselves.' (Hussey, 1927, p. 17)

It is not possible here to do more than single out from the picturesque a few ideas which we need to look at later, and one of these is its concern with the weaving together of material drawn from the two main sources of our present discussion: the observation of landscape and the formulation of aesthetic theory.

In the observation of landscape an immense step forward was made by the Reverend William Gilpin. Gilpin was a clergyman, a Cumbrian by origin though he lived all his adult life in the English lowlands. After leaving Oxford he went for a time to London, then spent twenty-six years in Surrey (as head-master of Cheam School) and another twenty-six in the New Forest as Vicar of Boldre. From these bases in the south he made between 1768 and 1776 a number of tours, during which he executed innumerable sketches, with the specific objective of discovering which parts of the countryside of Britain best furnished the 'picturesque' type of scenery. Subsequently he wrote up descriptions of these tours for the benefit of his friends who persuaded him to publish them. For this purpose some of the sketches were finished or re-drawn to accompany the descriptions. The first volume appeared in 1782, the last in 1809, some five years after Gilpin's death. They referred, therefore, to observations made several years previously, and indeed Gilpin had shown an interest in picturesque landscape earlier still.

Whether Gilpin could be said to have directed public taste in landscape or whether he merely displayed a susceptibility to the kind of visual environment in which the public was increasingly discovering aesthetic pleasure may be questioned. What he undoubtedly did was to present descriptive accounts of actual places, relating their physical attributes to the emotional response they aroused. To do this he employed with little or no inhibition a terminology derived from Burke and the chroniclers of the sublime. For instance,

> 'Nothing conveys an idea of *beauty* more strongly, than the lake [Derwent Water]; nor of *horrour* than the mountains; and the former *lying in the lap* of the latter, expresses in a strong manner the mode of their combination.' (Gilpin, 1786, vol. 1, p. 191)

What gave the 'picturesque' controversy such a direct relevance to the aesthetics of landscape—though, as Hussey pointed out, it affected all the arts—was its obvious bearing on the art of landscape gardening. Whereas the chief contribution of Gray and other writers had been to arouse a poetic sensitivity to landscape, whereas Gilpin's principal service was to point out how and where nature had disposed beautiful and sublime features, and whereas Burke's chief objective was to explain the causes of the satisfaction to which they gave rise, a fourth stream of ideas proceeded from the practical problems of making the environment conform to those standards of excellence which derived from the other three. Many of the participants in the controversy were also owners of land. Even Pope practised landscaping on a small scale in his garden at Twickenham (Hussey, 1927, p. 129) and, at a time when patronage of the arts came from the landed nobility and gentry, the study of landscape aesthetics was by no means a matter of mere academic interest. The discussion of philosophical ideas, the stimulus of the Grand Tour, the fashion for collecting the works of seventeenth-century Italian painters and their later imitators, all contributed to an urge among the aesthetic élite to try out new ideas in their own estates. If one could identify the source of beauty in nature it should be possible, by selecting only the most beautiful and eliminating the rest, to improve on nature and create even more beautiful landscapes. Indeed it was generally acknowledged that this is what the landscape painters had done, and the leaders of the 'picturesque' school turned enthusiastically to them for a scale of values by reference to which they could link the abstract concept of beauty to the arrangement of trees and grass, rocks and water, within the actual environment. Such guidance they sought in the works of landscape painters generally, but by common consent the supreme authority was to be found in the work of that group of painters who, whatever their respective national origins, painted landscapes in peninsular Italy in the seventeenth century, and particularly Claude Lorrain (1600–1682). (See Figure 4.)

When these advocates of the 'picturesque' looked at the work of the professional landscape designers recently and currently active in England, they did not like what they saw. Throughout the eighteenth century there were many such designers, but the acknowledged leadership passed successively through the hands of three men, William Kent (1684–1748), Lancelot ('Capability') Brown (1715–1783) and Humphry Repton (1752–1818) (see Jourdain, 1948; Stroud, 1950, 1962; Hyams, 1971). When Kent began practising he found the fashion still entirely dominated by the style of André le Nôtre (1612–1700), designer of Versailles and leader of landscape taste in Europe. Regular geometrical patterns dominated large parks as well as smaller gardens. Ornamental water was confined by circular or rectangular margins. Avenues linked up one focal point with another. Vistas were so devised as to convey the impression of strictly ordered regularity (Figure 5). All this Kent modified and eventually replaced by a more flexible and fluent approach.[7] The shapes of paths, avenues and ornamental water-bodies became curvilinear and irregular. The groupings of trees and open spaces were designed to emphasize the natural lines of the landscape, where

33

FIGURE 4. CLAUDE LORRAIN (1600–1682): LANDSCAPE WITH APOLLO AND THE MUSES
Alternatively known as *Landscape with the Parnassus* (Röthlisberger, 1961, p. 308 and Fig. 215). Reproduced by
permission of the National Gallery of Scotland

34

previously they would have been employed in an effort to efface them. This was an accommodation between art and nature in which each made the maximum concession to the other, and the result was a harmonious blend of those three components which flourish so felicitously under the English climate, trees (especially deciduous trees) grass and water. Among these were set occasional small structures such as bridges, gateways, temples perhaps, and of course the big house.

By the time Capability Brown arrived on the scene the changeover of style

FIGURE 5. VERSAILLES
Photograph by the author

had already taken place. Brown's role was to consolidate the position which Kent and others had pioneered, and this he did, in part at any rate, by rationalizing the technique into a few simple rules and devices. Thus the serpentine belt of trees commonly enclosed the view, leaving in front a great expanse of grass punctuated by 'clumps' of trees grouped together in a somewhat stereotyped fashion. Well before the end of the century this style had become part of the establishment, and compositions carried out in it, charming as they were within its limitations, lent themselves very easily to the kind of criticism which the cliché so easily attracts in any form of expression. It was this establishment which formed the target of the devotees of the picturesque.

While there is plenty of room for argument about when the picturesque view of landscape first emerged,[8] the year 1794 is a landmark in the controversy which raged about its application in the field of landscape gardening. In that year Uvedale Price published his *Essay on the Picturesque* in which he expounded his philosophy and discussed those properties of landscape which he felt should form the guide-lines for the art of landscape gardening. Up to a point Price accepted Burke's hypothesis, but he argued that the Beautiful and the Sublime did not encompass the whole of human feeling even in so far as it was aroused by landscape. Accordingly he postulated a third category which he called 'The Picturesque'. The term itself originally denoted the properties of paintings, and if the picturesque were to be attained in landscape gardening, the same principles should rule, he argued, as those which governed the composition of a landscape painting, though he admitted that there might be important differences in their application.

In drawing attention to the potentialities for landscape improvement latent in the tastes of the picturesque school, Price might be said to have implied that the orthodox landscape gardeners were at fault inasmuch as they had failed to implement his own ideas. But he was certainly not content with an implication. He went on to make a strong and very explicit attack on 'the professors'. Of Kent, he said:

'Kent, it is true, was by profession a painter, as well as an improver; but we may learn from his example, how little a certain degree of mechanical practice will qualify its possessor to direct the taste of a nation in either of those arts.' (Price, 1794, p. 184)

Among many uncomplimentary passages on Brown perhaps the most offensive is that in which he quotes with evident approval if not relish the opinion of

'a gentleman, whose taste and feeling, both for art and nature, rank as high as any man's. . . . "Former improvers", said he, "at least kept near the house, but this fellow crawls like a snail all over the grounds and leaves his cursed slime behind him wherever he goes".' (Price, 1794, p. 268)

One may add a certain finesse to a personal attack if one has the skill to deliver the thrust in rhyming iambic pentameters, and in the same year, 1794, Richard Payne Knight wrote a didactic poem called *The Landscape*, in which he attempted in verse much the same objective which Price (to whom, incidentally, the poem was addressed) had achieved in prose.

Price, Payne Knight and Gilpin differed considerably in detail over their interpretations of the picturesque. Payne Knight, for instance, never accepted Price's tripartite system. Nevertheless they had sufficient community of interest to form with their adherents something like a School of the Picturesque. Their bête noire was a style of landscape gardening which they regarded as insipid, monotonous and destitute of all excitement, characterized by a few stereotyped devices,[9] such as the 'clump' and the 'belt' and a lot of open space. For them the qualities to be sought in landscape were roughness of texture, irregularity, asymmetry, partial concealment, the unexpected and above all the impression, whether deserved or not, of natural occurrence rather than artificial contrivance (Figure 6). In the words of Richard Payne Knight:

> 'For as the cunning nymph, with giddy care
> And wanton wiles, conceals her study'd air;
> And each acquired grace of fashion tries
> To hide in nature's negligent disguise;
> While with unseen design and cover'd art
> She charms the sense, and plays around the heart:
> So every pleasing object more will please,
> As less the observer its intention sees:
> But thinks it form'd for use, and placed by chance
> Within the limits of his transient glance.'
>
> (Knight, 1794, Bk. II, lines 314–323)

In contrast with the beautiful, which required variation to be accomplished gradually and undramatically, the qualities admired by the champions of the picturesque were sudden change and a degree of variation wide enough to encompass extremes, even incorporating features which were on the one hand beautiful, on the other sublime. If the source of their inspiration was Nature herself, their supreme arbiters of taste were the seventeenth-century painters.

Curiously enough, although it is generally Claude who emerges as the doyen of the picturesque school, the qualities they most consistently praise are often to be seen more dramatically represented in the paintings of Salvator Rosa (1615–73) and Gaspar Dughet (1615–75),[10] both highly favoured, it is true, but generally hailed as the lieutenants rather than the peers of Claude. Their skies are blackened by real clouds; their woods are darker and more menacing; their light is sharper than the golden glow of serenity which permeates so many of the landscapes of Claude.

Since by this time (1794) Brown had been dead for some eleven years, it fell to Humphry Repton to defend the establishment against the assault of Price and Payne Knight, and this he did in a letter addressed to Uvedale Price, Esq., dated 1st July, 1794,[11] as well as in a number of subsequent publications. In this role Repton clearly emerges as the successor of Brown, and undoubtedly he appeared so to Uvedale Price, but at the same time he saw himself as an innovator, basically sympathetic to the ideas of the picturesque. This paradoxical position of Repton has never been very satisfactorily explained and, tempting though it is to enquire further into such a fascinating subject, we must here resist the temptation and turn briefly to consider one other aesthetician whose contribution is, so to say, ancestral to a group of ideas the importance of which will later become apparent.

The word 'association' is to be found in the work of nearly all eighteenth century philosophers. Its meaning is not always the same. Hipple says it is '. . . employed by Hutcheson[12] in a rather pejorative sense, to suggest confusions which falsify the perceptions of sense, distort the passions, or mislead the reason'

FIGURE 6. THE PICTURESQUE
This picture by Montague Stanley appeared as the Frontispiece in Thomas Dick Lauder's edition of Uvedale Price's
*Essay on the Picturesque* (Lauder, 1842)

(Hipple, 1957, p. 29), and that it is found in the work of Locke and is used (in a different sense) by Hume, by Lord Kames and indeed by Burke, among many others (Hipple, 1957, p. 29). But as the basis of a system it is linked principally with the name of Archibald Alison who curiously enough, like Gilpin, became a prebendary of Salisbury Cathedral. Alison planned to write an exposition of a philosophical system, the essence of which was contained in his *Essays on the Nature and Principles of Taste*. On its appearance in 1790 the first edition made little impact, but the second, enlarged edition, published in 1811, followed by five others between 1812 and 1842, was more influential.

Among the main points to come out of Alison's treatment of the theory of association we may note,

(1) that aesthetic enjoyment arises, not from the intrinsic qualities of objects perceived, but from trains of ideas which they suggest by association;

(2) that such trains of ideas must be:

(a) uninterrupted by alien ideas (the mind must be free from preoccupation),

(b) not subjected to analysis by the critical faculty,

(c) productive of emotion, and

(d) connected by some linking principle.

'It cannot be doubted, that many objects of the Material World are productive of the Emotions of Sublimity and Beauty . . . On the other hand, I think it must be allowed, that Matter in itself is unfitted to produce any kind of emotion. The various qualities of matter are known to us only by means of our external senses; but all that such powers of our nature convey, is Sensation and Perception; and who-ever will take the trouble of attending to the effect which such qualities, when simple and unassociated, produce upon his mind, will be satisfied, that in no case do they produce Emotion, or the exercise of any of his affections.' (Alison, 1812 edn., vol. I, pp. 176–177)

We shall see later that, whether or not we accept Alison's doctrine in the terms in which he sets it out, much importance attaches to the idea that emotions may be aroused by some intermediate object, acting symbolically, with which the real source of emotion is connected subconsciously by some train of association.

'. . . The qualities of matter are not to be considered as sublime or beautiful in themselves, but as being the SIGNS or EXPRESSIONS of such qualities, as, by the constitution of our nature, are fitted to produce pleasing or interesting emotion.' (Alison, 1812 edn., vol. II, p. 176)

It is, I think, fair to say that the prolonged controversy about the Beautiful, the Sublime and the Picturesque is widely regarded today as somewhat tedious and not very directly relevant to modern aesthetics—a kind of stagnant backwater into which aesthetic thought found itself diverted and from which it eventually emerged without anything useful to show for so much expenditure of rhetorical energy. This is, I believe, an extremely ungenerous view which arises from too direct an assessment of the achievements of the participants in terms of their own avowed objectives. Naturally one cannot complain of having one's work assessed in such terms, but history is full of examples of attempts which, though unsuccessful in attaining their stated goals, nevertheless incidentally achieved other objectives the value of which became apparent only to posterity. When Columbus set out in 1492 his objective was to find a new route to China and the East Indies. He never reached his intended destination, but to dismiss the voyage as a failure would be a harsh and, most people would say, an erroneous judgment. By the same token those eighteenth-century aestheticians who set out to erect philosophical systems which would entirely account for aesthetic experience are bound to fare badly if judged within the terms which they themselves determined. They forged chains of reasoning out of the dubious material of abstract nouns on the precise meaning of which there was no agreement. As everyone knows, the strength of a chain is that of its weakest link, and even the relatively tight reasoning of Burke can be shown to contain demonstrable fallacies (Boulton, 1958, editor's Introduction). These philosophical systems, therefore, if judged as philosophical systems, have to be rejected.

But if the eighteenth-century aestheticians failed to defend convincingly the positions they had taken up, we have failed for another reason to appreciate the importance of what they achieved. Our mistake has been to reject them *in toto* on the grounds that they do not stand up to the claims which they made for themselves. We find ourselves exasperated by the triviality of their petty controversies. However, until we have forged our own chains of reasoning and constructed entirely acceptable hypotheses to explain the aesthetic appeal of landscape, we should do well to re-examine these eighteenth-century chains to see whether those links which have not proved fragile may yet be of use to us. When we look at the 'picturesque' controversy and its preamble, from Shaftesbury to Uvedale Price and Repton, we shall find a number of ideas to which, I believe, we must turn back if we are to make the kind of rapprochement between landscape and aesthetics at which we are aiming. We shall then discover not only that the thinkers of the eighteenth-century were aiming their enquiries more directly towards our target than were most of their nineteenth-century successors in Britain (though not, perhaps, in America), but also that many of the ideas which they introduced or developed contained the germ of what we may well regard as a modern view.

## Some Nineteenth-century Milestones

If we accept Hussey's definition of the Picturesque as 'an interregnum between classic and romantic art' I think we are likely to conclude that it had more in common with the latter than the former. Even if we cannot find a universally acceptable definition of the Romantic Movement we should agree that it was well under way by 1800. The reappraisal of the relative roles of reason and the imagination, the reaction against authority—academic, religious and secular— the preoccupation with liberty, the emphasis on the heroic and on the struggle of man to overcome the hazards which threatened to thwart him in the attainment of his ideals, all these found expression in an upsurge of interest in the place of man within the natural order. This is a theme wide enough to encompass a vast variety of approaches, and in the reaction against the supremacy of reason and formalism it is not surprising to find the front-running made, in Britain at least, not so much by the essayists and authors of logical discourses, set out in the orthodox format of philosophical treatises, as by the poets, novelists and painters, not forgetting the musicians (whose innovations, however, have not the same direct applicability to our present purpose). Thus Wordsworth concerned himself almost obsessively with man's experience of nature. Coleridge stressed the interaction between the human mind and its perceived environment. Scott, like many nineteenth-century writers after him, made topographical context an integral part of romance, often using real places as the theatre of action and setting different episodes in different places in such a way that location really mattered not only in his novels but also in his epic poems.

> 'Stirlingshire and Perthshire, Loch Lomond and Loch Katrine, form the scene for *The Lady of the Lake*; the Lake District for *The Bridal of Triermain* and North Yorkshire for *Rokeby*; the Hebrides for *The Lord of the Isles*. In each case, a large part of the poem's appeal is based upon its use of landscape; This is particularly the case with *The Lady of the Lake*, which started a tourist boom in the Trossachs, but in each poem a strong element of its flavour is supplied by Scott's ability to place the events in a setting which he knew well.' (Watson, 1970, p. 126)

Constable revolutionized the attitude of the landscape painter towards the process of converting observation into expression, while Turner discovered entirely new potentialities in the nature of colour and light. One senses in all the Romantics a recognition that the process of civilization, by which man masters his environment and seeks to liberate himself from servitude to the natural order may, if carried too far, substitute for natural laws a structure of artificial conventions and standards of reference. These deceive him into thinking of himself as a new species isolated from and independent of the world of nature, with the contemplation of which he may from time to time amuse himself as an outside observer. The trumpet-call of the Romantics summoned rational man back to the role of a participant in the events and processes of nature. In so far as he cut himself off from this experience he deprived himself of that satisfaction which can only come from involvement. This idea is central to Burke's theory of the Sublime, and indeed the more one looks at the aesthetic theories of the eighteenth century the more one recognizes in them the origins from which sprang the creative art of the nineteenth.

In America the situation was somewhat different. The impact of what has been called 'the Scotch school of psychological aesthetics' (Van Zandt, 1966, p. 152) certainly made itself felt through the agency of poets and painters, but it also became the cause of a great logical discourse not unlike that which had raged in

England and Scotland in the latter half of the eighteenth century, as Van Zandt makes very clear in the following passage:

'The romantic discovery of the American landscape was an intellectual as well as literary or artistic movement, and it was accompanied by one of the longest controversies in the history of American ideas. The American landscape, so to speak, was an *argumentum* as well as an object of praise or beauty; it had to be *argued* into a state of aesthetic respectability. The reasons for this were the formal philosophical aspects of European romanticism and the inevitable clash with the unique characteristics of the American landscape. The key word in this controversy is once again the word *wilderness*, for it was the unique quality of the American wilderness that became a major obstacle in the intellectual assimilation of European canons of aesthetic judgment. The European doctrine of "Association",[13] for instance, was intrinsically inimical to the American environment, for it defined an ideal landscape in terms of its rich association with the ruins and relics, myths and legends, of all past human history—a condition that could hardly be found in the raw American wilderness. The concomitant doctrine of "the picturesque" was also, in some of its aspects, a major stumbling-block: wherever it stressed the importance of human art and artifice in landscape, it encountered a severe American opposition.

'The debate concludes in what we may call "the romantic apotheosis" of the American landscape. The key word is still *wilderness*. If many aspects of European romanticism were intrinsically hostile to the characteristic primitivism of the American landscape, one of the most important of all was the source of unqualified approval. Dear to the heart of every true romantic was the over-riding belief in the transcendental world of nature—the belief that the visible landscape of the earth was an emanation of God, complete unto itself, without the need of human intervention for its own self-contained glory. It was a belief that Americans could accept with unmitigated pride. Where but in America was the world of nature more free from human association, more true to God's first intentions? What could be more "sublime", in the crucial word of the romantic era, than the deep virginal forests of this vast primeval landscape? Here in the highest category of nineteenth-century romantic philosophy the American landscape achieved an unequivocal apotheosis.'[14]

The landscape which in the American mind epitomized this 'romantic apotheosis' was that of the Hudson Valley, which even today is still largely forested until it reaches the outskirts of New York City. As a symbol of romantic landscape the Catskill Mountains became even more important in America than did the Lake District in England. As seen through the eyes of writers like Washington Irving and James Fenimore Cooper, and of poets, particularly W. C. Bryant, the Catskills and the adjacent parts of the Hudson Valley became

FIGURE 7. ASHER B. DURAND (1796–1886): KINDRED SPIRITS
This well-known painting (1849) portrays the painter Thomas Cole and the poet W. C.
Bryant in a picturesque 'Hudsonian' landscape. Reproduced, by permission, from
the Collection of the New York Public Library, Astor, Lenox and Tilden Foundations

established as the ideal type of primeval American landscape (Figure 7). The
painter Thomas Cole visited the district in 1825 and took up residence there in
1836, to be followed by those fellow-artists who together became known as the
'Hudson River School'. In the terminology of the British aestheticians of the

previous century this ideal concept of landscape drew heavily on the imagery of the 'sublime'.

By contrast with this 'Hudsonian' view of landscape there developed also a sympathetic appreciation of the aesthetic value of a tamed, cultivated environment. This alternative view is sometimes called 'Concordian' (Vance, 1972, pp. 189–190; Van Zandt, 1966) because of its particular association with Concord, Massachusetts, which became a nineteenth-century centre of cultural pre-eminence under the influence of Emerson, Thoreau, Hawthorne and other leading personalities of American philosophy, art and letters who lived there. Nash has described how Thoreau's early enthusiasm for wilderness was somewhat modified by his acquaintance with real wilderness when he visited Maine, and how this enhanced his appreciation of the cultural refinements of the civilized landscape.

> '. . . Could men live so as to "secure all the advantages [of civilization] without suffering any of the disa vantages?" The answer for Thoreau lay in a combination of the good inherent in wilderness with the benefits of cultural refinement. The excess of either condition must be avoided. The vitality, heroism, and toughness that came with a wilderness condition had to be balanced by the delicacy, sensitivity, and "intellectual moral growth" characteristic of civilization.' (Nash, 1967, p. 92)

Apart from the awakening of environmental consciousness stimulated by the Romantic Movement—a process started but not completed in the eighteenth century—the great contribution of the nineteenth century was the provision of those scientific ideas which made possible a new perspective in the rational comprehension, as opposed to the spontaneous enjoyment of landscape. Once again accuracy of observation was a prerequisite of progress, but whereas in literature and the arts it was the imagination which tended to take over, in the sciences observation provided the basis of strictly rational argument. A passage from Dorothy Wordsworth will serve to illustrate how close to each other these two avenues can be in the first, observational stage.

In August, 1803, she set out on a tour of Scotland in the company of her brother William. Coleridge began the tour with them but gave up at Loch Lomond. During the tour Dorothy kept a diary which was later published and which is a model for the description of keenly observed landscape detail. (To read her account of the Falls of Clyde is as good a way as any of capturing some idea of what they must have looked like before they were put into a pipe.) On the western shores of Loch Lomond she became much interested in a group of cottages some two miles south of Luss. Having given a description of them she goes on to write as follows:

> 'We were now entering the Highlands. I believe Luss is the place where we were told that country begins; but at these cottages I would have

gladly believed that we were there, for it was like a new region.'
(D. Wordsworth, 1874, p. 67)

Observation, in other words, led her to reject what she took to be the established view that the regional boundary, whatever this might mean and however it might be defined, was encountered at Luss, and to postulate for it a more southerly location. There is no attempt to follow this up scientifically; there is no rationalization, merely an empirical conclusion that, by the time she reached these cottages, she had already experienced a change in the environment which warranted the phrase 'like a new region'. I suggest that most travellers today would be perfectly satisfied with the proposition that Luss was the place of transition, if indeed they gave the matter any thought at all. As they approach it from the south they would have their eyes on the distant mountains to the north of Luss and perhaps on the lake, the shores of which do not undergo any dramatic change south of the village. The difference is to be seen in comparatively minor features which would escape the twentieth-century motorist but not Miss Wordsworth. She does not argue the case in terms of the Old Red Sandstone Conglomerates and the Schistose Grits, but if we look at a modern geological map we find that the Highland Boundary Fault does not pass through Luss, but crosses the road some three miles further south, and when she observed that it was 'like a new region' she must just have passed from the sedimentaries of the rift valley of central Scotland on to the metamorphics of the Highlands.

If we must distinguish the sciences from the arts, perhaps a satisfactory basis for the distinction lies in the fact that the sciences use this kind of meticulous observation not as a conclusion to explain experience but as a premise for further detailed enquiry. As a result of this process the biological and environmental sciences developed quickly. Already in the eighteenth century Linnaeus had devised his system of classification of plants, and throughout the nineteenth all kinds of natural phenomena were subjected to some comparable process of orderly arrangement as a result of which their mutual relationships could be more clearly established. Rapid progress was made in the classification of rocks and their constituent minerals; the systematic application of similar treatment to surface landforms came rather more slowly. Meanwhile, before the end of the century, scientific systems of classification had been applied to man-made features, for instance in Meitzen's great work on the morphology of agricultural land and settlement (Meitzen, 1895)

There is not time here to go into the contributions of Darwin and Freud beyond noting that no branch of environmental science escaped the influence of the former and no behavioural science was unaffected by the latter. But if we could find time to look a little more closely at one of the outstanding figures of the nineteenth century that figure should perhaps be Ruskin.

Ruskin's interests were so wide that what he wrote specifically on landscape forms only a modest part of his voluminous output, but his attitude to everything was deeply affected by a sensitivity to his physical environment. He com-

bined a talent for accurate observation with a keen aesthetic sense and a facility
for expressing his ideas which we should today regard as over-rhetorical but
which still has a power equalled by few writers in the English language. Clark
says of him:

> 'Ruskin approached art through nature. During the first half of his
> life he believed that nature—by which he meant the mountains, rocks,
> trees, plants, skies and rivers of Western Europe—was a direct revela-
> tion of God's glory, designed for the edification of man . . ..' (Clark,
> 1964, p. 85)

The theme of landscape keeps appearing throughout his work. Not unnaturally it is most consistently prominent in *Modern Painters*,[15] the book, or
rather series of books, in which he sought to establish the superiority of modern
painters, and in particular Turner, over the old masters. To the twentieth-
century reader much of Ruskin is impossibly 'dated'. We may reject the moral
assumptions which underlie his philosophy; we probably do reject most of his
theology; we would never dream of using his rhetorical extravagance in ordinary speech. But there is something compelling about the self-confidence of his
iconoclasm which commands attention if not assent, and there is probably no
writer on the theme of landscape who has entered the field of controversy with
more relish. It is perhaps worth quoting the following passage at some length
in order to convey the effect of Ruskin in full cry:

> 'Claude had, if it had been cultivated, a fine feeling for beauty of
> form, and is seldom ungraceful in his foliage; but his picture, when
> examined with reference to essential truth, is one mass of error from
> beginning to end. Cuyp, on the other hand, could paint close truth of
> everything except ground and water, with decision and success, but he
> had no sense of beauty. Gaspar Poussin, more ignorant of truth than
> Claude, and almost as dead to beauty as Cuyp, has yet a perception of
> the feeling and moral truth of nature, which often redeems the picture;
> but yet in all of them, everything that they can do is done for decep-
> tion, and nothing for the sake of love of what they are painting.
>
> 'Modern landscape painters have looked at nature with totally
> different eyes, seeking not for what is easier to imitate, but for what is
> most important to tell. Rejecting at once all idea of *bona fide* imitation,
> they think only of conveying the impression of nature into the mind of
> the spectator. And there is, in consequence, a greater sum of valuable,
> essential, and impressive truth in the works of two or three of our
> leading modern landscape painters, than in those of all the old masters
> put together, and of truth too, nearly unmixed with definite or avoid-
> able falsehood; while the unimportant and feeble truths of the old
> masters are choked with a mass of perpetual defiance of the most
> authoritative laws of nature.
>
> 'I do not expect this assertion to be believed at present: it must rest

for demonstration on the examination we are about to enter upon; yet, even without reference to any intricate or deep-seated truths, it appears strange to me, that any one familiar with nature, and fond of her, should not grow weary and sick at heart among the melancholy and monotonous transcripts of her which alone can be received from the old school of art. A man accustomed to the broad wild sea-shore, with its bright breakers, and free winds, and sounding rocks, and eternal sensation of tameless power, can scarcely but be angered when Claude bids him stand still on some paltry chipped and chiselled quay, with porters and wheelbarrows running against him, to watch a weak, rippling, bound and barriered water, that has not strength enough in one of its waves to upset the flowerpots on the wall, or even to fling one jet of spray over the confining stone. A man accustomed to the strength and glory of God's mountains, with their soaring and radiant pinnacles, and surging sweeps of measureless distance, kingdoms in their valleys, and climates upon their crests, can scarcely but be angered when Salvator bids him stand still under some contemptible fragment of splintery crag, which an Alpine snow-wreath would smother in its first swell, with a stunted bush or two growing out of it, and a volume of manufactory smoke for a sky. A man accustomed to the grace and infinity of nature's foliage, with every vista a cathedral, and every bough a revelation, can scarcely but be angered when Poussin mocks him with a black round mass of impenetrable paint, diverging into feathers instead of leaves, and supported on a stick instead of a trunk. The fact is, there is one thing wanting in all the doing of these men, and that is the very virtue by which the work of human mind chiefly rises above that of the daguerreotype or calotype, or any other mechanical means that ever have been or may be invented, Love. There is no evidence of their ever having gone to nature with any thirst, or received from her such emotion as could make them, even for an instant, lose sight of themselves; there is in them neither earnestness nor humility; there is no simple or honest record of any single truth; none of the plain words or straight efforts that men speak and make when they once feel.' (Cook and Wedderburn, vol. III, 1903, pp. 167–169)

I have selected this passage because it illustrates three important features of Ruskin's concern with landscape. Firstly it brings out the twin premises, nature and feeling, from which his aesthetic philosophy springs. He was himself a most acute observer of detail, so that he acquired not merely a layman's understanding of the generalities of his environment but, in some fields, such as geology, a scientific acquaintance of the subject which brought him face to face with the technical problems of its interpretation. Part of him, in short, was a scientist; one of the other parts, and there were many, was a person of outstanding artistic sensitivity who expressed himself not only as an art critic but as a practising artist. He drew subjects from natural history as well as from architecture with a high degree of accuracy, always seeking to blend what in the above passage he calls 'truth' with what he calls 'love'. For this reason, even if he had not contributed anything substantial towards the development of taste, the vigour and sincerity of his efforts to link the physical landscape with aesthetic feeling would have entitled him to a place of honour among the bridge-builders who have sought to span the gap between science and art.

Secondly, it shows the emphasis which Ruskin habitually gives to the criticism of technique. All these seventeenth-century painters are slated for their inability to translate accurate observation into an accurate reflection of reality. This may be a failure of observation, to be explained, perhaps, by a lack of enthusiasm and excitement in their experience of nature; at all events it is a technical failure of execution. They have not the competence to record 'truth'.

Thirdly, it illustrates Ruskin's style as a critic: assertive, authoritative, robust, but at the same time reliant upon these very qualities to sweep the reader along so precipitously that he will not have time to see the weaknesses in the argument. If we are not careful we may find ourselves assenting, for instance, to the assertion that Gaspar Poussin has '. . . a perception of the feeling and moral truth of nature . . .' without really questioning how this finds expression in his paintings or even if it means anything at all. Similarly, when Ruskin seems to sum up these various strictures in a general proposition, namely that what is wanting is 'Love', it turns out to be a more lightweight and, indeed, dubious hypothesis than we have been led to expect by such a flow of rhetoric.

Apart from his creative work as an artist, Ruskin's contribution to the aesthetics of landscape was essentially that of a critic. He sought to appraise, to evaluate, to put into perspective, but whatever his role as an innovator in the sociological or any other field, as a landscape aesthetician he never really enunciated any wide-ranging general principles significantly different from the party line of the romantics. Although he wrote a great deal on 'beauty', he was highly inconsistent, as can be seen, for instance, in the changing attitude which he displayed in *Modern Painters* towards the beautiful and the sublime (Landow, 1971, Ch. 3). Thus Clark says:

'The fact is that Ruskin continually, and increasingly, found his dogmatic statements falsified by his experiences, and not being a philosopher but a poet, he changed the definitions of his terms to suit the flow of his thought . . . We should be wasting our time to look for a coherent system of aesthetics (two words he hated) in his works as a whole.' (Clark, 1964, p. 132)

Sometimes Ruskin seemed to be on the brink of proposing an original theory of landscape aesthetics, for instance when he wrote:

'Landscape painting is the thoughtful and passionate representation of the physical conditions appointed for human existence. It imitates the aspects, and records the phenomena, of the visible things which are dangerous or beneficial to men; and displays the human methods of dealing with these, and of enjoying them or suffering from them, which are either exemplary or deserving of sympathetic contemplation.' (Ruskin, 'Lectures on Landscape', Cook and Wedderburn, vol. XXII, 1906, p. 12)

Here indeed is an idea which holds out great promise for the theoretical explanation of landscape aesthetics. If only it could be developed in some systematic way which would allow us to relate to it *particular* components of landscape—trees, cliffs, river-terraces! But if Ruskin clearly understood how this could be done he never clearly expounded it.

## The Advancing Fronts of Today

Whatever the importance of the nineteenth and early twentieth-century philosophers to the study of formal aesthetics, we do not find again that aim and direction towards landscape, which characterized the interests of their eighteenth-century predecessors, until we reach the school of 'American Naturalism' and its leading figure, John Dewey (1859–1952). Dewey had already made a reputation as one of the leaders of his day in the fields of philosophy and education before he turned more specifically to aesthetics with the publication of *Experience and Nature* in 1929; *Art as Experience* followed in 1934. His role as an aesthetician was partly destructive. He had to break down the various 'dualisms' which he found in aesthetics, and more particularly that which set aside art as something separate from the rest of life. The way had been paved by his immediate predecessors (who were actually younger than Dewey but applied themselves to aesthetics somewhat earlier in life), Benedetto Croce (1866–1952), with his concept of 'intuitive knowledge' and George Santayana (1863–1952).

Dewey's main message, for our purposes, is that beauty resides neither intrinsically in 'beautiful' objects nor 'in the eye of the beholder', but that it is to be discovered in the relationship between the individual and his environment, in short in what he calls 'experience'. From this there follow three important corollaries. The first is that since experience is a two-way contact between the creature and what he experiences, the distinction between perception and expression—for instance between enjoying a view and making a painting of it—is a meaningless distinction (cf. Croce's formula: intuition = expression); both are part of a single relationship.

The second corollary is, since there is an infinite variety of environmental conditions, there is also a possibility for aesthetic experience to take on innumerable forms. It rejects the idea that all aesthetic experience must be based on one single property inherent in man's relationship with his environment, such as 'order', 'harmony', 'proportion', etc., and opens up possibilities for deriving aesthetic satisfaction as wide as the possibilities of human experience itself.

The third corollary is that all experience presupposes certain mechanisms of a biological kind by which the relationship between man and his environment is maintained.

> 'The nature of experience is determined by the essential conditions of life. While man is other than bird and beast, he shares basic vital functions with them and has to make the same basal adjustment if he is to continue the process of living. Having the same vital needs, man derives the means by which he breathes, moves, looks and listens, the very brain with which he coordinates his senses and his movements, from his animal forbears. The organs with which he maintains himself in being are not of himself alone, but by the grace of struggles and achievements of a long line of animal ancestry.' (Dewey, 1958 edn., p. 13)

It is this aspect of Dewey's aesthetics, constantly reiterated in his argument, to which attention must be particularly directed. In this concept he brings us to the threshold of a new perception of landscape. As we have seen, the eighteenth-century aestheticians were feeling in this direction. Dewey, from a post-Darwinian viewpoint, was able to see a far more fundamental relationship between man and his surroundings because he could recognize it as basically the same as that which links any animal with its environment; since landscape is nothing more or less than the perceived environment, this approach to the aesthetics of landscape is of inestimable importance in the present discussion. Indeed, one of the 'dualisms' which was most profoundly shaken by Dewey was that which has so far hung like a cloud over our enquiry, namely that which separates 'science' from 'art'.

> 'The fact that science tends to show that man is a part of nature has an effect that is favourable rather than unfavourable to art when its intrinsic significance is realized and when its meaning is no longer interpreted by contrast with beliefs that come to us from the past. For the closer man is brought to the physical world, the clearer it becomes that his impulses and ideas are enacted by nature within him. Humanity in its vital operations has always acted upon this principle. Science gives this action intellectual support. The sense of relation between nature and man in some form has always been the actuating spirit of art.' (Dewey, 1958 edn., pp. 338–339)

Before leaving Dewey for the time being, although we shall return to his ideas later, we should perhaps dispose of two questions. The first is whether, in singling out landscape from other aesthetic objectives, we are not setting up precisely that kind of dualism which Dewey so devastatingly rejected. It must therefore be made clear that there is a difference between asserting that things are intrinsically different and isolating them pragmatically for a more detailed examination. Our present pursuit is of this latter kind. In enquiring into the nature of that aesthetic satisfaction which proceeds from our experience of landscape, we do not say that it is different from the satisfaction derived from our experience of other sources of aesthetic pleasure. We make no assertion about its relationship to such other sources. There is no postulated dichotomy, no 'dualism' in Dewey's sense. Our position is indeed entirely consistent with Dewey's view that the possible forms of aesthetic experience are infinite.

The second question is not about our enquiries but about Dewey's. Having brought us to the point of recognition that our aesthetic pleasures are to be seen in the context of an animal's relationship to its environment, why does he not press the point further? He does, of course, exemplify many of his subsidiary generalizations, but in doing so he is using examples to explain his generalizations rather than using general theory to explain individual cases.

I think the answer brings us back to what has been a fundamental problem all along. Dewey, writing as a philosopher, does not conceive it to be his job to extend his theories into the applied field further than is necessary to establish their general validity. 'Fortunately', he says, 'a theory of the place of the aesthetic in experience does not have to lose itself in minute details when it starts with experience in its elemental form. Broad outlines suffice' (Dewey, 1958 edn., p. 14). It is up to the art historians, the musicians, the literary critics and the students of landscape to work out the implication of his theories for their own fields, and as far as landscape is concerned this has not yet been seriously attempted. The philosophers who have succeeded Dewey have broken much fresh ground which is highly relevant to the experience of landscape, for instance in the study of symbolism, but we are still waiting for someone to work out in detail the connection between 'experience' as understood in Dewey's aesthetics and 'landscape' as understood by geographers, painters, landscape architects and the man with the rucksack.

Within the last few decades there have been signs that those who are concerned with the scientific explanation of landscape have felt an urge to cross the gulf, though most of them, deterred by the ingrained suspicions of their scientific training, have thought better of it before actually launching out. There are two possible ways in which the scientific student of landscape might feel that aesthetics had some relevance to his own work. In the first case he might argue that some aesthetic stimulus was at least partially responsible for leading him to his scientific interest.

'For many leading geomorphologists a deep sense of the beauty of the natural landscape has been the inspiration of a lifetime's devotion to its study.' (Pitty, 1971, p. 16)

In the second case it can be argued that the scientific pursuit of some aspect of landscape has led to an aesthetic experience. Such an experience may be ephemeral, possibly quite fortuitous. Yi-Fu Tuan describes such an incident:

'The geologist . . . may have clung precariously to an outcrop of the Chinle Sandstone in order to measure its dip. That work—that act of concentration—done, he turns around, relaxes, and perhaps in that momentary shedding of the will—experiences the beauty of what A. N. Whiteheads calls nature *in solido*.' (Yi-Fu Tuan, 1961, pp. 29–30)

Alternatively, such an association between the scientist and an aesthetic experience may be of a more permanent and eventually, perhaps, a less fortuitous character.

> 'In Medieval times the high mountains were looked upon with horror, by the modern man they are regarded as objects of beauty and inspiration. The new outlook was initiated towards the end of the eighteenth century by the geologists who explored the Alps. By the middle of the nineteenth century mountaineering had become a recreation . . ... Although people in general now spontaneously admire the high snow mountains, the study of their geology should not be entirely relegated to the specialists, for the knowledge of the anatomy of mountains contributes to the recognition of their beauty.' (Cornish, 1943)

This raises the question of how far, if at all, knowledge *does* contribute to aesthetic satisfaction; whether the approach to beauty is a matter of cognition or emotion or whether it involves a mixture of both. This is one of many questions too large to be discussed here in detail, but certainly if there is any validity at all in the 'theory of association' there are good grounds for arguing that cognitive experience probably does affect patterns of association, and that we cannot ever assert with conviction that our emotional reaction to something observed in the environment has nothing to do with what we know about it. There is, therefore, a good case for enquiring what geographers and other students of landscape have thought about its aesthetic attributes.

With the words, 'I have something to say which to old-fashioned geographers may appear as revolutionary . . ..' Sir Francis Younghusband, the explorer and traveller, began his Presidential Address to the Royal Geographical Society over fifty years ago (Younghusband, 1920, p. 1). The burden of this 'revolutionary' idea was that we should '. . . regard the Earth as *Mother*-Earth, and the *beauty* of her features as within the purview of geography' (Younghusband, 1920, p. 1). In the course of this address he put forward some ideas which were certainly likely to prove controversial.

> 'I am not maintaining that the actual enjoyment of the natural beauty of the Earth should be regarded as within the scope of geographical science, . . . Enjoyment is feeling, whereas science is knowing; and feeling and knowing are distinct faculties . . . I am not claiming more than that knowing natural beauty—being aware of it—is part of geography. But I *am* claiming liberty to extend our knowing up to the extreme limit where it merges into feeling.' (Younghusband, 1920, pp. 3–4)

Younghusband's address was a cogent plea for geographers to turn their attention to a serious consideration of the beauty of natural scenery, and among his audience was Vaughan Cornish, then aged 57, a kind of academic free-lance researcher who was already well known for his work on physical and political geography. The effect of hearing this address was that Vaughan Cornish '. . . now turned his main attention to the "analytical study of beauty in scenery"' (Gilbert, 1965, p. 3; see also Goudie, 1972). Within this field his themes fall into two main groups which may be broadly termed academic enquiry into the aesthetics of scenery and practical campaigning for its preservation. Important as was the latter—and virtually all the post-1945 measures to do with National Parks and the countryside in Britain owe something to his ideas—it is with the former that we are here principally concerned.

Apart from his shorter papers and his studies of more limited areas, Vaughan Cornish's principal contributions to the aesthetics of landscape are to be found in four books (Cornish, 1931, 1932, 1935 and 1943). In the third of these, *Scenery and the Sense of Sight*, he deals principally with the scientific basis of the perception of landscape; it is to do with such things as the apparent magnitude of the sun and moon, with the physics of light in so far as this affects colour, with the geometry of the field of vision, and so on.

The other books treat more specifically of situations in which the author himself has experienced emotional responses of an aesthetic kind. In the Foreword to *The Scenery of England*, which was published by the Council for the Preservation of Rural England, its President, Lord Crawford and Balcarres, says that Dr. Cornish '. . . provides us with a philosophic basis for the aesthetics of scenery . . .' (Cornish, 1932, p. 7). Yet this is what he conspicuously fails to do. It is really a book of reminiscences, of recollections in tranquillity, anecdotal, poetic, in places sentimental; it has some excellent word pictures, but it has no clearly enunciated philosophical message.

It is interesting to compare these aesthetic excursions of Vaughan Cornish, full of rich, descriptive detail and emotional footnotes, with the more-or-less contemporary writing of John Dewey, full of theory but rarely touching on the details of landscape. Dewey writes about the difference between 'experience' and 'an experience'; Cornish about the difference between Grindelwald and Camberley. Neither can really get to grips with the language of the other, and when Dewey died in 1952, Vaughan Cornish having predeceased him by some four years, the gap between their disciplines may have been narrowed but had certainly not been eliminated.

The aftermath of the Second World War brought many new developments involving first, a more general awareness of environment and the problems of its protection and secondly, a number of more specific measures aimed at crossing those interdisciplinary boundaries which had proved so inimical to its serious study. Among the landmarks symptomatic of this new climate we may note particularly the appearance, from 1951, of a periodical entitled *Landscape*, published from Santa Fe by the University of New Mexico. This provided a much-needed forum in which architects, landscape designers, geographers and others could present and exchange ideas of mutual interest on the theme of landscape. It is particularly important from our point of view because it actively encouraged a speculative approach, at least in its earlier years. In a short valedictory note on relinquishing his office the first editor wrote as follows:

'. . . I would be deceiving myself if I believed that the exploratory and speculative point of view which has hitherto been the magazine's characteristic was still widely acceptable.' (Jackson, 1969, p. 1)

To this I should be tempted to add 'More's the pity', but, while the mood lasted, *Landscape* presented some exciting, if occasionally undisciplined ideas and there will be many references in the following pages to its contents. Not only did it encourage discussion of practical questions and of historical subjects, but its pages are also penetrated by arguments of an aesthetic kind. It is here also that we find a number of examples of that particular kind of interdisciplinary liaison to which I have already referred and which is generally distinguished by the term 'environmental perception'.

The basic concept which underlies all studies in environmental perception is that where behaviour seems to be influenced by environment, that influence does not operate directly, but through an intermediate stage or stages. Behaviour, in fact, is influenced by a person's attitude towards the environment, not as it is, but as he thinks it is. In other words, the image of an environment is what counts,[16] and this image may be distorted in all sorts of ways. This 'perception' approach was borrowed from the psychologists and indeed fundamentally belongs to their discipline. Geographers have applied it to the study of the interaction between people and places and, although this is a comparatively recent field of enquiry, there is already a voluminous literature on the subject. There are also two or three review articles which would serve as a useful introduction to this literature. L. J. Wood, for instance, has attempted a concise summary (Wood, 1970) in which he recognizes six main categories into which perception studies in geography can be placed, namely 'landscape studies, hazard studies, recreation studies, urban studies, movement studies and space preference studies' (Wood, 1970, p. 131), and concludes '. . . there is no accepted theoretical base to perception studies in geography. These studies are still of an exploratory nature. There exists a mass of ideas, yet the exposition of general principles for the scientific treatment of perception in geography seems distant.' (Wood, 1970, p. 136)

In a later publication, Brian Goodey presents a fairly comprehensive survey of work which can reasonably be regarded as falling in this field (Goodey, 1971). His categories differ from those of Wood, but in neither case can one rule out any of these categories as being irrelevant for our purpose, nor identify any particular one as exclusively concerned with perception in the aesthetic sense. Indeed, Goodey expressly denies that he is dealing with this aspect:

'An issue which is largely avoided in this paper is the relationship between perception of the environment and the philosophy of beauty, although this must be an element in our understanding of man–environment relationships. Suffice to say, our ability to organize our perceptions probably gives us a satisfaction which is at the root of our aesthetic judgments.' (Goodey, 1971, p. 3)

Anyone acquainted with the literature of aesthetics will realize that this last remark is, to say the least, controversial, but neither this nor the author's rejection of aesthetics as a part of his declared objective prevents the paper from being an invaluable guide to the literature.

From the dozens of authors who have already concerned themselves with perception studies, Goodey singles out two for special mention. From 1958 onwards David Lowenthal has contributed many ideas which have not only proved important in themselves but have also prompted further work by others, while in the last few years Kenneth Craik, with his 'environmental psychology' has urged a more directly psychological approach. Of Craik's work Goodey says, 'He sees three major topics for examination: (a) what does the everyday physical environment do to people? (b) how do people comprehend the everyday physical environment? and (c) what do people do to the everyday physical environment?' adding 'Under these three heads we can fit almost all of the topics discussed in this paper.' (Goodey, 1971, p. 15)

Within the general field of perception studies there are certain approaches which have impinged closely upon aesthetics. The attitudes of various culture groups towards their physical environment (e.g. Yi-Fu Tuan in Lowenthal, 1967), the basis of 'taste' in landscape (e.g. Lowenthal and Prince, 1964, 1965), the evaluation of scenery as a prerequisite of a preservation or development policy in planning (e.g. Linton, 1968; Fines, 1968, 1969; Brancher, 1969), the psychological aspect of movement through landscape (e.g. Appleyard, Lynch and Myer, 1964), these and many other approaches are important and will be referred to again.

But perhaps the most important contribution of perception studies to landscape aesthetics so far is the momentum which has been generated towards an understanding of landscape in terms of the way in which people look at it, what they see in it and how its components combine to stimulate responses of an emotive as well as of a cognitive kind. It is significant that, in a recent British venture which has appeared under the title *Progress in Geography*, the first three annual volumes have each included extensive review articles in which perception is a central theme (Brookfield, 1969; Downs, 1970; Prince, 1971). Other periodicals relevant to the theme of environmental perception have recently been instituted. (*Environment and Behaviour*, 1969 *et seq.*)

Among the literature of environmental perception it is generally recognized that a special place of honour is reserved for Glacken's monumental study of 'nature and culture in western thought from ancient times to the end of the eighteenth century.' (Glacken, 1967) As his subtitle implies, he is not concerned with modern interpretations of man's environmental perception, but this is undoubtedly the standard work on the historical background to the subject. Yet there is in Glacken comparatively little direct reference to aesthetics as such, and this may well reflect the difficulty which all cultures and societies have experienced in finding plausible interpretations of the links between 'feeling' and landscape. Needless to say, aesthetic question marks are rarely absent from his discussion of what he calls 'physico-theology' and 'environmental theory', but his book tends to confirm the conclusion that human interest in, indeed fascination with, the role of man in his environment has proved more effective as a stimulus to argument than as a key to understanding, at any rate in its aesthetic implications.

One important manifestation of the post-war revival of interest in landscape has been the renewed activity of writers on 'the American Myth', 'The Arcadian Myth', 'the American Ideal' and various other titles under which is comprehended the theme of the American attitude to nature. Sometimes the emphasis is historical, a retrospective reappraisal of the role of the wilderness in the emergence of American landscape taste (e.g. Nash, 1967) or in the colonization and settlement of the continent (e.g. Van Zandt, 1949 and Vance, 1972). Sometimes it has strong sociological undertones, particularly in its concern with the attitudes of present-day urban communities in the United States towards the primeval vegetation of the continent. The struggle between the modern industrial town, with its attendant mechanization, violence, overcrowding and other social problems, and the unspoilt world of nature, into which civilization has brought these things, presents a dramatic theme of contrasts which have been exploited, for instance, by Leo Marx (Marx, 1964). But the emphasis which this 'wilderness' literature so often places on the self-consciously 'American' character of the phenomenon tends to direct attention away from, rather than towards, any explanatory linking principles of universal applicability.

> 'Americans sought something uniquely "American", yet valuable enough to transform embarrassed provincials into proud and confident citizens. Difficulties appeared at once. The nation's short history, weak traditions, and minor literary and artistic achievements seemed negligible compared to those of Europe. But in at least one respect Americans sensed that their country was different: wilderness had no counterpart in the Old World.' (Nash, 1967, p. 67)

The last sentence is perhaps not strictly true. Parts of Europe, particularly in the north and east, still contained forests occupied by the wolf, for instance, but the general point may be conceded that America was different. The question is 'how different?' Are we dealing with some different aesthetic principle or merely with different idiomatic expressions of the same principle?

If we are to find some plausible hypothesis it must be able to embrace questions of this sort, and we have not as yet found a convincing hypothesis proposed within any of the disciplines we have encountered. What about the contribution, then, of social anthropology to an understanding of the aesthetics of landscape? From the time of Frazer (see Frazer, 1890–1915) onwards there have been numerous enquiries into the attitudes of man to nature. Levi-Strauss, for instance, has emphasized the highly complex systems of classification of natural objects to be found among many so-called 'primitive' people, protesting that '. . . the savage has never borne any resemblance either to that creature barely emerged from an animal condition and still prey to his needs and instincts who has so often been imagined nor to that consciousness governed by emotions and lost in a maze of confusion and participation' (Levi-Strauss, 1966, p. 42). We may perhaps be permitted to make certain reservations about this, but we can scarcely fail to be convinced that by dubbing simple-living tribal societies 'primitive' we must not attribute to them an inability to frame quite elaborate concepts of environmental phenomena. The very complexity of totemism, how- ever, tends to obscure rather than clarify the explanation of aesthetic sensitivity to scenery, while the rich symbolism commonly found in it tends to reflect properties and values ascribed to nature by people whose view of it is very different from that of the scientifically trained observers who have set themselves the task of interpreting it. I think it would not be unfair to the anthropologists to say that they are still a long way from postulating a generally accepted hypo- thesis to explain the emotive satisfaction which human experience finds in the contemplation of landscape.

I cannot help feeling that, in the previous chapter, I left the impression that the landscape architects have not pulled their full weight in the investigation of landscape aesthetics. If this is so it will by now be apparent that they share the company of their colleagues in other disciplines. In any case such a judgment would be too harsh. The published works of landscape architects must be, and indeed are, rooted in aesthetics. But I have already drawn attention to their pro- fessional preoccupation with the solving of practical problems (p. 14), and much of the aesthetic theory which enters into their textbooks tends to be introduced almost incidentally into discussions of the challenges presented by individual cases and commissions.

This methodology is not peculiar to the landscape architects of today. It was the basis of the published works of Humphry Repton, who drew very heavily on the 'Red Books' which he had prepared for, and presented to, his land- owning clients. And since his general writings were intended as manuals for the guidance of those involved in the practice of landscape gardening it is probable that this was the most effective form they could have taken. It is interesting, however, to find the same approach in a book like Jellicoe's *Studies in Landscape Design*, in which he groups essays and lectures on a wide variety of subjects. Some of these are quite openly problem-oriented in the sense that they are case studies very much like the 'Red Books'; they summarize the problem, and sug- gest the solution, making such diversions as are necessary to review the prin- ciples involved.[17] Others aim more directly at the discussion of aesthetic prob- lems, such as 'Landscape from Art' (Jellicoe, 1966, vol. II, pp. 1–16), but even here heavy emphasis is laid on two case studies very much as in Repton.

This preoccupation with the practicalities of landscape design is both the strength and the weakness of the distinctive contribution which the landscape architects have made to the subject of our enquiry. It is a source of strength for two reasons. First, because the landscape architects have the authority which comes from experience. They alone have the right to bring the rest of us down to earth. Secondly, they have concerned themselves with a very wide range of experience of landscape aesthetics which has taken them into the arts and the sciences. They have encountered the thinking of the philosophers, the writing of the poets and the painting of the landscape artists, and they have sought to relate what they have found there to their knowledge of botany, geology and soil science. The weakness of their contribution lies in the fact that all these forays into so wide a field of human experience are made for the purpose of retrieving information and ideas which are directed towards the attainment of a limited end: the creation of an aesthetic composition out of a particular environment. They have done much to synthesize in a practical context the discoveries of the human race about its own attitude to its own environment. What is needed now is some simple hypothesis which will carry this synthesis one stage further on a theoretical plane. Let us see, then, whether we can find one.

# CHAPTER 3

# Behaviour and Environment

## The Ethological Approach

> 'It is early one Sunday morning at the beginning of March, when Easter is already in the air, and we are taking a walk in the forest whose wooded slopes of tall beeches can be equalled in beauty by few and surpassed by none. We approach a forest glade. The tall smooth trunks of the beeches soon give place to the Hornbeam which are dotted from top to bottom with pale green foliage. We now tread slowly and more carefully. Before we break through the last bushes and out of cover on to the free expanse of the meadow, we do what all wild animals and all good naturalists, wild boars, leopards, hunters and zoologists would do under similar circumstances: we reconnoitre, seeking, before we leave our cover, to gain from it the advantage which it can offer alike to hunter and hunted—namely to see without being seen.'
>
> KONRAD LORENZ (1964 edn., p. 181)

At this point in the twentieth century Dewey's philosophy commends itself as the most promising starting point for any further enquiry into the aesthetics of landscape. The change of approach implicit in making experience the central theme was a prerequisite of further progress in understanding the aesthetic satisfaction which people find in their visible environment. But Dewey's approach remained essentially an explanation in general terms. Furthermore, it tended to be 'process-oriented' towards man's experience of the environment rather than 'object-oriented' towards the composition of the landscape itself. The next step must necessarily face the problems of applying the general principles of Dewey's aesthetic philosophy to actual environmental situations. Dewey comes as far as his allegiance to philosophy will allow him. Indeed, many of his phrases contrast sharply with the traditional language of the subject; but he still employs the terminology of aesthetics. At some point we have to move across to the terminology of landscape—foregrounds and distances, sloping and horizontal surfaces, arboreal and other kinds of vegetation, and the play of light and shade on these things. About these Dewey had very little to say except where they conveniently entered into examples chosen to illustrate some facet of perception, comprehension or emotional response. He did, however, repeatedly point the way towards the next stage of the journey, as is clear from the passage quoted in the previous chapter (p. 49, lines 3–12).

It is not merely the physical sense-organs which man inherits from his forebears. We can see also similarities in patterns of behaviour.

'To grasp the sources of the esthetic experience it is, therefore, necessary to have recourse to animal life below the human scale. The activities of the fox, the dog, and the thrush may at least stand as reminders
and symbols of that unity of experience which we so fractionize when
work is labor, and thought withdraws us from the world.' (Dewey,
1958 edn., p. 18)

A little later Dewey goes even further:

'I do not see any way of accounting for the multiplicity of experiences
of this kind . . . except on a basis that there are stirred into activity
resonances of dispositions acquired in primitive relationships of the
living being to its surroundings, and irrecoverable in distinct or intellectual consciousness.' (Dewey, 1958 edn., p. 29)

What are these dispositions? What are these primitive relationships? Is
Dewey saying that the basis of aesthetic experience is innate? If so, our gratitude
to him for pointing the way forward may be somewhat diminished when we
find that it leads directly into one of the most controversial areas of modern
behavioural science. Of course, Dewey does not say that aesthetic taste itself is
innate; that it can be genetically transmitted from one generation to another.
He seeks to explain aesthetic experience in terms of behaviour characteristics,
some of which, he implies, can be so transmitted. This is a very different matter,
and it is this proposition which we must follow into the territory of landscape
analysis. Even so, it is clearly necessary to dwell for a moment on the implications which it raises, and to satisfy ourselves that we are not embarking on the
pursuit of an idea which from the outset can be shown to be incompatible with
the findings of the behavioural sciences.

There are, I think, three main areas of controversy surrounding the question
of heredity and environment. The first is semantic. Words like 'instinct', 'learning', 'genetic', etc., are susceptible of different shades of meaning. The second
concerns the mechanisms by which behaviour characteristics are transferred
from parent to offspring. The third deals with demarcation disputes in the
attribution of behaviour characteristics to heredity and environment—the inborn
and the learned—respectively. (For instance, how much does a skilful tree-
monkey owe its skill to its genes and how much to its parents' training or its
cumulative experience of trial and error?) Obviously this is not the place to
become embroiled in these controversies. Provided we can satisfy ourselves
first, that there are behaviour characteristics as well as anatomical characteristics which are capable of being genetically transmitted, and secondly that some
such characteristics may have a role to play in relating the individual creature to
his environment, we can feel justified in looking more closely at these characteristics and in enquiring how they carry out this role.

On the first point there is ample evidence that certain behaviour characteristics can be 'inborn'. As an example let us consult the work of Thorpe on
chaffinches (Thorpe, 1956). By using oscillograms in the study of the songs of

chaffinches Thorpe was able to demonstrate that '. . . individual differences are not the expression of genetic differences but develop by learning during the early life of the bird.' (Thorpe, 1956, p. 5)

In these experiments it was shown that a young chaffinch, reared separately out of hearing of all chaffinch song, developed a very restricted song devoid of the usual phrasing and of the elaborate final flourish. 'The simple, restricted song of the isolated bird can be taken to represent the inherited basis of a chaffinch's performance.' (Thorpe, 1956, p. 5)

Two or more birds put together after babyhood develop more elaborate songs as complex as, but quite different from, that of a wild chaffinch.

> 'In nature young chaffinches must certainly learn some details of song from their parents or from other adults in the first few weeks of life . . ..
> But not until the critical learning period, during the following spring, does the bird develop the finer details of its song. This is the time when the young wild chaffinch first sings in a territory in competition with neighboring birds of the same species, and there is good evidence that it learns details of song from these neighbors.' (Thorpe, 1956, p. 5)

Thorpe concludes:

> 'So the full chaffinch song is a simple integration of inborn and learned song patterns, the former constituting the basis for the latter.' (Thorpe, 1956, p. 5)

A great deal of animal behaviour can be seen to be of this type; that is to say it is made up of two components, inborn and learned, and various experiments have been set up to separate these components in particular cases of observed behaviour. The methods by which lovebirds carry their nest-building materials have been studied by Dilger (1962) with a view to establishing the relative importance of inborn and learned characteristics in the acquisition of habits.

> 'All female lovebirds prepare their nest materials in much the same way: by punching a series of closely spaced holes in some pliable material such as paper, bark or leaf. The material is held between the upper and lower portions of the bill, which then works like a train conductor's ticket punch. The pieces cut out in this way vary in size and shape among the various lovebirds. So do the forms of behaviour that now ensue.' (Dilger, 1962, pp. 94–95)

Dilger then goes on to describe these forms of behaviour, which are of two different kinds. The birds in one group tuck the pieces of nesting material into their feathers and fly off with them. Those in the other group carry the pieces in their bills.

By crossing a bird from the former group (the peach-faced lovebird) with one from the latter group (Fischer's lovebird) Dilger produced a hybrid which displayed conflict in behaviour between the tendency to follow one method or the other.

'When our hybrids first began to build their nests, they acted as though they were completely confused. They had no difficulty in cutting strips, but they could not seem to determine whether to carry them in the feathers or the bill. They got material to the nest only when they carried it in the bill, and in their first effort at nest building they did carry in their bills 6 per cent of the time. After they had cut each strip, however, they engaged in behaviour associated with tucking. Even when they finally carried the material in the bill, they erected the feathers of the lower back and rump and attempted to tuck. But if they were able to press the strips into their plumage—and they were not always successful in the attempt—they could not carry it to the nest site in that fashion. Every strip dropped out.' (Dilger, 1962, pp. 97–98)

Dilger then describes how, over a period of two or three years, carrying in the bill gradually replaced the unsuccessful procedure of carrying in the feathers.

'Today the hybrids are behaving, by and large, like Fischer's lovebird, the more recently evolved of their two parents. Only infrequently do they attempt to tuck strips into their plumage. But it has taken them three years to reach this stage—evidence of the difficulty they experience in learning to use one innate pattern at the expense of another, even though the latter is never successful.' (Dilger, 1962, p. 98)

Now that we have established that certain habits of chaffinches and lovebirds have been demonstrated to be derived partly from inborn characteristics and partly from learning and that such a dual origin is therefore not impossible in nature, we can turn to those patterns of behaviour which express an even more direct relationship between an animal and its environment. That such patterns of behaviour are commonplace could hardly be denied by anyone who has observed the phenomenon of 'territoriality' in, for instance, the English robin, or the selection of nesting sites in almost any species of bird. Even more complex habits are to be found in bird migration (Sauer, 1957 and Ricard, 1969) and in the remarkable practice of 'sun-compass-orientation' (see, e.g. Ferguson, 1967). Many phenomena of this kind have been described in some detail, yet the mechanisms by which they are achieved have scarcely begun to be understood. Most of them seem to involve the acquisition of some inborn basic urge which becomes regularized by practice and experience into a set of habits. The individual creature interacts with its environment in a manner which, in the most general sense, is common to its species, but in detail is peculiar to itself.

Lorenz has described by reference to the water-shrew how such a set of habits is built up (Lorenz, 1964 edn., Ch. 9). This little animal, having acquired 'path-habits', can proceed quickly along familiar routes, but if it is confronted with a situation unfamiliar in even the smallest detail (such as if a pebble is displaced from a known path), it becomes immediately disoriented and has to set about building the new situation into its path-habit. To describe such path-habits as 'innate' would clearly be an abuse of the term, but at the same time the observation of these little animals laboriously building up their 'path-habits' by trial and error, and learning only to repeat movements precisely as they have made them before, suggests that the mechanisms by which an animal establishes a relationship with its environment are made up of two components (inborn and learned) as is the song of the chaffinch or the method by which lovebirds carry their nesting materials.

Almost all animals living in a natural environment display some forms of behaviour which reveal a use of their environment such as suggests a connection with the realization of their biological needs.

> 'The closer our study of behaviour becomes the more we are convinced that numerous details of behaviour are "adaptive", that is to say they play a part in the relations between the animal and his environment. Although this is self-evident to every ecologist acquainted with such phenomena as, for example, habitat selection, host selection, reactions to predators, food preferences, etc., only few workers recognize the amazingly high degree of adaptiveness to be found in numerous behavioural characteristics.' (Tinbergen, 1969 edn., p. 13)

Even where the relationship between animal and environment has not been subjected to scientific examination, such a relationship may be attested from observation, even to the point where environmental behaviour may be predicted.

> 'It is often true to say that a good naturalist knows more about his subject, at least within a narrow range of species, than the best-equipped student of the physical environment with all his micro-climatic apparatus and other devices, and most people who have studied a group of animals will have had the experience of being able to tell "intuitively" that this or that is an area where a given species will be found—and have been right. It is often difficult to explain such intuitions to others and to make them objective.' (MacFadyen, 1963 edn., p. 10)

The livelihood of a ghillie in a deer forest depends absolutely on an understanding of this relationship, an understanding based on the observation of recurring movements related to the topographical characteristics of the environment. Mortimer Batten, even if his scientific interpretations of behaviour were sometimes suspect, was a meticulous observer of wild life. This is what he wrote about the roe-deer.

> 'The roe-deer is a creature of more or less regular habits and regular runways, and even a two-mile range may contain many miles of visible track. Also, it will contain at least three harbours in regular use. One of these is probably an open, sunny plateau, where the bracken above affords sufficient cover for safety, while not excluding the sun. The

other two beds may be on comparatively swampy ground, in the heart of the densest cover, and comfortable only in so far as they afford adequate shelter from the wind. At these recognized resting-places dung is dropped more liberally than elsewhere, the wild deer having no need for sanitation. The roe-deer can, therefore, be said to have at least one dry sunning-bed on its range in addition to other harbours used when the luxury of warm sunshine is not obtainable, and chosen with a view to obtaining shelter, food, and freedom from disturbance.

'To and from these harbours the runways extend, and the following is typical. Coming down from the north end of the wood the deer hold the highland, close to the boundary wall, but on the forest side, and thus on to the beechwood. Here there is a harbour, much frequented by does with their fawns, which are very limited in range. The trail then drops to the burn-edge, and winding in and out of the rich undergrowth, turns straight back to the northern boundary, where it crosses the burn and turns southward down the opposite bank, encompassing every willow-swamp and traversing the thickest growths of forest. Here it taps a new planting, there it encompasses a small loch, and so on till the southern boundary is again reached, where it again doubles back, keeping near the opposite border, and terminating finally at the sunning plateau. All the runways are, of course, interconnected, but if left undisturbed the deer keep more or less to the same paths.' (Batten, 1920, pp. 41–42)

In this passage we have a description of a system of geographical associations which can only be explained in terms of both inborn and learned behaviour. It is impossible to believe that all roe-deer behave in a manner which is so similar that it can be described in general terms but yet have no common inborn behaviour characteristics. At the same time their *precise* reaction to their environment must be unique to the individual; for one thing no two environments can be identical. To understand how the process of adaptation works it will be as well to consider some primitive kinds of behaviour and enquire into their environmental implications.

Under the heading 'Behaviour' the *Encyclopedia Britannica* sets out the basic situation:

'Behaviour is closely related to function. There are four primitive kinds of behaviour having obvious adaptive results: ingestive behaviour, including eating and drinking; shelter seeking; sexual behaviour; and investigatory or exploratory behaviour. In addition to these, certain types of behaviour are found chiefly in the more complex animals, including man; agonistic behaviour, including fighting and escape behaviour; allelomimetic behaviour or mutual imitation, including the co-ordinated movements of flocks and herds; care giving or epimeletic behaviour; and care soliciting or et-epimeletic behaviour. Eliminative behaviour, concerned with disposal of bodily wastes, has importance in some animals.' (*Encyclopedia Britannica*, 1969 edn., vol. 3, p. 395)

It will be seen that *all* these forms of behaviour may implicate the environment to some degree. Even those forms which do not at first sight seem to do so, such as sexual behaviour, may, in some cases, lead to a very particular association. Many species of animal will not embark on the process of raising a family until they have made provision by adapting a micro-environment for the purpose. This process, known technically as *nidification*, has implications also in terms of the macro-environment, because the selection of a suitable site for the nest involves the identification of a place whose general characteristics are conducive to the requirements of other forms of behaviour. Indeed, it would be very unusual for any animal action to be explicable solely in terms of one of the above categories of behaviour. Some of these categories, however, have particularly important associations with the environment.

*Ingestion*, for instance, is a requirement which asserts a most powerful control over animal distribution. All animals are to some extent limited by the geographical occurrence of their food supply. *Shelter-seeking* also clearly involves the animal in a very close relationship with the environment. It is an extremely common phenomenon. Indeed, Scott says:

'The tendency to seek out optimum environmental conditions and to avoid dangerous and injurious ones is found in almost all animals and may be called *shelter-seeking*.' (Scott, 1958, p. 15)

And later:

'Any animal which can move at all and can discriminate between different parts of its environment will show some shelter-seeking behaviour.' (Scott, 1958, p. 59)

*Investigatory* or *exploratory* behaviour is of particular significance because this is the form of behaviour on which the successful selection of places which afford the optimum conditions for other forms of behaviour largely depends. *Escape* behaviour again links the animal very intimately with its surroundings. Anyone who has observed a mouse trying to escape from a cat will have noticed how it seeks to take every advantage which its environment affords, looking for easy paths of movement by which to reach a place of refuge accessible to itself but not to its pursuer, and concealing itself as best it can behind any object which happens to be available.

Animals show a general tendency to prefer and, in so far as they are able, to select an environment which affords opportunities for satisfying all the requirements, under these various headings, peculiar to their species. Places which afford such opportunities and which are commonly occupied by such creatures we call 'habitats'.

It is a characteristic of many species, particularly of birds, that the individuals seek to assert exclusive rights over habitats and will fight to preserve them from intrusion by other members of the same species. Tinbergen and Falkus, in a picture of birds nesting in a gullery, have schematically drawn in territorial boundaries marking off the territories around each nest. The caption comments: 'the territorial boundaries, so real to the birds, are invisible to us . . . but if we *could* see them, they would look rather like this' (Tinbergen and Falkus, 1970, p. 15). I doubt whether any ornithologist could be found who would be prepared to assert that the phenomenon of 'territoriality' was not based on an inborn behaviour mechanism, though the establishment of *particular* territories must clearly be the product of the application of these mechanisms to a unique context.

## The Atavistic Argument

In a moment we shall return to Dewey and his assertion that, to grasp the sources of the aesthetic experience, it is necessary to '. . . have recourse to animal life below the human scale' (p. 59). Desmond Morris has shown that, if we are to take a meaningful interpretation of the patterns of human behaviour, we must start from the premise that *Homo sapiens* is merely one of 193 living species of monkeys and apes (Morris, 1967, p. 9). And if his feeding habits, his aggressiveness and his sexual practices are to be studied as developments of equivalent behaviour patterns in other species of ape, surely it is logical to suppose that the attitudes of more primitive creatures to their visible and tangible environments may throw light on human attitudes towards the same things. Berlyne seems to think so and to suggest that such an approach can be carried into the field of aesthetic experience.

'We must naturally concern ourselves principally with experiments on human adults and, to a lesser extent, on children of school age, since these are the only organisms credited with "aesthetic taste" or "appreciation of art". Nevertheless, we must not forget that the aesthetic behaviour of the human adult has emerged out of an evolutionary process lasting millions of years and out of an intricate, gradual unfolding of psychological functions in the individual. So we must not overlook the presages of aesthetic behaviour that can be in the playful and exploratory activities of animals and human infants.' (Berlyne, 1971, pp. 181–182)

Yet it must be admitted at once that such an assumption would not be universally accepted without qualification. In an address given to the Institute of Landscape Architects, Lee stressed the adaptability of man in adjusting himself to his environment.

'It can be argued that the inspiration and uplift we get from certain qualities in the scenery have been contrived by conditioning, therefore we could learn to obtain aesthetic satisfaction from other conditions.' (Lee, 1972: see under Race, 1972, p. 15)

In the ensuing discussion, the speaker was asked if the perception of neighbourhood had any relation to territorial behaviour in animals.

'Professor Lee considered that some of the generalizations made by biologists tended to be rather wild; there may be vestiges remaining but these are quickly overlaid by learning.' (Race, 1972)

It will be remembered, however, that we have already accepted a major role for 'conditioning' and 'learning'. The question is whether the 'vestiges remaining' can be so completely 'overlaid by learning' as to be totally obliterated. David Stea certainly seems to think that the study of 'territorial behaviour' does not bear this out. He says:

'We have reason to believe that "territorial behaviour", the desire both to possess and occupy portions of space, is as pervasive among men as among their animal forebears—witness the attitude of slum-area street gangs towards their "turf". There is some suggestion, coming largely from the animal world, that territorial possession is not less fundamental than sexual possession, as had originally been supposed, but is equally or even more fundamental.' (Stea, 1965, p. 13. See also Cullen (1961) on 'possession' of place, pp. 21 et seq.)

Stea, it will be noted, is concerned with an aspect of *fundamental* behaviour. Of course it is easy to demonstrate the absurdity of comparing human and animal behaviour if we confine our enquiries to superficial details. If, for instance, we were to search our own habits for traces of a compulsive desire to tuck pieces of leaf or bark under our non-existent lumbar feathers we should not expect to find such evidence of a behavioural affinity with the lovebirds. Although this practice has been shown to be inborn it relates to a particular way of solving the problem of building a particular kind of nest from a particular kind of building material, all of which is restricted, not only to lovebirds, but even more narrowly to certain species of lovebirds. If, then, we cannot even draw inferences about the behaviour of one species of lovebird from that of another, no wonder that psychologists counsel caution in extending such inferences to the behaviour of man!

However, we are not concerned with this level of particularity but with much more basic manifestations of behaviour. At a more fundamental level we *do* share inclinations to achieve certain objectives not only with all species of lovebird but indeed with other animals generally. We are born with a capacity for feeling hungry and, if not with sexual desires, at least with mechanisms which ensure that most of us acquire these later. We experience the desire to drink in response to an impulse different from that which induces us to insert solids through the same orifice. We become sleepy; we feel protective towards our young and, if we are prevented from breathing, we have a sensation of discomfort, anxiety and, if the condition lasts long enough, fear, even panic, resulting in violent convulsions which we interpret as an effort to remove the impediment to respiration and restore conditions in which we can survive. Even if we can explain and perhaps control these actions by reason, we recognize that it is not reason which prompts us to attempt them in the first place. All the evidence points to the fact that the motivation which impels us is of the same kind as that which impels the animals. We do these things because we want to.

The question which confronts us, then, is this. If we share with animals a desire to eat, to drink, to sleep, to mate, to seek shelter and to escape from danger, is it reasonable to believe that we have inherited all these inborn desires but that, for some reason, the spontaneous awareness of the perceived environment, which is such a conspicuous feature of all the higher animals, has 'dropped out'? It is true that we are no longer as dependent on it for our survival as were our animal, or even our more primitive human, ancestors. It is true also that faculties which are not used may become less efficient. The human sense of smell, for instance, is less acute than that of many animals. But it has not disappeared in 'normal' human beings, and where those in whom it has been destroyed, by injury, for instance, are able to survive, we should not expect their children to be born without it merely because a parent had demonstrated that it was no longer essential. It takes many generations for underused faculties to disappear altogether and, allowing twenty-five years as a statistically average generation gap, a hundred generations in Britain would take us back to the Bronze Age; two hundred well into the Stone Age. It is therefore not very long since a keen sensitivity to environment was a prerequisite of physical survival. Any creature born without it would be less likely to live long enough to procreate its species and, by the principle of natural selection, such a sensitivity would continue to be a distinctive attribute of surviving members of that species. Even if one could reasonably believe that in the last hundred-or-so generations human nature has fundamentally changed, man still finds himself from time to time in a situation—in jungle warfare, for instance—in which the mechanism needs to be brought into use again in something like the circumstances in which, until civilization pronounced it to be a luxury, it was as indispensable to the survival of the species as hunger or the sexual impulse.

Many writers on landscape have been convinced that some such assumption lies behind our aesthetic enjoyment of landscape. Thus Brenda Colvin:

> 'Humanity cannot exist independently and must cherish the relationships binding us to the rest of life. That relationship is expressed usually by the landscape in which we live.' (Colvin, 1970 edn., p. 108)

In an article which questioned the basis of this relationship in a very direct form Searles made it clear that he had no doubt about the importance of the biological environment in landscape aesthetics.

> 'It is my conviction that there is within the human individual a sense *of relatedness to his total environment* [Searles' italics], that this relatedness is one of the transcendentally important facts of human living, and that if he tries to ignore its importance to himself, he does so at peril to his psychological well being.' (Searles, 1961–2, p. 31)

Man, says Searles, is constantly seeking to refresh his association with this biological background, for instance through recreational activities and through his interest in such things as gardens and gardening, nature haunts, pets, zoos, landscape in movies, in painting, in literature and in dreams. He stresses the relation of 'primitive' man to his physical environment and quotes the example of the pleasure which Vedda cave-dwellers derived from getting wet in the rain.

> 'It seems to me', he concludes, 'that, in our culture, a conscious ignoring of the psychological importance of the nonhuman environment exists simultaneously with a (largely unconscious) *overdependence upon* that environment. I believe that the actual importance of that environment to the individual is so great that he *dare* not recognize it.' (Searles, 1961–2, p. 33)

The idea that the aesthetic enjoyment of landscape is based on a kind of atavistic sensitivity is not by any means new. It was stated quite explicitly in 1900 by Sitte:

> 'Our ancestors since time immemorial were forest dwellers; we are apartment-house dwellers. This alone suffices to explain the irresistible craving for nature on the part of the residents of cities—to get out into the open air, out of the dust-mill and the crush of houses, into the greenery of the great out-of-doors.' (Sitte, 1965 edn., p. 167)

Even in medieval times, according to Glacken, we find a related idea:

> 'The basic objection to hunting and the reasons for trying to control it—among the lay and clergy alike—was that it embodied atavistic instincts which should be kept at bay.' (Glacken, 1967, p. 347)

Hunting, it may be noted, will emerge as an important linking theme in the association between behaviour, landscape and aesthetics.

## Habitat Theory

The point at which we always seem to run up against a brick wall is in understanding more precisely how the actual ingredients of landscape operate on the aesthetic sense. Even Searles does not reach a point where he can provide us with the tools for making a detailed analysis of an actual landscape in terms which can precisely relate biological and psychological experience with the aesthetic satisfaction derived from the observation of natural and man-made objects distributed in a particular fashion. If, then, we allow that human beings are born with a tendency to be immediately and spontaneously aware of their physical environment; if they experience pleasure and satisfaction from such an environment when it seems to be conducive to the realization of their biological needs and a sense of anxiety and dissatisfaction when it does not, how can we analyse those properties of an environment which are capable of producing this effect?

The important phrase is 'seems to be'. What matters is not the *actual* potential of the environment to furnish the necessities for survival, but its *apparent* potential as apprehended immediately rather than calculated rationally. In a sense we see the objects which comprise our environment as symbols suggesting by association properties which are not necessarily inherent in the objects themselves. There is nothing improbable in this; it is a very well attested phenomenon in animal behaviour. Some forty years ago Lack concluded that

'. . . the distribution of Breckland birds seems explicable only on the assumption that each species selects its ancestral habitat, recognizing it by conspicuous features.' (Lack, 1933, p. 256)

A little later he adds:

'Most distributions can be explained only by postulating the existence of specific habit selection—that each species selects its ancestral habitat, instinctively recognizing it by the conspicuous, not necessarily the essential, features.' (Lack, 1933, p. 259)

More recently Hinde has said:

'Habitat selection among birds usually depends on characters of the habitat which are not essential to survival, but which are visibly prominent characteristics of the landscape and which thus serve as sign stimuli.' (Hinde, 1966, p. 445)

All this leads to the proposition that aesthetic satisfaction, experienced in the contemplation of landscape, stems from the spontaneous perception of landscape features which, in their shapes, colours, spatial arrangements and other visible attributes, act as sign-stimuli indicative of environmental conditions favourable to survival, whether they really *are* favourable or not. This proposition we can call *habitat theory*. It brings within the orbit of aesthetic experience such features as suggest, even if by a remote association, the satisfaction of those basic behavioural requirements outlined above (p. 63). 'Ingestive' requirements, for instance, are very directly suggested by the smiling cornfields, the browsing flocks and the limpid brooks of the classical poets and their latter-day disciples. Outstandingly important, however, in this elementary relationship between man and his perceived environment is the extent to which he is able to exploit it in securing an advantage in his relations with his fellow humans, with the other creatures of the animal world, and with those inorganic forces of nature which used to be poetically called 'the elements'.

All this is, in general terms, implicit in what Dewey wrote forty years ago. To study its particular relevance to the aesthetics of landscape we need a further signpost. We shall find it, I suggest, in that little phrase which concludes the quotation from Konrad Lorenz at the beginning of this chapter: '. . . *to see without being seen*'.

'Habitat theory' thus asserts that the relationship between the human observer and the perceived environment is basically the same as the relationship of a creature to its habitat. It asserts further that the satisfaction which we derive from the contemplation of this environment, and which we call 'aesthetic', arises from a spontaneous reaction to that environment as a habitat, that is to say as a place which affords the opportunity for achieving our simple biological needs. When we attain a sufficient control over our environment to render the mechanisms by which we make this spontaneous appraisal of it no longer essential to the achievement of these biological needs, the mechanisms do not immediately die out in the species but continue to be transmitted from one generation to another and may, if needed, be called upon again to discharge their primitive function. More often, however, they are released from this function, which is to ensure the survival of the individual and the species, and we are then able to enjoy the satisfaction which results from the perception of a biologically favourable environment without uncomfortably exposing ourselves to the hazards against which this sensitivity to our surroundings would protect us in a 'state of nature'. Habitat theory, in short, is about the ability of a place to satisfy *all* our biological needs.

### Prospect–Refuge Theory

Lorenz' phrase 'to see without being seen' reduces the scope of the habitat concept. It provides a kind of shorthand reaction to environment by latching on to a facet of behaviour which automatically exploits the advantages latent in a creature's surroundings.

Let us briefly go back to some of the primitive kinds of behaviour referred to above (p. 63) and consider the position of a creature engaged in hunting, escaping, shelter-seeking and exploring, and let us, by way of an explanatory exercise, rationalize the attitude of such a creature to its environment, making it very clear, of course, that we are not asserting that any such rationalization actually takes place.

A creature *hunting* says to itself, 'If I wish to catch my quarry I must do so before it can reach a place which is inaccessible to me. Such a place may be a hole in the ground, a pond, a tree-top, or simply, if the quarry has greater speed and stamina than I, a distant location from which it can move further as I approach. To minimize its chances of doing this I must approach as close as possible before it sets in motion the mechanism for achieving this escape, which means, in practice, before it notices me.' *Per contra* a creature *escaping* says to itself, 'If I am to escape successfully, I must ensure that I can reach a place inaccessible to my pursuer before he can prevent me. When, therefore, I am engaged in activities such as feeding, which involve the diversion of my attention from the activities of a potential pursuer, I must so position myself, if possible, that either he will not see me or, if he does, I will perceive him threatening me while I yet have time to reach safety.'

In both these cases it is in the creature's interest to ensure that he can see his

quarry or predator, as the case may be, without being seen, and the achievement of these conditions becomes a first objective which renders more likely
the achievement of the second, to catch or to escape.

A creature *seeking shelter* has a somewhat different objective. Its concern is to
escape from the threat, not of an animate pursuer, but of an inanimate hazard,
such as the wind or the rain or the excessive heat of the sun, but it very frequently happens that a place which will serve the function of providing shelter
from the elements, a rabbit hole, for instance, will also provide concealment from
the hunter. If, indeed, the place of shelter has to accommodate the creature when
sleeping or rearing its young, it may be important that both objectives be
achieved at the same time.

All these kinds of advantage can be more certainly secured if a creature is
familiar with the opportunities afforded by its environment for observing
animate and inanimate threats and protecting itself from them.[18] The creature
*exploring* is seeking to acquaint itself with the widest range of options to exploit
its environment so that, if the necessity arises, it can act from a basis of information and not of ignorance. Exploring is the master activity which lies behind the
successful accomplishment of the others and it can be observed in all the higher
animals.

Even in the course of this activity, however, the creature must be constantly
aware of the possibility of exposure to some hazard, and the escape equipment
must be kept in working order. The creature exploring is always potentially the
creature escaping. Let us return for a moment to Lorenz' shrews.

> 'Exactly as mice and many other small rodents would do under similar
> conditions, the shrews interrupted their careful exploration of their
> new surroundings every few minutes to dash wildly back into the safe
> cover of their nest-box. The survival value of this peculiar behaviour is
> evident: the animal makes sure, from time to time, that it has not lost
> its way and that it can, at a moment's notice, retreat to the one place
> it knows to be safe. It was a queer spectacle to see those podgy black
> figures slowly and carefully whisker their way forward and in the next
> second, with lightning speed, dash back to the nest-box.' (Lorenz,
> 1964 edn., pp. 100–101)

It can now be observed that seeing and hiding have a unique complementary
role to play in all these 'primitive' activities. But the spontaneous appraisal
of the landscape can only be successful in safeguarding the observer if it is followed by the inducing of anxiety or restlessness which will prevent the creature
from relaxing its attention to potential danger until it has found an environment
which furnishes the conditions for protecting itself from such danger and, whatever these conditions may ultimately be, they are first apprehended in terms of
the ability to see without being seen. Where these conditions are present their
perception is attended with pleasure; anxiety is set aside and relaxation is possible. Where they are absent anxiety continues and there is no relaxation.

At this point in the argument we have an obligation to remind ourselves again of the dubious validity of drawing inferences about the behaviour of humans from that of animals. The question is whether this spontaneous satisfaction, obtainable from a strategically favourable environment, is one of those basic experiences, like eating, sleeping and mating, which we share with the higher animals, or whether it is one of the more particular phenomena of behaviour which are restricted to certain species or groups of species, excluding man.

Certainly, among so-called 'primitive' communities whose livelihood depends on hunting, there can be no doubt that a combination of searching and hiding, whether these are rational or spontaneous activities, is fundamental to success, as reference to almost any account of tribal hunting activities will show.

> 'The men will perhaps set off armed with spears, spear-throwers, boomerangs and shields in search of larger game such as emus and kangaroos. The latter are secured by stalking, when the native gradually approaches his prey with perfectly noiseless footsteps. Keeping a sharp watch on the animal, he remains absolutely still, if it should turn its head, until once more it resumes its feeding. Gradually, availing himself of the shelter of any bush or large tussock of grass, he approaches near enough to throw his spear . . . Sometimes two or three men will hunt in company, and then, while one remains in ambush, the others combine to drive the animals as close as possible to him. Euros [*Macropus robustus*, a small kangaroo] are more easily caught than kangaroos, owing to the fact that they inhabit hilly and scrub country, across which they make "pads", by the side of which men will lie in ambush while parties of women go out and drive the animals towards them. On the ranges the rock-wallabies have definite runs, and close by one of these a native will sit patiently, waiting hour by hour, until some unfortunate beast comes by.
>
> 'In some parts the leaves of the pituri plant (*Duboisia Hopwoodii*) are used to stupefy the emu. The plan adopted is to make a decoction in some small waterhole at which the animal is accustomed to drink. There, hidden by some bush, the native lies quietly in wait. After drinking the water the bird becomes stupefied, and easily falls a prey to the black fellow's spear. Sometimes a bush shelter is made, so as to look as natural as possible, close by a waterhole, and from behind this animals are speared as they come down to drink.' (Spencer and Gillen, 1899, pp. 19–20)

The importance of a strategic use of the environment in hunting is constantly emphasized in anthropological literature.

> 'The Washo hunter was successful not because of uncanny accuracy but because of his stalking ability. The purpose of the hunt was to get close enough to the game so that a miss was virtually impossible.' (Downs, 1966, p. 26)

Or again,

'The hunting of land mammals offers nothing exceptional. The Tlingit Indian is generally a poor shot, and therefore he tries to come as close to his prey as possible, waiting for hours in a blind until the game approaches.' (Krause, 1956 edn., p. 125)

Having established, then, that there is much evidence to show that at both human and sub-human level the ability to see and the ability to hide are both important in calculating a creature's survival prospects, we must next see whether we can find some means of erecting a system for classifying the components of landscape according to this simple principle, whether or not they are conducive to the observer seeing and hiding. Where he has an unimpeded opportunity to see we can call it a *prospect*. Where he has an opportunity to hide, a *refuge*. And just as we can identify the desire to see without being seen as something conducive to, but more limited than, the desire to satisfy *all* our biological needs, so we can recognize its aesthetic basis as more limited than the aesthetic basis of that more comprehensive ulterior objective. To this more limited aesthetic hypothesis we can apply the name *prospect–refuge theory*.

At the risk of repetition, and because it is important to understand the precise senses in which our terms are used, let us briefly recapitulate. Habitat theory postulates that aesthetic pleasure in landscape derives from the observer experiencing an environment favourable to the satisfaction of his biological needs. Prospect–refuge theory postulates that, because the ability to see without being seen is an intermediate step in the satisfaction of many of those needs, the capacity of an environment to ensure the achievement of *this* becomes a more immediate source of aesthetic satisfaction.

From the recognition of prospects and refuges as the twin bases of our hypothesis we may at first sight appear to have set up a dichotomy of opposites, and before we can explore the implications of the hypothesis in terms of the actual components of landscape it is essential to enquire more closely into the relationship between the two terms. That there is an element of contrast between them is obvious. 'To see' is clearly not the same as 'not to be seen'. But it would be quite fallacious to regard them as 'opposites' as we might regard good and evil, bigness and smallness, light and darkness, and so on, as opposites.

The point can perhaps be made clearer by an analogy. The tactics in a football match can be seen in terms of 'attack' and 'defence', and any press report will serve to show how indispensable this concept is in the analysis and description of the game. But the primary dichotomy is not between attack and defence, but between a team and its opponents. The *objective* is for 'us' to beat 'them'. The means of achieving this objective lies in scoring goals without conceding them and a failure in either department, attack or defence, can result in defeat. Similarly, the concepts of prospect and refuge are antagonistic only in tactical terms, and just as 'attackers' and 'defenders' are equally essential in a football team, so prospect and refuge must work in combination within the context of the real conflict. In a football team strength is a virtue both in attack and defence. Weakness in one may be compensated for by strength in the other. Similarly, a landscape which affords both a good opportunity to see and a good opportunity to hide is aesthetically more satisfying than one which affords neither, but again weakness in prospect or in refuge may be compensated for by strength in the other. In short 'prospect' and 'refuge' do not constitute a dichotomy or 'dualism' in the sense which would have offended Dewey.

## Variables in the Experience of Landscape

The strategic value of a landscape, therefore, whether natural or man-made, is related to the arrangement of objects which combine to provide collectively these two kinds of opportunity, and when this strategic value ceases to be essential to survival it continues to be apprehended aesthetically. The number of possible arrangements of prospects and refuges which are capable of inducing aesthetic satisfaction is obviously infinite. The potential variety of aesthetic experiences which can be derived from the contemplation of landscape can be achieved in many ways, but principally by varying (i) the objects employed to symbolize prospects and refuges, (ii) the manner and intensity with which they symbolize them, (iii) the spatial arrangement of the symbols, (iv) the equilibrium of prospect and refuge symbols, and (v) the physical media by which such an arrangement is communicated to the observer. Let us briefly amplify these points.

(i) The objects employed to symbolize prospects and refuges and the relationships between objects and their symbolic values will be examined in more detail in the next chapter.

(ii) The variable manner and intensity with which objects, or groups of objects, symbolize prospects or refuges leads to the use of a terminology which can indicate, in general if not precise quantitative terms the extent to which such symbolism is potent in an object. Thus, we can meaningfully say that an object is 'a strong prospect symbol' or 'a weak refuge symbol', or that it has a 'high prospect value', a 'low refuge value', etc.

(iii) The variable spatial arrangement of the symbols is the basis of landscape composition. What has been said of 'objects' under (ii) above can equally be said of the whole composition. There is no absolute line of demarcation between symbolic objects and their arrangement. Thus trees (=objects) arranged collectively comprise a wood (=another object). The spaces between trees, or between woods, may comprise a 'prospect', and so on.

(iv) The variable equilibrium of prospect and refuge symbols may lead to the emphasis of one or other of these concepts in a landscape. Thus we can talk about a 'prospect-dominant' landscape or a landscape in which prospect and refuge are 'well balanced'. While most human beings seem to be sensitive to aesthetic stimuli arising from prospect and refuge elements combined in varying proportions, individuals may display preferences for, or more strikingly, perhaps, antipathy towards the 'prospect' or 'refuge' components.

Such antipathy may, indeed, amount to a neurosis, which we call 'agoraphobia' or 'claustrophobia' depending on whether the symptoms display an aversion to 'prospect' or 'refuge'.

These four variables will be considered in much more detail in the following chapters. The fifth variable can more usefully be discussed now.

(v) The variations in the physical media by which the details of a landscape are communicated to the observer may be highly complicated, but basically they can be reduced to variations affecting the passage of light. Light is the one fundamental requirement for the realization of any prospect, and if we are to enquire further into the nature of prospects and the differences between them, it will be necessary to make a brief excursion, at the most elementary level, into the physics of light in order to make sure that we understand those of its properties which have a bearing on the appearance of landscape.

For a sighted person to be able to see the component parts of his environment the essential requirement is that light shall be able to pass from its source to the observer's eye. Where the object perceived is itself a source of light, such as the sun or the flame of a candle, the light passes directly to the eye and the observer sees an image of that object. But by far the greatest number of objects are perceived as a result of light from some other source being reflected from them. This reflected light reaches the eye from different directions according to the distribution of the objects from whose surfaces it is reflected. Interruptions to the passage of this light may take place at either stage, that is between the source and the reflecting surface or between the reflecting surface and the eye, and they may be partial or total.

This process is illustrated in Figure 8. Light from a source (S) falls on a landscape-feature (L) and part of this light is reflected to be 'caught' by the eye of the observer (O). The maintenance of a prospect, visible to the observer, depends on the maintenance of the passage of light through the sequence $S \rightarrow L \rightarrow O$ (Figure 8a). It can be destroyed by a breach either of the line SL or of the line LO.

At the same time, if light from the same source, or from some other source, illuminates the observer (Figure 8b), he in turn will be visible from such places within the landscape (L) as the light reflected from him can reach. This visibility will be maintained as long as the passage of light is maintained through the sequence $S \rightarrow O \rightarrow L$. It can be destroyed by a breach of either the line SO or the line OL.

In the prospect–refuge situation, therefore (Figure 8c), the observer seeks to ensure that the passage of light is maintained from L to O but not from O to L. This can be achieved by interrupting SO but sustaining SL and LO (Figure 8d) or by sustaining SL and SO but so interfering with the line LO that light can pass along it in one direction ($L \rightarrow O$) but not in the other (Figure 8e). A theoretical solution would be to interpose a plate of 'one-way glass' which would allow the passage of light in one direction but not in the other. 'One-way glass', however, is not a substance encountered by creatures in a state of nature, and if the observer is to be rendered invisible by an interference with the passage of light

76

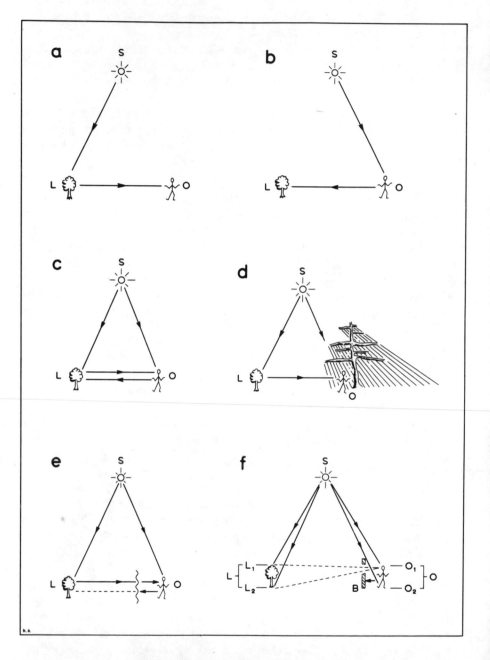

FIGURE 8. SEEING WITHOUT BEING SEEN
S = source of light. O = observer. L = landscape feature. B = barrier. For further explanations see text. Drawn by Keith R. Scurr

between O and L it must be by some means other than the total elimination of light moving in one direction, because an obstruction which achieves this, except by cutting off the source of light between S and O, will also cut off light moving in the direction $L \rightarrow O$.

In discussing this problem so far we have argued as if L and O were points having position but no magnitude. In fact both the observer and the object he perceives do have magnitude. Light from L to O and from O to L is reflected not from a point but from an area and, if a barrier (B) is placed near the observer, as in Figure 8f, with an opening large enough to admit the passage of light reflected to the observer's eye from all points between $L_1$ and $L_2$, he will still be able to see the whole image of L. At the same time a substantial portion of the light reflected from the observer (between $O_1$ and $O_2$) will be impeded by the interrupting screen and will render such a small portion of his person visible that he will have achieved at least partial concealment. Theoretically the law of intervisibility asserts that, if X is visible from Y, then Y is visible from X, X and Y being points. As soon as X and Y acquire magnitude, however, a condition is set up in which the kind of interference illustrated in Figure 8f becomes possible, and prospect and refuge can be at least partially achieved simultaneously.

In trying to explain the achievement of prospect and refuge in terms of the behaviour of light we began by making a false assumption that the landscape-object (L) and the observer (O) were points. This exegetic simplification we have now rectified by recognizing that L and O are not points but areas. In so far as this little model is intended to represent an actual landscape situation, however, we have not yet rectified certain other oversimplifications which we have made in the cause of explanation. Thus we have assumed that the source of light (S) is also a point, whereas in fact it must have magnitude. Even an apparently infinitesimal 'point' of light, such as a star, has magnitude; indeed it may well have a real magnitude vastly greater than that of our own sun, but distance renders its apparent magnitude diminutive. The sun itself, being much nearer, has a larger apparent magnitude, and one consequence of this can be seen in the indefinite edge of a shadow cast in sunshine by the definite edge of an object. The larger the apparent area of the source of light becomes, the more does this effect come into operation. Where light from the sun is diffused, for instance by being passed through a cover of cloud, virtually the whole sky becomes the equivalent of a source of light. On a cloudy day there are no sharp shadows, though there may be differences in the intensity of light falling on the ground, as for instance when a large overhanging tree cuts off the light from the overhead sky and allows the penetration of light only from a low angle. It will still be darker under the tree than under the open sky. But since the variations of diffusion as well as of the intensity and angle of incidence of light from the original source are infinite, the extent to which a prospect can be interrupted (Figure 8) or a refuge created by obstructing the lines SL and SO respectively will depend on all the circumstances, including the nature of the interrupting object. A thin layer of cirrus cloud, for instance, will have a very different effect from a thick layer of stratus or cumulus cloud or from the canopy of a cedar, and much of the variation in prospect and refuge within a landscape is achieved by such variations in the passage of light. We all know how different the same landscape can look under different weather conditions as a result of differences in the behaviour of light.

One corollary of this phenomenon of diffusion is that, even on a sunny day, an object which casts a shadow does not necessarily destroy the visibility of objects within the shadow. It may render them less conspicuous without totally concealing them. Some light always reaches the shaded object by reflection from environmental objects, including particles of dust or water in the atmosphere. Such reflected light is of so low an intensity compared with the direct light of the sun that we are still left with the impression that all the light is coming directly from a single source, but we can nevertheless manage to distinguish, even if only dimly, objects within the shaded area. The degree of efficacy of an obstacle casting a shadow will therefore depend on such considerations as the size of the object, the extent to which it is truly opaque—trees, for instance, commonly allow the penetration of some light between the leaves, causing 'dappled shade' and the presence or absence of lateral screens to cut off the penetration of reflected light approaching from other directions. The shadow of a large horse-chestnut is likely to provide a more effective hiding-place than that of a silver birch. A cave will be more effective than either because its roof is totally opaque and its walls cut off the lateral intrusion of reflected light except through its mouth.

Before leaving this elementary digression into the physics of light it may be as well to mention that certain other properties of light can have important implications for landscape. When, for instance, we referred to an interruption in the passage of light the term may have suggested a total impediment, and there are many substances which have the power to preclude absolutely the passage of light. But not all substances behave like this. A layer of cloud, for instance, will reflect a proportion of the sun's light back into space, so that there will be not only a diffusion of that light which succeeds in passing through it but also an actual loss of light intensity, as any photographer will tell you.

Again, under favourable atmospheric conditions the loss of light may not take place from the whole spectrum but selectively from different parts of it, thereby altering the colour perceived. The red and orange of the sunset is the most obvious example of this. Also, an impediment may simply bend or 'refract' light. We are all familiar with the way in which refraction affects the appearance of a river-bed as seen through water, but it may occur also when layers of air of different temperature refract the rays of light passing through them. The phenomenon known as a 'mirage' is caused by refraction under these conditions.

Similarly, where water particles are suspended in the air they may interfere with the passage of light, not only between the sun and the earth, as in a cloud layer, but also between a reflecting object (L in Figure 8) and the observer (O). The effect is then to blur the details of the object; the edges become indistinct; the outline begins to look like an ill-defined silhouette. A distant horizon seen through a shower of rain looks like this.

A similar effect to that of diffusion of light by water particles in suspension may also be achieved by particles of dust. In detail the effect tends to be somewhat different, for instance in colour selection and in the extent and occurrence of the interference. Anyone who has watched the sun set over the smoke haze of an industrial town will be familiar with this. Sometimes the effects of interference by dust particles may be highly spectacular. It is recorded that a succession of remarkable sunsets was seen all over the world after the eruption of Krakatoa in 1883. More often, however, the effect is to be seen locally, even, maybe, in the smoke of a bonfire and it is not always aesthetically satisfying. In the whole field of meteorological terminology it would be hard to find a word with more unpleasant associations than 'smog', that hybrid derivative of smoke and fog which so diffuses such light as can penetrate it that the observation of the clear outlines of objects beyond the immediate environment of the observer becomes impossible.

Prospect–refuge theory should provide us with a frame of reference for examining the aesthetic properties of landscape from one particular theoretical base. There is no suggestion that it should supersede other frames of reference which have been successfully employed in the various disciplines concerned with this problem. All such frames of reference involve a measure of classification according to the properties which are deemed to be important. In the traditional description and criticism of landscape painting, for instance, in which perspective has been accepted as a fundamental characteristic, the division of a landscape into foreground, middle ground and distance is practically inevitable.

A geographer interested in landscape would not be content with quite the same basis of differentiation. In so far as it is his concern to explain the character of a place in terms of the principles governing the distribution and interrelation of what he finds in it, he will probably see a primary significance in the dichotomy between those features which have been disposed by nature and those whose origin has involved also the work of man. The theoretical division between the 'natural' and the 'cultural' landscape (p. 6), though quite untenable if pressed too far, provides at least a meaningful starting point from which an approach can be made. Other terminology may be appropriate for indicating the dominant features of a landscape by allocating it to a type. Thus we can talk of 'a mountain landscape', 'a desert landscape', 'a winter landscape', even 'a Mediterranean landscape', and so on. Such terminology is extremely imprecise, but at least it imposes some limitation on the imagination of the listener when he tries to reconstitute in his mind a picture of the landscape which he has heard described by such a term.

An architect or town-planner would probably see landscape in terms of other classifications depending on the function and associated appearance to which it could be referred. He will see a major contrast between 'residential areas' and 'public open space', for instance, or between 'high-rise' and 'low-rise' buildings. A landscape architect again has his own terminology. For him a major distinction is to be seen between 'voids' and 'masses', by which he means respectively clear, open spaces, allowing the penetration of the line of sight, and impediments to vision such as might be interposed by trees, cliffs, buildings, etc.

A moment's reflection will show that all such systems of classification of landscape features can be equally valid for their respective purposes. They are not mutually exclusive, and we do not have to demonstrate the invalidity of one before we can propose another. Indeed, even the most sophisticated examination of a vast amount of data classified in one way could totally overlook the significance which might be immediately apparent were it classified in another. Just as a classification of human beings by race, pigmentation, age, sex and other physical characteristics (all important for some purposes) would be useless for the Blood Transfusion Service which, nevertheless, needs a precise and highly exacting system of classification for its own ends, so a division into foreground, middle ground and distance, or into mountain and valley, or into permanent grass and arable, does not by itself evaluate a landscape in terms of its capacity for providing the opportunity to see without being seen. For this purpose we need a framework of classification based on the complementary concepts of prospect and refuge, and when we have provided ourselves with this, and when we begin to refer to it actual features of the environment, then an explanatory link between aesthetic concept and actual landscape suddenly seems attainable. Let us therefore set up such a framework.

# CHAPTER 4

# A Framework of Symbolism

### The Symbolic Interpretation of Landscape

> 'Psychologists class the problem of picture reading with
> what they call "the perception of symbolic material"'
>
> E. H. GOMBRICH (1960, p. 202)

Reference has already been made more than once to the importance of symbolism in the interpretation of a creature's behaviour within the environment. Before we examine the symbolism of prospect and refuge in more detail, it will be as well to reflect a little further on certain aspects of symbolism in general, and the first point is that symbols vary in their degrees of precision. Mathematical symbols may be extremely precise, but the symbols with which we are concerned are typically much more vague.

One consequence of this is that the symbolic analogy must never be pressed too far. There is always a credibility gap between what the symbol actually is and what it is supposed to represent. This gap can be bridged only if we accept the validity of the symbolic link even when reason tells us that it is invalid. The rituals of religion, of folklore, of superstition are full of examples. The Easter egg may be used to symbolize the resurrection of Christ; but in so far as it purports to represent the emergence of life from death we know very well that biologically the egg is not dead. Symbols are used, in fact, to convey ideas to which rationally they are only very loosely related. In just the same way the symbolic representation of danger may be only vaguely and quite irrationally related to a real danger; a 'refuge' may afford no real guarantee of security, and a 'prospect' which visually satisfies the observer that his immediate environment is free from danger, may be permeated with radiation hazards or alive with poisonous snakes. Yet the symbolic impact of these environmental phenomena can induce in us a sense either of ease and satisfaction or of unease and disturbance, and it is on these emotional responses rather than on the real potency of the danger, the refuge or the prospect that our aesthetic reactions will depend.

Another characteristic which applies to all symbolism is that, in so far as objects are used to suggest ideas, there need not be, as it were, a one-to-one ratio. That is to say, one object may represent more than one idea and conversely one idea may require a number of associated objects through which to be represented. Let us take the first case first.

A Romanesque church in an Italian village may suggest a number of associated ideas, such as the antiquity of religion, the 'assurance' of solid, round-arched construction, the continuity of settlement, the simple faith of an agricultural community or simply a place of shelter from the rain. In the symbolism of habitat theory we constantly encounter this phenomenon, and frequently in a form where two or more apparently conflicting ideas are symbolized in a single object. A cloud, for instance, if it is dark and threatening and emitting rain, or if it has assumed some dragon-like shape, may symbolically suggest a threat. On the other hand, if it affords some shade from the blinding sun, it may suggest a refuge. A distant cumulus cloud rising out of the evening shadows to reflect the rays of the setting sun can be a prospect symbol. It is even possible, and indeed extremely common, for an object to symbolize prospect and refuge at the same time. A turret of a castle does this. It suggests a place of safety whose function is to provide a vantage-point.

The opposite case, in which the symbolic expression of one idea requires several objects, needs to be particularly stressed in connection with landscape. In the painting of stories or episodes a single symbol, placed somewhere in the picture, often suffices to communicate its message. Most of the Christian saints, for instance, had their own distinctive marks of identity (such as Saint Peter's keys or Saint Catherine's wheel). But in landscape painting the symbolism may lie not in the objects themselves so much as in the spatial relationships between them, or in the way in which some objects are seen in shadow and others in the full glare of the sun.

Yet another characteristic of symbolism is that it can be manifested at what we may call different levels. An illustration will explain what I mean by this. A model of a lighthouse can be said to 'symbolize' a real lighthouse. We know perfectly well that it *isn't* a lighthouse and that it could not be used as one in a real situation, but if I were to ask 'What is this?' you would probably reply, 'A lighthouse', even though, strictly speaking, you would mean 'A model of a lighthouse', because you accept the convention by which an accurate scale model may be understood to represent or 'symbolize' the object to which it has been made to bear a resemblance.

If, again, I were to show you a lighted candle standing by itself on a table, and if I were to ask 'What is this?', you would probably say, 'A candle.' But if I were to place the candle among model ships, standing it on the end of model breakwater and were again to ask 'What is this?', the reply 'A candle' would suggest a dismal lack of imagination, because, in that setting, it would obviously be intended to discharge a symbolic function in representing a lighthouse. The imitation of the original lighthouse is in this case much less accurate than in the case of the model, but we can hardly say that the symbolism is weaker. Rather it is expressed at a difference level.

Applying this idea, then, to the experience of landscape, we see that environmental objects can symbolize hazards, prospects, refuges, etc., at different 'levels of symbolism'. When we talk of a 'hazard' we may mean, on the one hand, a crocodile, a bush fire or a human enemy or, on the other, simply a feeling of exposure to an unidentifiable or even an imaginary and perhaps non-existent threat. When we talk of a 'prospect' we may mean, on the one hand, what we can see from an observation post specially selected or even constructed to command a view of a piece of country in which there may or may not be some potential threat or, on the other, simply the sense of not being shut in, such as may be experienced, for instance, when one looks upward to a bright sky. When we talk of a 'refuge' we may mean, on the one hand, a hiding-place screening us from a hostile observer, or a cottage sheltering us from the real adversities of the weather or, on the other, a sense of being enclosed, over-shadowed, protected by some ineffective barrier, such as a cloud, against an unidentified and perhaps wholly imaginary source of danger.

In all these cases we can distinguish between those levels of symbolism which relate the observer to his immediate environmental situation and those which operate merely symbolically by suggesting environmental situations which are not actually realized. After we have considered in more detail the various kinds of symbol employed in prospect–refuge theory we shall be in a better position to see how these 'levels of symbolism' apply in practice and we shall therefore re-turn to the subject again, but throughout the discussion we must recognize that there is no clear-cut line of demarcation between those environmental objects which suggest a strategic advantage or disadvantage *directly* and those which achieve a similar effect *symbolically* at different 'levels' of symbolism.

The idea of a physical object being, as it were, the manifestation or representa-tion of some ideal equivalent is fundamental to the philosophy of Plato and is found recurring in one form or another throughout the history of human thought. It has played a central role in all religions, because religion deals with areas of existence which can only be reached through symbols. At certain periods, for instance in the Romantic Movement, its importance in the aesthe-tics of landscape may have increased, but there has never been a period or an art form which has not depended to some extent on the use of symbols.

During the nineteenth century the symbol began to acquire a new significance when the psychologists addressed themselves to the scientific investigation of processes of thinking and communication. In particular the work of Sigmund Freud opened up a field of enquiry based on the assumption that ideas and images entertained in the conscious mind were indicative, or representative, of other ideas, recollections, relationships or experiences which were never consci-ously recognized. That is to say they were symbolic. And since one of the most startling disclosures of Freud was that many features of human behaviour were to be explained in sexual terms, symbolism in psychology came to be thought of by the layman as principally sexual.

It is therefore not unnatural that anyone looking for a symbolism by which human feelings are linked with the physical environment should first turn to the symbolism of sex. It will be remembered that Edmund Burke had done just this over a hundred years before Freud was born (p. 28) and had come up with a clearly defined set of symbols which, he thought, explained the Beautiful in nature in terms of the Beautiful in womanhood. The idea therefore is not new, but inevitably any present-day attempt to pursue this line would have to be based on a much more direct, even clinical, approach to sexual symbolism of a Freudian rather than an eighteenth-century kind. Thus, in a study of what he calls 'the cross-valley syndrome' (Shepard, 1961), Shepard has examined the persistent aesthetic interest taken in river valleys at the point where they pass through ridges or mountains, and after discussing the common features of their morphology comes up with the suggestion that gorges are vagina symbols and pleads for further study of the primitive view that the relationship of man to his place of habitation is basically that of the child to the 'Earth-Mother'.

It may well be that Shepard is right when he argues that further investigation of such imagery is needed and that a subconscious anthropomorphism may be the real basis of the aesthetic appeal of landscape. After all, the common English word for a narrow ravine of the kind he describes in his paper is the French word for the throat, and what about those imaginative place names like the Paps of Jura! But one danger of pursuing a theory which is superficially promising is that its attraction may lure one away from other theories which in the long run could prove more fruitful still. The clever criminal, at least in fiction, takes good care to leave some clue which will throw the detective off the scent.

Once we have made up our minds that sexual symbolism lies at the root of the aesthetic pleasure we take in landscape, a whole feast of possibilities opens up, and if Gray's 'ivy-mantled tower'—destined to feature so prominently in the landscape painting of the romantics—is to be seen as a phallus, every dark cavern, partially concealed by foliage or, as in Shepard's example, every cleft and chasm, can as certainly be recognized as a vagina.

Habitat theory, however, proposes a relationship between man and the landscape which is based on quite different, and much simpler, premises, namely that he is descended from ancestors who, being at risk as soon as they were born into the world, reduced the danger of premature extinction in proportion as they knew how to use their environment to further their biological needs. Just as this is based on different assumptions from those which underlie the 'Earth-Mother' concept, so it therefore demands a different symbolism. While not disdaining the idea that sexual symbolism may be a key to a deeper understanding of the aesthetics of landscape, we should not be deterred from enquiring into the implications of the hypothetical assumption that a universal characteristic of primitive man, transmitted innately to his modern descendants, is the desire to see without being seen. The imagery of the prospect and the refuge is, I suggest, much simpler, more logical and more effective in providing explanations of familiar experience (dare one say 'more penetrating'?) than any symbolism erected on a sexual hypothesis.

What, then, is this imagery? What are its symbols, and how do they achieve the effect of satisfying us aesthetically through the representation of ideas or relationships which cannot be directly perceived?

Any system of classification must be based on clearly defined principles which in turn must be related to the purpose for which the classification is to be used. In setting up a framework of symbolism for the analysis of landscape in prospect–refuge terms we are fortunately concerned with principles of the most elementary simplicity. We need to be able to identify those features, objects or situations which are conducive to seeing and those which are conducive to not being seen, never forgetting that any one such feature, object or situation may combine both attributes in an infinite variety of degrees. We are not arbitrarily attributing particular cases to particular categories. We are not saying, 'Let this be a prospect because I say so', or 'Let that be a refuge because it suits my argument so to describe it'. We are bound throughout by the application of the principle. Any feature, object or situation which directly facilitates observation or indirectly suggests an opportunity to extend the field of vision fits into the category of the prospect. Any which actually affords, or symbolically suggests, an opportunity to hide or to shelter fits into the category of a refuge. We are concerned, in short, with functional definitions, proposed in strategic terms. How far this strategic concept is relevant to our physical survival in the modern world is a question to which we shall return later.

## The Imagery and Symbolism of the Prospect

'*Der Gipfel des Berges funkelt*
*Im Abendsonnenschein*'

HEINRICH HEINE (*Die Lorelei*, lines 7–8)

From what has already been said there is clearly a *prima facie* case for associating light with the symbolism of the prospect and darkness with that of refuge. At this stage, however, we shall concentrate on that symbolism which relates, not directly to the source of light itself, but to the opportunities which the environment affords for the light to reach the eye of the beholder, because, in looking at any view, we are first conscious of the shapes and arrangement of the reflecting surfaces and of the intervening obstructions, and we tend to think of what we can see rather than of the source of light which enables us to see it. Any useful classification of prospects, therefore, must be made principally in terms of the relationship between the observer and the observed landscape in so far as his view is encouraged or impeded by the content of the intervening environment.[19]

In the first main category of prospect we can group together *direct prospects* (see Table 1), and within this definition are included all views directly observed from a given point of observation. The logical criterion of further differentiation is the extent of the view and the manner in which it is restricted by the interference of objects in the landscape.

The *panorama* is a wide view from a good vantage-point. Strictly speaking, it implies the ability to see the surrounding landscape through 360° of arc. In practice the word is used quite commonly to denote a broad view even of a restricted extent provided that breadth is a striking characteristic. The term *interrupted panorama* may be used to describe a view into which minor obstacles intrude but not on a sufficiently large scale to destroy the general impression of a panorama. The interruptions are small enough to allow the imagination to complete the picture of what is obscured, so that one is left with the impression of one partially obscured view, rather than of two or more separate views divided by an impediment or impediments.

The *vista* is a view which is restricted by conspicuous bounding margins. In a *simple vista* the general view is obscured by some intervening screen which contains a limited breach through which the eye can penetrate further. Often a vista

86

FIGURE 9. DIDACTIC LANDSCAPE

The landscape has the general form of an interrupted panorama, but within it there can be recognized two contrasting vistal themes (V). That on the left is highly regular and employs the technique of reduplication to emphasize the vistal axis (arrowed) by the convergence of several lines on a vanishing point within the magnetic area (MA). Here the prospect symbolism is further strengthened by several devices. These include a conspicuous spire starkly silhouetted against a fragment of the sky dado (S-D) and underlined by the dark horizon of the plain and the escarpment (right). The magnetic area also corresponds with the direction of maximum fetch (MF), while the inferred position of the sun accentuates the vertical margin of the arboreal screen which forms the left-hand flank of the vista. The right-hand of the picture is less overpoweringly vistal, but the river line introduces an irregular vistal axis (V) with a deflection (DV) to the left. The prospect symbolism is strengthened by falling ground below the primary vantage-point. Abbreviations are as follows:

| | | | |
|---|---|---|---|
| Aq S | Aquatic Surface | MF | Maximum Fetch |
| Arb H | Arboreal Horizon | ML | Magnetic Line |
| Arb R | Arboreal Refuge | NS | Naked Surface |
| Arb S | Arboreal Surface | O | Offset |
| Arch S | Architectural Surface | P+R | Prospect + Refuge Symbol |
| C | Coulisse | S-D | Sky Dado |
| CC | Cloud Canopy | SVP | Secondary Vantage-Point (indirect prospect |
| CS | Carpeted Surface | | symbol with strong reduplication) |
| DV | Deflected Vista | V | Vista |
| MA | Magnetic Area | | |

The original painting in oils by the author makes no pretence to artistic merit but is certainly the first painting deliberately conceived and executed with a view to illustrating the symbolism discussed in this book

TABLE 1. THE IMAGERY AND SYMBOLISM OF THE PROSPECT

TABLE 1A. TYPES OF PROSPECT

1. **Direct Prospects**
   A. *Panoramas*
      (i) Simple panoramas
      (ii) Interrupted panoramas
   B. *Vistas*
      (i) Simple vistas
      (ii) Horizontal vistas (incl. sky dados) ⎫ may occur in multiple form
      (iii) Peepholes ⎭
      (Panoramas and vistas may be either 'open' or 'closed' with varying length of 'fetch'.)

2. **Indirect Prospects**
   A. *Secondary panoramas*
   B. *Secondary vistas*
      (i) Deflected vistas
      (ii) Offsets
   C. *Secondary peepholes*

TABLE 1B. TYPES OF VANTAGE-POINT

1. **Primary Vantage-points** (commanding direct prospects)

2. **Secondary Vantage-points** (commanding, in the imagination, indirect prospects)
   A. *Natural*                    C. *Composite*
   B. *Artificial*
   (*Horizons* comprise a special type of secondary vantage-point).

is accentuated by the arrangement of the objects which comprise the screen. A view down an avenue, for instance, is contained by lines of trees which, though parallel, appear to converge because of the application of the laws of perspective. The impression of the confinement of vision to a restricted passage is thus enhanced. It is perfectly possible, however, to achieve a vista without such a device. A gap in a hedge, for instance, will produce the same restricting effect, though perhaps in a less dramatic form.

Where an opaque screen is breached by more than one opening the term *multiple vista* may be used. Multiple vistas are to be distinguished from interrupted panoramas by the dominance of the screen rather than the continuity of the view. Where two or more distant views are separated by such a large impediment that the eye sees them as two or more separate entities rather than as a single landscape partially obscured, then the term multiple (or double, triple, etc.) vista is more appropriate.

Vistas are normally bounded by vertical or near-vertical edges, but in some circumstances a comparable effect may be achieved in a horizontal plane and here the term *horizontal vista* may be used. Such a phenomenon may occur, for instance, where there is a narrow gap between arboreal vegetation and the ground. Certain trees with conspicuous horizontal elements in their habits of growth, such as cedars, may give rise to this effect, which may also be found in parks, for instance, where trees have been eaten by stock up to the limit of their reach; they block out the view of the sky while allowing a wide but vertically restricted view beneath. Such a prospect could therefore alternatively be thought of as a kind of panorama limited in a particular way.

In true vistas and horizontal vistas the limitations of vision are imposed in either the vertical or the horizontal plane. Where such restrictions apply in both planes simultaneously a further reduction of the field of vision takes place and the resulting prospect may be called a *peephole*.

In all these kinds of prospect, except a true panorama, one is left with the impression that distant vision can be achieved in some directions but not in others. There remains, however, the case in which it cannot be achieved in any. The window of a house, for instance, may command a clear view across a lawn to an encircling belt of trees. To say that in such a situation no prospect at all is achieved would be an exaggeration. Bearing in mind the concept of seeing without being seen, a restricted view of this kind, if uninterrupted in the immediate foreground, may suffice to induce that sense of security which comes from the knowledge that one has power to detect a hazard even in the comparatively near vicinity. The term *closed prospect* may be used to describe cases of this kind. Not only panoramic views but vistas also may exhibit such features. An avenue which leads up to a small temple backed by a screen of trees or by the side of a hill may be termed a *closed vista*.

In referring to the length of vision obtainable in any direction from a viewpoint it may be helpful to borrow a term from the geographers. This is the word 'fetch', and it has been defined thus: 'The distance of open water over which a wind-blown sea-wave has travelled, or over which a wind blows' (Monkhouse, 1965, p. 122). The word can be applied by analogy to the prospect, indicating the distance over which visibility can be achieved. We can speak of a closed vista as having 'a short fetch'. In many landscape paintings the direction of maximum fetch has an important significance in attracting the eye towards a certain part of the composition.

All direct prospects are views actually achieved by the observer from his position of observation, which we can call his *primary vantage-point* (Table 1B). A very important role, however, is discharged by other potential vantage-points. It must be remembered that the satisfaction of seeing is only a part of the satisfaction of achieving an advantageous position within one's habitat, and clearly the belief that one's field of vision can be further extended if one moves to another observation-point will accentuate the sensation of environmental advantage. Such alternative observation-points we may call *secondary vantage-points*, and the potential views which it is inferred may be obtained from them we may term *indirect prospects*. Secondary vantage-points always symbolically suggest the expectation of an indirect prospect; they are indirect prospect symbols.

One of the most common and effective kinds of secondary vantage-point is the *horizon*. A horizon marks the edge of an impediment to the line of vision, and such an edge invariably invites the suggestion that the impediment may not be effective, or as effective, beyond the point where it appears to end. It is a matter of common experience that the arrival at a horizon is followed by the opening up of a further field of vision, and the contemplation of a horizon therefore stimulates the expectation that such an extension of the field of vision is probable, if not certain, wherever a horizon is reached. This expectation relates particularly to that field of vision which lies beyond, that is, in the same direction as, but further than, the horizon concerned. After all, in so far as it is further vision in *this* direction which the horizon frustrates, it is the resumption of vision in this direction which is most immediately suggested by the surmounting of the obstacle. The contemplation of a horizon therefore directs the attention particularly to speculation about what lies *beyond* it, and the horizon itself seems to be the key which can provide the answer to such speculation. Potentially, therefore, the horizon has a major role to play in the imagery of the prospect.

Just as a sense of satisfaction can be derived from the belief that the field of vision may be extended beyond the horizon, so it may be stimulated by any situation which gives ground for anticipating an extension of the field of vision in other directions. The observation-points from which such extensions are possible may indeed lie on the horizon, and if the latter is formed by a mountain, for instance, or by a skyline elevated generally above the surrounding country, it is highly probable that it will afford a general extension of the view in many directions. But such observation-points need not necessarily be at places which appear from the original viewpoint to be on the horizon. The entire three-dimensional geometry of the environment will determine whether this is so or not.

*Natural* secondary vantage-points commonly include the summits of hills, mountains, crags, etc., especially when steep, conical, or overhanging an area of low ground, as an escarpment overhangs a vale. They could also include trees, particularly if they are of a strikingly vertical habit of growth, such as the Scots Pine (*Pinus sylvestris*), the Lombardy Poplar (*Populus italica*) and various kinds of Cypress (*Cupressus*). Off-shore islands might suggest viewpoints from which a wider view of the coastline might reasonably be expected. *Artificial* secondary vantage-points include all man-made structures which have the effect of providing an observation-point from which an extended field of vision could be achieved. Thus towers may be seen to be powerful indirect prospect symbols. Artificially constructed viewpoints or 'lookouts', or even clearings on forested hills, add the stamp of aesthetic approval to natural vantage-points. Tapering spires have a particular potency as indirect prospect symbols; their whole design and structure is aimed at expressing elevation above the surrounding country. The distinction between natural and artificial secondary vantage-points is not necessarily important and may indeed be difficult or even impossible to establish, but it will do no harm to recognize that conspicuous vertical objects may derive from either source, or from both, in view of the subsequent discussion of landscape aesthetics in the context of man's modification of the natural environment.

Indirect prospects are essentially symbolic. They symbolically invite the speculation that they command a further field of vision. Whether they actually do so is less important than whether they appear to do so. Whether they are attainable by the observer is also a matter of secondary importance. It is true that we have postulated that the prospect has a strategic importance for the survival chances of the individual in nature, and if this is really relevant to an aesthetic evaluation of a vantage-point it could be argued that it matters very much whether the vantage-point really does afford an extended view and whether it is really attainable. But just as those visibly prominent characteristics of the landscape on which habitat selection among birds usually depends are not necessarily essential to survival (p. 69) so, it may be replied, landscape features perceived by man may act as sign stimuli to attract him, whether or not they fulfil their spontaneous initial promise. Let us briefly lapse again into the dubious device of expressing a spontaneous experience in rational terms. The observer who says 'That hill attracts me because if I were on top of it I might be able to see further' does not reject it aesthetically merely because he *could* say 'If I were on top of that hill I might *not* be able to see further.' The apprehension of its promise is immediate and spontaneous, and this kind of rationalization does not in fact take place.

By the same token, once he has apprehended an indirect prospect symbol as attractive, because of the expectation of an extended field of vision, the observer does not proceed to reject it on the grounds that it is unattainable. He does not say 'Because I cannot sit on the top of that cloud, therefore the probability of attaining an extended field of vision does not attract me'. If he rationalizes at all, it is to exclaim 'If only I could sit on that cloud, what a fantastic view I should have!'

Secondary vantage-points of the kind referred to above (hills, towers, etc.) commonly suggest extensions of the field of vision which are panoramic in character and may indeed be called *secondary panoramas* (Table 1A). Where such extensions are vistal the term *secondary vista* may be employed. Secondary vistas make their most dramatic aesthetic impact within the framework of direct or 'primary' vistas. Vistas are limited channels of vision which, unless they are completely closed, give rise to the expectation that, if the observation point is moved forward along the vista, further vistas (or perhaps panoramas) will be revealed by which the field of vision can be further advanced. Secondary vistas, like secondary panoramas, are suggested or inferred. They are never experienced, because the moment the observer reaches such vantage-points they afford direct or primary prospects which may in turn contain further secondary vantage-points.

Secondary vistas comprise a very wide range of suggested visual experiences, but it may be useful to distinguish two particular kinds. In the first case, the secondary vista continues the line of vision in the same general direction and can therefore be thought of not merely as an extension of the field of vision but as an extension of the direct prospect, particularly if this is vistal in character. As an analogy we may consider the common shape of an electricity transmission line, which every now and then undergoes a slight angular deflection but nevertheless maintains the same general direction. Secondary vistas of this kind may be called *deflected vistas*. They are, as it were, continuing channels of vision which

A

B

FIGURE 10. DEFLECTED VISTAS

A and B; deflected vistas with offsets (left). In the first the vistal channel is formed by the aquatic surface of a shallow lake (Thorpeness Meare, Suffolk) from which the reeds emerge on both sides to bound the vista. In the second the geometrical arrangement is similar but the vistal margins are of firm ground with a light arboreal cover. In C and D the arboreal cover is much heavier, and it is this which forms the bounding margins

C

D

of the vistas. Note how the opening up of the woodland by the carriage drive in C and by the river in D creates the 'edge-of-the-wood' effect on both sides. In D (and in a more subdued form in B) the prospect symbolism of the conical peak provides a measure of reduplication by drawing the eye in the same general direction as the deflected vista. All the drawings are by Keith Scurr from photographs by the author have become slightly bent, so that continuity of perception cannot be achieved instantaneously but only serially. The angles of deflection are the potential vantage-points of the next primary vistas. The passage of a slightly serpentine road through a forest affords a good example of the deflected vista (Figure 10).

A somewhat different aesthetic sensation is aroused where the line of a vista is joined laterally by other vistas. Imagine oneself in a forest looking along a straight section of forest road. The angle of the sun is low and only the tree-tops are directly illuminated by it. Some distance along the shaded road a little patch of sunlight proclaims that a breach in the flanking forest allows the penetration of the sun. If the observer is alive to an awareness of his environment he will, perhaps without consciously recognizing it, sense the probability that, at this point, his field of vision may be extended, not merely within the confines of the direct vista but also at least in that other direction from which the sunlight enters. It is, in short, a point which, in terms of prospect symbolism, affords a particular advantage. To this kind of indirect prospect the term *lateral vista* or *offset* may be applied. The word 'offset' is perhaps the more appropriate. It is borrowed from the terminology of the surveyor. One of the simplest kinds of field survey is the chain-and-compass traverse. From the starting point a straight line or 'leg' is first measured by chain. From the end of this the traverse is continued by a second leg. The angle between the two legs is recorded, the length of the second leg is measured, and so on to a third and fourth leg until the traverse is completed. This enables the surveyor to fix the position of any point along the line of the traverse. To relate outlying points to this framework of measurement he constructs what he calls 'offsets' between such points and the nearest point on the line of traverse. In this way he extends the very limited coverage afforded by his line of measurement to embrace a wider field. This system of traverse and offset presents us with an arrangement closely parallel to that of a chain of 'deflected' vistas with 'lateral' vistas co-ordinated into it, hence the application of the term 'offset' to this type of indirect prospect.

It is important to remember that these categories of indirect prospect are neither discrete nor are they necessarily mutually exclusive. They are intended rather to underline certain attributes of different kinds of indirect prospect. The horizon, for instance, can only achieve realization in relation to one particular viewpoint. Viewed from elsewhere it has no existence; another takes its place. The secondary vantage-point, on the other hand, whether panoramic or vistal, is not directly affected by the position of observation. The view *from* a church tower may be presumed to be the same no matter from what primary vantage-point the tower is observed.

Anything which makes for improved visibility is conducive to the achievement of a prospect, and visibility can be improved in several ways. In particular the clarity of the atmosphere makes for prospect orientation in a landscape. The use of distant blues with sharp skylines is a very common feature of Italian Renaissance painting, for instance. The depicting of distant trees, spires, etc., as tiny objects on the canvas, minutely delineated, is a favourite device of many periods. One finds it in the earliest Renaissance painters, in Rubens, in Constable.

To take the fullest advantage of a clear atmosphere, however, it is important that there should be long distances free from visual interruptions between the observer and these distant landscape details, and the chances of achieving this tend to be improved where the point of observation is raised. Elevation of the viewpoint is also characteristic of many periods and styles of painting. Of course, there is more than one possible explanation of the elevated viewpoint. Where large numbers of figures are involved, a low viewpoint would result in the more distant figures being obscured by those in the foreground. It becomes geometrically necessary to lift the viewpoint if all the figures are to be visible as may be observed, for instance, in the early Flemish painters. But what applies to figures in the foreground applies also to the middle ground and the distance. Their details are rendered more visible by the elevation of the viewpoint. In extreme cases the curvature of the earth's surface is sharp enough to limit visibility from low vantage-points, as can be demonstrated by looking out to sea from a beach. Even a large ship does not have to be very far away before the hull becomes invisible and only the masts project above the horizon. On the other hand, too great an elevation may result in loss of contact with the perceived environment. The observer of a landscape from an aircraft may obtain an extreme sensation of 'prospect' but at the cost of any sense of participation in the landscape he observes. Its refuges, as seen from a great height, seem impotent to protect him. It is like looking at a remote world from outside rather than feeling the real world from inside. But any aesthetic experience can be impaired by excess, and within the normal limits of the experience of landscape the elevation of the viewpoint enhances its prospect value. *Falling ground*, that is to say ground which slopes downward away from the vantage-point, is a hallmark of prospect symbolism. It is particularly effective in panoramic prospects but can also add to the prospect value of vistas. Since elevated places figure prominently in the symbolism of indirect prospects, it goes without saying that falling ground can give expression to the prospect value of secondary vantage-points.

Because the distinctive character of prospects is often determined by the shapes and dispositions of the objects which limit them, such objects enter into the symbolism of the refuge as much as that of the prospect. Indeed they constitute the 'interface' between those parts of the environment which are visible and those which are not, and we shall encounter them again in connection with the symbolism of the refuge. First, however, a word about hazards.

### The Imagery and Symbolism of the Hazard

> 'The nearer we get to a bit of disaster without getting hurt, the better we like it.'
>
> JOHNNY MORRIS, 1973 (on the Falls of Schaffhausen)

The argument that the desire to 'see without being seen' is related to the individual's expectation of survival can only be sustained if we see this 'hide-and-seek' reaction as a counter-mechanism which protects the individual against those dangers to which, in a more primitive state of existence, he is exposed.

Similarly, if we seek to interpret our aesthetic response to the landscape in terms of these same reactions, albeit refined and perhaps re-stated in symbolic rather than direct behavioural forms, and if this process leads us to postulate a 'system' of prospect and refuge symbols for this purpose, how are we to deal with the hazards against which, we infer, it is a function of such mechanisms to defend us? To 'abolish' the hazard altogether is to deprive the prospect and the refuge of their meaningful roles, since they cannot be expected to react against a stimulus which is no longer there. Burke realized, and stated very explicitly, that exposure to a sense of the power of nature, or better still to a sense of the infinite, was indispensable to the experience of the Sublime (p. 28), and this is simply stating, in eighteenth-century terms, that prospect symbolism and refuge symbolism also demand a hazard symbolism to make them work.

However, Burke also realized that there was a difference between the kind of 'pain' which distinguished the Sublime from the Beautiful and the kind of 'pain' which a creature might experience at the hands of a merciless Nature if he presumed to trifle with her. To experience the sublimity of a storm wave one does not have to plunge into it and taste the real sensation of being smashed to pieces. To stand on a cliff and be gently shaken with it, to feel the sting of the spray on the face and the clammy chill of wet cheeks, to hear the ponderous thud, something between a bang and a rumble: these will suffice. The knowledge that we can see the wave and assess its potential before it breaks, and that we can observe it from a place of safety just, perhaps only just, beyond the reach of that potential, this is what enables us to find meaning and excitement in the whole experience. Exposure to the hazard is matched by perception of the hazard and followed by refuge from it.

Unless, therefore, we are to expose ourselves recklessly and irresponsibly to the hazards which, if we seek them, we can surely find even in an allegedly 'tamed' environment, we must find a means of cutting down the risk to an acceptable degree of severity. How best we can do this will depend to some extent on the character of the hazard. This suggests that we should attempt another classification and this is embodied in Table 2.

TABLE 2. THE IMAGERY AND SYMBOLISM OF THE HAZARD

| | |
|---|---|
| **1. Incident Hazards** | **2. Impediment Hazards** |
| A. *Animate hazards* | A. *Natural* |
|    (i) Human hazards | B. *Artificial* |
|    (ii) Non-human hazards | |
| | **3. Deficiency Hazards** |
| B. *Inanimate hazards* | |
|    (i) Meteorological hazards | |
|    (ii) Instability hazards | |
|    (iii) Aquatic hazards | |
|    (iv) Fire hazards | |
|    (v) Locomotion hazards | |

Within the concept of habitat theory all hazards pose some sort of a threat to the achievements of our biological needs. In terms of experience, however, we may identify three main types of threat which we can call respectively 'incident hazards', 'impediment hazards' and 'deficiency hazards'.

By *incident hazards* I mean those threats to a creature's well-being which seem to him to be occasioned by some external incident. The agent or instrument by which harm may be inflicted is always an element of the environment, but it may be either animate or inanimate, and *animate hazards* may be further divided into human and non-human hazards.

It would be quite fallacious to suppose that *human hazards* have been eliminated since our primitive ancestors defended themselves and their families with clubs and staves. We are all too well aware that violence between humans assumes the magnitude of a major problem, whether it occurs catastrophically in the form of out-and-out warfare, or chronically in the form of robberies with violence, vendettas or simply punch-ups. In any case it must be remembered that the operation of the prospect–refuge mechanism does not depend on the certainty of there being a real hazard just round the corner. Even the possibility of a real hazard may be too strong a stimulus to allow that freedom from interruption by alien ideas without which Alison said aesthetic experience could not be achieved (p. 38). Minor hazards may lend an air of additional satisfaction to one's relationship with the environment. I well remember as a little boy having a 'den' in the top of a thick yew hedge. In this I was totally invisible. The hazard from which I sought refuge might be another little boy with whom I did not wish to play or a well-meaning lady who, I calculated, might at best prevent me from doing what I wanted for the rest of the afternoon and at worst want to kiss me. There in the yew hedge I could keep the situation under close observation, so that when the hazard departed I knew that it was safe to emerge. 'To see without being seen!' I have often wondered how far my liking for the yew was 'reinforced', as the psychologists would say, by early environmental experience.

In a slightly more risky situation we may picture the young lovers creeping off to some remote corner of the common in search of a thick patch of bracken. The hazard against which they seek protection is less likely to be the purposeful pursuit of an ill-wisher than the involuntary intrusion of an embarrassed passer-by. Indeed, to bring the prospect–refuge mechanism into operation it may be sufficient for the observer to conjure up no more than the idea that, if he wished to maintain his privacy in the physical environment in which he found himself, he would have sufficient mastery over that environment to ensure that he could do so.

*Non-human* animate hazards are perhaps less easy to envisage in the real situation of civilized man, though I suspect the young lovers in the bracken would have less cause to fear intrusion from a fellow human than from his little dog, whose exploring instincts would not be put out of action by any sense of delicacy. Anyone who has had a picnic in a field with a bull will subscribe to the point of view so unscientifically attributed above to 'the creature escaping' (p. 70).

The point about hazards at the animate level, whether human or non-human, is that the person who is confronted by them is placed in a situation in which he has the opportunity to exploit his environment to his own advantage in terms of 'seeing and not being seen'. It is the type of hazard which most closely impinges on the true 'prospect–refuge' complement.

The *inanimate* type of incident hazard differs fundamentally from the animate; it is subject to entirely different principles of occurrence. Whereas the animate hazard potentially involves the process of pursuit and escape and invokes the mechanism of seeing and hiding in furtherance of these processes, the inanimate hazard is not directly involved with such challenges or responses. It asserts its threat through the *un*selective operation of the laws of physics. This means that, whereas the potential victim, in seeking to inform himself of the approach or presence of such a hazard, employs much the same methods as when threatened by an animate hazard, and whereas the symbolism of the prospect may therefore be equally relevant to the process of detection, in the process of protecting himself against it he must necessarily employ an entirely different range of refuges.

Among the various hazards of this kind the most common are those which adversely affect the regulation of the temperature of the body. Extremes of heat can be dangerous in low and middle latitudes and, where all the circumstances are conducive, direct exposure to the sun can prove fatal within minutes. Similarly, exposure to extreme cold can quickly result in death from loss of body heat. In practice, exposure to extremes of both heat and cold normally induces irritation, discomfort or pain which leads to shelter-seeking before serious damage is done.

*Meteorological* phenomena, therefore, which are most commonly concerned with this temperature regulation, constitute an important group of inanimate hazards. They include wind, cold static air and atmospheric moisture, whether absorbed in the air (relative humidity can have a powerful effect on physiological response), or occurring as large or small drops of water, hailstones, or crystals of ice or snow. All of these may appear under a wide range of conditions. The term 'wind', for instance, comprises not only gentle zephyrs and devastating cyclones, but hot, dessicating winds like the *sirocco* and destructively cold winds like the *mistral* of Southern France and the *bora* of the Adriatic. Similarly, snow may be delivered either vertically to settle undisturbed on an accumulated bed, or horizontally in a blizzard, being deposited and picked up over and over again. The kind of measures a man may take to protect his person against such hazards will depend on his ability to observe accurately the patterns of these phenomena and to devise effective defences to render enough living-space immune from them to keep himself comfortable until the hazard has passed. Meteorological hazards may be taken to include other atmospheric phenomena, such as electric storms, or the very unpleasant conditions which arise when strong winds are rendered even more destructive by the material they pick up. Dust storms and sand storms, for instance, bring problems of survival very different from those associated with other winds.

*Instability hazards* arise from various causes of instability in the earth's crust. Earthquakes and volcanic eruptions, for instance, are serious hazards in some parts of the world, but the consequences of lesser instabilities may be felt much more widely, for instance in landslides and avalanches of snow or mud.

*Aquatic hazards* vary greatly in their character and incidence. Even calm water can be a fatal hazard to a victim who cannot swim, but the destructive potential of water is more eloquently expressed when it is moving, and waterfalls, rapids and storm waves figure consistently in the landscape furniture of the Sublime. The unexpected distribution of water in unusual quantities and in places where it is not normally found, as in floods or tidal waves, is a cause of many of the most spectacular disasters.

*Fire* is another powerful hazard of which most creatures seem to have an innate fear, since they flee from it even if they have never previously experienced it. The smell of smoke in a forest fire has frequently been observed to induce panic and terror among animals. The symbolism of fire is extremely powerful, especially as it is intimately related, as a source of light, to the symbolism of the prospect.

In being exposed to all the above types of hazard a creature is at the mercy, so to speak, of forces over which he has no control, except in so far as he may take evasive action or channel them into some other course, as when he diverts the wind by a windbreak. In every case the 'incident' is provoked by some external agency, whether belonging to the animate or inanimate parts of nature. A charging rhinoceros, a blizzard, a falling rock, an advancing wall of flame: these are all 'incident hazards' which may overtake a victim without the necessity of any action on his part to trigger them off. Another category of incident hazard arises, however, as soon as he begins to move. His passage through the environment may be fraught with all manner of dangers which we call *locomotion hazards*. One of the most prevalent is that of falling. We all know that fatal falls can be sustained even on level surfaces, but generally serious falls are associated with high elevations, and it is these which have the power of suggesting danger and arousing fear for those who encounter them. Here again, those landscape features which display this property, 'beetling cliffs', chasms, precipices of all sorts, are among the hallmarks of the Sublime.

The role of locomotion in achieving the mastery over habitat has been constantly commented on by ethologists, and its implication for prospect–refuge symbolism will be amplified later. Already, however, it must be apparent that any threat to freedom of movement will be accompanied by frustration and an awareness that a favourable relationship with the environment is being to that extent impaired. *Impediment hazards* are not quite the same as those we have considered so far because they do not directly pose threats to the survival or well-being of the creature. They do not of themselves initiate 'incidents' and if an impediment hazard is involved in a disaster at all, that disaster will come from some other hazard whose superiority or advantage over the victim has been favoured by its intervention.

*Natural* impediment hazards may take a number of different forms. In nature dense vegetation, cliffs, ravines, etc., may impede movement, as also may waterbodies of all sorts or land surfaces rendered impassable by instability or by a high water content. Rivers play a particular role in this respect, because under normal conditions they continue as lines of physical separation over long distances. It may be objected that rivers are not really lines of separation but rather of intercommunication. In fact they may perfectly well perform both functions simultaneously, since they can favour locomotion for those who are equipped to exploit them and inhibit it for those who are not. The transport system of any estuary will illustrate this; it provides a linking function for shipping, a dividing function for land-based traffic.

To those impediment hazards encountered in nature we must add the important group of *artificial* structures which have the effect of hindering movement. Some of these are deliberately constructed for this purpose and they range from military installations, mural fortifications, prison walls, etc., at one end of the scale, to fences, field-boundary walls, hedges, etc., at the other. Impediments, however, may also be provided incidentally where there is not necessarily an intention to obstruct. Artificial ditches, navigation canals, railway cuttings and embankments: these may be very effective in severing communication, though their construction does not necessarily imply such a purpose.

It is a general rule in the prospect–refuge situation that the creature who seeks to exploit his environment to his advantage does so by making the most effective strategic use of features which are available to his adversary as well as to himself. The prospect which enables him to see may equally well be employed by his enemy. The refuge in which he seeks cover may already contain a lethal hazard. By way of recompense, so to speak, the impediment which threatens his escape may also hamper his pursuer. It is a common assumption in military operations that the river line which may be exploited to hold back the enemy is the last kind of physical feature one would choose to have behind one, because it cuts off retreat or, as one might say, denies refuge.

One final point about the impediment hazard may be noted for later reference. It is that particular significance attaches to those places where such a hazard is terminated or interrupted. A crossing-place of a river, for instance, by a bridge or ford, focuses the attention on the opportunity which it presents for circumventing or surmounting the hazard. Gateways, stiles, staircases, paths up cliffs and similarly the heads of estuaries or inlets, the ends of buildings, of walls or of other structures, they all signal opportunities for movement which is elsewhere impeded or denied.

All these kinds of hazard to some extent imply a deficiency, whether of the essential requirements for survival or of some less essential but nevertheless desired objective, such as privacy or physical comfort. By *deficiency hazard* I have in mind rather a chronic deficiency, which does not manifest itself in some dramatic incident or conspicuous symbol but nevertheless threatens the achievement of a creature's biological needs. The provision of food and drink is the principal need which may be threatened by hazards of this kind. The need for warmth and shelter is no doubt equally important, but where these are threatened there are generally perceptible manifestations of a hazard in the landscape, such as a storm, an environment devoid of conspicuous refuges, etc. Hunger and thirst are not necessarily symbolized in this way. They are not exactly events but rather conditions, and if they find symbolic expression it is frequently when the condition is terminated, that is, when the provision is eventually made. Nicolas Poussin's 'Moses striking water from the rock' (The Duke of Sutherland's Collection in the National Gallery of Scotland) is an example of a painting in which a deficiency, in this case of water, provides the hazard which is so dramatically terminated by the incident.

> 'Individually the figures portray gratitude, relief, wonder and eagerness by turns. Their arrangement in coherent lines, crossing each other and receding into the depth of the picture, provokes at first glance by its agitation the mood of the subject.' (Thompson (n.d.), p. 25)

The deficiency hazard, if it is rarely explicit in the symbolism of landscape painting, is constantly implicit in the symbolism which proclaims the capitulation of want in the face of plenty. The cornfields and the vineyards, the browsing oxen and the bleating sheep, the gushing fountain and the limpid brook, the swain with the sheaves and the milkmaid with the pail, the flagon and the cornucopia, in short, all the provisions of a bountiful nature and their symbolic representations: these are the perpetual reminders that it is the function of a creature's habitat to provide first and foremost for his alimentary needs, and that the environment of civilized man is still basically a habitat.

### The Imagery and Symbolism of the Refuge

'Rock of ages, cleft for me,
Let me hide myself in Thee.'
A. M. TOPLADY (*Hymns Ancient and Modern*, No. 210)

It will have been noted that the bases of classification of Tables 1 and 2 differ markedly, because prospects and hazards are different kinds of concept, and the things we need to know about them are discovered by asking different kinds of question. Similarly, the things we need to know about refuges are different from both, and consequently the classifications of Table 3 bear little resemblance to those of the others. Since the refuge necessarily involves protection against some hazard, and since, in our hide-and-seek aesthetics, it is complementary to the prospect, we have inevitably already touched on its role in both these contexts. It remains to tidy up these ideas by setting out systematically the main criteria by which we can assess the symbolic value and meaning of refuges, and Table 3 may help us to do this. It sets out different bases of discrimination by which refuges may be distinguished. These bases are not mutually exclusive; indeed any refuge can be referred to all five.

The most important single basis of differentiation between refuges concerns the kind of hazard against which they afford protection; it is, in short, a differentiation by *function*. We have seen already that those hazards which we call 'animate' rely on the ability of the pursuer to see his quarry or to detect him

TABLE 3. THE IMAGERY AND SYMBOLISM OF THE REFUGE. BASES OF CLASSIFICATION

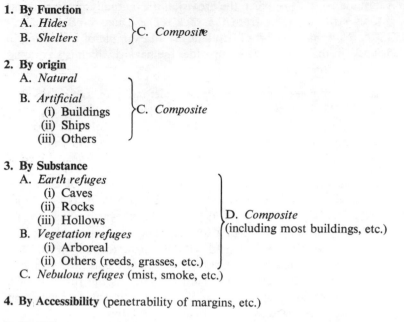

**1. By Function**
  A. *Hides*
  B. *Shelters*  }C. *Composite*

**2. By origin**
  A. *Natural*

  B. *Artificial*
    (i) Buildings
    (ii) Ships       }C. *Composite*
    (iii) Others

**3. By Substance**
  A. *Earth refuges*
    (i) Caves
    (ii) Rocks
    (iii) Hollows                  D. *Composite*
  B. *Vegetation refuges*          (including most buildings, etc.)
    (i) Arboreal
    (ii) Others (reeds, grasses, etc.)
  C. *Nebulous refuges* (mist, smoke, etc.)

**4. By Accessibility** (penetrability of margins, etc.)

**5. By Efficacy**

through one of the other senses. In such a situation the essential feature of a refuge is to impair visibility. The yew hedge of my childhood (p. 97) was such a refuge, but since my den was in the top of it, it was largely ineffective in keeping me dry when it began to rain. The efficiency of a refuge in achieving protection from the elements depends on quite different considerations, such as, if it is a tree, the size, shape and arrangement of the leaves, the direction of the wind and so on. Whether the sheltering creature can be *seen* sheltering is not directly relevant to the efficiency of a refuge as a protection against a meteorological hazard. In other words, we can distinguish between the functions of a *hide* and a *shelter*. It was noted above (p. 71) that a creature may need both kinds of protection at once, and many refuges, both natural and artificial, are of this kind, from the rabbit hole to the castle.

A significant basis of differentiation is that which distinguishes the *origins* of refuges. We can distinguish first between those refuges which are of *natural* origin (forests, caves, ravines, for instance) and those which are constructed as *artificial* refuges. Principally we are concerned in the latter case with construction of human origin, but man is not, of course, alone in making purpose-built refuges.

'Environmental adaptations also include those behaviour patterns with which an animal creates a shelter against bad weather—structures and nests that protect it against heat as well as cold. It is known that many desert mice can only survive the midday heat by retreating to their dens ... The earth mounds around the dens of prairie dogs protect them against flooding. Beavers dig dens into the riverbanks, but if the bank is so low that no cave can be dug, then the beaver will put its den into a large mound of twigs.' (Eibl-Eibesfeldt, 1970, p. 270)

The category of artificially constructed refuges of human contrivance contains a vast range of *buildings*—huts, hovels and other rough shelters, cottages, mansions, castles, cathedrals and what you will. All have the power of suggesting symbolically the idea of 'refuge'. The fact that they have been constructed is in itself symbolic of man's assertion of his emancipation from subjugation by the powers of nature, however illusory that emancipation may be. Buildings, as refuges, seem to offer not the fortuitous sanctuary of a cave or forest, but the planned sanctuary contrived with care and forethought for the express purpose of shielding vulnerable and sensitive man from the hostile forces to which he would otherwise be exposed.

A particular and highly specialized kind of artificial refuge is the *ship* or boat. Masts and sails, like all objects which reach up towards the sky, are suggestive of the promise of 'prospect', but the hull of a vessel, whether a small boat or a liner, is a refuge symbol rendered more potent by the immediacy of its exposure to hazard. The sea, as we know, can quickly become unfriendly and dangerous, and a ship is specially constructed to afford protection against it. In many a seascape the ship is the only refuge symbol in the whole picture. On the other hand, just as houses and other buildings can be grouped together to form larger refuges, like towns and villages, so groups of ships can be assembled and distributed in such a way as to build up a more complex composition of prospect–refuge symbols.

While ships fall clearly into the category of artificially constructed refuges, the distinction between natural and artificial cannot always be so sharply maintained. We can therefore recognize a category of composite refuges. Just as a bird may build its nest in a hole in a tree, constructing a refuge of its own making within another fortuitously available, so man will habitually take advantage of naturally occurring refuges to facilitate the task of making his own provision. Perhaps the building of houses within natural caves, though perfectly well attested, is too unusual to be convincing; but reference to any textbook on the geography of settlement will disclose less dramatic examples where protection in one form or another is an important contributory factor in site selection.

Differentiation on the basis of the *substance* or fabric of a refuge can also be significant. *Caves, chasms, ravines*, in short any orifices which allow a creature to enter physically into the fabric of the earth, are obviously potent refuge symbols. Perhaps this is the vindication of Shepard's 'Earth-Mother' concept (p. 84). At any rate the cave is the most complete general purpose sanctuary provided by nature, and vestiges of human habitation all over the world testify to the supremacy as well as the antiquity of the cave as a refuge. Less extreme forms of earth refuge may be provided by rough or irregular *rocks*. *Hollows* in the ground, affording shelter from wind as well as concealment from view, occur commonly in landscape painting.

By contrast, *vegetational refuges* have their own distinctive advantages which derive from the nature of their fabric. The *forest* provides a less complete, less enveloping hiding-place than the cave; one into which more light can penetrate, rendering concealment less effective, but permitting also a measure of prospect within the refuge. The forest tends to be vastly more extensive, and therefore more easily attainable than the cave, and to permit escape by the facility of movement through the trees, whereas the cave is often a cul-de-sac with no back door. In short, the cave and the forest illustrate two extreme but strongly contrasting forms of refuge symbol and when one considers the infinite variety of forms which each can take, it is small wonder that their popularity in the landscape paintings of civilized man has been commensurate with the importance of their role in the habitat of his ancestors. Arboreal refuge can be provided by quite small groups of trees, such as copses, spinneys, shrubberies and so on.

In the contrivance of landscape for aesthetic ends it would be difficult to exaggerate the importance of arboreal vegetation. There are, however, other kinds of growth which may be highly effective in their own way. Reeds and rushes, for instance, can provide striking refuge elements, particularly since they tend to occur in or immediately adjacent to, water surfaces, which are strongly prospect-oriented (Figure 10). Just as there is an immense range of variation of types of vegetation, from grasses and bracken to forest trees, all potentially affording refuge, so there is an infinite possibility of combining their different shapes in a single composition. Vertical components can be provided, for instance, by the cypress; horizontal components by the cedar or the creeping shrubs. Vines and climbing plants can fill in gaps, cover surfaces and tie the composition together. The size and texture of leaves and the degrees of opaqueness they provide can all affect the general impression conveyed by a refuge as well as the aesthetic response of the observer, and all these variations stem from the nature of the substance or fabric of which the refuge is composed.

Refuges, whether natural or artificial, may well consist of more than one substance (most buildings, in fact, employ many) and to these we may give the designation *composite*.

A particular kind of refuge (nebulous), which seems to be capable of arousing a powerful aesthetic response is that created by mist. A wisp of it among the trees, or on a lake, especially when seen from a higher elevation, suggests a kind of veil, whose significance in the art of concealment is self-explanatory. A thin smoke haze at evening provides a gratuitous increment to the refuge symbolism of the town which lies beneath it, just as a skein of peat-smoke may spread a symbolic blanket above the cottage from whose chimney it rises. But smoke and mist are substances which must be employed in moderation. To be immersed in a fog is one of the bleakest of sensations. It does not create a refuge; it rather frustrates a prospect. It leaves the observer with the feeling that he may be exposed to a hazard which could be very near and still unperceived.

It is our constant theme that the arrangement and interrelationship of prospect and refuge are basically strategic, or perhaps 'tactical', in character, and in so far as the refuge is envisaged in terms of its ability to afford protection, its *accessibility* is an important attribute. All kinds of irregularity tend to facilitate the act of hiding. Rough, broken ground, through which one may move easily from one boulder to another, provides a more effective cover than a much larger feature, such as a cliff, which denies access. Anything which suggests ease of penetration is conducive to the symbolism of the refuge. Thus, whereas a wall devoid of openings appears as an impediment hazard, the same wall, if breached by entrances, embellished by porticos or surmounted by staircases, becomes less formidable as an obstacle and more inviting as a retreat. Windows, alcoves, recesses, balconies, heavily overhanging eaves—all these suggest a facility of penetration into the refuge. Even if actual access is not practicable the suggestion of accessibility can stimulate the idea of refuge. Just as an indirect prospect symbol, such as a tall, bright cloud, may be unattainable except by the imagination, and yet may suggest symbolically an extension of the field of vision, so apertures of all kinds which invite penetration only by the imagination can be to that extent effective. It is, after all, the imagination which is principally involved in experiencing the environment aesthetically. A woodland surrounded by a wall or fence is less satisfying than one which is open to the adjacent sward, because the impediment hazard frustrates the concept of the refuge. Even a straight boundary of a wood or forest suggests a 'margin' which is more forbidding than an irregular or 'frayed' edge, with the occasional outlying tree or bush suggesting the protection of sporadic cover as gradual access or egress is achieved.

This interpretation of prospect and refuge reaches an intense and at the same time very common form in the device known as the *coulisse*. In its original usage this term denotes the side-pieces of scenery used on the stage. They serve a dual function in the stagecraft of the theatre. In the first place they can help to create an impression of three-dimensional space. Whereas the backcloth can achieve this only by employing the rules of perspective as applied to the problem of the representation of three dimensions on a two-dimensional surface, the side-pieces actually stand forward on the stage. They not only look nearer than objects in the distance; they *are* nearer, and they can therefore be used to accentuate the impression of perspective created by the scenery depicted on the backcloth.

The *coulisse*, however, has another function; it covers the entrances and exits of the actors. By projecting on to the stage it extends the area of concealment provided by the wings into the scene of the action and, because the actors can normally pass either in front or behind, it suggests more than one place where escape from view is possible. The use of more than one *coulisse* accentuates even further the impression of refuge.

What the scenery designers can do on the stage, artists can do, and for centuries have done, in landscape painting, and art historians and critics have borrowed from the theatre the term *coulisse* to describe

'. . . the type of composition in which the effect of recession into space is obtained by leading the eye back into depth by the overlaps, usually alternatively left and right, of hills, bushes, winding rivers, and similar devices.' (Murray and Murray, 1968 edn., p. 97)

It is a reasonable inference that if one of the theatrical purposes of the *coulisse*, to contribute to perspective, is implied by its use in painting, the other purpose, to facilitate the process of escaping from view, should also be implied.

Finally, refuges can be distinguished by their *efficiency*. Reference has already been made to this characteristic and it has been noted, for instance, that an efficient refuge from one hazard may be very inefficient in relation to another. It is not, therefore, merely a question of degrees of opaqueness or of impermeability, but of the particular capacity of a refuge to afford protection against a particular hazard operating from a particular quarter. Thus we can distinguish between uni-directional and multi-directional refuges, between continuous and interrupted refuges, and so on.

### Surfaces

'. . . A gently sloping bank of soft and smooth turf, must, I imagine, suggest the idea of the quality of smoothness . . .: on the other hand a rough, abrupt, and stony bank, with stumps and roots of trees mixed with thorns and briers, would most certainly present ideas of a very opposite kind . . .'

UVEDALE PRICE (in Lauder, 1842, pp. 112–113)

This discussion of the imagery and symbolism of prospect and refuge has so far been concerned with the shapes of the major elements in the landscape composition. A tree may be said to have 'shape', but if we observe from a distance a mountain covered with trees, what strikes us is not the shape of individual trees but the general effect which they achieve collectively in altering the appearance of the mountain. The 'shape' we see is that of the mountain; the quality imparted to it by the vegetation we call 'texture'. Both are properties of the land surface.

Surfaces may therefore be distinguished in two principal ways (Table 4). *Surface configuration* is a geometrical property of the surface as a whole. Surfaces distinguished in this way may be said to be, for instance, 'horizontal', 'undulating', 'precipitous', etc. *Surface texture*, on the other hand, is a property which distinguishes the capacity of a surface (of whatever configuration) to reflect light, which in turn derives from the substance of which the surface is formed.

There may well be difficulties in drawing an exact distinction between surface configuration and surface texture. The ruggedness of a mountain peak, for instance, may be described as a property of its shape, so that we can properly regard the indentations and projections, by which we recognize this ruggedness, as contributing to its outline or configuration. At the same time we could legitimately say that it had a rugged texture. The further our observation point is

## TABLE 4. SURFACES AND HORIZONS

**TABLE 4A. CLASSIFICATION OF SURFACES BY CONFIGURATION**
Surfaces may be classified according to ordinary geometrical terms, e.g. 'horizontal', 'vertical', 'inclined', 'convex', 'undulating', etc., some of which suggest an affinity with particular kinds of symbolism; e.g. convex surfaces suggest prospect values; concave surfaces refuge values; undulating surfaces an alternation of both.

**TABLE 4B. CLASSIFICATION OF SURFACES BY TEXTURE**
**1. Terrestrial Surfaces**
  A. *Open surfaces*
    (i) Naked
        a, b, etc.; sub-categories by lithology, natural/artificial, etc.
    (ii) Carpeted
        a, b, etc.; sub-categories by genera, species, etc.
  B. *Arboreal surfaces*
    (i), (ii), etc.; categories by genera, species, habit of growth, natural/artificial, etc.
  C. *Architectural surfaces*
    (i), (ii), etc.; categories by components (e.g. walls, roofs, etc.), materials (e.g. masonry, timber, etc.).

**2. Aquatic Surfaces**
May be classified by various properties, e.g. roughness/smoothness, flow/stagnation, ice formation, cover of aquatic vegetation, etc.

**3. Nebulous Surfaces**
May be distinguished by general descriptive terms, e.g. 'clouds', 'fog', 'smoke', etc.

N.B. All the above terminology may be equally well applied to *horizons*, and all categories of surface except No. 3 (Nebulous Surfaces) may take on very different appearances under a cover of ice or snow with consequent changes in the balance of symbolism.

from the mountain the more we shall be inclined to regard this ruggedness as a property of its texture. The closer we approach the more clearly do the irregular components of the surface of the mountain appear as surfaces in their own right, each perhaps with its own distinctive texture.

Provided we bear in mind that there is a basis of differentiation between surface configuration and surface texture we shall find in practice that it does not generally inconvenience us in the verbal description of landscape. Price, in the passage quoted above, refers to two features whose surface configuration is sufficiently similar to allow them both to be described by the same word 'bank'. They are, however, distinguished, still in terms of surface configuration, by the terms 'gently sloping' and 'abrupt'. All the other descriptive terms relate to their textures, which are sharply contrasted.

Irregularities in configuration may well endow surfaces with very different potentialities in prospect–refuge terms. Convex surfaces, for instance, tend to be prospect-dominant; they achieve elevation and they create horizons. Concave surfaces, because they form hollows and depressions, tend to be secluded and are refuge-dominant. These dominant characteristics may, of course, be cancelled out and even reversed by differences in texture. A convex surface covered with dense forest may afford a better hiding place than an open, grassy amphitheatre, and a classification of surfaces by texture may therefore tell us more about their symbolic roles than a classification by configuration.

In the context of the prospect–refuge complement we may distinguish five principal types of surface according to their texture. Of these the first three may be grouped together as *terrestrial surfaces* inasmuch as they consist of 'solid' substances.

*Open surfaces* are those which carry no vegetation large enough to provide effective refuges. They may be *naked*, consisting of bare rock, sand, earth, shingle, gravel, concrete, etc., or they may be *carpeted*, covered with vegetation, provided it is sufficiently short to suggest a sense of 'exposure'. Surfaces of this type are prospect-conducive almost by definition in that they facilitate rather than impede the view. One thinks first of mown or closely cropped grass, a highly important source of aesthetic satisfaction alike to the fell-walker and the connoisseur of landscape painting from the Middle Ages to Seurat and on to the present day. It is frequently used as the basic prospect symbol in landscape design. Heather, sage-bush and many short agricultural crops are examples of 'carpet' vegetation.

Naked terrestrial surfaces are prospect-conducive when smooth and free from crannies or other irregularities. Sand surfaces can communicate a striking sense of visibility. One recalls the popularity of beach scenes in certain schools of landscape painting and the great panoramic prospects of the desert. The gravel paths and drives of stately homes, the paved surfaces of terraces, not least, perhaps, the ribbon of the arterial road, all these are rich in prospect imagery and contrast markedly with those kinds of surfaces which we associate with the refuge.

*Arboreal surfaces* are generally far more suggestive of the symbolism of the refuge. They can be subdivided on the basis of genera and species, habit of growth, etc. Thus it is easy to distinguish, even at a distance, between coniferous and deciduous forest surfaces; a mixture of these two types creates a variety which many find aesthetically satisfying. Within the arboreal category we can also include tall grasses or bamboos, or other kinds of vegetation which, though perhaps not 'arboreal' in the botanist's usage of the term, nevertheless have more affinity with trees than with the shorter grasses when it comes to providing refuge.

*Architectural surfaces* are those which owe their texture to human construction; they are formed as new surfaces, erected independently of the shape of a landform, though clearly they can be superimposed on a landform in such a way as to reflect, at least partially, its general configuration, as in a hilltop town. To press the distinction too far would be pointless and impracticable; in landscape design, for instance, 'open' surfaces may well be artificial.

A very special kind of prospect-conducive surface is provided by water. The significance of *aquatic surfaces* is that they ensure a clear passage for the line of sight. Interruptions may occur in the form of ships which, if numerous, as in some of the seascapes of Cappelle and Willem van der Velde, can considerably interfere with visibility and even destroy the impression of a prospect-dominant view; also, exceptionally, the surface may be so disrupted by storm waves that the distant prospect is cut off. But normally water surfaces may be thought of as guaranteeing a very high probability of uninterrupted vision; they are therefore strong prospect symbols.

*Nebulous surfaces* include, for instance, surfaces of fog and mist patches, or of low clouds lying on mountains. Such atmospheric 'obstacles' can form almost indistinguishable extensions of terrestrial forms quite apart from any role they may have to discharge in the sky, a subject on which more will be said later.

Terrestrial and aquatic surfaces may be considerably altered by ice and snow. Generally the shape of the surface is not fundamentally affected except where deep accumulations are able to form, as in ice-sheets and glaciers, but even a shallow cover of ice or snow can, by imparting whiteness to the surface, add a large measure of prospect orientation to an outdoor scene.

Nowhere does the importance of surface texture assume more significance than when seen in horizons. Indeed the symbolism suggested by a horizon can be profoundly altered by, for instance, an arboreal cover. Anyone brought up in those latitudes where mountains are normally bare experiences a curious unfamiliarity when confronted by mountains which are forested. The extreme prospect symbolism of a horizon of bare rock, or of grass, peat or heather, is not conjured up if, on closer examination, it proves to be covered by forest. The total aesthetic effect may actually be enhanced, but the balance between prospect and refuge will be altered so that quite a different *feeling* is aroused, even though the *shape* of the horizon is not perceptably altered.

All the terminology applied to surfaces in Table 4 has meaning when applied more specifically to horizons. Thus we can speak of 'an arboreal horizon', 'an aquatic horizon', and so on.

## Light and Darkness

> '. . . And God divided the light from the darkness. And God called the light Day, and the darkness he called Night. And the evening and the morning were the first day.'
>
> *Genesis:* i:4–5

We have so far considered the imagery and symbolism of the prospect and the refuge in so far as they may be studied in terms of the shapes by which they may be recognized, the functions which they discharge and various other bases of differentiation. The prospect–refuge complement, however, requires one essential ingredient to bring it to life, namely light, and there is a whole field of imagery which is concerned not so much with illuminated objects as with light itself, though obviously there are limits to the lengths to which the distinction can be pressed.

Within the solar system the supreme prospect symbol is the sun, which is not only by far the most powerful source of light but is also symbolic of distance on a supra-terrestrial scale. By casting shadows, brightening clouds and realizing the differentiation of colours it makes its impact on landscape, but more often than not this impact is indirect. There is a distinction to be made between illuminating a landscape and participating as a component of it. There are two principal difficulties which commonly prevent the orb of the sun from appearing as an integral part of the landscape. The first is simply one of geometry. When the sun stands high in the sky and therefore subtends a wide angle from the horizontal plane near which most of the landscape components tend to be concentrated, it is necessarily separated from these components and therefore cannot easily be visually related to them within a formal composition. Only when the sun is near the horizon is this geometrical problem resolved.

The second difficulty is more fundamental. The intensity of the sun's light when viewed without any intervening screen is such that the eye cannot contemplate it except at the risk of great discomfort and even physical damage. Even when its brightness is so diminished that it is just possible to look at it, the difference in intensity between the light received direct and that reflected from terrestrial surfaces is such that the brilliance of the former obliterates everything else, as Burke pointed out (p. 29), and for this reason the participation of the sun in the composition of a landscape is again impossible. A considerable reduction in the intensity of light is a prerequisite of such participation, and this can be brought about when some screen or veil is interposed. Dust or water particles, when they occur in sufficient concentration in the atmosphere to form thin cloud or haze, can have this effect on the sun even at noon, but it is when the angle of the sun is low in the sky, at sunrise and sunset, and its light intensity is correspondingly weakened by the passage of light rays diagonally through the atmospheric envelope, that the incorporation of the sun itself within the composition becomes most practicable.

The participation of the sun within a landscape totally dependent on it can perhaps be usefully compared with the Christian doctrine of the Incarnation. The quality of God is so far superior to that of man, so the argument goes, that there can be no meaningful intercourse between them, and unless man achieves a measure of divinity which brings him within reach of God (which he cannot do), God must assume such human limitations as are necessary to bring him within reach of man. Only then can they participate in a common experience.

There is much in the mythology of the Sun god which is based on the same imagery. The sun is at first so blindingly bright that we can see nothing. Some limitation must be placed on its brilliance so that it approaches the same scale of light intensity as the landscape it illuminates. Gradually and inevitably it sinks, to be drowned or buried as the case may be beneath the western horizon, only to rise again in the dawn. Never during the whole process does it lose its essence. It is just as much 'sun' at every stage of the cycle. But in terms of the terrestrial environment it becomes for a time manageable, assimilable, comprehensible.

It is small wonder, therefore, that the sunrise and sunset assume great importance in the experience of landscape. They allow the supreme prospect symbol to enter for a time into the composition and take its place alongside the mundane, terrestrial shapes. The process is accompanied by a change in the balance of light of different colours, so that the general effect is to move towards the yellow-orange-red sequence of the spectrum, whereas under normal conditions we should associate blue with distance and therefore with prospect symbolism. Often, at sunset, the blue of distant objects such as hills persists even under a golden light, thereby accentuating the impression of prospect orientation.

There are certain differences between the sunrise and the sunset. The dust content of the atmosphere often tends to be higher in the evening than in the morning, while the atmospheric moisture tends to be somewhat differently distributed according to whether the condensation processes have taken place at the conclusion of a warm day or during the gradual cooling-off normally characteristic of night. It is no mere fanciful association which leads us to think of the golden light of Claude or Cuyp as belonging to morning or evening, depending on our experience. One feels one recognizes the mood of one or the other, even though there is nothing in the angle of elevation of the sun to indicate which it is.

Since light is essential to the realization of all prospects, surfaces or substances which reflect light acquire thereby a measure of prospect orientation. The effect of this can easily be studied in traditional landscape painting. Bright clouds, patterns of light reflected in water, snow surfaces, patches of clear blue in an otherwise overcast sky, all have something of the prospect symbolism of the sun. Because, on reflection even from bright objects, some light is invariably absorbed, this automatically brings about that limitation of the range of intensity which, as we have seen, is essential if other objects are not to be swamped by solar light. Brightly reflecting objects have an additional advantage over the sun itself in that they can occur in many different shapes and may also reflect colours or tones differentially, thereby contributing to the variety and interest of a composition or arrangement.

A particular example of a reflecting surface acting as a secondary source of light is to be found in the moon. Its behaviour in the matter of elevation above the horizon and its apparent cyclic motion are not unlike those of the sun, though it does have the additional attribute of its surface being covered by varying amounts of light and shade on a monthly cycle. But it differs from the sun in one important respect: the intensity of its light never reaches an intolerable level. It is always subdued, not only at the time of its rising and setting but even at its maximum elevation in the sky. To become a constituent part of the landscape it does not have to be 'cut down to size'. If, therefore, the hours of sunrise and sunset acquire an emotional association for the reasons suggested above, and if comparable circumstances apply to the moon all the time it is visible, this may go a little way towards explaining the 'poignancy' of sunrise and sunset (p. 21) and the 'romantic' quality of moonlight. Light, like any other commodity, becomes more precious when it is in short supply.

In addition to the primary source of light which we equate with the sun, and to those other primary sources, the stars, which may well figure as objects in the 'skyscape' (after all one of them was prominent enough to give its name to a well-known Turner) (*The Evening Star*, The National Gallery, No. 1991) but collectively contribute a negligible amount of light to illuminate a landscape, there are also 'artificial' sources of light, such as fires, lamps and torches. These have very important roles to play in landscape painting, but we shall be in a better position to examine them later on.

In very general terms it can be said that what light is to the prospect darkness is to the refuge. Just as light is conducive to seeing, so deprivation of light is conducive to not being seen. Refuges, at least in the sense of 'hides', may be made effective either by the interposition of some obstacle to interfere with the passage of light reflected from the observer (Figure 8) or by the cutting off of light from the observer so as to render him inconspicuous. There is therefore a very direct functional association between darkness and concealment and a *prima facie* case for symbolically equating darkness with the refuge as light with the prospect. It also frequently happens that those refuges which afford protection against meteorological hazards also preclude the intrusion of light, so that in the imagery of the cave or the forest, for instance, or even the cottage, interior darkness becomes associated with seclusion from every hazard against which such a haven provides protection and its refuge symbolism is thereby strengthened.

## Levels of Symbolism

'. . . Like far-off mountains turned into clouds.'
W. SHAKESPEARE (*A Midsummer Night's Dream*, Act IV, Scene 1, line 194)

In referring earlier to 'levels of symbolism' we noted that it would be advantageous to defer more detailed consideration of this subject until we had clarified the basic imagery of prospect, hazard and refuge. We have now looked at examples of these various kinds of imagery but chiefly at what may be called the 'tangible' end of the symbolic scale. Features which embody this kind of symbolism may be reflected or imitated in other media. For instance, the silhouette of a distant mountain backed by the fading evening sky would be a strong prospect symbol. But what if we cannot be sure whether it is a mountain or a cloud? What is received in the eye is an impression of contrasting shapes of different colours. From our experience of observing similar features elsewhere we may form the impression that we are looking at a mountain. But even if we do not—if we know, for instance, that there is no mountain there—we are prepared to accept the illusion in much the same way that we accept the illusion implicit in a painting.[20] In the following passage we find clouds fulfilling the role of prospect symbols, hazard symbols, even refuge symbols:

'Perrin thought that he had never seen the clouds assume such curious shapes—perhaps they were not clouds at all, but rather creatures of the sky that only his eye could see, just as it was only his eye that could see the other Mr. Perrin. There were birds with long, bending necks, and fat, round-faced animals with only one eye, and stiff, angular creatures with wings and legs like sticks, and then again there were splendid galleons with sails unfurled, and cathedral towers and trees and mountain ranges—they were all very strange and beautiful, and perhaps this was the last time that he would see them.' (Walpole, 1919 edn., p. 243)

Thus a cloud has the power of suggesting or, if you like, 'symbolizing', terrestrial forms and even the undulations of the counterpane, dimly perceived in the first moments of waking, or the pictures contemplated in the dying embers of the fire can evoke the same sort of feelings which we experience in our contact with 'real' prospects in our 'real' habitat.

Examples of this power of a stimulus to retain an element of ambiguity while at the same time achieving an aesthetic effect may be found in the following two passages. The first refers to Gauguin's *Jacob wrestling with the angel*:

'Viewers couldn't decide whether the Breton girls were looking at a crazy red sky or at a still crazier red meadow . . . It is equally plausible to speculate that the wrestling takes place on red soil, the kind Gauguin was working in as a ditch digger for the Lesseps Canal Company in Panama.' (Jenny, 1968, pp. 956–957)

The second refers to Kandinsky's *Improvization N.26, 1912*:

'Bits of nature still remain, the brown outlines of hills, clouds, an orange-yellow field placed next to a blue lake—or is it a window of sky?' (Jenny, 1968, p. 957)

In Jenny's interpretation of these pictures, and perhaps it is worth remembering that these are the views not of a professional art critic but of a soil scientist, vastly different parts of nature are interchangeable as regards their visual effect on the eye. In the first a piece of sky is interchangeable with a meadow or red soil; in the second with a lake. All these objects, it will be noted, are prospect symbols: the meadow or red soil being an 'open' surface (Table 4), the lake an aquatic surface further characterized by the (distance) colour blue, the red sky, suggestive of the prospect symbolism of the sunset, and the blue 'window of sky' being an unmistakeable example of that type of direct prospect which we have called the 'peephole vista'.

In a reference to *Snowstorm: Hannibal Crossing the Alps* in the Tate Gallery, Kitson stresses the interchangeability of very different forms in the paintings of Turner.

'He even adapted the curving shapes, the repeated arcs of light and shade, which he had used in his early Gothic interiors—e.g. "Ewenny Priory", a watercolour exhibited in 1797—to express the effect of sunlight breaking through the storm clouds; the clouds seem to share the mysterious, cavernous atmosphere of the medieval vaults. It should be noticed, too, how the same curves are echoed in the foreground below, thereby linking the ground and the sky in a continuous pattern on the surface.' (Kitson, 1964, p. 73)

We must surely all have experienced the sensation of perceiving phenomena of one kind which can be worked on by the imagination in such a way that we can see them as objects of a very different kind. A very personal anecdote will serve to illustrate this.

In November, 1971, I was sitting on the top floor of the Library in the University of Hull at about half-past four in the afternoon, writing one of the early chapters of this book. My attention was caught by a sunset so striking that I could concentrate on nothing else. I therefore stopped what I was doing and wrote out a description of the sky using the words which came immediately to mind. It is not surprising that such a hastily composed piece of writing is devoid of literary merit, but I quote a passage from it, without amendment, to illustrate how easily and indeed how willingly, the eye may be deceived into interpreting one kind of stimulus as if it were another.

> '. . . in the lowest part of the sky is a dull, purple-brown haze over which appear two or three long, flat clouds, little more than lines, of flaming orange. Next there comes a break-through—a long horizontal vista of duck-egg blue which spans the whole sky from north-west to south-west where it is closed by the junction of the upper and lower cloud-layers. This "junction area", together with all the upper cloud, is lit by the most brilliant orange light which each minute grows more red, complementing the change from blue to green in the distant sky. The shape of cloud layer is more or less flat, but it consists of various surfaces reminiscent of skeins, bundles of sinews, and ripple-marks.
>
> 'The whole of this surface gives the impression of being lit from underneath by some distant flame, the actual source being obscured by the lower haze. Black shadows, where the surface recedes upwards, set off the brilliance of smooth orange shapes.
>
> 'Turning the head upside down one can see the upper cloud surface like a huge tract of flaming desert landforms. The sharp junction between cloud-layer and distant sky now becomes a horizon. The general sensation is much the same as when it is viewed right way up, but the cloud forms now suggest terrestrial symbols. One seems to be looking over the edge of the world. The emotional impact is intense. Looking at it again the right way up, one seems to be aware of a new concept of distance. Has this been added by "association" in Alison's sense of the word?'

In an experience like this we have clearly come a very long way from that simple association between a creature and his environment which induces a feeling of satisfaction through the spontaneous appraisal of a biologically advantageous relationship to a habitat. The flaming sands of this nebulous desert afford no protection by rendering visible the approach of a hazard, animate or inanimate, because in reality there is no such hazard. But to dismiss the experience on these grounds as unconnected with the 'real' prospect–refuge situation of the creature in his terrestrial habitat is as illogical as to say that we cannot feel ourselves to be face to face with a real personality when we look at a Rembrandt portrait merely because we know it is an illusion contrived in oil and pigment on canvas. An apparent similarity between shape, colour, light and shade as perceived in a portrait and the equivalent features perceived in the face of a living person is sufficient to create an opportunity for the imagination to reconstruct, as it were, that person. In the same way the occurrence of shapes and colours and the distribution of light and shade as perceived in patterns in the sky can evoke a sensation similar to that which we experience from our relationship to real and functional prospects and refuges.

The passage itself, it will be noted, is markedly prospect-oriented (if one will allow the application of this terminology to the sunset!). The 'dull, purple-brown haze' is certainly a refuge symbol, as also are the 'black shadows, where the surface recedes upwards' which, notice, 'set off' the 'brilliance of smooth orange shapes'. This last phrase, in common with all the rest of the terminology employed, clearly belongs to the symbolism of the prospect. One phrase in particular may be noted, the 'long, horizontal vista of duck-egg blue'. We encountered horizontal vistas as exemplified, for instance, by the view in a park where cattle had eaten the leaves of the trees up to the limit of their reach, leaving a slice of visibility under the surviving foliage (p. 89). The most striking examples of this kind of prospect, however, are afforded by the phenomena of the sky. The sensation of being enclosed by a cloud-cover which, above the horizon, is slit open to allow the eye to penetrate to a vast distance, is a common source of aesthetic satisfaction wholly consistent with the complementary symbolism of prospect and refuge. Read the following passage paying special attention to such symbolism. It comes from the pen of one of the most landscape-sensitive of twentieth-century poets, and yet another prebendary, this time of Chichester Cathedral:

'But the Cotswold edge added a new memory. Driving over the edge in twilight. I saw what was apocalyptic. Dark cloud shadowed the sky and the Severn Valley lay in deep shade, but between the cloud and shadow burned a sunset, a long sea of fire. There, if anywhere, were "the flaming ramparts of the world". Or was I seeing farther, not a sunset, but a sunrise on another world? No, it was too lurid; it was a reflection from some infernal region. And I was hastening down to it, leaving not only the Cotswolds, but the earth itself.' (from 'Cold Cotswolds' in Young, 1967, p. 51)

This description of a horizontal vista draws heavily on the imagery, first, of the refuge, 'dark cloud . . . Valley . . . deep shade', then of the prospect, '. . . burned a sunset, a long sea of fire'. From here on practically every word is intensely charged with prospect symbolism, so much so that the length of vision, the 'fetch' of the prospect, seems to carry him right out of this world. The imagery indeed is too strong; the refuges of dark cloud and deep shade are no longer competent to protect him and he capitulates in the face of the rich hazard symbolism which swamps the last two sentences.

The horizontal vista as encountered in the sky takes us back to the most simple and primitive of refuge symbols. To stand under a canopy of black clouds with a narrow belt of clear, bright sky surmounting and sharpening the horizon is like standing under cover of the forest but near enough to its edge to obtain a view into the open ground beyond. Even more, perhaps, does it resemble the experience of being in a low cave with a wide, flat mouth, almost totally enclosed and protected, yet affording in one direction the opportunity of visual contact with the outside world. It is indeed such a common feature of landscape that it will be convenient to find a special name for it. *A sky dado*, then, is a layer of bright, clear sky between a horizon and a darker covering of cloud. The darkness of the upper layer, which we can call the *cloud canopy*, is caused by the cloud impeding the passage of light, whereas in the lower layer light can enter without interruption.

A common variant of the sky dado can be caused by precisely the opposite conditions. In this case, when the sky is comparatively free from particles of dust or moisture, it is the upper layer which affords the least impediment to the passage of light, so that its colour appears as a deep blue. Only near the horizon, where light has to pass for a greater distance through the lower levels of the atmosphere, does it encounter enough interference to suffer that diffusion which produces a whitish layer in the lower sky. For this feature the name *false sky dado* may therefore be appropriate. So common is the false sky dado on fine days in Western Europe that it becomes a normal feature in medieval painting immediately after the abandonment of the practice of depicting the heavens in gold.

An important feature of the sky dado, whether true or false, is that, by bringing the lighter-coloured parts of the sky into juxtaposition with the horizon, it contributes powerfully to the prospect symbolism and draws the eye into the distance. It may also be used to accentuate the difference between the sky and distant terrestrial forms where these are of the same colour. Titian (1487/90?–1576), for instance, frequently introduces streaks of cream-coloured cloud in the lower sky thereby separating two fields of blue, one in the heavens and one in the far-off hills.

**Scale**

> '"I should like to be a *little* larger, Sir, if you wouldn't mind," said Alice: "three inches is such a wretched height to be."
> '" It is a very good height indeed!" said the Caterpillar . . .'
> LEWIS CARROLL (1925 edn., pp. 69–70)

Although it must be forty years since I have seen it, I well remember an illustration in a children's edition of *Gulliver's Travels* depicting the hapless Gulliver pegged out on the ground while the disconcerted Lilliputians peered at the apparent giant from behind bushes which, in size, bore a closer relationship to themselves than to him. The point which I particularly recollect is how Gulliver, even when prostrate, projected above the surrounding vegetation and was therefore denied even the consolation of concealment which his puny adversaries enjoyed.

The idea of physical concealment obviously implies that the size of a screen must be related to the size of a person which it can effectively hide. Yet we have just suggested that the shapes, patterns and colours in the sky may evoke sensations similar to those evoked by refuges of a terrestrial kind, such as may be found in a forest or a cave.

The problem is not as difficult as it might at first seem. The advantage of a creature, human or non-human, in a pursuit or escape situation in the field depends very closely on his correct appraisal of the environmental opportunities at his disposal. To misjudge distance, to overestimate the size of a hiding-place, to allow a hazard to approach too close before setting in motion the escape mechanism—these may indeed prove disastrous, and the question of scale is therefore a very important one. When, however, we transfer the *whole* situation into its symbolic equivalent, when the clouds become our sheltering canopy and the low streak of clear sky our means of peeping out from under it, it would clearly be as absurd to peg the scale of intervening distances at the level at which they were originally effective as it would be to make a half-size reproduction of the *Mona Lisa* in which everything had been reduced by fifty per cent except the blandly smiling mouth.

If, coming nearer to the subject, the reader were to select some object in the middle distance of any of the landscapes reproduced in this book and were to ask himself how far away it was, although we should not expect a very precise answer, anything between a quarter of a mile and two or three miles might, I suggest, be reasonable. In fact, unless the reader were myopic, the answer would probably be nearer fifteen inches, that is, a distance of a different order of magnitude and, incidentally, the same distance as that of all the other features in the picture from the foreground to the most remote horizon, since they all lie in the same two-dimensional plane. But once the eye has accepted the conventions of perspective, it can attribute different distances to the various objects portrayed, even though their images on the page are actually equidistant from the eye itself. Once a system of proportionate relationships has been set up we can magnify or reduce the picture as much as we like and it will still be recognizably the same. Thus it is reasonable to argue that the sensation of obtaining cover from the edge of a wood while commanding a view over open ground can be stimulated, not only by the actual occurrence of these features in a real-life relationship to the observer, but also by a sky picture of the same sort of environmental situation. The idea, therefore, that the scale imparted by the human form is important in the prospect–refuge context does not inhibit the realization of an imitative composition in which the actual distances are vastly greater.

At the 'tangible' biological end of the scale, the human form does act as a kind of modulus establishing a framework of perception from which observed features cannot be divorced. It is a common experience to go back to a place one has known well in childhood but not visited since, to find that all the buildings have shrunk and now stand closer together. The appraisal which we made of our environment when we were six or seven was made on an entirely different assumption about height and distance in relation to the size of our persons. When we visit such places again we feel that they have 'shrunk'. What we now perceive is not in tune with what experience had taught us to expect.

What seems to be important is that we recognize the possibility of environmental features acting in the capacity of prospect, refuge or hazard symbols, or some combination of each, at very different scales. A depression in the ground can be a refuge symbol, whether it is the shallow pit which shelters the charcoal-burner or the Severn Valley as perceived by Andrew Young from the Cotswold Edge. A parting through an opaque screen can be a vista whether it is a firebreak in a young fir plantation or the Grand Canyon of the Colorado. Falling water can symbolize the power of the forces of nature whether in Niagara or in the absurdly genteel 'cascade' of the eighteenth-century landscape gardeners. In our behavioural experience of our habitat the limitations imposed by scale may matter very much; in our aesthetic experience of landscape those limitations may be transcended.

## Locomotion

'He ran through the desert; he ran through the mountains; he ran through the salt-pans; he ran through the reed-beds; he ran through the blue gums; he ran through the spinifex; he ran till his front legs ached. He had to!'

RUDYARD KIPLING (1930 edn., p. 87)

An obvious corollary of the hypothesis that the aesthetic enjoyment of landscape is based ultimately on the establishment of an advantageous relationship between the observer and his environment is that he must be free to move within the environment in such a way as to achieve that advantage. Concealment within a refuge affords a measure of satisfaction, particularly if that refuge affords a clear field of vision over the surrounding area. Yet the process of escape is clearly facilitated if it is possible to vacate a refuge when the moment seems opportune and to attain another, better situated in relation to any new challenge consequent on a change in the spatial relationships between the fugitive and the hazard or hazards from which protection is sought.

In the situation of pursuit, on the other hand, the necessity for freedom of movement is even more apparent. We all know that there are certain plants which, though literally rooted to the spot, can trap their prey as it visits them, and certain predatory animals to whom the process of pursuit and capture may involve only an extremely limited movement, but normally pursuit in nature implies a fair measure of mobility.

It follows, therefore, that if the eye makes a spontaneous appraisal of the environment as a strategic theatre for survival, this must include some assessment of the opportunity for movement between the various key-positions in the prospect–refuge complex. We have already touched on many examples of this and have noted in particular the role played by 'impediment hazards' (p. 100), the function of which is to put the creature, whether escaping or pursuing, at a disadvantage in relation to his adversary. We also noted that particular strategic importance attached to those places where an impediment hazard ceases to be effective; gateways, staircases, bridges, heads of estuaries, ends of buildings, etc., were cited as sign symbols suggestive of opportunity for movement in an area where such movement generally is limited or denied.

It is but a short step from the opportunity for movement symbolized by a breach of an impediment hazard, a gap in a wall, for instance, to the more positive suggestion of locomotion indicated by paths, roads, etc., and these play a very important role in landscape and particularly in the composition of landscape painting. Because they tend to be conspicuous, elongated features they often assert an influence on landscape composition disproportionate to the actual area of canvas they occupy. They therefore have a way of attracting the attention of those art critics who employ a predominantly two-dimensional descriptive system. The 'diagonals' which discharge connecting or separating functions are frequently lines of communication. Their continuity, their gentle curvature, and their liability to link distinctive features of a landscape have been constantly exploited by artists and landscape gardeners alike. But in addition to their geometrical significance in the two-dimensional geometry, of the canvas, they may be seen as potent invitations to movement within the three-dimensional environment of the observer.

In contemplating the pattern of communications in a landscape the eye tends to fit together the visible components in such a way as to construct imaginary paths between its various parts. A carriage drive in a park, for instance, which dips out of sight into dead ground and reappears on a rising surface farther off, suggests a continuous channel of movement, even though its continuity cannot be perceived, and leads the eye forward towards its destination. Again, the linking of paths with breaches in impediment hazards can strengthen the impression of ease of movement within the landscape and therefore of the achievement of an environmental advantage. A path leading to a bridge conveys a more potent suggestion of movement opportunity than either the path or the bridge alone. Two paths converging on a bridge are even more effective in suggesting potential for freedom of movement within the habitat.

Probably, when we think of channels of movement in landscape, we most readily call to mind the sylvan path or the spacious gravel drive, but once the principle is accepted that routes and channels of communication of all sorts symbolize the concept of movement within an environment, we may well recollect the moments when we have paused on a railway bridge to look along the receding tracks into the distance, when we have watched a boat chugging placidly along a canal, or when we have achieved an unmistakeable satisfaction in perceiving landscape from the motorway. Locomotion, either in achievement or in imagination, is an essential ingredient of participation in the experience of landscape.

The question of participation, of involvement, raises wider issues which we shall consider later. But first we must look more closely at the way in which the different kinds of symbolism are combined in a composition, that is to say how effectively and in what way they may be balanced.

# CHAPTER 5

# Balance

## The Idea of 'Balance'

'The Wood supports the Plain, the parts unite,
And strength of Shade contends with strength of Light'
ALEXANDER POPE (*Moral Essays: Epistle to Lord Burlington*,
lines 81–82. See Bowles, 1806, vol. iii, p. 339)

The proportions in which the symbolism of prospect, refuge and hazard are combined in a landscape establishes its equilibrium or 'balance'. Symbols can vary both in strength and in frequency, and the 'feel' of the landscape is largely determined by the 'mix' of symbols of like, opposite or complementary kinds.

Where we find two symbols of the same kind reinforcing each other, we can call the process *reduplication*. Reduplication is such a widespread phenomenon that it would be difficult to find a landscape which did not furnish examples of it. There are, however, certain combinations of symbols which constantly recur and we can soon learn to recognize these as conforming to a common pattern. We have already noted the road-plus-bridge partnership; in addition we frequently encounter the road (or path or track or railway line) associated with some other prospect symbol which leads the eye in the same general direction.

The avenue is an obvious partner for the road in achieving the effect of reduplication. Hobbema's famous painting *The Avenue at Middelharnis* (Figure 11) provides a good example. The flanking hedges, the grass verges, the wheel-ruts and the little bobbles of foliage at the tops of the trees all converge on the same vanishing point. Yet so powerful is the prospect imagery on the flanks of the panorama that even this central channel has to fight hard to secure the observer's attention. The left-hand side contains the longest fetch and the most prominent tower; the right-hand side a sharply defined roof-horizon, only partially obscured by closer trees, and the brightest cumulus cloud in the sky. The road needs the support of the converging lines to enable it to hold its own against these inviting expanses on either side.

It is a common characteristic of lines of communication that they are accompanied by other features which accentuate their linear character. Flanking grass verges, ditches, hedges, fences, kerbs, telephone wires all discharge supporting roles which are even more effective when they introduce a colour contrast. Thus a white road can acquire emphasis from green verges and a brown fence, or a bed of grey ballast from its gleaming silver railway lines.

Another very common case of reduplication occurs when indirect prospect symbols, such as towers, are placed on hills. The Greeks had a phrase 'mounting

122

FIGURE 11. MEINDERT HOBBEMA (1638–1709): THE AVENUE AT MIDDELHARNIS
Reproduced by courtesy of the Trustees, The National Gallery, London (No. 830)

Pelion on Ossa'—that is, achieving the cumulative effect of elevation by adding together the two conspicuous mountains which lay to the south of Olympus. If, then, the observer's viewpoint is such that the tower-on-the-hill appears as a horizon a further strengthening of the prospect imagery is achieved.

In the same way, reduplication can be employed to accentuate refuge symbolism. Hobbema again would furnish plenty of examples; indeed the reduplication of refuge symbolism, rather than prospect symbolism, would be much more characteristic of his work. Cottages and woods are both powerful refuge symbols. When Hobbema places one inside the other the effect is enhanced (Figure 12).

The reduplication of refuge symbols is one of the most common devices in painting, in landscape design and in verbal landscape description. Farmsteads are not uncommonly situated within shelter belts. This is no mere aesthetic affectation; there is a very good reason for it. Consequently when we see a farmstead so situated in a landscape we are impressed by the exaggerated sense of shelter. Similarly, houses in hollows or ravines, towns in valleys, caves overhung by trees, summerhouses backed by tall hedges: all aim to augment the feeling of seclusion, of refuge.

Reduplication in this sense always involves two or more symbols of the same kind which can be seen to reinforce each other. The 'cottage-in-the-wood' is a partnership of refuge symbols either of which could stand on its own and still suggest the idea of refuge, although much less effectively and intensively. One symbol fortifies another and in so doing adds directly to the strength of its symbolism.

A picture which seeks to emphasize the hazard will tend to employ a number of symbols to this end, while at the same time keeping down the refuge imagery. Shipwreck scenes, for instance, tend to pile on the agony by enlisting the aid of several hazards. The disintegration of a dismasted ship pounded on a sandbank by giant waves would be terrifying even against a clear blue sky, which could, with meteorological authenticity, perfectly well accompany gale-force winds. But what a waste of the sky! A romantic artist would, in practice, be likely to fill it with tempestuous clouds and driving rain, leaving perhaps a few brighter patches to give emphasis to its menacing blackness and also to taunt the vicarious participant with the merest suggestion of a prospect symbolism adequate to invite the idea of escape from the present hazard but wholly impotent to procure it. The chances are also that he would replace the sandbank with jagged rocks. Refuge symbols, it need hardly be said, are not wanted unless, again, to tantalize. The inclusion of a distant harbour, perceived but unattainable, suggests almost a streak of artistic sadism. A striking example of reduplication in hazard symbolism is described by Kenneth Clark in the phenomenon of 'Fire in the Flood'. (Clark, 1949, p. 41)

By comparison Claude invariably reduces his hazard symbols to a very low level. The symbolism of prospect and refuge may be intense. Black shadows under massive canopies of foliage balance long, open views, providing a satisfying equilibrium of complementary strategic components (Figure 4). And all

124

for what? To safeguard the observer from a hazard which scarcely exists. The most menacing animals are browsing sheep, the wind has no bite when the air is motionless, the clouds which catch and purify the golden sunlight are incapable of emitting rain. Even the sense of approaching darkness is accompanied by the soothing assurance that there is nothing there to be afraid of. No wonder that so many connoisseurs of landscape painting have for three centuries subscribed to the opinion that Claude is incomparable in creating a world of tranquillity, security and repose. Whether it is the real world is another matter. Ruskin thought not (p. 45).

Not all painters, however, would be tempted to aim at such an objective. For some a balance of symbolism would need to be sought in very different values. Just as Hobbema is generally a refuge-dominant painter, so Philips Koninck is the opposite (Figure 13). His landscapes of estuarine levels viewed from a moderate elevation are the products of lavish prospect imagery—extreme forms of panorama, in which wide, flat alluvial surfaces, laced with smooth, reflecting watercourses, are surmounted by capacious skies. Whatever the title of the picture, visibility is the theme. Refuge symbols are there in plenty, but they are inconspicuous, generally distant and totally overwhelmed by the expansiveness of the open view.

A landscape may be said to be 'in balance' when each type of imagery is represented in roughly equal strength. When the power of one type of symbolism is increased the whole becomes prospect-dominant, refuge-dominant or hazard-dominant as the case may be. This 'mix' of symbolism which applies to whole landscapes may apply also to their individual components. We have already noted that a castle turret is a symbol both of prospect and of refuge (p. 82); if manned by a hostile force it may also symbolize a hazard. There are certain other types of building which have recognizable dual roles of this kind. A distant church spire, for instance, is certainly a common form of indirect prospect symbol. Its purpose seems to be to achieve elevation for its own sake and in doing so it frequently breaks the horizon. But it also suggests 'refuge' in a number of senses. It implies the presence of a large building which provides physical shelter against meteorological hazards. It symbolizes, through historical association, the idea of 'sanctuary' provided by ecclesiastical authority against hostile powers, both temporal and spiritual. It generally indicates the whereabouts of a settlement, often concealed from view, by trees, for instance, or by the lie of the land, and thus it symbolizes the comfort of civilization within an open landscape which may be still largely possessed and dominated by the forces of nature.

Another type of building constantly recurring in the history of art is the mill. A refuge it certainly is, but one which, at least before the age of steam, had of necessity to be itself exposed to nature as a source of power. This sense of exposure is dominant in the windmill, invariably a prospect symbol because it is functionally required to reach upwards into the moving air. In this objective it is frequently assisted by an elevated site, either the crest of a hill or, as so often in Dutch paintings, the raised bank of a river, canal or dyke. Almost invariably it

126

indulges in the trick of horizon-breaking. The refuge aspect, though present, is suppressed.

The watermill, on the other hand, combines the same essentials in very different degrees (Figure 14). Its source of power is here more concentrated. It is almost invariably low-lying and therefore the mill site is more liable to be sheltered from atmospheric hazards. The building itself does not need to be tower-like in structure. It can be sheltered by trees and neighboured by other buildings which could not be tolerated in the immediate vicinity of a windmill because of the loss of efficiency which would inevitably result. In the windmill the power of nature must be caught as it asserts itself, free, unchannelled and at full force. In the watermill it may be captured inconspicuously in a pool, led quietly captive through a leet and then put to work at the moment of liberation to come to life again as an orderly, manageable hazard symbol in a modest cascade, whose splash and rumble may excite with no more than a token suggestion of real danger. The watermill is almost as popular as the windmill in seventeenth-century Dutch painting. We find one, two and even more watermills named in the titles of paintings, and innumerable examples occurring in pictures whose titles make no mention of them.[21]

Up to a point symbolic meanings may be attached to particular objects, caves, towers, etc., wherever they occur; but from the very nature of the prospect–refuge concept it follows that much of the symbolism is to be seen in the relationships between them. There are, furthermore, certain general directional or positional associations which are to be found in most landscape situations. For instance, the upper part of a landscape naturally tends to be associated with the idea of 'prospect', the lower part with 'refuge'. The sky is usually the principal source of light, whether this comes direct from the sun or whether it is diffused by a cloud cover over the whole area. As an observer raises his eyes progressively upwards from the ground in front of him his line of vision encounters objects increasingly far away. Similarly, on the canvas of a painting the more distant horizons are higher than the nearer ones. There are, of course, exceptions to this. Above the horizontal the converse rule begins to operate. The overhanging canopies of trees are nearer than objects which are perceived through horizontal vistas underneath. The nearer clouds in the sky also generally appear more overhead than those which are successively farther away; but in general we tend to associate elevation with prospects while refuges tend naturally to occur in the lower parts. Caves, ravines, sheltered hollows, etc., all add weight to this association.

It can be seen, therefore, that composition in landscape painting is already preconditioned towards certain tendencies by general rules which govern the arrangement of prospect and refuge symbols in particular ways. Just as the top and bottom of a picture tend to have their own associations, so the flanks of a picture are very commonly filled with refuge symbols which 'frame' the view. There are, of course, very good reasons for this which can be perfectly well explained in terms of the orthodox rules of perspective and the physics of light. If we place a large refuge symbol in the centre foreground, the chances are that

128

Figure 14. Meindert Hobbema (1638–1709): A Landscape with a Stream and Several Watermills

Reproduced by courtesy of the Trustees, The National Gallery, London (No. 832)

we block the view. 'Interest', in the form of buildings or foliage in the foreground, is therefore more usually confined to the flanks, and such objects intrude only in the middle distance where they appear small enough not to get in the way.

If, however, we look at the same phenomena from the standpoint of prospect–refuge symbolism we can see that the *coulisse* is something more than a compositional convention. In a behavioural context it is functionally crucial (p. 105). The proximity of refuge material in the flanks of the foreground ensures some measure of 'cover' for the apparent vantage-point. Even if the observer is actually exposed to a counter-view along the fetch of the prospect, he is reassured that the opportunity for concealment is not far away. The provision of some kind of cover in at least one of the flanks of the foreground, if not in both, is an almost invariable habit of Claude as of many other painters. It is also to be found in many styles of landscape gardening. The view from the house is often covered at the flanks by some constricting vegetation or, in landscape architect's terms, voids are flanked by masses. The professional photographer again makes effective use of this device, 'framing' his prospect by the symbolism of the refuge.

'Framing' in this sense is used figuratively, but we can see the application of prospect–refuge theory even in a literal interpretation of the word. The frame of a picture is like the frame of a window, and what better expresses the prospect–refuge complement than the old lady peering out on to the street from the gloom of an interior, veiled perhaps by net curtains, and hiding the greater part of her person behind the walls! By edging sideways beyond the frame of the window she can in a trice achieve complete concealment. Strategically her situation is superb!

A very common practice in painting is to make a concession towards equilibrium by introducing into a composition 'token' representations of the symbols complementary to those which dominate it. This is particularly true of refuge-dominant pictures into which prospects are allowed to intrude. The phenomenon may easily be studied without looking further than the National Gallery in London. Perhaps the best known example is the *Ansidei Madonna* of Raphael (Figure 15). The Madonna and Child occupy the centre of the composition. They are backed by the large canopied throne on which the Virgin is seated, and which does, in fact, block the view. In the foreground on either flank stand the figures of St. John and St. Nicholas respectively. The throne is not quite wide enough to obscure the aperture of the great rounded arch which spans the whole composition, so that, between the throne and the walls supporting the arch on either side, only partially obscured by the figures of the saints, there is room for two narrow vistal glimpses into a distant landscape of gently rolling hills. The general 'feel' of the composition is one of refuge. The throne behind and the canopy over the Virgin and Child, the 'framing' of the flanks with (male) protective figures also backed by plastered masonry screens, the sensation of seclusion achieved by the grouping of the figures in the immediate vicinity of the observer: all these dictate the mood of refuge. But the idea of seclusion is

130

FIGURE 15. RAPHAEL (1483–1520): THE ANSIDEI MADONNA
A very common environmental situation for a Madonna of the period. The dominant
refuge symbolism is balanced by two token prospects. Reproduced by courtesy of the
Trustees, The National Gallery, London (No. 1171)

strengthened rather than weakened by the introduction of these two token prospects which establish a context for the refuge and offer an assurance that beyond this inner core of sanctuary there lies an outer strategic zone of good visibility.

A charming example of this type of composition is to be found in the *Virgin and Child* by Lorenzo di Credi (Figure 16). This painting contains two tiny landscapes, each asymmetrically divided by the pillars, but not so much as to destroy the unity of each composition within its Romanesque frame. Each landscape is based on a central vistal axis represented by a river and an avenue respectively. In both cases there is a suggestion that the vistal axis is continued in a valley beyond. Other prospect symbols include the towers, the horizons, largely open but broken by occasional trees, and the clear sky with a false sky dado.

The device of a marginal vista flanking a central refuge is extremely common in paintings of this most popular of all subjects in the late fifteenth and early sixteenth centuries. A wide range of variations in this compositional arrangement can be studied in the collection of the National Gallery. Sometimes the flanking vistas are broad, sometimes ludicrously narrow, as in Boltraffio's *Virgin and Child* (Giovanni Antonio Boltraffio, c. 1466/7–1516, No. 728). In Bergognone's *Altarpiece: the Virgin and Child with Saints Catherine of Alexandria and Siena* (Ambrogio Bergognone, active 1481, d. 1523? No. 296), the margins are occupied by vistas less than one inch in breadth and over forty in height! Sometimes the vistas are asymmetrical, as in Bramantino's *Adoration of the Kings* (Bartolomeo Suardi, known as 'Bramantino', living 1490, d. 1530, No. 3073) in which a peephole vista on the left contrasts with a much larger vista on the right. In Gerolamo dai Libri's *Madonna and Child with Saint Anne* (Gerolamo dai Libri, c. 1474–1555? No. 748) the conventional central refuge symbol is replaced by a lemon tree which allows room for two wide flanking vistas of almost panoramic extent, thereby conveying a much greater sense of prospect in the balance of symbolism than is usual in these paintings. Within the whole group, however, prospect and refuge, and the balance between them, are represented in a highly stylized fashion, which sharply separates their complementary roles and exaggerates the functions which each discharges.

There are, of course, many other arrangements of prospect and refuge symbolism in paintings of the Madonna. In Jan van Eyck's *Madonna of Chancellor Rolin* (Figure 17) the three apertures occupy the centre rather than the flanks of the composition and, because they are placed close together, the landscape appears as a single whole. It is, in short, an interrupted panorama, rather than a series of separate vistas (p. 85 and Table 1) and, incidentally, contains many features we have already encountered. Notice the deflected vista in the river, the central place accorded to the bridge, and the two little figures peeping through the wall from a position of refuge.

The device of the 'token' prospect can be found in a very different but equally distinctive form in the 'courtyard' paintings of the seventeenth-century Dutch school, of which one of the best known examples is Pieter de Hooch's *Courtyard*

FIGURE 16. LORENZO DI CREDI (1457–1537): VIRGIN AND CHILD
Reproduced by courtesy of the Trustees, The National Gallery, London (No. 593)

FIGURE 17. JAN VAN EYCK (d. 1441): THE MADONNA OF CHANCELLOR ROLIN (*La Vièrge au Donateur*)
Reproduced by permission of the Director of the *Musées de France, Musée du Louvre,* Paris

*of a House in Delft* (Figure 18). Here the 'fetch' of the token vista tends to be very short, but its function is manifestly the same—to put out a kind of feeler from the refuge area into the wider environment. If danger is to come, this is the route by which it must enter, and the defensive situation of the observer is strengthened by the assurance that he can see down the alley, if that is the right word, and into the world beyond.

From the enclosed courtyard it is but a short step to the 'interior' which became a favourite theme with many Dutch painters, and here again the token

134

FIGURE 18. PIETER DE HOOCH (1629?–post 1684): COURTYARD OF A HOUSE IN DELFT
Reproduced by courtesy of the Trustees, The National Gallery, London (No. 835)

prospect (vista or peephole) is an almost universal feature in one form or another. It is not, of course, peculiar to this type of painting. Leonardo's *Last Supper*, it may be remembered, contains three tiny rectangular apertures with landscape fragments visible in each. But the Dutch interiors are distinguished by the way in which light is exploited within the confines of enclosed space. Doors and windows are frequently employed to afford prospects of trees and sky, as in the earlier group portraits of Frans Hals. (In the later groups, the St. Hadrian

(1633), Amsterdam (1637) and St. George (1639) Militias, Hals relieved the dominance of the refuge symbolism by moving his milieu into the open air.)

Vermeer's interiors, on the other hand, make their token concessions to prospect symbolism even less ostentatiously. In the very large number of interiors in which windows are shown they are invariably so positioned and angled that no landscape is visible through them, only an infusion of light. This is to be explained, no doubt, primarily in terms of the effect required from light falling on the subjects in the room, but at the same time anyone familiar with the symbolism of the prospect as experienced in the open air will have little difficulty in recognizing Vermeer's windows as indoor versions of the 'secondary peephole' (Table 1) and the prospects they suggest (cf. 'offsets') as the imagined token links between the interior and the outside world.

We have already seen that certain effects can be achieved by consolidating particular kinds of symbol in certain parts of a painting. The flanking token vistas of those medieval Madonnas which concentrate the refuge symbolism in the centre relegate the prospect symbols to the sides. Compositions based on the *coulisse* reverse the arrangement; a central prospect is flanked by refuge symbols on one side or both. Yet another variation can be introduced by bringing the prospect–refuge interface in to the centre of the composition. This is what happens in the 'edge-of-the-wood' phenomenon which has intrigued so many painters. Pictures of this kind are divided into two contrasting parts, often roughly equal, in which the open view on one side is balanced by the woodland on the other. The woodland itself is usually depicted with an unenclosed, penetrable edge and often a path, or paths, leading invitingly into the trees. The effect is enhanced by accentuating the details of the symbolism in either half; the prospect is distinguished by clarity, distance and sometimes falling ground, the refuge by an impression of the darkness, depth and capaciousness of the woodland in which the observer can, at his own choosing, be swallowed up.

A different effect can be achieved by *contraposition*, which is the opposite of reduplication. In contraposition individual symbols of *different* kinds, such as buildings and open space, are juxtaposed. A refuge symbol, such as a house, may be placed on its own, unprotected by supporting vegetation and surrounded by a naked or carpeted surface. Capability Brown frequently carried his 'shaven lawns' right up to the mansion with no encircling garden. His use of 'clumps' of trees also illustrates the same sort of arrangement; a clearly defined refuge is set conspicuously within a matrix of strong prospect symbolism.

Variation in the choice and appearance of refuge symbols can also induce aesthetic satisfaction. Many observers prefer mixed woodlands to stands of single species. Contrast of colour, shade or tone is invariably commented on by those who praise the spring in England and the fall in the north-eastern United States; 'variety' was one of the virtues most consistently valued in 'The Picturesque'. It is a fact that the greater the variegation of the environment the less conspicuous is a person located within it. Compare the dappled shade of a mixed vegetation of trees, bushes, grasses, etc., with the uniform background of a sunless pine forest, where a much lower level of light intensity affords less effective concealment. Even if the survival value of a variegated background cannot be demonstrated, such a background is certainly not inconsistent with the idea of 'seeing without being seen'.


## Inversion

> '"How strange!" I said to one I saw;
> "You quite upset our every law.
> However can you get along
> So systematically wrong?"'
> W. S. GILBERT (1887 edn., *My Dream*, pp. 228–233, verse 18)

A special type of balance of symbolism is to be found in what may be called the phenomenon of *inversion*. Notwithstanding the very tenuous nature of the associations which we have so far noted between environmental objects and the concepts of 'prospect', 'refuge' and 'hazard' we have, I suggest, established at least a *prima facie* case for regarding certain phenomena as having appropriate symbolic roles to discharge. It is true that many environmental objects and situations have ambiguous or ill-defined roles in the prospect–refuge complement, but this does not invalidate those associations which can be recognized as regular. Thus horizons invariably suggest 'prospect', caves 'refuge', and so on.

The moment we begin to recognize that the terms 'prospect', 'refuge' and 'hazard' really indicate roles played by environmental objects in a dramatic process in which the observer interacts with his environment, it becomes clear that each situation in which we find ourselves presents us with some variation of a limited number of basic themes. Just as in the theatre we can recognize a number of stock situations, the jealousy of a husband, the unwelcome intrusion of a mother-in-law, the downfall of the over-confident tyrant, which are re-created by different characters in different plays set in different periods with different lines and different scenery, so in landscape we find recurring the same basic situations in which the details are peculiar to the particular occasion while conforming to a regular general pattern.

In human relationships one of the most common devices for producing a dramatic effect is to be found in role reversal. The characters who are assigned to a particular role do not comply with all the behaviour patterns we normally associate with that role. In sexology, for instance, the male, whose stereotyped image marks him as the dominant, masterful, even aggressive partner, sometimes derives satisfaction from assuming the submissive role conventionally attributed to the female. Role reversal may take place between children and parents, between master and servant, or between superior officer and subordinate, as for instance in certain units of the British Army when, on Christmas Day, the officers traditionally wait on the other ranks. There is scarcely a story in the whole of fairy-tale fiction which does not exhibit some example of this trend; the all-powerful ogre is exposed as impotent, the beggar turns out to be a magician or the wizened old woman a beautiful princess. The 'rags-to-riches' and 'log-cabin-to-White-House' type of story casts a character in a stereotyped role which immediately invites expectations which in that case are not fulfilled.

For a more sophisticated example we may turn to Macbeth, which is really a drama about role reversal. To begin with, the driving power comes from Lady Macbeth, who makes it her business to dispel the infirmity of purpose of a reluctant accomplice. Already we have a reversal of the conventional husband–wife role. It is the lady who, so to say, wears the trews. But as the play proceeds this role reversal gradually breaks down. Macbeth grows increasingly aggressive as his wife relapses, not into the submissiveness of wifely feminity, but into the incapacity of neurosis, collapse and eventual death.

All tragedy has an element of role reversal, if it is only a suggestion of weakness in the powerful, the vulnerable heel of Achilles. The life work of Charlie Chaplin has demonstrated its indispensability in comedy. And just as in social relationships we can create a sense of the dramatic by setting up roles and peopling them with characters who display aberrations from the behaviour we expect, so we can find the same kind of anomalies in those environmental relationships in which the components of landscape raise expectations in terms of the symbolism of prospect, refuge and hazard, only to frustrate them. 'He hath put down the mighty from their seat and hath exalted the humble and meek' becomes in translation 'Every valley shall be exalted and every mountain and hill made low.'

Inversion involves the intrusion of one kind of symbol into a situation which we should normally associate with another kind. If, for instance, the upper part of a landscape is normally suggestive of prospect and therefore associated with distance, openness and light, while the lower part is associated with the symbolism of refuge, the representation of one of these areas in terms of an alien symbolism would constitute an inversion.

The most common and dramatically effective inversion is to be found in the landscape of night. The sky, which we normally think of as containing, if not constituting, the principal source of light, is now deprived of it. The upper part of the field of vision, which is normally to be thought of as prospect-dominant, is now occupied by the extreme refuge symbol of darkness. Where prospects are developed at all they are to be found in pools of light from artificial sources. Instead of a landscape of refuges set within the wider prospect, we have limited or 'contained' prospects set within an infinite refuge. Almost all the values we can attach to an environmental object are the opposite of what we should normally expect. They are, like the values in Gilbert's Topsy-Turveydom, 'systematically wrong'.

Because light and darkness are themselves potently charged with prospect and refuge symbolism respectively, inversion can easily be achieved if we use one or other of them to infuse environmental objects commonly associated with the symbolic complement. Fires in caves, lanterns in forests, shafts of light streaming from open doorways, all transmute common refuge symbols into limited and localized prospects. Per contra inversion can be achieved in a direct prospect when a vista of inky blackness is opened up between the pillars of a candlelit banqueting hall, or in an indirect prospect symbol when a floodlit church tower, projecting into the night, proclaims a vantage-point but denies the expectation of a view.

The idea of situating minute sources of light within an envelope of darkness is not, of course, confined to what we traditionally think of as 'landscapes'. It is a device associated with the *chiaroscuro* technique favoured by Caravaggio and perfected by Rembrandt, generally in portraits or groups depicted in 'interiors'. But there must be thousands of Nativities which exploit the opportunities latent in a situation in which the refuge of the stable is illuminated as a tiny prospect contained within the all-enveloping refuge of the night.

In his chapter on 'The Landscape of Fantasy' Clark devotes a long paragraph to 'Night Pieces' in which he says:

'A large area of dark paint cannot be made to look convincing by optical processes alone; it must have been transmuted into the medium of the poetic imagination. . . . It was Elsheimer who brought to a new stage of realization the nocturnal fantasies of a hundred years earlier. In his picture of the *Flight into Egypt* in Munich . . . he carried them as near to the limits of truth as such subjects can go without entirely sacrificing the element of decoration which must exist in any picture. No student of English poetry need be reminded that the early seventeenth century was profoundly excited by the beauty of the night. *Romeo and Juliet*, *A Midsummer Night's Dream*, even *The Merchant of Venice*, contain those poetic scenes which the Venetian artists used to call *notte*, in the same way that Herrick and other lyricists used the expression "a night piece" in description of a poetic subject.' (Clark, 1949, pp. 51–52)

The Elsheimer painting (Figure 19) to which Clark refers provides a very good example of the symbolism of inversion in prospect–refuge theory. The picture is divided roughly into two halves by the irregular diagonal outline of a wood. Above this line and to the right is a partially cloud-covered moonlit sky. Below it and to the left is a massive arboreal screen. In the centre foreground the holy family forms a little group in a tiny pool of light. To the left and in the mouth of a small vista opening into the wood, a fire creates a brighter source of light illuminating a little group of people and animals and bringing to life the surface of the trees. To balance this the full moon appears on the right through a 'peep-hole' in the clouds just above the rounded outline of the wood and, as if this were not enough, it appears again in reflection on the unruffled water which occupies the middle and foreground of the picture on the extreme right flank.

At a later period the Romantics not unnaturally revived the interest shown by earlier painters (Stechow, 1966, devotes some ten pages to what he calls 'Nocturnes') in the device of inversion. Fires, torches and lanterns were all pressed into service. The working fires of manufacturing industry were superbly exploited by Loutherbourg in a well-known painting of Coalbrookdale by night (in the Science Museum, London; reproduced as Plate 46 in Clark, 1969).

139

FIGURE 19. ADAM ELSHEIMER (1578–1610): THE FLIGHT INTO EGYPT (*Die Flucht nach Ägypten*) Reproduced by permission of the *Bayerische Staatsgemäldesammlungen*, Munich (Alte Pinakothek, Munich, No. 216)

Conflagrations of disaster offered the opportunity for achieving greater dramatic effect by combining the source of light with a potent hazard symbol, as in Turner's *Fire at Sea*.[22]

The use of inversion perhaps reached its culmination in the work of John Martin who so reversed the natural order as to set quite large prospects inside enormous caves (Balston, 1947). Even where the scene is obviously intended to be out of doors, he frequently depicts the sky as if it were the roof of a stupendous cavern (Figure 20), sweeping up the clouds into huge, rock-like canopies broken by an orifice through which a flash of lightning or the sun itself strikes into the refuge to reveal a rich and terrifying fantasy of light and shade (cf. Kitson on Turner, p. 113).

We have already noted that the sunrise and sunset are distinguished, not only by a particular geometrical relationship between the sun and the horizon, but also by diminution of the light intensity, and that this latter phenomenon is also found in moonlight (pp. 110–111). This diminution of light may be thought of as a partial inversion, a half-way house to the real thing. The symbolism is not reversed but the balance is significantly altered, principally by the accentuation of the refuge symbolism. Trees and bushes which in broad daylight afford little concealment may, in moonlight, cast heavy shadows with less contrast but little less definition than shadows cast in sunlight. In the pre-dawn and post-sunset 'glow' the light level may be sufficiently reduced for the 'rods' of the eye to take over from the colour-sensitive 'cones', reducing vision to black-and-white as in moonlight.

Under these conditions favourably situated prospect symbols can retain their potency and even increase it. A horizon, for instance, is at its most effective when its surface is so starved of light as to appear black against a background of crepuscular light which has just enough brightness to be perceived in colour—green, blue, yellow or even bright pink, as in Bellini's *Garden* (Figure 24). Woodland glades and clearings, lawns, parkland, the sea-shore, in short all open surfaces, may secure enough light to make them recognizable as prospects, having, however, a different and less familiar relationship to the total balance of symbolism. In a complete inversion such open spaces, even the sky itself, become a part of the dark enveloping refuge. Any prospects have to be created by artificial light within them.

**Magnets**

'To lead, with secret guile, the prying sight
To where component parts may best unite,
And form one beauteous, nicely-blended whole,
To charm the eye and captivate the soul.'
R. PAYNE KNIGHT (1794, Bk. I, lines 193–196)

It is a matter of common experience that in any landscape, whether observed directly in nature or recorded in a painting, certain parts attract our attention more forcibly than others. We can talk of 'dominant figures', 'focal points', and

FIGURE 20. JOHN MARTIN (1789–1854): JOSHUA COMMANDING THE SUN TO STAND STILL
The device of 'inversion' here provides an opportunity to develop the symbolism of prospect, hazard and refuge to a level of intensity rarely achieved and never surpassed in the painting of dramatic landscapes.
Reproduced by permission of the Trustees of the British Museum

so on, using a terminology which implies that not all parts of a landscape are of equal importance. The recognition of these differential values is the concern of art critics, and almost always in explanatory or analytical descriptions of paintings one will find distinctions being drawn in terms of the relative significance attached to the various parts of the composition. Let us have a look at a 'typical' explanatory description of this kind. The author, T. M. Greene, is seeking to bring out the contrast between 'unitary' and 'repetitive' ideas in painting, and the work to which he refers is Nicolas Poussin's *Et in Arcadia Ego* from the Duke of Devonshire's Collection at Chatsworth (Figure 21).

'The three figures of the shepherdess and the two shepherds are, considered severally, unitary ideas. Taken as a group, they constitute a closely knit and powerfully rhythmic repetitive idea of the developmental type. The eye is quickly caught by the vertical figure of the shepherdess on the left and moves irresistibly from her to the shepherd nearest to her and then on to the second shepherd, whose main axis, intensified by gesture and gaze, is strongly inclined towards the sarcophagus on the extreme right. This repetitive idea or motif, whose basic "figure" (to use a musical analogy) might be said to be the second shepherd's crook, is repeated in reverse by the trees, which are quite vertical at the extreme right and incline more and more as the eye moves from right to left. (Their basic "figure" is the first shepherd's staff which is so clearly silhouetted behind his head.) These two repetitive motifs, then, combine almost in contrapuntal fashion to constitute an unusually clearly defined unit of marked developmental complexity.

'The seated male figure in the foreground, meanwhile, is an example of a unitary idea. It is itself a rhythmic and somewhat repetitive organization of more or less self-contained units (note the shoulder, arms, and foot). It also epitomizes, with remarkable economy of means, the complicated contrapuntal idea just mentioned. The right edge of the torso recalls the vertical tree trunk above the sarcophagus. The lighted axis of the torso, with the head, carries out the diagonal of the leaning tree trunk and the first shepherd's crook. The draped foreleg is parallel to the diagonal legs of the shepherds. Thus the natural structure of his body provides the resolution for the vertical and diagonal motifs otherwise only contrasted, and the figure as a whole, itself a very complex unitary idea, sums up the whole picture.' (Greene, 1940, pp. 134–135)

There are, of course, many other ways in which this painting could be described. One could concentrate on the story which Poussin is representing. Thus Blunt writes:

'A group of shepherds and shepherdesses in the idyllic land of Arcadia suddenly come upon a tomb above which is a skull and on which they

FIGURE 21. NICOLAS POUSSIN (1594–1665): *Et in Arcadia Ego*
Reproduced by permission of the Trustees of the Chatsworth Settlement (Devonshire Collection)

decipher the inscription *Et in Arcadia ego*. This shocks them into recognition of the fact that even in complete happiness death is ever present.' (Blunt, 1967, p. 114)

In identifying the important features of the painting, much will depend on how we look at it. If we are interested in it as a story, the skull may be said to play a crucial part as one of the two principal symbols of death. It is an essential focal point. If we look at it as a matter of geometry, the skull is so unimportant that Greene does not even mention it. In his description it is the seated figure in the foreground which 'provides the resolution for the vertical and diagonal motifs otherwise only contrasted' and which '. . . sums up the whole picture'.

Here, then, are two quite different ways of assessing the important points in a picture; one picks out the geometrical *foci*, the other the thematic *foci* of the narrative. (There are indeed many other ways. We have said nothing, for instance, about the balance of colour.) But neither approach employs the system of prospect–refuge symbolism which we are supposed to be examining. An analysis of the picture along *these* lines would present yet another ranking of priorities. We should note first a division of the picture into two parts. Virtually all the prospect symbols—the 'open' surfaces and horizons, the maximum fetch, the bright cloud-symbols, and so on—are on the left; the refuge symbols—the trees, the shadows, the masonry wall, the tomb itself—are on the right. A small area of overlap occupies the centre. We might then take up Greene's point that the eye is quickly caught by the vertical figure of the shepherdess. Greene assumes this; he does not venture an explanation why it should be so. Neither do I pretend we can explain it; but we might at least point out that the whole of the upper part of the shepherdess forms a horizon against the distant sky. Of the other three figures only the head of the first shepherd is so positioned as to achieve this. When we see the composition in terms of prospect on the left and refuge on the right, it is the shepherdess who is in the most exposed position, most deprived of refuge, most deeply in danger of being seen. We should then note that the three standing figures are all facing away from the prospect and towards the refuge area. That they find in it the alarming symbols of death introduces a suggestion of the idea of inversion.

Greene's phrase 'The eye is quickly caught . . .' suggests the idea of magnetism and spontaneous attraction. We do not need to be able to explain magnetism in order to recognize it. As we have seen, Greene does not explain the instant attraction of the eye to the shepherdess, but he is so certain of it as a *fact* that he bases his description on the assumption that we share his reaction to the painting. The success of his subsequent description depends on our acceptance of this as the proper starting-point.

All descriptions of landscape paintings assume an attraction of the eye towards certain parts of the composition and these we may call 'magnets'. Depending on their character we may further distinguish them as 'magnetic points', 'magnetic lines' or 'magnetic areas'. A magnetic point could be exemplified by the vanishing point of the converging lines of Hobbema's avenue (Figure 11), a magnetic line by an aquatic horizon, a magnetic area by the glade-like amphitheatres or the sunlit distances set off against each other in so many of the landscapes of Claude (see also Figure 9).

The idea of magnetism, whether referred to by this or some other name, is basic to the art critic's technique. It concerns us particularly in the present context because, if we postulate a kind of complementary antithesis between prospect and refuge as relevant to the explanation of our aesthetic response to a landscape, the magnetic features which emerge as important in terms of 'seeing without being seen' may well be different from those which we should recognize from an examination of either the geometry of the picture surface or the story content of the composition. We have seen from Greene's description of the Poussin that the placing of the seated figure not only in a particular part of the composition but also in a particular attitude 'provides the resolution for the vertical and diagonal motifs otherwise only contrasted', from Blunt's description that it is the skull and sarcophagus of the story which draw the figures' attention towards the right-hand side of the picture, and from the 'prospect–refuge' approach that the shepherdess occupies a more dramatic position than any of the other figures in terms of behavioural opportunities (potentially hiding, seeing, escaping, being exposed, etc.).

It cannot be too strongly emphasized that the prospect–refuge approach does not invalidate either of the other approaches. Rather it reinforces them. Just as Greene's assumption that the eye moves first from left to right derives support from Blunt's explanation of the role of the skull and sarcophagus, which accounts for the turning of the heads towards the right, so his assumption that it is first caught by the shepherdess derives support from her position in relation to the interface between the prospect-dominant left and the refuge-dominant right.

The real significance of magnetism, therefore, brings us back to the phenomenon of reduplication. By setting a human figure or an animal, for that matter, in a position where its importance in the 'story' and/or the geometrical structure coincides with some magnetic feature of the habitat, the artist can accentuate the magnetism derived from these other scales of value.

The same basic rules can be seen to apply also to landscape design. In the accepted style of the seventeenth and early eighteenth centuries the obelisk, strategically set at the intersection of a number of straight paths, discharged the function of a geometrical focus. The impact of a conspicuous columnar structure was accentuated by the pattern of converging lines. But its position also gave it the unique advantage of visibility along each radial vista. From no other point could such an effective command of the grounds be achieved. The reduplication achieved by the interaction of the prospect symbols (obelisk and vistas) ensures a powerful magnetism for this particular point in the design. The judicious placing of temples, sundials, colourful flower beds, and so on, would furnish other examples.

In painting or photography the intrusion of a human or animal subject into the scene allows the further development of magnetic features. The placing of a pair of lovers in a glade or in the entrance of a cave, or the silhouetting of a horseman on a horizon, augments the magnetic effect which such figures would naturally have. The 'Willow Pattern' motif places the figures strategically in relation to the bridge, the fence, the trees, and so on (Figure 22). In orthodox compositional terms we can explain the magnetism of the bridge in relation to the geometry of the surface of the plate. In terms of habitat theory we can approach the explanation through a different analytical system, recollecting that bridges, fences, water-surfaces, trees, vessels and buildings, not to mention the distant *coulisses*, have all been encountered in the previous pages in connection with the symbolism of the prospect, the refuge and the hazard.

'Balance', then, in prospect–refuge theory, is concerned not merely with establishing the morphology of outlines, with relating areas of sunshine and shadow or of dark and light paint, with analysing geometrical patterns on a two-dimensional surface. Rather, it is to do with interpreting the mood or 'feeling' of a landscape in terms of its predominant symbolism. Let us then look at some examples to see whether the ideas we have discussed in theory can be seen to work out in practice.

## Prospect-Dominant Landscapes

> 'As for an extensive view: a great change has taken place since Petrarch's ascent of Mount Ventoux, and, with the exception of love, there is perhaps nothing else by which people of all kinds are more united than by their pleasure in a good view.'
>
> KENNETH CLARK (1949, p. 74)

All sorts of considerations enter into the determination of a prospect-dominant landscape. Even the condition of the atmosphere can destroy a potential prospect if it impedes the passage of light. In north-western Europe prolonged conditions of high atmospheric pressure may give rise to hazy visibility in summer and to fog in winter. The warm sector of a depression may well bring rain or drizzle. The best visibility is often achieved in the north-westerly air stream which commonly follows the passage of a cold front, and the walker who can then brave the drop in temperature is likely to be rewarded with the longest views.

It is, however, the relationship of the observation-point to the land-surface and the sum of all visible objects on it which constitutes the main potential of a prospect. High mountains naturally tend to afford wider and more distant prospects, but even quite modest elevations can afford superb views where the adjacent area is free from obstruction. Low hills commanding views over flat land or over aquatic surfaces can afford better prospects than higher summits in hillier country, as can be seen in the paintings of Koninck (p. 125). Absolutely flat land, as exemplified in marsh country, can achieve a high prospect value if its surface is free from arboreal vegetation. The following passage presents a picture of a marsh landscape on the eastern coast of the United States as seen through the eyes of Sidney Lanier, who was so sensitive to this type of environment that he earned the title of 'the poet of the marshes'. The experience he here describes begins in the woods, and one can hardly fail to be struck by the contrast between the oppressive refuge symbolism which he uses to describe them and the prospect symbolism which takes over as soon as he emerges on to the open marsh.

FIGURE 22. WILLOW PATTERN
A landscape composition which achieves its effect by combining basic symbols of prospect and refuge in a simple and straightforward arrangement

'Beautiful glooms, soft dusks in the noon-day fire,—
Wildwood privacies, closets of lone desire,
Chamber from chamber parted with wavering arras of leaves,—
Cells for the passionate pleasure of prayer to the soul that grieves...'
    (Lanier, *The Marshes of Glynn*, lines 12–15; Young, 1947, p. 14)

Outside the wood lie the marshes, but the poet shrinks from the exposure by which alone he can enjoy their prospect-dominant mood, recalling

'... when length was fatigue, and when breadth was but bitterness sore,
And when terror and shrinking and dreary unnameable pain
Drew over me out of the merciless miles of the plain.'
                (Lanier, *The Marshes of Glynn*, lines 32–34)

Now the apprehension of the hazard symbolism has been overcome and, like Lorenz in the Austrian forest, he is ready to break out from refuge to prospect. Watch the transition in the language as he does so.

'Oh, now, unafraid, I am fain to face
   The vast sweet visage of space.
To the edge of the wood I am drawn, I am drawn,
Where the gray beach glimmering runs, as a belt of the dawn,
For a mete and a mark
   To the forest-dark:—
      So:
Affable live-oak, leaning low,—
Thus—with your favor—soft, with a reverent hand,
(Not lightly touching your person, Lord of the land!)
Bending your beauty aside, with a step I stand
On the firm-packed sand,
   Free
By a world of marsh that borders a world of sea.
Sinuous southward and sinuous northward the shimmering band
Of the sand-beach fastens the fringe of the marsh to the folds of the land.
Inward and outward to northward and southward the beach lines
      linger and curl
As a silver-wrought garment that clings to and follows the firm sweet
      limbs of a girl.
Vanishing, swerving, evermore curving again into sight,
Softly the sand-beach wavers away to a dim gray looping of light.
And what if behind me to westward the wall of the woods stands high?
The world lies east: how ample, the marsh and the sea and the sky!
A league and a league of marsh-grass, waist-high, broad in the blade,
Green, and all of a height, and unflecked with a light or a shade,
Stretch leisurely off, in a pleasant plain,
   To the terminal blue of the main.
Oh, what is abroad in the marsh and the terminal sea?
Somehow my soul seems suddenly free
From the weighing of fate and the sad discussion of sin,
By the length and the breadth and the sweep of the marshes of Glynn.'
                    (Lanier, *The Marshes of Glynn*, lines 35–64)

We have seen that the prospect-orientation of a landscape can be enhanced by a cover of ice or snow (p. 109) and this is particularly the case in flat country where extensive horizontal surfaces tend to arouse the kind of response which Lanier felt in the marshes. The painter Hendrik Avercamp frequently combined ice and snow surfaces with the flat polderlands and one thinks of him, therefore, as a prospect-dominant painter. In his ice landscapes colour variation is largely obliterated; people and animals show up conspicuously, and in a country like Holland (*sensu stricto*) the few trees tend to be of deciduous species and are therefore devoid of leaves during these winter conditions. The provision of refuge imagery is therefore left largely to the buildings, which usually include some, notably churches and windmills, which add significantly to the 'prospect' as well as the 'refuge' side of the account.

Figure 23 illustrates most of these points and in addition shows a variation of the device of splitting the picture into prospect- and refuge-dominant halves. On the prospect-dominant left the tower rising out of the trees is an example of a common formula for combining the two kinds of symbolism; but as a refuge area it is remote and the only immediately attainable hiding-place is among the buildings on the right. Several features of these buildings, however, conspire to suppress the refuge imagery. There is only one entrance door depicted which leads directly into the building and that is closed; the building is made as 'impenetrable' as possible; there are no balconies, staircases or other signs of linkage between the interior and exterior; the overhang of the roof at the eaves and gables, always suggestive of shelter, is virtually absent; there is little vegetational screen near the house and such as there is appears pathetically ineffective in its leaflessness. This refuge area is therefore only a weak antidote to the prospect symbolism which controls the mood of the painting.

This technique of accentuating the prospect symbolism of a landscape by suppressing its refuge symbolism can also be seen in word pictures. In the following poem only the vantage-point (the orchard seat) introduces the concept of refuge. Every other idea which Wordsworth introduces is loaded with prospect symbolism. The simple imagery of the mountain is reduplicated successively by the symbolism of sunlight, distance, meteors, the planet, the heavens and the clouds.

> 'There is an Eminence,—of these our hills
> The last that parleys with the setting sun;
> We can behold it from our orchard seat;
> And, when at evening we pursue our walk
> Along the public way, this Peak, so high
> Above us, and so distant in its height,
> Is visible; and often seems to send
> Its own deep quiet to restore our hearts.
> The meteors make of it a favourite haunt:
> The star of Jove, so beautiful and large
> In the mid heavens, is never half so fair
> As when he shines above it. 'Tis in truth
> The loneliest place we have among the clouds.
> And She who dwells with me, whom I have loved
> With such communion that no place on earth
> Can ever be a solitude to me,
> Hath to this lonely Summit given my Name.'
> (Wordsworth, No. III of *Seven poems on the naming of places*,
> 1800, as given in Hutchinson, 1895, p. 148)

The association of loneliness with this intense prospect-symbolism provides

150

FIGURE 23. HENDRIK AVERCAMP (1585–1634): ICE SCENE NEAR A TOWN

An example of emphasis by contraposition. The refuge symbolism is largely confined to the building on the right and its immediate appendages. Almost all the remaining symbolism is highly prospect-dominant. Reproduced by courtesy of the Trustees, The National Gallery, London (No. 1479)

us with the excuse to remind ourselves again of the danger of regarding prospect and refuge as opposites. I have tried throughout to stress their complementary rather than antagonistic roles. Nevertheless, when the prospect imagery is built up, as in this case, by the exclusion of refuge symbolism, there is a tendency for the idea of prospect to become associated *in this context* with the idea of 'non-refuge', and however forcefully one asserts that this is not a universal rule, it may certainly be admitted that Wordsworth's interpretation of prospect-dominant landscape invites the intrusion into his word pictures of a strong dose of the symbolism of the hazard. The association in Wordsworth is powerfully emphasized by Wesling who writes of '. . . scenes of visionary exposure on waste moor or open road, mountain or ocean' (Wesling, 1970, p. 36; see also Noyes (1968) and Salveson, 1965). In Wesling's analysis Wordsworth's landscape is to be interpreted, not in terms of prospect and refuge, but of 'exposure' and 'seclusion'. 'Seclusion' we may well equate with 'refuge', but 'exposure' means something more than 'prospect'. It is 'prospect-plus-hazard'. 'One way of reading *Tintern Abbey*', says Wesling, 'is as a dialectic between exposure and seclusion, between youthful receptivity to experience and the mature man's tendency to formulate experience.' (Wesling, 1970, p. 30).

## Hazard-Dominant Landscapes

'High on some cliff to Heaven up-piled,
Of rude access, of prospect wild,
Where, tangled round the jealous steep,
Strange shades o'erbrow the valleys deep . . .'
WILLIAM COLLINS (*Ode on the Poetical Character*,
lines 55–58; in Blunden (Ed.), 1929, p. 84)

The 'landscape of exposure' is a useful phrase because it presents a true opposite to the landscape of refuge which can find expression through the symbolism of the prospect, even though, as we have seen, prospect and refuge are not fundamentally opposed. A striking example of the use of this prospect-plus-hazard symbolism is to be found in the *Agony in the Garden* by Giovanni Bellini (Figure 24). In spite of the refuge overtones generally implicit in the word 'garden', the imagery here is intensely prospect-dominant. The theme of the story involves hazard, exposure, absence of protection. Even the rock on which Christ is kneeling is singularly devoid of nooks and crannies. The fence (right) offers no protection and symbolizes, if anything, an impediment hazard. The buildings are remote and the surfaces generally of the open ('naked' or 'carpeted') type. The absence of trees and foliage of all sorts is as striking as it is unusual in a garden. By contrast the prospect imagery is very powerful indeed and is based on a sky dado in which the surmounting clouds form a weak canopy, gently illuminated from the underneath, while the terrestrial surface is heavy and dark. The stark contrast between this dark surface and the brilliance of the lower sky produces one of the most exciting horizons in all landscape painting. On the extreme left the dark hill is backed by a sky of a darker tone,

152

Figure 24. Giovanni Bellini (c. 1430–1516): The Agony in the Garden
Reproduced by courtesy of the Trustees, The National Gallery, London (No. 726)

and here Bellini introduces a light-coloured architectural horizon to balance it, whereas in the central part, where the sky is bright, such buildings as break the horizon are vertically developed and sharply silhouetted. The towers in the very centre are so tiny yet so sharp that they suggest at once great distance and very clear visibility. Finally, as if to spell out the message that earthly refuge is not to be found in this bleak Gethsemane, Bellini links the figure of Christ with the ghostly divinity in the heavens by raising the head and the praying fingers to break the horizon and appear silhouetted against the brightest part of the sky, where the prospect symbolism of distance is at its most intense. The angle from which the light falls on the foreground and on the buildings at the left is inconsistent with the angle from which it illuminates the sky and the clouds, but maintaining consistency with nature and the physics of light is less important than building up the prospect imagery to the highest degree of intensity.

Needless to say, the landscape of exposure can be employed to good effect in the novel. As an example, let us consider one or two passages from Rölvaag's *Giants in the Earth* (1927), first written in his own language by a Norwegian immigrant to the United States in the nineteen twenties. It is a story of Norwegian pioneers, of fifty years earlier, Per Hansa and his wife Beret, who have settled in the plains of South Dakota. While Per Hansa is caught up in the challenge of his work, Beret is overwhelmed by a sense of isolation and loneliness which the author ties up closely with the vast, featureless landscape (Lanegran, 1972).

'With a common impulse, they went toward the hill; when they had reached the summit, Beret sat down and let her gaze wander aimlessly around . . .23 In a certain sense, she had to admit to herself, it was lovely up here. The broad expanse stretching away endlessly in every direction, seemed almost like the ocean—especially now, when darkness was falling. It reminded her strongly of the sea, and yet it was very different.

'This formless prairie had no heart that beat, no waves that sang, no soul that could be touched . . . or cared . . .

'The infinitude surrounding her on every hand might not have been so oppressive, might even have brought her a measure of peace, if it had not been for the deep silence, which lay heavier here than in a church. Indeed, what was there to break it? She had passed beyond the outposts of civilization; the nearest dwelling places of men were far away. Here no warbling birds rose on the air, no buzzing of insects sounded; even the wind had died away; the waving blades of grass that trembled to the faintest breath now stood erect and quiet, as if listening, in the great hush of the evening . . . All along the way, coming out, she had noticed this strange thing: the stillness had grown depressing, the farther west they journeyed; it must have been over two weeks now since she had heard a bird sing! Had they travelled into some nameless, abandoned region? Could no living thing exist

out here, in the empty, desolate, endless wastes of green and blue? . . .
How *could* existence go on, she thought desperately? If life is to
thrive and endure, it must at least have something to hide behind!'
(Rölvaag, 1927, pp. 37–38)

Rölvaag here uses strong prospect symbolism to emphasize the feeling of
exposure and hence of vulnerability. 'Something to hide behind!' To Beret
unimpeded prospect, 'endless wastes of green and blue', becomes virtually
synonymous with refuge-deficiency; the clarity, the visibility, the horizon, the
panorama itself begin to assume the character of hazard symbols threatening her
very existence.

'Beret had now formed the habit of constantly watching the prairie;
out in the open, she would fix her eyes on one point of the sky line—
and then, before she knew it, her gaze would have swung around the
whole compass; but it was ever, ever the same . . . Life it held not; a
magic ring lay on the horizon, extending upward into the sky; within
this circle no living form could enter; it was like the chain enclosing
the king's garden, that prevented it from bearing fruit, . . . How could
humans continue to live here while that magic ring encompassed
them?' (Rölvaag, 1927, pp. 126–127)

The total absence of refuge symbols in the landscape is the counterpart of the
absence of any refuge against the hazards of her own oppressive fears. In the
face of an increasing sense of hopelessness she has nothing to protect her.
Refuge-deficiency becomes a neurosis.

Per Hansa has found the door of his own house barricaded.
'Pulling himself together, he shoved against the door with all his
strength—shoved until red streaks were flashing before his eyes. The
door began to give—the opening widened; at last he had pushed it
wide enough to slip through.
'. . . "*Beret*!" . . . The anguish of his cry cut through the air . . .
"Beret!"
'Now he stood in the middle of the room. It was absolutely dark
before his eyes; he looked wildly around, but could see nothing.
'. . . "Beret, where are you?"
'No answer came—there was no one to be seen. But wasn't that a
sound? "Beret!" he called again, sharply. He heard it now distinctly.
Was it coming from one of the beds, or over there by the door? . . .
It was a faint, whimpering sound. He rushed to the beds and threw off
the bedclothes—no one in this one, no one in that one—it must be
over by the door! . . . He staggered back—the big chest was standing
in front of the door. Who could have dragged it there? . . . Per Hansa
flung the cover open with frantic haste. The sight that met his eyes
made his blood run cold. Down in the depths of the great chest lay
Beret, huddled up and holding the baby in her arms; And-Ongen was

crouching at her feet—the whimpering sound had come from her.'
(Rölvaag, 1927, pp. 347–348)

In fact what Beret was hiding from was the plague of locusts outside—a real,
animate hazard—which she firmly believed was of supernatural origin, but it is
no accident that, when the refuge symbolism is introduced, it comes in this
melodramatic and absurdly exaggerated form, an overcompensation for the
total lack of it in the landscape itself. The imbalance of prospect–refuge imagery destroys for Beret the aesthetic potential of a landscape in which others
found great beauty; indeed it does much more, as one may find out by reading
the novel.

Perhaps a better known passage illustrative of this use of the landscape of
exposure is the opening page of *Great Expectations*. The effect of loneliness is
built up by the prospect imagery of consecutive references to increasingly
remote and inhospitable environments linked with the isolation of bereavement.
The language of the hazard is strongly represented, but note also the token
concession to the idea of refuge introduced by the churchyard. Note also,
incidentally, that alluvial marshlands are again employed as the basis of this
landscape of exposure.

'Ours was the marsh country, down by the river, within, as the river
wound, twenty miles of the sea. My first most vivid and broad impression of the identity of things, seems to me to have been gained on a
memorable raw afternoon towards evening. At such a time I found out
for certain, that this bleak place overgrown with nettles was the
churchyard; and that Philip Pirrip, late of this parish, and also Geor-
giana, wife of the above, were dead and buried; and that Alexander,
Bartholomew, Abraham, Tobias and Roger, infant children of the
aforesaid, were also dead and buried; and that the dark wilderness
beyond the churchyard, intersected with dykes and mounds and gates,
with scattered cattle feeding on it, was the marshes; and that the low
leaden line beyond was the river; and that the distant savage lair
from which the wind was rushing, was the sea; and that the small
bundle of shivers growing afraid of it all and beginning to cry, was
Pip.' (Dickens, *Great Expectations*, 1860–61; Chapman and Hall edn.,
1881, vol. XII, p. 2)

In Turner's well-known painting, *Rain, Steam and Speed—the Great Western
Railway*, in the National Gallery, London, the common association of hazard
and prospect is again brought into play. The elevated viewpoint produces a
landscape potentially as prospect-dominant as any work of Koninck, but the
potentiality is not realized owing to the obscuring of the distance by the rain.
The sense of exposure is, however, intense, being exaggerated by the absence of
any firm ground for the viewer to stand on. There is no foreground, apart from
the near end of the viaduct, and the displacement of the viewpoint to the side
makes even this seem unattainable. One might be looking at the scene from a

helicopter. There is a vistal element, the railway line, inserted into a panorama. The idea of 'hazard' finds expression not only in the rain but also in the sense of height which accentuates the idea of 'prospect'. The straight edge of the parapet and the threading of light through the space of the arch arouse the fear of falling. There are, however, in this picture many other ideas which we have already encountered, particularly pertaining to locomotion. Freedom of passage through the landscape is symbolized by the railway and the bridges, and the attention is irresistibly caught by the chimney and smokebox of the engine so conspicuously privileged in the colour scheme. Apart from some very ill-defined trees in the middle distance, the only real refuge symbol is the train, a little haven of shelter able to enjoy the opportunity of movement through, even escape from, this bleak and inhospitable environment.

The alliance with the symbolism of the prospect, which gives rise to the landscape of exposure, is perhaps the most common form in which we find the symbolism of the hazard dominating a landscape. But the alliance is not indispensable. Meteorological hazards in the form of storm clouds, rain, lightning and other natural sources of discomfort and terror are used by many painters, including Salvator Rosa, Gaspar Dughet and again Turner in his terrifying storm scenes. Here one can really see what the eighteenth century meant by the Sublime.

> 'That Turner was possessed by the Romantic attachment to nature— its power, its mystery and beauty—there can be no doubt. He was exhilarated by nature's violence, as has been seen from his reaction to Switzerland on his first foreign tour and to the storm at Farnley [described in Kitson, 1964, pp. 18 and 73] which inspired "Hannibal crossing the Alps". He was equally excited by storms at sea. It must never be forgotten that Turner began his career as a devotee of the picturesque. This coloured his view of natural scenery all his life.'
> (Kitson, 1964, p. 75)

The remarkable thing is that the unprecedented range of styles and techniques which he employed to express this view of natural scenery never involved the abandonment of concepts which, at every stage in his development, can be easily fitted into a common framework of symbolism. The terminology of prospect and refuge can be as meaningfully applied to his later landscape abstractions as to his earlier essays in the style of Claude.

The juxtaposition of hazard and refuge is a favourite theme in painting and poetry. Let us kill two birds with one stone by citing a few lines from Wordsworth's verbal description of Beaumont's pictorial description of such a theme. The poet is contrasting his own recollection of Peele Castle as seen 'sleeping on a glassy sea' with the same subject portrayed in the painting under conditions of storm.

> 'That hulk which labours in the deadly swell,
> This rueful sky, this pageantry of fear!

>And this huge Castle, standing here sublime,
>    I love to see the look with which it braves,
>—Cased in the unfeeling armour of old time—
>    The lightning, the fierce wind, the trampling waves.'
>(Wordsworth, *Elegiac Stanzas*, comp. 1805, lines 47–52;
>                                 Hutchinson, 1895, p. 579)

The significance of the imagery is in no way weakened by the fact that it is used as a premise for an observation on a different dimension of life:

>'But welcome fortitude, and patient cheer,
>    And frequent sights of what is to be borne!
>Such sights, or worse, as are before me here:—
>    Not without hope we suffer and we mourn.'
>(Wordsworth, *Elegiac Stanzas*, lines 57–60)

Or, in Wesling's words, 'Exposure and seclusion are combined in the heroic images of consciousness as a fortress.' (Wesling, 1970, p. 51)

## Refuge-Dominant Landscapes

>'A sweet but absolute Retreat,
>'Mongst Paths so lost and Trees so high,
>That the world may ne'er invade,
>Through such Windings and such Shade,
>My unshaken Liberty.'
>ANNE, COUNTESS OF WINCHILSEA (*The Petition for an Absolute Retreat*,
>                                 lines 3–7; Murry, 1928, p. 74)

A refuge symbol can be given emphasis by setting it in a prospect-dominant or hazard-dominant landscape. This is the emphasis of contraposition, which makes the refuge symbol conspicuous by being different and is a ubiquitous and deep-seated source of pleasure.

>'Whenever the younger children in the school had an opportunity, they would arrange the chairs and tables so as to make a "cosy place" with a defensive rampart . . . The defensive element comes out clearly here and there—"so that nobody can look in", "to keep us warm", or "to keep the tigers out", or "to keep the foxes out". Sometimes the children added to the intensity of their feeling of security by asking a grown-up to "be a tiger—and come from a distance, so that we can hear you growling".' (Isaacs, 1933, pp. 362–363)

A refuge-dominant landscape, on the other hand, communicates its message by the cumulative effect of grouping together different refuge symbols to reinforce each other, in other words by reduplication. There are many examples of refuge-dominant landscapes in painting. Woodland scenes generally tend to be of this kind, though almost invariably they contain at least token prospects to introduce an element of balance (Ogden and Ogden, 1955, p. 41). Reference has already been made to the 'cottage-in-the-wood' and also to the nocturnal refuges of 'inversion'. Both these themes enjoy great popularity in landscape painting. Aert van der Neer (1603/4–'77) specialized in evening or night scenes in which moonlight plays a conspicuous part, and in these the refuge values are accentuated by the darkness of the shadows (Figure 25). Prospect symbols there are, of course, but these tend to be concentrated in the sky and in those restricted water surfaces which catch and reflect the moonlight. Towers, tall buildings, trees and ships' sails often break the horizon, and moonlit clouds are effectively used to strengthen the prospect imagery, but the general impression is of a landscape in which it would not be difficult to move from shadow to shadow, from refuge to refuge, with a reasonable chance of remaining unseen—a feat which could not possibly be achieved in any of Avercamp's ice panoramas. The comparison between Avercamp's prospects and van der Neer's refuges[24] is the more interesting because they both found inspiration in the same flat country in the environs of Amsterdam.

Deprivation of light can add a measure of refuge value to any scene, but what generally marks a landscape as 'refuge-dominant' is the arrangement of screening material, particularly of an arboreal kind. Most impressions of refuge rely heavily on trees, shrubs or bushes.

> '. . . O'er pathless rocks,
> Through beds of matted fern, and tangled thickets,
> Forcing my way, I came to one dear nook
> Unvisited, where not a broken bough
> Drooped with its withered leaves, ungracious sign
> Of devastation; but the hazels rose
> Tall and erect, with tempting clusters hung,
> A virgin scene!'
> (Wordsworth, *Nutting*, lines 14–21; Hutchinson, 1895, p. 185)

Notice how the arrival at the 'dear nook unvisited' is prefaced by the passage through foliage, an idea which we find in a somewhat extended form in the following lines, still from Wordsworth:

> 'Our walk was far among the ancient trees:
> There was no road, nor any woodman's path;
> But a thick umbrage—checking the wild growth
> Of weed and sapling, along soft green turf
> Beneath the branches—of itself had made
> A track, that brought us to a slip of lawn,
> And a small bed of water in the woods.
> All round this pool both flocks and herds might drink
> On its firm margin, even as from a well,
> Or some stone-basin which the herdsman's hand
> Had shaped for their refreshment; nor did sun,
> Or wind from any quarter, ever come,

FIGURE 25. AERT VAN DER NEER (1603/4–1677): MOONLIGHT
Reproduced by courtesy of the Trustees, The National Gallery, London (No. 2536)

But as a blessing to this calm recess,
This glade of water and this one green field.
The spot was made by Nature for herself;
The travellers know it not, and 'twill remain
Unknown to them; but it is beautiful;
And if a man should plant his cottage near,
Should sleep beneath the shelter of its trees,
And blend its waters with his daily meal,
He would so love it, that in his death-hour
Its image would survive among his thoughts:
And therefore, my sweet MARY, this still Nook,
With all its beeches, we have named from You!'
(Wordsworth, No. V of *Seven poems on the naming of places*,
— 1799; Hutchinson, 1895, pp. 149–150)

There is much in this passage beside the imagery of refuge. It is a good example of the Arcadian version of a habitat furnishing effortlessly a number of biological needs. ('And blend its waters with his daily bread'.) But the refuge symbolism provides the essential background to the 'slip of lawn' which, like the keep of a medieval castle, is only attained after the outer protective screens have been breached. It is worth noting the familiar 'cottage-in-the-wood' image and also the way in which terms with prospect-symbolic overtones (sun, road, path), are introduced only in association with negatives.

In case it should be thought that I have deliberately picked on a poet or even a period with a style and idiom to suit my case, let us take a couple of stanzas from the Faery Queene. Belphoebe has discovered the wounded squire and has him conveyed to a place where she can reduce his foul sore to fair plight. The use of reduplication of refuge symbols is again conspicuous. Within the encircling mountains are the woods. Within the woods is the glade with its little embayment among the myrtles and laurels. Eventually, in the middle of these protective shells, we come to the equivalent of the 'cottage-in-the-wood'.


### XXXIX

'Into that forest far they thence him led,
    Where was their dwelling, in a pleasant glade,
    With mountains round about environed,
    And mighty woods, which did the valley shade,
    And like a stately theatre it made,
    Spreading itself into a spacious plain.
    And in the midst a little river plaid
    Emongst the pumy stones, which seem'd to plain
With gentle murmur, that his course they did restrain.

### XL

'Beside the same, a dainty place there lay,
    Planted with myrtle trees and laurels green,

In which the birds sung many a lovely lay
Of God's high praise, and of their loves sweet teen,
As it an earthly paradise had been:
In whose inclosed shadow there was pight
A fair pavilion, scarcely to be seen,
The which was all within most richly dight,
That greatest Princes living it mote well delight.'

(Spenser, Tonson edn., 1758,
Bk. III, Canto V, Stanzas XXXIX and XL)

A variation of the imagery can be found in a later passage in which Spenser describes the garden of Adonis. This obviously has all the features of a man-made refuge (including a prospect mount), but so important is it to Spenser to stress the susceptibility of human emotions to the aesthetic stimuli of the *natural* environment that he goes to increasingly absurd lengths in asserting the natural origin of his heavily charged refuge symbols.

### XLIII

'Right in the middest of that paradise,
There stood a stately mount, on whose round top
A gloomy grove of Myrtle-trees did rife,
Whose shady boughs sharp steel did never lop,
Nor wicked beasts their tender buds did crop,
But like a girlond compassed the height,
And from their fruitful sides sweet gum did drop,
That all the ground with precious dew bedight,
Threw forth most dainty odours, and most sweet delight.

### XLIV

'And in the thickest covert of that shade
There was a pleasant arbour, not by art,
But of the trees own inclination made,
Which knitting their rank branches part to part,
With wanton Ivy-twine entrayld athwart,
And Eglantine, and Caprisole emong,
Fashion'd above within their inmost part,
That neither *Phoebus*' beams could through them throng,
Nor *Æolus*' sharp blast could work them any wrong.'

(Spenser, Tonson edn., 1758,
Bk. III, Canto VI, Stanzas XLIII and XLIV)

Finally, a little gem from the fifteenth century. I quote it at some length because it shows so many of the devices we have previously encountered in these pages, fully-fledged already before the end of the Middle Ages. Notice the description again of successively encountered refuge symbols in the approach phase. Notice the contrast between the natural wilderness of the oak wood, where the path 'forgrowen was with grasse and weed', and the care which had been lavished on the contrivance of the arbour (herber) to afford seclusion within that natural wilderness. Notice, too, in the closing lines how skilfully the author describes the 'one-way-screen' effect of the hedge (p. 75), amplifying in round Chaucerian phrases the elementary formula 'to see without being seen'.

> 'And, at the last, a path of little brede,
> I found, that greatly had not used be;
> For it forgrowen was with grasse and weede,
> That wel unneth a wighte might it se:
> Thought I, "This path some whider goth, parde!"
> And so I followed, till it me brought
> To a right pleasaunt herber, well ywrought,
>
> 'That benched was, and with turfes newe
> Freshly turved, whereof the grene gras,
> So smale, so thicke, so short, so fresh of hewe,
> That most like unto grene wool, wot I, it was:
> And closed in al the grene herbere,
> With sicamour was set and eglatere,
>
> 'Wrethen in fere so wel and cunningly,
> That every branch and leafe grew by mesure,
> Plaine as a bord, of an height by and by.
> I see never thing, I you ensure,
> So wel done; for that he took the cure
> It to make, y trow did all his peine
> To make it passe alle tho that men have seine.
>
> 'And shapen was this herber, roofe and alle,
> As a prety parlour; and also
> The hegge as thicke as a castle walle,
> That who that list without to stond or go,
> Tho he wold al day prien to and fro,
> He should not see if there were any wight
> Within or no; but one within wel might
>
> 'Perceive alle tho that yeden there withoute
> In the field, that was on every side
> Covered with corn and grasse.'[25]

We may not, I fear, dwell so long on examples of refuge-dominant landscape in prose. One must suffice. The potency is achieved by building up a picture of concentric protective rings around the 'magnetic' object, which in this case is a patch of water-lilies and the shafts of light in the water beneath them. The build-up begins from the outside and works inwards.

'So the mere was three times ringed about, as if it had been three times put in a spell. First there was the ring of oaks and larches, willows, ollern trees and beeches, solemn and strong, to keep the world out. Then there was the ring of rushes, sighing thinly, brittle and sparse, but enough, with their long, trembling shadows, to keep the spells in.

'Then there was the ring of lilies, as I said, lying there as if Jesus, walking upon the water, had laid them down with His cool hands, afore he turned to the multitude saying, "Behold the lilies!" As if they were not enough to shake your soul, there beneath every lily, white and green or pale gold, was her bright shadow, as it had been her angel. And through the long, untroubled day the lilies and the angels looked one upon the other and were content.' (Webb, 1924, p. 216)

## Integration and Differentiation

'Here Hills and Vales, the Woodland and the Plain,
Here Earth and Water seem to strive again,
Not *Chaos*-like together crush'd and bruis'd,
But as the World, harmoniously confus'd:
Where Order in Variety we see,
And where, tho' all things differ, all agree.'

ALEXANDER POPE (*Windsor Forest*, lines 11–16;
Bowles, 1806, vol. i, pp. 124–125)

We have now looked at a number of examples in which artists or writers have employed particular kinds of symbolism to achieve a dominant mood in the portrayal of landscape. Not all landscapes, however, display a dominance in any one direction, and the 'balanced' landscape should perhaps be regarded as the norm from which the mood can shift one way or the other.

'. . . To more than inland peace,
Left by the west wind sweeping overhead
From a tumultuous ocean, trees and towers
In that sequestered valley may be seen,
Both silent and both motionless alike;
Such the deep shelter that is there, and such
The safeguard for repose and quietness.'

(Wordsworth, *The Prelude*, Bk. II, lines 108–114;
Hutchinson, 1895, p. 643)

Here the balance is, perhaps, marginally towards the refuge side, but terms like 'sweeping overhead' or 'trees and towers' clearly suggest the symbolism of the prospect, while the 'tumultuous ocean' brings us back to Wordsworth's favourite imagery of 'exposure'.

Sometimes a deliberate play is made of the alternation of the contrasting symbolism of prospect and refuge, as in the passage from Pope quoted above, and its continuation, which goes as follows:

'Here waving Groves a checquer'd Scene display,
And part admit and part exclude the Day;
As some coy Nymph her Lover's warm Address
Nor quite indulges, nor can quite repress.
There, interspers'd in Lawns and opening Glades,

> Thin trees arise that shun each other's Shades.
> Here in full light the russet Plains extend;
> There wrapt in Clouds the blueish Hills ascend:
> Ev'n the wild Heath displays her purple Dies,
> And 'midst the Desert fruitful Fields arise
> That crown'd with tufted trees and springing Corn,
> Like verdant Isles the sable Waste adorn.'
>
> (Pope, *Windsor Forest*, lines 17–28;
> Bowles, 1806, vol. i, pp. 125–126)

Here the alternation is rapid; the poet flits about from waving groves to opening glades, oscillating on a short wavelength, so to say. By contrast, let us look at a poem which alternates no less from prospect to refuge but on a longer period—a kind of ocean swell which holds the mood for several lines before passing the emphasis over to the complementary symbolism. In it John Dyer (1700–1758) extols the virtues of a four-hundred-foot hill in the Ordovician some five miles down the Towy Valley from Llandeilo in his native Carmarthenshire. There are a few lines at the beginning and towards the end where the landscape imagery is somewhat suppressed, but otherwise practically every line can be seen to make a contribution to the build-up of an environmental picture in prospect–refuge terms. The poem is reproduced as Appendix B and will serve not merely to show how much eighteenth-century poets were subject to the symbolism of prospect and refuge, but also how one may set about analysing a poem in these hitherto unfamiliar terms. Just as a musical composition consists of several variables—pitch, volume, tone, tempo, etc.,—combined in a particular way, so a landscape poem uses an imagery which varies, for instance, in the strength, the level and the balance of its prospect–refuge symbolism. With its emphasis principally on the last, an elementary analysis of the structure of this poem might follow the pattern shown in Table 5.

TABLE 5. TRENDS IN THE BALANCE OF SYMBOLISM IN
*GRONGAR HILL*
(See Appendix B)

| Lines | Dominant symbolism |
| --- | --- |
| 1–14 | Introductory; weak P. |
| 15–18 | Strong R. |
| 19–26 | R emerging into P. |
| 27–30 | Reversion to weak R; into P. |
| 31–40 | Steadily increasing P. |
| 41–56 | Strong, maintained P. |
| 57–76 | R emerging into P. |
| 77–92 | R dominant, with strong 'ruin' imagery. |
| 93–128 | Short-period alternations of P and R. |
| 129–136 | Weak R. |
| 137–145 | Dominant P with weak R allusions. |
| 146–158 | Weakening landscape symbolism rallying to R at finish. |

P = prospect    R = refuge

The tendency in this poem to group together prospect and refuge symbols respectively in larger 'blocks' moves somewhat in the direction of the phenomenon of the 'edge-of-the-wood' in landscape painting, where the balance of the whole composition is achieved by creating prospect-dominant and refuge-dominant halves (p. 135). Rubens' *Landscape with a Rainbow* (Figure 26) is an excellent example of this type of composition. It could be described as a 'balanced landscape', since it is rich in the symbolism of both prospect and refuge. Yet if we were to cut it down the middle, we should be left with two very unbalanced pictures. That on the left might remind us of the compositional technique of Koninck, with its moderately elevated viewpoint and resultant picture of 'falling ground'. Refuge symbols there are—trees, a haystack and dark shadows, for instance—but they are not strong enough or near enough to destroy the overwhelming sense of openness and distant vision created by the brown and gold of the fields and the blue of the distant hills.

The right-hand picture might perhaps be more reminiscent of one of Hobbema's woodland scenes. The ground here also falls away, but the prospect is effectively closed by the arboreal mass. Although the edge of the wood is comparatively straight, it will be noted that Rubens has been at pains to suggest its penetrability by picking out, for instance, a few of the tree trunks, thereby accentuating the sense of dark space behind, by omitting any kind of fence or other impediment hazard, by depicting the individuality of the trees which make up the margin of the wood, and by playing enough light on to their upper surfaces to create an impression of a canopy so dense and opaque as to furnish a highly effective refuge which, however, is easily accessible.

Rubens has not, of course, painted two pictures here but a single composition with a particular kind of balance. He is at pains to link the thematic material of the two sides, for instance with the rainbow and the streaks of light which he carries across from the open ground on the left into the forest: yet another device for suggesting 'penetrability'. These horizontal elements in the colour pattern help to proclaim a panoramic rather than a vistal prospect. Rubens, in other words, is telling us that his landscape affords opportunities for seeing and for hiding, that these opportunities are not uniformly distributed throughout his composition, but that we are presented with a particular kind of arrangement in which, if we keep to the left we can see further and if we keep to the right we can hide better.

A very common variation of the 'edge-of-the-wood' phenomenon on a small scale is to be found in those outdoor portraits of individuals or of family groups in which the background is divided into prospect-dominant and refuge-dominant sides. This arrangement can be seen in many of the portraits of van Dyck (1599–1641)[26] and in the following century Reynolds (1723–92) and Gainsborough (1727–88) led a fashion which was emulated by almost all their lesser brethren. It is usual, though by no means the universal practice, to place the subject or subjects of the portrait facing either towards the observer or towards the prospect-dominant side, that is to say with the refuge symbols behind them (Figure 27) an arrangement wholly consistent with a strategic interpretation of

166

FIGURE 26. SIR PETER PAUL RUBENS (1577–1640): LANDSCAPE WITH A RAINBOW
Reproduced by permission of the Trustees of the Wallace Collection, London (No. 63)

FIGURE 27. THOMAS GAINSBOROUGH (1727–1788): MRS. HAMILTON NISBET
Reproduced by permission of the National Gallery of Scotland

the environmental context. It is the reversal of this direction of attitude which is one of the striking features of Poussin's *Et in Arcadia Ego* (Figure 21).

The 'edge-of-the-wood' presents contrasting landscape types, prospect-dominant and refuge-dominant, within a single composition which prominently features the interface between them. In the novel it is possible to set off such contrasting landscape types even though they may not occur in juxtaposition. Each landscape is employed as an appropriate setting for a different part of the narrative in such a way as to give emphasis to contrasts of moods or of personalities.[27] The classical example is to be found in *Wuthering Heights* (Emily Brontë, 1847). The association of each family with the landscape of prospect-plus-hazard and of refuge respectively is one of the central themes of David Cecil's well-known essay.

> 'The setting is a microcosm of the universal scheme as Emily Brontë conceived it. On the one hand, we have Wuthering Heights, the land of storm; high on the barren moorland, naked to the shock of the elements, the natural home of the Earnshaw family, fiery, untamed children of the storm. On the other, sheltered in the leafy valley below, stands Thrushcross Grange, the appropriate home of the children of calm, the gentle, passive, timid Lintons. Together each group, following its own nature in its own sphere, combines to compose a cosmic harmony. It is the destruction and re-establishment of this harmony which is the theme of the story.' (Cecil, 1934, p. 164)

Just as the landscape symbolism of Wordsworth is used to reinforce assertions of a moral kind, so the contrasting landscape types of Emily Brontë express a symbolic affinity between each family and the 'personality' of the environment within which it lives. The 'balance' here is achieved, if at all, only within the framework of the whole novel. To maintain the integrity of the two landscape-types is as essential as to perpetuate the separate identity of the Earnshaws and the Lintons.

# CHAPTER 6

# Involvement

## Man in Nature

The idea that our aesthetic sensitivity to landscape is derived ultimately from inborn behaviour mechanisms does not mean that there is a direct, utilitarian relationship between those landscapes which afford us satisfaction and those which afford us safety. The relationship is much more remote. It would be absurd to insist that a lover of landscape walking on the mountains is actually reducing the risk of death or injury at the hands of an enemy because he can get a better view, or that his wife, strolling in a sequestered garden, is a better insurance risk if she is surrounded by rhododendrons, which might, indeed, be harbouring all sorts of undesirable characters bent on doing her all kinds of mischief. But just as your gourmet, roundly savouring his caviare or his Burgundy, has come a long way from the ancestor who spiked saliva-drenched incisors into the raw, quivering flesh, so your connoisseur of landscape is living in a very different world from that of the primitive man whose very survival depended on that ability to see without being seen which was afforded him by a functional disposition of foliage and open space. In both cases, however, to by-pass the antecedents is to begin after the logical premise. The removal of urgent necessity does not put an end to the machinery which evolved to cope with it; rather it frees that machinery to achieve different objectives which themselves are constantly changing with the aspirations and caprices of society. What was a functional disposition of environmental objects becomes conventionalized into a type or series of types which we regard as harmonious because they continue to give us satisfaction, even though we may not recognize that satisfaction as the counterpart of the assurance and sense of security which was more than an aesthetic extravagance when physical survival was an urgent preoccupation.

To say that the transmission of a desire to see without being seen was originally *causally* related to biological survival and that, when the need for it passed, it became the *cause* of aesthetic satisfaction in the experience of landscape would be putting too simple an interpretation on the idea of causality. I do not suppose my philosopher friends would let me get away with the proposition that the possession of sexual inclinations is a *cause* of the perpetuation of the species, much less that the necessity to perpetuate the species is a *cause* of the possession of sexual inclinations, because causality implies a very particular relationship between two or more events or circumstances. Let us therefore side-step this exacting term and say of those creatures who perpetuate their species by sexual union that there is a consecutive relationship between those processes which culminate in sexual intercourse and those which begin with conception and progress through gestation to parturition. The severance of this chain of linked processes at any point would result in the frustration of the 'end-process' which produces another individual physically separate from its mother. Such a severance could be brought about, for instance, by the introduction of a contraceptive device in sexual intercourse with the express purpose of frustrating the 'end-process', but the behaviour mechanisms which prompt the earlier processes in the chain would continue to operate as if nothing had happened. The partners who practise contraception do not say that, because conception cannot now take place, therefore there is no point in attempting sexual intercourse. They say rather that contraception enables them to gratify their inborn inclinations in isolation from any ulterior functional process.

In much the same way those other mechanisms, which seem to prompt forms of behaviour conducive to the achievement of other biological requirements through the encouragement of favourable environmental relationships, do not peter out simply because what we infer to be the 'end-process' is no longer attainable solely through their agency. We do not say that because our survival does not depend on our catching a rabbit or eluding a cannibal, therefore there is no point in attempting to see without being seen. We say rather that release from the obligation to use these mechanisms for self-preservation enables us to gratify these biological inclinations in isolation from the exposure to real, uncontrollable hazards, such as was probably experienced by our ancestors and is still experienced by most animals and some human beings today.

This interpretation of aesthetics in terms of survival mechanisms becoming available for aesthetic ends when they cease to be needed for some practical, utilitarian purpose, exposes us to another line of criticism, namely that it is a form of 'play theory'. We have placed a heavy emphasis on the philosophy of Dewey, and it is true that he rejected the assertion that 'art is play'.

> 'The philosophical implications of the play theory are found in its opposition of freedom and necessity, of spontaneity and order . . . Its underlying note is the idea that aesthetic experience is a release and escape from the pressure of "reality". There is an assumption that freedom can be found only when personal activity is liberated from control by objective factors . . . The contrast between free and externally enforced activity is an empirical fact. But it is largely produced by social conditions and it is something to be eliminated as far as possible, not something to be erected into a differentia by which to define art.' (Dewey, 1958 edn., pp. 279–280)

It is merely as a *criterion* for differentiating between aesthetic and non-aesthetic activity, therefore, that Dewey rejects 'play', that is to say the practice of activities in isolation from the *immediate* achievement of material ends. Play can, of course, discharge an essential role, through training, in the *ultimate* achievement of material ends. It is one thing to say 'all aesthetic experience is play'; it is quite another to say 'some aesthetic experience may be play'.

Indeed, Dewey himself sought to minimize the distinction between 'aesthetic' and other types of experience. Of 'art' he says that it has been

'... remitted to a separate realm, where it is cut off from that association with the materials and aims of every other form of human effort, undergoing, and achievement. A primary task is thus imposed upon one who undertakes to write upon the philosophy of the fine arts. This task is to restore continuity between the refined and intensified forms of experience that are works of art and the everyday events, doings, and sufferings that are universally recognized to constitute experience.' (Dewey, 1958 edn., p. 3)

Thus in the experience of landscape there is no fundamental difference between the perception of the foxhunter, the deer-stalker, the mountaineer, the fell-walker, the poet, the painter. There may be differences in the 'intensity' and 'refinement' of their activities, in the practical application of their energies to material ends, and in the intimacy of the connection between their behaviour and their environment. But 'aesthetic' is not a discriminatory term which includes some activities and excludes others on the basis of their purpose. The pleasure derived from an experience of environment cannot be meaningfully classified on the basis of whether it results in some material improvement or whether it does not. The probability that seeing and hiding can, under certain circumstances, have a practical value is consistent with our enjoying an experience of landscape which affords the opportunity to engage in these activities. To insist that a particular experience must or must not have a practical outcome in order to make it 'aesthetic' is to set up a false distinction.

If, then, we accept this view of the meaning of aesthetic experience it follows that such experience cannot be achieved except by the involvement of the observer in his habitat. This involvement has two related but distinct facets which we must now investigate further. First it concerns the changes which man has collectively introduced into his environment. Secondly, it concerns the continuing necessity for each individual to accept the acquisition of inborn behaviour mechanisms as a part of his biological make-up and to develop them through experience into more complex habits by which he may regulate and express his own relationship to that environment.

## Nostalgia for the Primeval

The first facet is epitomized in the words of Seyyed Hossein Nasr:

'Today, almost everyone living in the urbanized centres of the Western world feels intuitively a lack of something in life. This is due directly to the creation of an artificial environment from which nature has been excluded to the greatest possible extent.' (Nasr, 1968, p. 17)

This takes us back to a basic predicament of man in nature. The history of civilization is basically concerned with the ability of *Homo sapiens* to assert enough control over his environment to render him so immune to its hazards, whether these take the form of famine, exposure, physical assault or whatever, that he has the opportunity to devote at least part of his time to other activities. We have postulated that his ability to achieve this control depends, at least in part, on the acquisition of certain inborn mechanisms which lead to the establishment of fixed behavioural patterns relating the individual to his environment. We have cited evidence that certain objects may act as sign-stimuli quite independently of any experience in the individual which could explain such stimuli in terms of association with past behaviour. It is fundamental to habitat theory that such stimuli continue to operate even after they have ceased to be biologically indispensable. There comes a time, however, when man is so successful in mastering his environment that he virtually creates a new one in which those natural objects which, we have inferred, act as sign-stimuli, are in grave danger of being replaced by other environmental objects. How far can man create for himself an environment of new shapes in new media and still expect them to induce the same kinds of response which an animal displays towards its natural habitat? At what point does artificiality render a landscape no longer 'authentic' in terms of the mechanism of environmental stimulus and response which, we have suggested, is as immutable as the innately transmitted syndrome of stimulus and response in sexual behaviour or alimentary hunger? If we see man in these terms, endowed innately with a mechanism for building a behavioural relationship with one kind of environment but living in another, we can hardly be surprised if he finds himself constantly hankering after a visible environment in which he can recognize those sign-stimuli to which he naturally reacts. This is the point Sitte was making in the passage quoted above (p. 68).

Yi-Fu Tuan, in an article which has much to say on symbolism in landscape, comes to the heart of this problem when he says: 'It has been said that we are in need of new symbols and images, of a freshly integrated vision that does justice to the newly revealed aspects of nature.' (Yu-Fu Tuan, 1966, p. 35). He goes on to quote Gyorgy Kepes: '. . . Small electronic tubes rival flowers in their delicacy and order' (Yi-Fu Tuan, 1966, p. 35). But are delicacy and order the properties in landscape which stimulate aesthetic reaction? Or should we be looking for components of an environment which, in toto, is capable of arousing those who actively participate in it by subjecting them to those stimuli to which they react by nature?

There is a wealth of accumulated experience to be culled from the whole history of civilization which suggests that we are constantly harking back to simpler and more direct associations with nature. This phenomenon is at least a part of the antiquarianism which Lowenthal and Prince have shown to be so important in English landscape taste (Lowenthal and Prince, 1965). One finds it also in the common preference for architectural concessions to naturalism such as thatched roofs and local stone and timber, which blend into the landscape. Regional vernacular building styles in England, for instance, however much they may embody more widespread principles of design (Sheppard, 1966) have, through their use of locally available building materials, established recognizable styles, which have made such an impact on public taste that, in some parts of the country, planning restrictions forbid the construction of buildings in any substance other than quarried or reconstituted local stone. Thus masonry surfaces are suggestive of cliffs or rock surfaces such as might occur naturally in that particular environment.

To the sentimental this device of binding the artificial into the natural offers all sorts of possibilities. The stone walls of cottages can be further 'naturalized' by clothing them with ivy or more ornate creepers. Of the Villa Negroni, in Italy, Uvedale Price wrote:

> 'The more broken, weather-stained, and decayed the stone and brick-work, the more the plants and creepers seemed to have fastened and rooted in between their joints, the more picturesque these gardens become.' (Uvedale Price, *On decorations near the house*, in Lauder, 1842, p. 300)

Cheapness of construction is not the only advantage which the crude dry-stone wall has over its more sophisticated masonry counterpart; its texture can more easily be mistaken for the work of nature. In reconciling the artificial with the natural we are seeking to reconcile the symbolism of our emancipation from the tyranny of the environment with the symbolism of that same environment; and we are driven to do this because it is in this environment that we still find the sign-stimuli which activate our aesthetic responses. We need the assurance not just that we really are emancipated but also that we have not lost that half of our inheritance, namely our habitat, which can uniquely provide for the satisfaction of that other half, namely the behavioural mechanisms which forge our relation-ships with it. Thus the more romantic manifestations of landscape aesthetics reserve a special place for those devices which seek to link the architecture of civilization with the phenomena of nature untamed. Temples are set in groves, gravel paths lead through groomed jungles and 'rustic' bridges span water-courses which meander 'naturally', even if at the bidding of the engineer. Deceit is fundamental to the exercise (p. 36), for emancipation from, and subjugation to, nature are inevitably contradictory.

Supreme among the devices for linking the artificial with the natural is the ruin, in which the harsh functionalism suggested by its form is tempered by its manifest incorporation within the natural order. A castle, manned and patrolled by hostile occupants, must be a forbidding sight. The powerful symbolism of both prospect and refuge which such a structure embodies cannot be aestheti-cally apprehended as long as it represents a real and possibly lethal hazard. But empty it of its garrison and it takes on a very different role. Reduce it to impo-tence still further by physical disintegration and there comes a time when a balance is struck between the functional but unacceptable symbolism of a wholly artificial contrivance and the inoperative but 'naturally' plausible stone surface rising out of a bed of 'natural' vegetation.

It is not necessary here to dwell on the role of the ruin in landscape history.

In painting it is to be found in the work of artists of all periods. Not unnaturally it had a particular appeal for the devotees of the Picturesque. To make an elegant Palladian structure picturesque Gilpin advocated the use of the mallet. '. . . we must beat down one half of it, deface the other and throw the mutilated members round in heaps.' (Quoted by Hyams, 1971, p. 159). Where ruins were not available they could always be constructed. An inventory of 'follies' would contain many which were never intended to reach such a stage of completion as would warrant the remedy of Gilpin's mallet (Barton, 1972). It is easy enough to dismiss these extravagances with a scorn which, we feel, absolves us from making serious enquiry into the motives which led to such apparently absurd and irrational luxuries. But at least one can find in the problem of reconciliation between the artificial and the natural some partial explanation for these quixotic attempts to live in two worlds at the same time.

These exercises in retracing our steps along the path of civilization by dramatically proclaiming the repudiation of functional efficiency in favour of the natural order are a constant reminder that we do not rate our emancipation as an unmixed blessing. We do not, however, have to rely exclusively on the retrieval of paradise by the rejection of the artificial. As more and more of us commit ourselves to an increasingly urban environment, we are at least becoming aware that we can build into it something of the world we have left behind so that we may be able to find in it counterparts which resemble the sign-stimuli of the prospect and refuge of nature closely enough to resuscitate our aesthetic responses. The importation of nature into the city in parks, gardens and other public open spaces, the planting of avenues, the provision of hanging flower baskets or window boxes outside our houses and of rubber plants or aspidistras inside them, all indicate that we have not altogether forgotten. There is indeed a gradual transition from the rural to the urban which can be observed in any city. The woodland ride is soon transmuted into the urban avenue—the chaussée of the Bois de Boulogne gives way to the Champs Elysées. Here the trees are demoted from an enveloping matrix to a row of token refuge symbols. They are but the lining of a masonry trough in which the vistal element is paramount as it steers the eye west to the Arc de Triomphe or east to the Place de la Concorde. It is but a short step from the Champs Elysées to the Rue de Rivoli, but the transition marks the next stage towards the architectural replacement of the prospect–refuge vegetation. The arcades suggest the avenue, their masonry 'trunks' affording a hint of lateral openings to offset the harsh perspective of converging lines. Further east the arcades are less in evidence and at the next stage of transition we find ourselves in a maze of streets in which the tree symbol gives way to a landscape of urban canyons reflecting the symbolism of the rock rather than of the forest.

To argue that this intrusion of 'natural' sign-symbols into the urban architectural forms of Paris springs from a conscious and deliberate policy of design would be extremely dangerous, but certainly there have been many architects who have gone out of their way to bring about a more intimate blending of the two than is implied in the lip-service paid by all architects to environmental congruity. Antoni Gaudí, for instance, incorporated into his buildings all sorts of natural morphological designs from tree trunks to rock pinnacles.[28]

Even in ordinary domestic architecture the complement of prospect and refuge asserts itself. The modern, centrally heated flat or maisonette affords a far better protection against meteorological hazards than the more primitive shelters of earlier days. Where the picture window links this cosy living-space with the world of nature symbols in the garden, a satisfying balance between prospect and refuge may be achieved. But where large windows face streets, squares or public open spaces, and especially if the internal structure of the house is based on the 'open plan', the physical protection provided against the weather may not be matched by the visual protection against the eye of the intruder. The refuge may be successful as a 'shelter' but ineffective as a 'hide'. It is this circumstance which gives rise to the expression 'living in a goldfish bowl' and which revives our affection for the low ceiling, the small windows and the subdued light of the country cottage.

If the march of civilization leads our urban society to substitute an artificial for a natural environment with only the occasional nostalgic backward glance, a parallel trend may be noted in the stylistic development of the visual arts. A characteristic of the last few decades has been the search for means of communication which do not involve the exact imitation of the observed phenomena of nature but rather employ an artistic vocabulary uncontaminated by association with such observed phenomena. To talk of 'representation' in the world of abstract art is to ask for trouble, but even here it may well be that others, more familiar with this field, will discover some application of the ideas which underlie prospect–refuge theory. After all, even the most abstract work of art complies with the same laws of physics which govern all the rest of our environment. Its various parts are related to each other by the same geometrical principles, its colours can be explained in terms of the same spectrum, and once one has established that, even in traditional landscape painting, the interpretation of aesthetic response in terms of the observer's 'habitat' involves a large measure of symbolism, one can never eliminate the possibility that even the most abstract forms of art may lie at the end of an avenue which leads to the primitive game of hide-and-seek. This was clearly in Jellicoe's mind when he wrote of the human body that it is

'. . . still the same as ever, and within this body, but very deep down under layers of civilization, are primitive instincts that have remained unchanged. It is probably true that the basic appeal of the rolling downlands is a biological association of ideas.' (Jellicoe, 1966, vol. II, p. 14)

What exactly this association of ideas amounts to is a question to which he makes no answer, but it is worth noting that in the essay from which this passage is taken he is putting the case that not only representational but also abstract art is of relevance and indeed importance to the landscape architect. Of abstract art he says, 'with what, in fact, are the instincts endeavouring to make contact, and what are the paintings endeavouring to convey? Here we must turn to the primitive for guidance, because these instincts still lie within us, however dormant, and it is these which the modern artist is endeavouring to reach and release.' (Jellicoe, 1966, vol. II, p. 4)

The similarity, not only of theme, but even of style and phraseology, with some of the writing of John Dewey can hardly escape us. The 'instincts . . . however dormant' are frankly acknowledged but only vaguely apprehended and certainly not identified, much less named.

In the experience of landscape, then, it is not only unreasonable but also pointless to argue a clear-cut distinction between representational and abstract art. A series of equally-spaced, elongated ellipses, erected perpendicularly from a horizontal base, each painted in light green on one side and a dark shade on the other, could well be recognizable in a landscape painting as a row of Lombardy poplars even if they were smoothed off to perfect geometrical shapes such as would most improbably occur in nature. If a similar arrangement of elongated ellipses figured in an abstract painting, the artist might rightly and reasonably deny that they were intended to represent poplars, or even trees, or even anything at all in the sense in which 'representation' is generally understood in art. But he would be unlikely to claim, and certainly unable to demonstrate, that his use of this pattern of geometrical shapes owed nothing to some past experience of poplar trees, even though the experience itself might be beyond recall (p. 51). In the same way, if the abstract artist has inherited a sensitivity to habitat as experienced in prospect–refuge terms, as we infer the rest of us have, it would be difficult to assert with conviction that the arrangement of shapes, patterns and colours in ways which satisfy him has nothing whatever to do with a sense of exposure, of strategic movement, of participation in a three-dimensional environment, of 'seeing without being seen.'

> 'Who knows the individual hour in which
> His habits first were sown . . . ?'
> (Wordsworth, *The Prelude*, Bk. II, lines 206–207;
> Hutchinson, 1895, p. 645)

If we can go no further than equating areas of bright, light colours with the concept of 'prospect', and dark, subdued colours with that of 'refuge', we have begun to inject into an abstract composition an element of 'meaning' in habitat-theory terms, though we should probably not be thanked for it by the artist.

It is against this background that one must note the frequency of 'representational revivals' in modern art. Just as the process by which man achieves his emancipation from nature through architectural, economic and urban advancement is periodically interrupted by the retracing of his steps in search of the natural habitat he is leaving behind, so the general twentieth-century trend towards the abstract in art has frequently been punctuated by reversals, in which the representational approach to landscape painting has reasserted its importance. The surrealist movement, for instance, though producing strange and unfamiliar associations of shapes and objects, frequently drew on a fairly orthodox 'representational' landscape as the framework for a composition, and the same kind of reversion is apparent in the various manifestations of 'neo-realism' (see, for instance, Galerie Mokum, 1970) and in the work of several contemporary artists. This twentieth-century phenomenon is not, of course, unique. The degree of abstraction which it seeks to counteract may be unprecedented in earlier years, but the works of such heterogeneous artists as Wordsworth, the Pre-Raphaelites and Sir Giles Gilbert Scott all display something of this quest for the lost world from which we have made such desperate efforts to escape but which now evokes in us as exiles a compulsive nostalgia. Though few of us would give up the emancipation we have already won, all of us long to get back, when the opportunity arises, to that proper environment to which our inborn behaviour mechanisms are still tuned, and in it to live and move and have our being.

## Recreation as Environmental Experience

It is now time to turn to the second of those facets of man's involvement with his environment to which we referred earlier, namely 'the continuing necessity for each individual to accept the acquisition of inborn behaviour mechanisms as a part of his biological make-up and to develop them through experience into more complex habits by which he may regulate and express his own relationship to that environment' (p. 171).

Problems which come in this category are not of man's own making and basically are not peculiar to his species, but concern all individuals, whether human or not, who find themselves subject to this sort of environmental relationship. It will be remembered that these behaviour mechanisms seem to be derived from two sources which we have called 'inborn' and 'learned' (p. 62). The inborn component is crude, simple, fundamental. It becomes refined and elaborated by learning, by practice, by experience. When lambs leap and gambol in a field they are doing what Lorenz' water-shrews were doing in his experiment (p. 61). They are turning basic inborn urges into an efficient machinery for survival. A strategically favourable environment is inadequate unless the participant has acquired the ability to make effective use of it. If, therefore, man needs to be aesthetically reminded of the favourable nature of his environment, equally he seeks assurance that he has a mastery over that environment. Exploration is an important part of this mastery, but it is not all. The ability to move swiftly from one part to another is also an essential ingredient, and therefore the perfecting of skilled, controlled movements of the body can also be seen to have a survival value in the primitive existence. Just as the ability to see without being seen becomes a source of satisfaction in itself even when isolated from any ulterior questions of survival, so the ability to run fast, to climb with agility or to take to the water persists as a source of satisfaction when it is no longer needed as a prerequisite for survival.

The whole question of recreational activity therefore impinges very closely on our subject. Sometimes techniques of body movement are developed for the satisfaction which they afford for their own sake. Environment is then relatively unimportant. The running track, the gymnasium, the swimming baths, which provide a milieu for these activities, are not judged primarily by their capacity for giving visual pleasure but for providing the opportunity for cultivating excellence in particular skills.

There are, however, many recreational activities which involve the fitting of bodily movements into a context in which they can more effectively evoke the satisfaction which comes from the creature's successful strategic participation in his entire environment. For this kind of activity the race-track and the boxing-ring are not enough, and we shall now examine some examples to illustrate this.

At one end of the scale may be found those kinds of recreation which involve little or no special equipment, for example, walking. As walking develops from the stroll in the park, through fell-walking to mountaineering, the need for special equipment increases. Efficiency of locomotion can be improved by enlisting the aid of animals, particularly the horse, or of simple mechanical apparatus to facilitate movement by skating, skiing or cycling, or to open up alien environments by sailing, rowing or canoeing. Similarly the swimmer, who needs no equipment at all, can with the provision of the proper apparatus, explore new regions by sub-aqua diving.

The application of mechanical power to locomotion not only makes possible enormous increases in speed, as in motoring or motor-cycling, but also opens up quite new kinds of recreational activity, such as flying (and hence parachuting), water-skiing and the racing of power-driven vehicles.

I do not think that these different kinds of locomotion constitute significantly different kinds of aesthetic experience; rather they open up the possibility of experiencing familiar environments in unfamiliar ways or of viewing them from unusual angles. It is worth noting, however, that by increasing the speed at which we pass through a landscape, they may greatly alter the time-sequences which are an integral part of our perceptive experience of it. Brenda Colvin says of the beech avenue at Clumber Park, Nottinghamshire,

> 'The scale of such avenues is adapted to the pace of horse or pedestrian rather than the motor car. At faster speeds the repetition of the trunks is confusing to the traveller.' (Colvin, 1970 edn., p. 125)

Skiing is an example of an activity which combines skilled, controlled movement with the aesthetic experience of landscape. Much of the exhilaration of this sport can be attributed to the sensation of rapid movement over snow. That the skier is not actually pursuing a quarry or escaping from an enemy does not prevent him from enjoying the experience of using a skill which could be highly beneficial in the real pursuit or escape situation. When the objective of pursuit or escape is missing, the achievement of perfection in the means becomes the end. Probably some of the satisfaction of skiing could be experienced on a featureless inclined surface, but the satisfaction is greatly enhanced by the environment within which it takes place. Consider a long ski-run in an Alpine setting. The run begins in an environment whose features pertain strongly to the symbolism of prospect: the elevation of the site, the distant view with clear, refuge-free horizons, the surface devoid of hiding-places, the brightness and whiteness of the gleaming snow. If the sun is shining through a clear sky the imagery is further strengthened. Finally there is that hallmark of the prospect sensation, falling ground.

The refuge symbols all lie below; the valley itself, the trees, the signs of human habitation, in short, everything needed to restore the missing elements in the prospect–refuge complement. The actual run achieves the transfer of the participant from the world of the prospect to the world of the refuge. It is analogous to a rabbit reaching a hedge from an open field. A distinctive feature of the achievement is the great distance which has to be covered before the refuge can be attained and which therefore gives rise to a keen sense of hazard. This, however, is compensated by the speed at which the operation can be performed, a speed far in excess of that which is attainable by the ordinary process of walking or even running.

Something of the exhilaration of this rapid movement within the environment can be experienced by the ordinary motorist. In fact this was one of the earliest areas of landscape aesthetics to be invaded by the environmental perceptionists of the nineteen sixties. In *The View from the Road* three architects with a particular interest in environment set out to discover how the motorist perceives the landscape through which he passes and what sort of environmental experiences impress themselves upon him and cause aesthetic satisfaction. To do this they devised a system of notation by which the essential experience of the highway could be recorded. This 'essential experience' consisted, they said, 'in the perception of roadside detail, the sense of motion and space, the feeling of basic orientation, and the apparent meaning of the landscape'. (Appleyard *et al.*, 1964, p. 21)

Having devised such a system they subjected various observers to the experience of travelling along highways in different parts of the north-eastern United States.

'The basic technique used was the one common to all artistic criticism: numerous repetitions of the experience, and its analysis and evaluation both on the spot and from memory. The process was aided by the use of tape recorder, camera, and sketch pad to record momentary impressions . . .

'A similar graphic technique was used on the Northeast Expressway only, and was carried out by a somewhat wider sample of people (twenty subjects: mostly, but not entirely, middle-class and professional). Here the subject was given a small pad of paper and required to

sketch the scene at an extremely rapid tempo, averaging three drawings
per minute. Again he is under such pressure that he cannot consciously
control what he records. The sketches were timed to indicate the location in which each was made; they could then be arranged in rows one
above another, all drawn to a common scale. Thus it was possible to
see what the entire set of subjects recorded at similar points on the
road.' (Appleyard *et al.*, 1964, p. 27)

From the resulting sketches the authors then compiled '. . . something of a
composite view of what the sketches say; that is it reproduces a sketch (in a
simplified style which approximates the most usual detail) whenever a majority
of observers were making the same drawing at approximately the same point'
(Appleyard *et al.*, 1964, p. 37). This composite view (Figure 73 in the original)
is reproduced here as Figure 28. Finally, as the outcome of the whole exercise,
the authors draw some conclusions which, they argue, could form guide-lines
for the aesthetic improvement of expressway design.

*The View from the Road* therefore is a study of the aesthetics of landscape as
perceived under particular circumstances. It seeks to record and as far as possible to measure the aesthetic responses of observers; it does not attempt to
explain systematically the origins of these aesthetic responses. Yet it does present
an account which is highly consistent with the basic ideas of prospect–refuge
theory (Table 6). A few passages quoted from the text will reinforce the impression that, behind a difference in terminology, there lies a unity of message. At
several points, for instance, a comparison is drawn with the movement of a
skier.

'One of the strongest visual sensations is a relation of scale between an
observer and a large environment, a feeling of adequacy when confronted by a vast space: that even in the midst of such a world one is
big enough, powerful enough, identifiable enough. In this regard, the
automobile, with its speed and personal control, may be a way of
establishing such a sense at a new level. At the very least, it begins to
neutralize the disparity in size between a man and a city . . .

'The sense of personal mastery of space is strongest on skis or on
a motor-cycle, where the vehicle is small and delicately controlled,
where one is "outside" in contact with the environment, and where it is
impossible to make body motions within the vehicle which are irrelevant to the motion through the landscape. The sense of mastery is the
product of both maneuverable velocity and a sensuous contact.' (Appleyard *et al.*, 1964, p. 13)

Or again:

'Particularly if the road swings smoothly from point to point of a
fine and rather open natural landscape, it gives the same sense of
vital rhythm and movement as a skier's track.' (Appleyard *et al.*,
1964, p. 10)

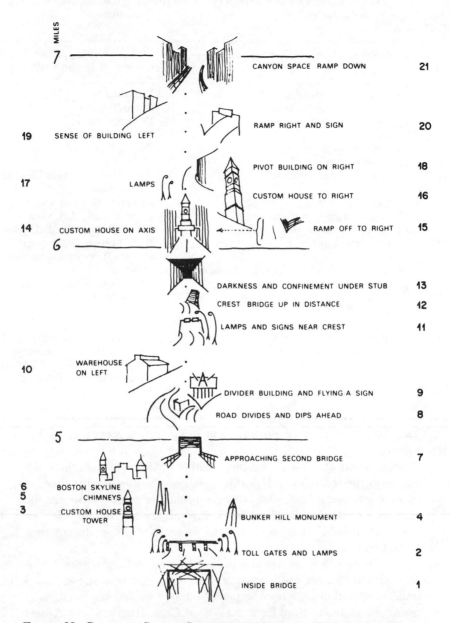

MILES

7 ———————————— CANYON SPACE RAMP DOWN 21

19 SENSE OF BUILDING LEFT RAMP RIGHT AND SIGN 20

17 LAMPS PIVOT BUILDING ON RIGHT 18

CUSTOM HOUSE TO RIGHT 16

14 CUSTOM HOUSE ON AXIS RAMP OFF TO RIGHT 15

6 ————————————

DARKNESS AND CONFINEMENT UNDER STUB 13

CREST BRIDGE UP IN DISTANCE 12

LAMPS AND SIGNS NEAR CREST 11

10 WAREHOUSE ON LEFT

DIVIDER BUILDING AND FLYING A SIGN 9

ROAD DIVIDES AND DIPS AHEAD 8

5 ————————————

APPROACHING SECOND BRIDGE 7

6 BOSTON SKYLINE
5 CHIMNEYS
3 CUSTOM HOUSE TOWER

BUNKER HILL MONUMENT 4

TOLL GATES AND LAMPS 2

INSIDE BRIDGE 1

FIGURE 28. COMPOSITE SKETCH SEQUENCE OF NORTHEAST EXPRESSWAY (DETAIL) FROM THE VIEW FROM THE ROAD
Part of Figure 73 reprinted from *The View from the Road* by Appleyard, D., Lynch, K. and Myer, J. R. (1964) by permission of the M.I.T. Press, Cambridge, Massachusetts. Copyright © 1964 by the Massachusetts Institute of Technology. (The marginal numbers have been added to facilitate reference to Table 6; they do not form part of the original)

TABLE 6. NOTES ON THE SYMBOLISM OF FIGURE 28

| Ref. No. L-H R-H | Identification | Symbolism |
|---|---|---|
| | 21 CANYON SPACE. RAMP DOWN | Orthodox vista; falling ground; R symbols left and right |
| | 20 RAMP RIGHT AND SIGN | Deflected vista |
| 19 | SENSE OF BUILDING LEFT | R symbolism of vistal flank |
| | 18 PIVOT BUILDING ON RIGHT | Deflected vista |
| 17 | LAMPS | Minor P symbols |
| | 16 CUSTOM HOUSE TO RIGHT | Strong P symbol |
| | 15 RAMP OFF TO RIGHT | Deflection |
| 14 | CUSTOM HOUSE ON AXIS | Strong reduplication effect in regular vista |
| | 13 DARKNESS AND CONFINEMENT UNDER STUB | Inversion effect in vista |
| | 12 CREST. BRIDGE UP IN DISTANCE | P symbol and defl. vista |
| | 11 LAMPS AND SIGNS NEAR CREST | Minor P symbols; defl. vista |
| 10 | WAREHOUSE ON LEFT | Roof-horizon (P); potential R but (?) poor penetrability |
| | 9 DIVIDER BUILDING AND FLYING A SIGN | P symbol |
| | 8 ROAD DIVIDES AND DIPS AHEAD | Split vista; falling ground |
| | 7 APPROACHING SECOND BRIDGE | Peephole effect in vista |
| 6 | BOSTON SKYLINE ⎫ | ⎧Powerful P symbols in |
| 5 | CHIMNEYS ⎪ | ⎨distance; strong |
| | 4 BUNKER HILL MONUMENT ⎬ | ⎪reduplication deriving |
| 3 | CUSTOM HOUSE TOWER ⎭ | ⎩from horizon location |
| | 2 TOLL GATES AND LAMPS | Breached impediment hazard with minor P symbols |
| | 1 INSIDE BRIDGE | Peephole effect |

P = prospect     R = refuge

The distinction between prospect and refuge symbols is never far beneath the surface.

'Confinements are always notable, whether made by cuts, tunnels, tall buildings, or the sides of hills. Overhead enclosures, such as bridges or even overhead signs, seem to be especially significant. So are the moments of spatial freedom, as when the road rides up over an eminence, the city falls away, and the driver is aware of the sky or a distant panorama.

'Spatial contrast, as when Boston's Central Artery passes North Station and "comes out" into the inner city, makes a strong visual impact. Spatial change may be perceived as a unified sequence, as in the approach to Hartford from the Wilbur Cross Highway: one crosses the river while elevated, descends into a cut, thence into a short tunnel, and finally bursts out into the central park. The road in Philadelphia's Fairmount Park and the Rockefeller Parkway in Cleveland share a simple effect of this kind: the repetitive experience of passing under a succession of bridges, each of different quality. The East River Drive in New York City subjects the driver to a dramatic series of riverside spaces, progressing from open to sidehill, to tunnel, to open-walled tunnel, to cut and sidehill again. Such a sequence can be a thrilling one.' (Appleyard *et al.*, 1964, p. 12)

As for 'the apparent meaning of the landscape' referred to above, if this is a 'meaning' in the sense of rational explanation, of cognitive experience, it emerges as of secondary importance in comparison with the spontaneous visual impact of the perceived environment. In drawing their study to a close the authors conclude:

'To some extent, this monograph has discussed the issue of meaning in the visual landscape, and the way in which this meaning is communicated to the driver. But our greatest emphasis has been on orientation and visual form, and on meaning primarily in reference to the meaning of motion and of the road itself.' (Appleyard *et al.*, 1964, p. 63)

In England canal cruising is a form of recreational activity whose popularity has vastly increased in recent years. A network of 'narrow' and 'broad' canals, with a minimum width of approximately seven and fourteen feet respectively, was constructed in England, mainly between the seventeen fifties and the eighteen thirties. Most of this network is no longer used for freight traffic, but it carries a large assortment of pleasure craft of all shapes and sizes, some converted from old narrow boats, some specially constructed, to bring luxurious living, with showers, refrigerators and gas cookers, to the old arteries of commerce. Economically the activity of the cruisers is quite useless in the sense that it achieves nothing by way of commercial distribution. It is certainly a form of passenger transport, but the vast majority of travellers eventually arrive at the same destination from which they started. The purpose of the exercise can only be explained, therefore, in terms of the pleasure to be derived from the experience itself.

This experience is made up of many activities whose novelty, at least in that particular form, no doubt adds interest. Even washing-up becomes interesting when the kitchen window glides slowly past green fields, browsing cattle and tangled bramble bushes. Playing at housekeeping is good fun for a short time, and steering a temporary home through very restricted water can be a stimulating challenge. But undoubtedly it is as an unfamiliar experience of landscape that this highly specialized form of vacation makes its principal impact on those who fall for it.

The perception of landscape from a canal boat involves the same principles of prospect and refuge with which we are already familiar, but it puts a premium on certain kinds of experience. The views which one obtains of the undulating lowlands through which most of these canals meander are generally panoramic in character, but the line of the waterway fore and aft introduces a vistal theme which is always there. The idea of participation is fostered by the opportunity for combining movement through the landscape with refuge in the boat, and a well-designed modern canal boat, with its rigid limitations of height and beam, can be a very cosy refuge indeed.

Whereas the earlier canals tended to meander a good deal, following the contours, some of the later additions to the system, especially after about 1820, were obliged to pursue more direct courses, since part of their purpose was to forestall competition from the railways. Accordingly, embankments and cuttings are common features of these later canals, and here the alternation of prospect-dominant embankments and refuge-dominant cuttings based respectively on panoramic and vistal forms introduces an interesting dimension into the visual experience.

There are many kinds of recreational activity which bring us even closer to the primitive 'habitat' situation—the world of pursuing, of escaping, of hiding and seeking—and our attention turns naturally to one of the oldest and most widely practised forms of outdoor recreation, hunting.

In England I suppose the word 'hunting' conjures up first and foremost a picture of foxhunting, though this is simply one conventionalized ritual manifestation of the basic urge to assert one's control over animals in their natural environment, in this case by chasing and killing them.

The process of foxhunting involves a highly organized, highly disciplined communal social activity, in which regular roles are assigned among the body corporate of pursuers, while the pursued enjoys, if that is the right word, his distinction without competition. The vocabulary of the chase is full of words heavily charged with prospect–refuge symbolism: 'view', 'covert', 'going to ground', etc.

Most accounts of a foxhunt succeed in conveying the sense of balance between prospect, refuge and hazard as reflected in the behaviour and movement of the fox. After all, the speed he can attain and the strategic use he can make of his own environment are the only weapons he has. In the following passage note how the link between activity and environment has been accentuated by a number of direct references to the hunters and the background sound-effects as well as to the orthodox aesthetic imagery of landscape:

'When all were assembled in the park, they presented a most uncommon and beautiful picture; dogs and riders sometimes at full speed over the few level spaces; and then cautiously stepping among the rocks, and over the summits of the bold high grounds—sometimes alighting and carefully descending their steep sides. At one time the hounds seemed not to be aware of the precipice before them, over which it was feared, in their eager pursuit, they would have been lost, but they turned short and escaped the danger. When all came in sight of Duddingstone, the scene was beautiful beyond description—dogs, huntsmen, ladies and gentlemen in scarlet uniforms, in the most pleasing groups, all over the picturesque scene which that side of the King's park at all times presents to the eye—while the echo of the horns, dogs, horses, and the voices of the riders, awakened a perfect contrast to the everyday stillness and solemnity of that region of comparative silence and solitude. Reynard found shelter in some retreat of the rocks, where he could not be found, when the whole hunt proceeded southwards towards Libberton; and the usual silence and solitude of the hills and glens of the royal park were restored, the sheep rested in peace, and nothing was heard but the whispers of the passing breeze.' ('Sporting Occurrences in October', *Annals of Sporting and Fancy Gazette*, 1823, vol. IV, p. 347)

The intrusion of the most blatant symbolism will not escape the reader. Prospect ('summits', 'bold high grounds', 'came in sight') is mixed with hazard ('cautiously stepping among the rocks', 'carefully descending . . . steep sides', 'precipice', 'danger'), and what could be more expressive of refuge than 'Reynard found shelter in some retreat of the rocks, where he could not be found . . .' ?

Intimate as is the association between foxhunting and the landscape, the application of the principles of prospect and refuge tends to be somewhat one-sided. Since the hounds, having picked up a scent, can flush a fox out of his cover into open ground, the pursuer does not need to seek the protection of invisibility. By contrast, deer-stalking imposes not only on the quarry but also on the hunter the necessity to squeeze every ounce of strategic advantage out of his environment. The scarlet uniforms and the 'echo of the horns, dogs, horses, and the voices of the riders' would add up to a poor recipe for a fruitful day in the deer forest. The very last thing the stalker has to do is awaken 'a perfect contrast to the usual every-day stillness and solemnity of that region of comparative silence and solitude'. Even the whispering of those sibilant abstract nouns would be better dispensed with where *both* parties in the confrontation are playing the game by the same rules. Each has an equal interest in seeing without being seen, and it is not surprising, therefore, to find the connection between successful deer-stalking and the imagery of prospect and refuge as we have previously discussed it very clearly exemplified in descriptive passages from the literature. Grimble's book will serve as well as any (Grimble, 1901). Here are a few selections which may be read with the symbolism of prospect and refuge in mind. The first illustrates the importance of a correct use of environment as part of the technique of shooting a stag.

'In getting near deer never come *over* a boulder or a hillock, but always creep *round* it. It is a sign of bad stalking if the stalker is continually stopping dead and suddenly bobbing down. Walking too fast is apt to produce this style, for in going at a great pace with deer in front it becomes impossible for the eye to guard three or four hundred yards on either side; the country is opened up *too quickly*, and frequently the deer get a good look at you before they themselves are seen.' (Grimble, 1901, pp. 55–56)

In this passage Grimble is concentrating on the technique of fieldcraft. In the next extract we find him describing a particular incident within its landscape context. The technique, however, is still his principal concern.

'From the position [the deer] were then in it was impossible to approach nearer till they moved, for there was a large flat between us and them, and the hill they were resting on commanded every inch of it. We pushed on, however, to the edge of this flat, which brought us to within about half a mile; here we had to halt, and creeping to a heathery knoll, we pulled out the glasses and examined them one by one at our leisure . . . The flat was simply a morass, and no hillock or watercourse to shelter us higher than two feet or deeper than one. Forth we crept, as if we had been own brothers to the serpent; in a moment we are wet from breast to knees, sinking well over our elbows at every movement, often having to wait motionless for many minutes . . .'
(Grimble, 1901, pp. 116–117)

It is hardly necessary to annotate this description with marginal references to the symbolism of prospect–refuge theory as set out in Tables 1 to 4. It is indeed a thin line of demarcation between the enjoyment which this deer-stalker derives from playing out the drama of pursuing his quarry within a wild environment and the aesthetic satisfaction communicated spontaneously by that environment itself, and in the next two passages he shifts the emphasis still further, until he is writing very little about the chase and very much about the aesthetics of landscape:

'Around the would-be deer-slayer spreads a sea of hills—some in curved symmetry of outline, others with their summits broken into jagged and fantastic peaks. Then as the pure mountain air finds its way into the lungs, the muscles seem to harden, the eyes grow clearer and more far-seeing, and a determination to do or die pervades the mind; and altogether a sensation is experienced that it is better fun to be alive at that moment than it was the same time the day before.'
(Grimble, 1901, p. 50)

And finally:

'We were soon off again, and after a scrambling walk of about two miles along the side of Loch Lyon, we reached the march. Then commenced the ascent of the overhanging hills, and in spite of the sharp east wind, I was something more than warm when we gained the first spying-place. Out came the glasses. Archie with his telescope, I with the binoculars. It was only a small corrie, and having made sure nothing was there, I could not help turning my attention to the prospect around me. The day was perfect—a steady breeze, a bright blue sky, a few white clouds drifting rapidly overhead; the outlines of the very distant hills clear and well defined—a very ocean of them meet the eye; and of course to me the beauty of it all was more than doubled, for each hill was the haunt of the wild red deer.' (Grimble, 1901, pp. 106–107)

How the reader reacts to Augustus Grimble is not my immediate concern. I suspect he may be amused by the earnestness of the purple passages and possibly nauseated by the whole business. But he cannot, I think, miss the point which I am trying to make in quoting the words of this enthusiast. For Grimble, at least, the hunting of the deer and the enjoyment of the mountains become merged in a single landscape experience, very closely consistent with the idea that innate urges to satisfy primitive requirements give rise to man–landscape relationships which continue to provide pleasure long after they have ceased to be biologically necessary for survival.

To those who find themselves revolted by the seeking of pleasure in the killing of animals there are many ways and means of salvaging the aesthetic experience while disposing of the slaughter. For instance, animals may be captured alive, and if most of us are able only to enjoy the experience of collecting for zoos vicariously on film and television, thousands of anglers seem content to catch fish, weigh them and throw them back. Alternatively plants, fossils, minerals and other natural objects may be substituted for animals and still provide a hunting incentive for a safari. Another solution, increasingly popular, is to substitute the camera for the rifle or shot-gun; yet another is to dispense altogether with even a synthetic capturing process and simply enjoy the landscape symbols associated with the environment of the chase.

In all these activities the element of exploration and discovery (p. 71) is important and this provides a constant source of satisfaction in such activities as rambling, fell-walking, etc. Pot-holing is a particular kind of environmental exploration with a powerful component of 'inversion'. The landscape to be explored consists of limited vistas and peepholes all set within the enveloping refuge of the cave.

Another way of accentuating the impact of an environmental experience is to emphasize the hazard element. This is, of course, implicit in pot-holing, but it is found also in rock-climbing, where the absence of fast movement (cf. skiing) is compensated by the satisfaction of overcoming incomparably more difficult impediment hazards in one's own good time. By carrying this emphasis still further one can set oneself undertakings in which the challenge itself has to make up for the severe paucity of variety in landscape symbols which one would have to accept, for instance, in crossing an ice-cap by sledge or an ocean in a small boat.

Within the whole range of what Kates calls 'pleasurable environmentally oriented activities' (Kates, 1966/7, p. 22) may be found many which have associations with particular kinds of landscape. The hunter who pursues the otter, for instance, is led into a very different environment from that in which his counterpart chases the hare. The grouse-shooter finds himself not only on moors but on heather-moors, while the duck-shooter will spend a whole day among the reeds and sedges. But while the visible features of the landscape will vary greatly, the basic concept of seeing and hiding will not. It is only the agencies through which these concepts are expressed that will appear different and thereby mislead us into thinking that there are no common general principles by which to link the aesthetic pleasures which some derive from one landscape and some from another.

Other kinds of recreational activity give emphasis to different aspects of the man–environment situation. Some, such as cross-country running, put a premium on the stamina which is so essential in the survival stakes. Skiing, we have already seen, accentuates the ability to move quickly and skilfully from a prospect area to a refuge area, a technique which is found in an even more dramatic form in parachuting. Sailing rewards the exercise of skill in harnessing the wind and tide. Gliding fulfils a similar function in one medium only. The recently popularized sport of orienteering affords a unique opportunity for combining the acquisition of topographical knowledge with the physical prowess by which such knowledge can be exploited to strategic advantage. Clearly, we cannot examine all outdoor sports in detail to see how well they stand up to the theory, but if the reader will do so himself he will find, I think, that such dissimilar activities as steeplechasing, bird-watching, rally-driving and riding on miniature railways are all expressions of the need to act out some role or roles in the continuing drama in which man still finds he is seeking to assure himself of his ability to hold his own in the perpetual confrontation with his environment.

Where the choice of a venue is not limited by the requirements of an activity such as deer-stalking or tobogganing the participant has greater freedom to choose where he will seek his recreation. The fact that we associate recreational land with certain kinds of visual form suggests that this choice of land use is governed by some basic principles. Not all of these principles are necessarily aesthetically based. The availability, accessibility and ownership of land, for instance, may affect its use (Patmore, 1970). But mention of walking, rambling or picnicking conjures up a picture of some piece of land which affords the opportunity not only for comfort (picnicking on grass is generally better than on ploughland!) but also for the contemplation and enjoyment of landscape. Beechwoods, gorse-covered commons or sand dunes would all serve well, and all tend to be rich in the imagery of both prospect and refuge.

In all these activities which we have broadly termed 'recreational' we see man at work first in cultivating and developing those rudimentary behaviour mechanisms on which, for his ancestors, survival may well have depended, and then, having shaped if not perfected them, seeking the opportunity of practising what has by now become a pleasurable act or occupation. It will be noted that, in terms of our concept of 'levels of symbolism', these activities span a wide range. Let us take two examples of 'strategic' activities to illustrate opposite ends of the continuum from the 'tangible', 'immediate' or 'real' end to the 'intangible' or 'symbolic' end of the scale.

We noted above that the spontaneous reactions to environmental objects, so important to survival under primitive conditions, may need to be resuscitated in conditions of war (p. 67). One can hardly pretend that the experience of landscape in conditions of jungle warfare is 'aesthetic' in any generally acceptable sense of the word. We have already seen, as Burke saw (p. 28), that the pleasure of any experience can be frustrated if the hazard element is allowed to become too strong, but we can find in the adjustment of a soldier to his field environment manifestations of attitudes, feelings and impulses recognizably related to those which regularly enter into landscape aesthetics. Manuals of infantry training tend to be restricted documents, and I had therefore better not quote page references, but I do not think I shall suffer incarceration for pointing out how much they are concerned with camouflage and concealment, with assessing the lie of the land and with fostering an awareness of every detail of an environment, on the effective use of which a soldier's life may depend. If you can get hold of such a manual you may well find an illustration of precisely that situation in which Grimble urges the advisability of coming round a boulder or hillock rather than over it (p. 185). You may well find instructions on how to plan a route through a landscape, looking for what the army calls 'obstacles' and what I have called 'impediment hazards', and paying particular attention to the gaps or passages through them. You may well find the advantages of 'ridges' (convex surfaces, Table 4), as areas of observation distinguished from 'hollows' (concave surfaces), as areas of concealment. Also, if you pick the right manual, you will find one sentence which, in view of the importance we have attached to that key phrase from Konrad Lorenz, I cannot refrain from quoting verbatim, even at the risk of incarceration. 'If you want to kill without being killed, learn to see without being seen.'

As a complete contrast to the experience of a real strategic use of the environment as a theatre for survival, consider the game of golf, in which the strategic basis of the man–environment relationship is re-stated in a symbolic, conventionalized or ritualistic form. The object here is to achieve the greatest possible mastery of movement through the environment, not directly or personally but vicariously. The ball becomes the representative of the player, almost a symbolic extension of his personality, so much so that he uses the personal pronoun to refer indiscriminately to the ball and to the player who struck it. 'It's all right for you; you're on the green, but I'm in the rough.'

A study of any golf course will reveal an extremely close parallel between the game and the experience of landscape as expressed in the terminology of prospect–refuge theory. The player takes his stance on the tee, an open and often somewhat elevated platform commanding a clear view (over falling ground) of the field through which he (represented by his ball) has to pass. From this prospect the goal can be seen as a clearing in a matrix of 'rough' to which a fairway (cf. vista) allows direct approach. Impediment hazards are introduced to right and left and very likely beyond the target. Other natural phenomena may influence his (or rather the ball's) passage, such as the wind, the wetness of the grass, the slope of the ground. That the player will reach his goal is almost certain—even a poor player is only occasionally denied that ultimate satisfaction[29]—but the process may be achieved with a greater or lesser degree of efficiency which can be measured arithmetically by a simple criterion. When eventually he reaches this objective, he, through the medium of his representative, disappears into that most fundamental of refuges, a hole in the ground.

Golf is a parody of primitive environmental experience in which the basic relationship of man to habitat is expressed in a system of stylized equivalents whose identity is very thinly disguised.

## Participation by Proxy

This idea of vicarious involvement, or participation by proxy, presents us with a device which can often help us in our efforts to recapture the experience of our primitive natural environment. When we have so modified the environment as to render it incapable of stimulating our proper responses towards it, we may recover something of the sensation of participation by identification with other creatures not similarly deprived. The popularity of watching animals in the wild may be at least partially explicable in these terms. A field mouse can find concealment in quite short grass which would afford us no protection whatever, and as we watch him extracting the maximum advantage from his tiny world of prospects and refuges we momentarily live his life for him, participating through him in an environmental experience which we *can* only enjoy at second hand. Anyone brought up on the works of Beatrix Potter knows that this kind of experience by proxy is one which offers to children, and not only to children, an immediate source of intense delight.

Animals which enjoy environmental opportunities denied to us seem to have a particularly potent influence on our aesthetic sensitivity. We have already noted the importance of locomotion in environmental experience, and those creatures which possess advantages of mobility which we cannot share seem to evoke a powerful response. Think, for instance, of the role played by birds in painting. One cannot explain the work of an artist like Peter Scott solely in terms of his competence in depicting the anatomical properties of geese, undeniable though that is. The sight of a flock rising from the reed-beds into a green, pre-sunrise sky invites more than a cognitive recognition of the species. If one can become a Brent Goose by affiliation, this is surely what momentarily and spontaneously happens! You and I would probably find little comfort, little protection, in the reed-bed. Yet our experience of prospect and refuge is sufficiently close to that of other members of the animal kingdom to enable us to feel a kind of affinity with these vastly different creatures. Up to a point we can understand, or we think we can, what it must feel like to take off into the cold morning air, emancipated for a moment from those limitations imposed on human environmental relationships by the laws of gravity.

The deer, as we have seen (p. 62), is another creature which exemplifies a close and highly regulated adjustment to its environment. It held—indeed still holds— a place of privilege in the landscape of parkland and it figured prominently in romantic painting of the 'monarch-of-the-glen' type. The red deer of Scotland was generously endowed with the qualifications required in a proxy. It inhabited a landscape rich in prospect and refuge symbols, particularly the former. It possessed a means of locomotion inferior to the birds but, especially in this type of country, superior to man. It was credited with an uncanny knowledge of its own territory and a capacity for exploiting its habitat through all its senses to its own advantage. It was popularly associated with 'the chase', that unique theatre for dramatizing the process of survival in terms of prospect, refuge and hazard; and in those pictorial situations which portray disaster, imminent in the 'stag-at-bay' type, complete in the 'packhorse-plus-carcass' type, it was, after all, only a proxy, and the vicarious participant could sever the association as soon as the yelping became too loud, the jaw-snapping too close, or the pressure on the trigger too critical.

From the vicarious participation in landscape through identification with the wild animal it is but a short step to the pathetic fallacy: the attribution of feelings (and the means of expressing them) to hills, clouds, rivers, trees or whatever. Once one accepts the idea not only of man participating in nature but also of inviting the inanimate environment to participate with him, the table is set for a veritable banquet of prospect–refuge imagery. The mountains become sentinels, the groves protectresses, the instrument becomes the agent and the whole environment is translated from a passive to an active role.

## CHAPTER 7

# Landscape in the Several Arts

'Possibly we should be humble enough to recognize that
in our comparisons between the arts we have not advanced
far enough to establish genuinely systematic approaches'

KARL KROEBER (1972, p. 76)

Just as we have stressed all along the need for an interdisciplinary approach;
just as we have not hesitated to make excursions into elementary ethology,
psychology or physics, so we have looked for expressions of landscape in prospect–refuge terms wherever they may be found: in the garden, the deer forest, the
art gallery, the library and so on. It is an essential part of our philosophy that a
common experience of landscape may be communicated in many different ways
and through many different media. The distinction between these various media
cannot therefore be in itself an important criterion of the symbolism of prospect
and refuge.

Nevertheless, subject to this necessary qualification, it is advisable to look at
these several media as vehicles for the experience of landscape. They do each have
certain characteristics proper to themselves. Some are better suited than others
for expressing different kinds of symbolism or for expressing the same symbolism
in different ways or with different emphasis, and if we are to turn to various
media for the evidence with which to support our hypotheses, we should at least
be aware of their several potentialities and limitations.

### Prospect and Refuge in Contrived Landscape

Of all the arts, landscape gardening, landscape architecture or landscape
design are those which come closest to the reality of natural landscape experience. Here we are concerned with the contrivance of actual landscape objects
and the arrangement of real trees and bushes on a real land surface in three-
dimensional space.

'Aesthetically contrived landscape' may be said to include all landscape which
has been altered or devised for the *principal* purpose of giving aesthetic pleasure.
Following a very loose definition we can employ the words 'garden' and 'park'
to a continuum in which size, scale of design, etc., are the criteria whereby we
decide which term is the more applicable.

The more limited extent of the garden as compared with the park inevitably
has implications for the balance of symbolism of prospect and refuge, as can be
seen throughout the whole history of the garden. Medieval gardens were of two
main kinds. The herb garden was concerned with the growing of plants for food.

The place set aside for recreation was known as the 'orchard' (the sense has changed considerably) or 'pleasaunce' (Crisp, 1924, Ch. III), and it is with the latter that we are principally concerned. Its whole character was that of a refuge, a kind of extension of the house or castle into the open air.

The most potent refuge symbol associated with the garden is the garden wall, but the sensation of refuge is often intensified by the careful placing of shrubs, bushes and trees and by the optional furniture introduced to provide shelter either from the elements or from the eye. Loudon distinguishes alcoves and arbours as places of shelter, the former being open to the sun for winter use, the latter being '. . . shaded with fruit-trees, as the vine, currant, cherry; climbing ornamental shrubs, as ivy, clematis, etc.' He also lists 'roofed seats, boat-houses, moss-houses, flint houses, bark huts and similar constructions . . . forming resting-places containing seats, and sometimes other furniture or conveniences in or near them' (Loudon, 1859 edn., p. 639).

At an early stage, however, we find various devices employed to counteract the sense of enclosure and to balance the refuge element with that of the prospect. Of these devices the most effective was the 'mount'. According to Crisp this feature of the medieval garden was copied from Roman gardens; it is found in the gardens of the Louvre as early as the time of Charles V (1350–1364), '. . . where there were four pavilions raised on artificial mounds of earth, giving a view over the walls of the garden' (Crisp, 1924, p. 84). It was a popular feature of Tudor gardens. The mount at Hampton Court, built in 1533, is described by Hadfield:

> 'Upon a foundation of over a quarter million bricks soil was piled, and planted with hawthorns. On the summit stood a many-windowed, three-storeyed building, roofed with a lead cupola surmounted by a vane in the form of an heraldic lion. This "lantern arbour" was reached by a pathway spiralling up like "the turnings of cockle shells", bordered by heraldic beasts carved in stone' (Hadfield, 1969, pp. 40–41).

The purpose of the mount was to provide a prospect without sacrificing the sanctuary of the garden. Hadfield continues:

> 'It took various forms, but in principle seems always to have consisted of some kind of seat or arbour raised on a pile of earth above the general level of the garden to a "pretty height", so that, having spiralled up, one might "look abroad into the fields" and over one's domain. The mount was planted with clipped shrubs, or perhaps low box hedges bordered the ascending path' (Hadfield, 1969, p. 41).

The mount was gradually superseded by the tower (a more efficient structure for providing a view out of the garden refuge), though it seems to have survived late enough to appear in Bridgeman's plan for Eastbury, Dorset (1716–20) (Hussey, 1967, p. 38) and even later in Pope's garden at Twickenham (Hussey 1967, pp. 41–42). 'The prospect-tower', says Loudon, 'is a noble object to look at, and a gratifying and instructive position to look from. [Note the distinction between a secondary and a primary vantage-point: Table 1.] It should be placed on the highest grounds of a residence, in order to command as wide a prospect as possible' (Loúdon, 1859 edn., p. 639). Among other devices for facilitating the view were the gazebo, a small building whose function was to provide a sheltered viewpoint, and the clairevoie, a gate-like structure of wrought iron 'piercing the walls at the end of walks' (Hussey, 1967, p. 18).

The extension of the prospect into the countryside beyond the refuge of the garden led logically to the modification of the wider landscape also for aesthetic purposes, initially by extending avenues beyond the limits of the enclosure (Hussey, 1967, p. 23). The technique of 'improving' parks was necessarily different from those most appropriate to the more restricted garden, but the balance of prospect and refuge was no less fundamental to landscaping on the larger scale. The opportunities for restoring the link with the Virgilian concept of an idealized if primitive human habitat were, if anything, greater in the more expansive park. 'Ancient authors afforded evidence, which Renaissance archaeology confirmed, for the existence in antiquity of both broad types of garden: the functional enclosure adjoining a man's home, and the sacred landscape of grove, rock and fountain associated with his survival and the supernatural' (Hussey, 1967, p. 14).

Because it was planned on a larger scale the park generally afforded greater opportunities than the more restricted garden for accentuating the prospect symbolism. Indeed the term 'prospect' permeates the literature of eighteenth-century landscape gardening. Just how the symbolism of prospect and refuge is employed in the park is a question to which we shall return in the next chapter. Here it must suffice to note that the principles of landscape design must not be assumed to be identical with those of landscape composition in painting. Practically all writers on landscape gardening make the point that while they can, and should, learn from the painters, they must exploit their freedom from those limitations to which the painters are subject. Most particularly they should take advantage of the opportunity, denied to the painter, for changing the vantage-point from which the composition may be viewed.

### Prospect and Refuge in Architecture and Urban Design

> 'Architecture is building which offers a comfortable—or otherwise stimulating—climate in physical, social, cultural and aesthetic terms.'
>
> GEOFFREY BROADBENT (1973, p. 387)

Since we have been concerned in the previous chapter with stressing the nostalgic attraction of a 'natural' environment for man, a species which is in process of so changing that environment as to impair its capacity for arousing inborn, behavioural responses, it may be thought at first that architecture must be an art hostile to the achievement of aesthetic satisfaction in prospect–refuge terms. Yet experience tells us that this is manifestly not the case. Whether my picture-image of a symbolic transition through the streets of Paris (p. 174) is sense or nonsense

—and there are many architects who would dispute the suggestion that architectural forms derive from, or even reflect, natural objects—two propositions emerge which would probably command general if not universal agreement. The first we have already considered. It is that the process of emancipation from nature, though regrettably involving the impoverishment and perhaps even the destruction of the 'natural' symbolism of the human habitat, is not in itself unwelcome. Indeed the normal concept of a refuge for modern man is very likely to take the form of a building. And since man is by nature gregarious, even the agglomeration of buildings in urban forms is not fundamentally at variance with the behaviour characteristic of his species.

'Towered cities please us then,
And the busy hum of men . . .'
(Milton, *L'Allegro*, lines 117–118)

The second proposition is that these replacements of the natural environment are also capable of arousing aesthetic pleasure or of communicating a sense of dissatisfaction, unease or even powerful dislike. The question is, then, can we also assess the aesthetic values of architectural forms within the framework of prospect–refuge theory? If a natural environment can afford or deny the basic needs for survival, the designer of an artificial environment must at least take account of what these basic needs are, as Broadbent has clearly shown (Broadbent, 1973; especially Ch. 8). If, furthermore, there are grounds for believing that conditions favourable for securing at least some of these basic needs are first apprehended in terms of seeing without being seen, then there must be at least a *prima facie* case for thinking that prospect–refuge theory is not irrelevant to the analysis and criticism of architecture as an important component of landscape.

It is not as if there were any alternative, universally accepted basis for the interpretation of the aesthetics of man-made environments. Perhaps this is a field in which the concepts of 'order', 'symmetry', 'proportion' and so on provide us with all that is necessary for an understanding of the basis on which to distinguish between the beautiful and the ugly. Yet, if this were so, we should expect the regularity of a planned settlement to be aesthetically more satisfying than the irregularity of one which has simply grown, and we know very well that this is not necessarily the case. Neither do the aesthetic properties of urban environments depend on the size of a town nor of its compositional parts. Both these points are made in the following passage.

'When one considers the "splendid" places of the world, one realizes how many (including the Place de la Concorde and the Place de l'Opéra in Paris) give a marvellous explosion of pleasure. They seem to show that architectural planning may be at its best where overblown to the point of wickedness.

'In towns, small unplanned places that have just grown may be the most enchanting. These may seem to contradict my previous examples:

the narrow winding streets of any Provençal village or Italian hill-town; the rich alleys and byways of Venice. Venice, a gorgeous town which no sensible planner would ever have designed, contradicts all definitions, but remains the most successful city in the world from an aesthetic, as well as a spiritual point of view. Venice the labyrinth is a dream city made visible in daylight' (Cunliffe, 1969, pp. 162–163).

If we accept in a general way the same values as Mitzi Cunliffe (though I am not sure what distinguishes an aesthetic from a spiritual point of view), we are faced in this passage with a number of contrasts, planned versus unplanned, regular versus irregular, large-scale versus small-scale, yet none of these affords any help at all in differentiating between beautiful and ugly. If we seek in its geometrical properties an explanation of what makes Venice beautiful we may well decide that it contradicts all definitions. But if we see it as creating in urban forms areas conducive to seeing and shapes conducive to concealing, far from contradicting all definitions, it proclaims itself to be richly endowed with prospect–refuge symbols of a kind which, in slightly different forms, are already familiar to us. The rich alleys and byways provide us with vistas which every now and then widen into little closed panoramas every time we come to a *campo* or open square—panoramas, furthermore, whose boundaries are pierced by innumerable further escape holes, like woodland paths leading between glades, each of which, as soon as we enter it, becomes yet another vista leading on to the next opening. This experience of moving through successive alleys and open spaces is described a little later in the same article.

'The most exciting vista I can cite is the view . . . of the Roman rock-cut temple at the end of a crevice at Petra. With a similar explosive sense of revelation, one is suddenly in an open square after emerging from a network of alleys in Rome' (Cunliffe, 1969, p. 165).

Here we are back with Konrad Lorenz in the Vienna Woods, pausing before we '. . . break through the last bushes and out of cover on to the free expanse of the meadow' to gain 'the advantage which it can offer alike to hunter and hunted—namely, to see without being seen' (p. 58). In Venice, Petra or Rome or, for that matter, in Soho or any well-designed pedestrian shopping precinct, it is the narrow streets which arouse the expectation of this 'explosive sense of revelation', affording the observer the security of lateral cover until the moment when he is ready to concede the refuge as the price of achieving a wider prospect. An even more dramatic refinement of this sensation can be experienced as one emerges from the tube of a spiral staircase at the top of a cathedral tower.

This alternation of experience, this setting-off of the prospect against the refuge to produce a balanced strategic environment, is a very well attested phenomenon in built-up areas as well as in the country. Thomas Sharp expresses it exactly.

'For people in towns, where views are close-focussed, restricted and canalised, an open view in a park or along a river can afford great pleasure. In the country the position is reversed. There, where views are wide-reaching and rarely closely directed, a limitation of the view may offer a kind of psychological refuge and a visual satisfaction by way of contrast. That is the pleasure of the walled garden. The enclosure should not, of course, be such as to produce a sensation of being shut in, of being imprisoned. That would be going to the other extreme. And almost always some of the windows of a house in a village should face out into the open country . . . But from inside the enclosed village the surrounding framework of buildings, confining the view and subtly conveying a sense of refuge, can give a great (though not perhaps very easily definable) visual pleasure and psychological satisfaction' (Sharp, 1946, p. 65).

It will be noted that in this passage Sharp is writing entirely within the symbolic framework of prospect–refuge theory. He is aware that the 'great pleasure' and 'psychological satisfaction' proceed from the 'open view', the 'enclosure' and the contrast between them. But why is the ensuing visual pleasure 'not perhaps very easily definable'? Can it be because, although Sharp recognizes the phenomena of prospect and refuge, he is not able to find any general principle by which he can relate them to an ulterior biological explanation? Once we accept the premises of prospect–refuge theory as a part of the wider habitat theory, then the great visual pleasure becomes very easily definable indeed. It is simply the consequence of the observer finding himself in a situation in which an imbalance in the symbols which proclaim opportunities for seeing and not being seen is rectified and a more favourable strategic environment is (symbolically) restored. Both 'visual pleasure' and 'psychological satisfaction' are precisely what one would expect from the attainment of a condition more conducive to biological survival, even though it is expressed through a symbolism which employs bricks and mortar rather than rocks and trees and even though biological survival may not be a real issue in the village street.

On a smaller scale Gordon Cullen comes to the very heart of the prospect–refuge complement in what he has to say about the enclave as an architectural feature.

'The enclave or interior open to the exterior and having free and direct access from one to the other is seen here as an accessible place or room out of the main directional stream, an eddy in which footsteps echo and the light is lessened in intensity. Set apart from the hurly-burly of traffic, it has yet the advantage of commanding the scene from a position of safety and strength.' (Cullen, 1961, p. 25)

It is interesting to test the imagery and symbolism of prospect–refuge theory against one's own experience of particular towns and villages and the emotive response they provoke. Let us take two examples. It is probably safe to say that most people would regard the street in Kersey (Figure 29) as more attractive than the alley in Merthyr Tydfil (Figure 30). The question is why? Any architect

198

FIGURE 29. KERSEY, SUFFOLK

Reproduced by permission of B. T. Batsford, Ltd., from a photograph by Herbert Felton

FIGURE 30. NANT-Y-GWENYTH STREET, MERTHYR TYDFIL, GLAMORGAN
Originally published as Figure 101 in Ewart Johns, *British Townscapes* (1965) and
reproduced by permission of Ewart Johns and Edward Arnold

or town planner could give you reasons in terms of his own technology, but how
are the two views to be compared in terms of prospect and refuge?

To begin with, one notes that they are both vistas terminating in deflections,
but it is difficult to find much common ground beyond that. In Kersey the main
vista is slightly deflected to the right. The prospect imagery is strengthened in
several ways. First there is falling ground, which is not only prospect-conducive
in itself, but also has the effect in this case of expanding the view of the opposite
hillside and widening the prospect from a restricted vista into at least a suggestion
of a panorama. Although the horizon is not very distant or distinguished by any
dramatic feature, it gives a sense of contact with what lies beyond, and it introduces the symbolism of a natural environment in the woodland. The arboreal
horizon is broken at the extreme left to create a tiny opening (cut off by the

chimney), which in turn suggests a further extension of the view over the hill. Other features of the prospect symbolism include strong suggestions of offsets on both sides (but particularly on the left, where patches of sunlight on the road proclaim the presence of openings between the buildings), the stark roof-lines in the left foreground, backed by bright sky, and the numerous bright architectural surfaces illuminated by direct sunlight.

Refuge symbols mainly take the form of buildings on both sides of the street, and it will be noted that there are many features which suggest penetrability. These include the inferred gaps already mentioned, the irregularity of the building line, the overhang of eaves, gables and upper storeys, the steps which symbolize the means of passage between the vistal street and the flanking doorway refuges and, in the foreground, a little screen of vegetation to provide additional cover in front of the entrances. The whole composition suggests a balanced co-existence between the symbolism of prospect and refuge. This is expressed not only in the facades of the buildings themselves, but also in the patches of light (prospect) and shadow (refuge) mingling in the street and, on the opposite hillside, in that familiar form of prospect–refuge interface, the edge of the wood.

By contrast the alley in Merthyr does not fall away. The vista therefore does not open out above the roof-tops, there is no arboreal vegetation visible at any point, there are no convincing offsets on either side and no bright sunshine, only an indication of recent rain on the shiny stone slabs. The only true refuge symbols are the buildings on the right, but the impression of penetrability is extremely weak. There are no gaps in the building frontage which has no recesses of any magnitude and no projections, no irregularity in the roof-line, no steps or other symbols of invitation. The one window visible is closed. The eaves have a minimal overhang, the upper storeys none. On the left there is a small gate in the foreground, but otherwise an apparently continuous wall, surmounted by a wire mesh fence, presents an impediment hazard affording little concealment but effectively preventing escape. There is no interweaving of sunlight and shadow, only a sense of imprisonment within a wholly artificial environment which in every way negates the proposition that the observer is here experiencing the natural habitat of man, though it is only fair to add that Ewart Johns, from whose book the picture is taken, and who has a more penetrating eye than most of us, defends this row of cottages to the extent of urging that it '. . . does, at least, have an intimate and friendly air, not to be despised in the bleak wet climate of the Welsh Hills' (Johns, 1965, p. 104).

Even in Kersey the aesthetic advantage is achieved with a minimum of devices such as trees, grass or water. Spreading chestnut trees, village greens and duck ponds are all common features of 'calendar' pictures and all fit into the prospect–refuge imagery. Compare the leafy villages of the south of England with those bleak little towns, so common in Scotland and Ireland, where trees are banished from the streets together with many of those other features of 'penetrability' which are so conspicuous in Kersey but absent from the back-alleys of Merthyr Tydfil.

Reverting, then, to the question whether architectural forms do or do not, should or should not, 'represent' natural features such as trees, cliffs or caves, we can now see that we are in a position to side-step this controversial issue. The creation of an artificial environment capable of stimulating an aesthetic response in prospect–refuge terms does not depend on the slavish imitation of natural forms in man-made structures. All that is required is that buildings should be so designed and so positioned as to provide effective symbolic substitutes for those environmental features which, in their natural forms, suggest an opportunity for seeing without being seen. The landscape architects have long recognized this and have discovered in their 'masses' and 'voids' a simple system of identification to which natural and man-made objects may equally be referred. In view of what we have previously seen to be the danger of man eliminating from his visible environment those natural sign-stimuli to which he is attuned by his biological inheritance, it is to be expected that the introduction of trees and other plants will help the observer to accept artificial objects as symbolic substitutes, but it does not by itself guarantee an aesthetic experience. Most people would accept that *part* of the attraction of the buildings of Trent University (Figure 31) lies in the use of foliage, but the positioning of the buildings

FIGURE 31. TRENT UNIVERSITY, PETERBOROUGH, ONTARIO
Note how powerfully the symbolism of prospect and refuge is combined in the buildings and how the prospect is maintained on the nearer side by the River Trent and on the farther side by the carpeted surface of the drumlin with only occasional bushes to provide cover. The trees are pushed back to form the arboreal horizon, creating a nest-like setting. Within this the building can exploit these advantages of both prospect and refuge for which their design seems to fit them so admirably. Photograph by the author

202

within the environment, the suggestion of numerous indirect prospects ('secondary vantage-points') and the provision of *penetrable* refuges are no less important in arousing a sense of pleasure in the contemplation of this architectural composition.

The applicability of the symbolism of prospect–refuge theory to the interpretation of architectural forms can be exemplified in the medieval cathedral. Parallel rows of pillars, leading the eye to a vanishing point, invoke the prospect imagery of the vista. Reduplication may be provided by the apparently converging lines of aisles, clerestory windows, bosses in the roof-vaulting, etc. In England, as compared with France, unbroken string courses above the arcades commonly add to the effect. At the 'crossing' the openings into the transepts at either side provide a striking example of the 'offset'. By contrast the cloister employs a vistal theme only along its margins. The central open square, like the secular courtyard and the college quadrangle, affords a closed panorama.

## Prospect and Refuge in Painting

'Poet and artist alike have . . . to interpret nature's appeal to the imagination, and to utter her response to human feeling. The special office of the artist is to render this interpretation, by means of lines and tints, a language addressed to the eye . . .'

JOSIAH GILBERT (1885, p. 4)

The *Oxford English Dictionary* tells us that the word 'landscape' or 'landskip' was '. . . introduced as a technical term of painters'. The process by which landscape was first employed as a background to the representation of actions and events, often, though not always, of a religious kind, and only later became regarded as a proper subject for painting in its own right, is explained very clearly in Kenneth Clark's *Landscape into Art*. Here we are concerned not so much with the historical evolution of landscape painting as with its distinctive capacities and limitations, compared with the other arts, in representing the kind of symbolism which we have been discussing.

The painter enjoys two great advantages over the architect or landscape architect in his freedom to 'create' landscape. First he is far less limited by the laws of nature and the configuration of a given site. He may, for instance, accentuate his prospect imagery at will by elevating mountains, by ensuring, if he wishes, a perpetually clear atmosphere, and by selecting the most favourable viewpoint at which to set up his easel. He may indeed take almost any liberties he chooses in representing the scenery as he wishes it to be seen. Thus Emerson says:

'In landscapes the painter should give the suggestion of a fairer creation than we know' (Emerson, 'Essay on Art', in *The Complete Works*, Century Edn., 1903, vol. II, p. 351).

while Barbier says of Gilpin's later landscape sketches of the Lake District:

'In these drawings, where the last concession to topographical accuracy has been discarded, Gilpin was able at long last to find a formula which enabled him to express what the Lake District meant and had always meant to him' (Barbier, 1963, p. 108).

Secondly, the painter is not restricted to the same extent as the architect by considerations of finance. It is true that his work may be influenced by the availability of time, and there is a sense in which 'time is money', and by limitations placed on him by his patron, but if he wishes, let us say, to obliterate refuge symbols as represented by trees in a valley, he may, at no expense, remove them, and if he wishes to go even further he may flood the valley with ornamental water, achieving with a few strokes of the brush an exaggeration of the prospect symbolism which the landscape architect could achieve only if his client were willing to pay handsomely for it.

As against this the painter has one great disadvantage. Having chosen his viewpoint he must express everything he wishes to communicate about his landscape as if it were observed from a single point. He can, as we have seen, add to, or subtract from, what is actually visible from that point. He can move his easel, so that, having painted one object from one viewpoint, he may add something else not visible from the first viewpoint. But once he has introduced an opaque object into his composition he renders everything which lies behind it permanently invisible. This may present the painter with particular problems in the representation of refuge symbolism. Generally speaking, the reduplication of *prospect* symbols is not impeded by this limitation. If the painter purposes to place a tower on a hill he may accentuate the prospect value of the hill by increasing its elevation, clearing it of vegetation, playing on to it the most appropriate light for emphasizing visibility and using any device to sharpen and exaggerate the line of the horizon. None of these measures will interfere with the addition of his tower. If anything they will render it, too, more conspicuous and thereby make the reduplication more effective. But if he seeks to reduplicate his *refuge* symbolism he will inevitably find that one symbol tends to conceal another. Obviously he may go a long way in this direction. The device of 'partial concealment' was an important element in the landscape of the Picturesque and, as we have seen, the 'cottage-in-the-wood' is a constantly recurring theme in painting; but if each succeeding object partially obscures the one behind it, there is a limit to the possibilities of building up successive refuge symbols in the synoptic view of a landscape which is implicit in painting.

What we are saying, in other words, is that the painter is by the very nature of his art denied those advantages of 'serial vision' which make such an important contribution to the architect's technique (Cullen, 1961, pp. 17–21). This limitation restricts his freedom to exploit the gradually revealed prospect. The exciting aesthetic experience described by Mitzi Cunliffe (p. 196) is not available to him. He may arouse the expectation of such a revelation, this is what the 'deflected vista' is all about, but he can never realize that expectation except by painting another picture. The medieval painters sometimes sought to achieve a kind of serial vision by painting successive events, for instance in the life of Christ, inserting them as separate episodes within the same landscape. As a representation of a story the painting becomes a serial; as a landscape it does not.

These limitations, therefore, invite comparison between the techniques of the painter and those of creative artists who depict landscape through other media. But because these limitations may affect the balance and the representation of symbolism, it follows that the critical analysis of a painting (Figure 32) can easily fail to bring out its significance in prospect–refuge terms unless it concerns itself specifically with those relationships in which such concepts find expression. We have already noted the inadequacy for our purposes of a critical analysis which relies too heavily on a two-dimensional geometry. Such an analysis (Figure 33a) may actually impede an assessment in prospect–refuge terms by drawing attention away from those three-dimensional relationships (Figure 33b) which are essential to an understanding of landscape as a strategic theatre for biological survival.

Of course, it would be absurd to suggest that this element of three-dimensional analysis is absent in the criticism of landscape painting. What could be more expressive of three-dimensional space than the phrase, 'to . . . walk in the landscape and count the miles', which Richard Wilson applied to the paintings of Claude? (Kitson, 1964, p. 74). Of the same paintings Kitson says:

'Here was . . . a world designed for the imagination to enter and wander about in. This was achieved by means of an open foreground, like a stage, by framing trees on one side balanced by an answering motive on the other, and a circuitous path taking the eye by easy and varied stages to a luminous distance. This distance is the goal of the imaginary traveller in Claude's landscapes and is the point on which the whole composition depends.' (Kitson, 1969, p. 7)

Meanwhile Hendy says, in a commentary on Rubens' *Castle of Steen* (No. 66 in the National Gallery):

'The great landscape is something more than a single view of a natural scene, and yet one must feel able to set foot in it and travel to the horizon confident of firm ground.' (Hendy, 1971 edn., p. 196)

This kind of terminology obviously implies a strategic view of the landscape, with the observer participating in an experience of real three-dimensional spatial relationships. It is one thing, however, to make a general recognition of the strategic role of the observer; it is another to devise a system of critical analysis which can be used to describe a picture in prospect–refuge terms. Let us therefore attempt such a description, using one of Claude's seaport paintings as an example (Figure 34).

As in most of Claude's seaports the prospect is essentially a vista. The vistal axis is strongly reinforced by the low sun and its line of reflection. Other prospect imagery is found in the brightness of the lower sky, the long fetch and the

205

FIGURE 32. SALVATOR ROSA (1615–1673): RIVER LANDSCAPE WITH APOLLO AND THE CUMAEAN SIBYL. For analytical diagrams see Figure 33. Reproduced by permission of the Trustees of the Wallace Collection, London (No. 116)

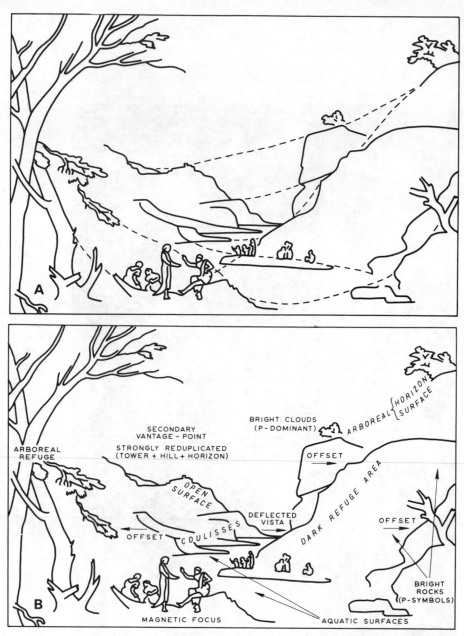

FIGURE 33. ANALYTICAL DIAGRAMS OF *RIVER LANDSCAPE WITH APOLLO AND THE CUMAEAN SIBYL* BY SALVATOR ROSA (FIGURE 32)

A. A geometrical analysis with two-dimensional emphasis (cf. Figure 3), indicating how the eye may be led to important 'magnets' by the linking of lines in the composition irrespective of their distance from the observer

B. An environmental analysis giving a three-dimensional emphasis of the setting of the figures within a landscape conceived in terms of the imagery and symbolism of prospect and refuge

Neither analysis is 'right' or 'wrong'. Each method has a different contribution to make to the understanding of the composition. Drawn by Keith R. Scurr

FIGURE 34. CLAUDE LORRAIN (1600–1682): SEAPORT
A vista flanked by *coulisses* in masonry (left) and timber (right)
Reproduced by permission of the Duke of Northumberland

aquatic horizon, all attracting the eye in the same direction. The high architectural horizons (left) introduce a number of contrasting forms in which prospect and refuge are closely intermixed. Penetrability is suggested by the steps, portico and balcony of the nearest building. At the same time the prospect values increase with elevation and culminate in the pediment horizon. In the second building the open arches of the towers invite access, and therefore refuge, in what are still strong prospect symbols with their balustrades silhouetted against the sky. Beyond, the slender tower and the vertical face, which concludes the group, balance the more squat tower on the right of the vista. On this side also there is a composite imagery. The refuge element, symbolized in the ships' hulls, becomes increasingly prospect-dominant as the eye rises with the masts to the 'crow's nests' and the crowning flags.

Among the other refuge symbols may be noted the tiny patch of foliage (extreme left), the various small boats and the groups of people in the foreground, whose darker colours break up the exposure of the shore. The clouds, which are unusually dark for Claude, begin to suggest the protective covering of the symbolic cave mouth, though they are not free from the symbolism of the hazard. Kitson points out that in the top right-hand corner it appears to be raining, adding that this is unique in the work of this artist (Kitson, 1969, p. 17). Even so it is a very feeble shower! Perhaps the most interesting feature of the composition, however, is to be found in the *coulisses*, created here, not by foliage, as is so common in Claude, but exclusively by buildings and ships.

A similar analytical approach could be applied to the study of paintings of any other school. I have chosen *Village Dancers* (Figure 35) by David Teniers the Younger (1610–1690) because it embodies so many features which we have already encountered and portrays them in such an obvious way; I am not arguing that it is typical of Flemish paintings generally in the richness of its prospect and refuge symbolism. It is a special kind of 'edge-of-the-wood' composition in which there is a general imbalance between a refuge-dominant right and a more open, prospect-dominant left, though it does illustrate the way in which numerous symbolisms of each kind can intrude into that part of the composition which is dominated by the other. The formal gardens (right) rely heavily on vistal prospect symbols consistent with the le Nôtre pattern (p. 32). There is a good example of reduplication of prospect symbols in the avenue (right centre) in which the path, trees, grass, etc., combine to create a strong vistal line. The moated castle in the centre stands within a walled enclosure and from this position of refuge introduces through its composite symbolism the theme of 'prospect', thereby proclaiming the change in emphasis between the symbolism of the two principal parts of the composition as one moves from right to left. From this point onwards the picture is dominated by a broad panorama, in which a number of familiar symbols combine to emphasize the idea of prospect. The falling ground is here given the scope which the refuge symbols deny it in the other half of the picture. The horizon, only partly arboreal, is broken by no less than three spires and a windmill and the whole is crowned by an expanse of open sky. Many other features, for instance the shallow hollow which provides

Figure 35. D. Teniers the Younger (1610–1690): Village Dancers
Reproduced by courtesy of the Trustees, The National Gallery, London (No. 5866)

a refuge for the dancers, will be found to furnish examples of the symbolism of prospect and refuge.

Since innovation invariably invites misrepresentation I must again emphasize that I am not advocating the abandonment of established techniques of criticism, analysis or description and their replacement by an entirely new system. I merely propose that the accepted approach be supplemented by another which lays stress on the observation of a landscape *as environment*, using a terminology which allows us to relate that observation to other experiences of environment as apprehended in other landscapes and through different media.

## Prospect and Refuge Through the Lens

'In making a photograph you take a piece of reality and cut it away from its ordinary surroundings by confining it within a frame . . .'

S. W. BOWLER (1956, p. 142)

The principles which govern the representation of landscape in painting are broadly applicable to photography also, and therefore I propose to leave the reader to explore their implications in this field for himself. He could well do worse than thumb through any pictorial calendar featuring landscapes which, from their inclusion in such a publication, are likely to be generally regarded as attractive. Reference may also be made to textbooks on the techniques of photography from an artistic point of view. I should be surprised if examples illustrative of prospect–refuge symbolism did not quickly come to light. There may well be important artistic differences between the techniques of good composition in photography and in painting, but they are, I suggest, merely differences in the application of common fundamental principles which underlie both arts as they underlie all experience of landscape.

This is not to say, of course, that there are not important *practical* differences. The photographer does not enjoy the same opportunity as the painter to move his viewpoint in the course of producing a single picture; much less can he, like Gilpin, discard '. . . the last concession to topographical accuracy' (p. 203). In manipulating his composition he is even more rigidly limited than the landscape designer, who may inject a liberal infusion of his own imagination. The photographer of landscape can do little more to determine the balance of his picture than select his vantage-point with care and wait for the most favourable conditions of light and perhaps even of season.

It could well be argued, however, that a more important difference than that which separates the photograph from the painting is that which distinguishes between the 'still' and the motion picture. The latter shares with landscape design, architecture and literature the advantage of being able to use 'serial vision'. It is not bound by the limitation of the single viewpoint, and any cinemagoer or television viewer will easily call to mind occasions on which the cameraman has cleverly employed a change of position, gradually unfolding a panorama or closing up a refuge by the exploitation of parallax.

One need look no further afield for evidence than the 'Western', and surely any house with a television set is daily invaded by the cowboy culture. Here, within a very limited range of constantly recurring landscape types, some of the most powerful symbolism is to be found. Wide-ranging panoramas with horizons reinforced by hills and mountains often of tower-like shape (for instance the *buttes* of Monument Valley) alternate with the vistas of forest paths and rocky ravines. Refuges of tree trunks and broken rock are pressed into service as soon as the shooting begins. The mood of exposure is built up by the furious chases across open ground, by the silhouetting of horsemen on horizons and by the distant magic of 'them thar hills'. The complement, refuge, is set in the woods, the stockades, the log-cabin homesteads and, not infrequently, the cave itself.

In the screen versions of great romances and historical novels directors usually go to great lengths to ensure suitable landscape backgrounds either in the studio or on location. Again it must be left to the reader, the next time he goes to the cinema, to make his own observations. Some directors have a clearly expressed predilection for certain types of landscape. Miklós Jancsó's *Agnus Dei* and *Red Psalm*, for instance, both exploit the imagery of the Great Hungarian Plain (Melly, 1973): one of the most extreme examples of a prospect-dominant landscape to be found in Europe.

Even the most imaginative director, however, is to some extent limited in his choice of location by the actual character of real places. In the cartoon his imagination is allowed much more freedom. Walt Disney's *Fantasia* (1940) will serve to illustrate how, even when released from the limitations of real places, with only the musical stimuli to guide him, the creative film artist is still circumscribed by an inescapable framework of symbolism.

Consider, for instance, Disney's handling of Beethoven's Pastoral Symphony. From this unrestricted workshop of landscape composition there emerges a veritable gallery of pictorial representations of prospects and refuges. The imagery employed to accompany Beethoven's thunderstorm, when the centaurs, cupids and baby Bucephalids seek shelter from the hazards of Jove's thunderbolts in trees and bushes and under the cornices of temple roofs, embraces clouds and the more tangible landscape furniture as if they were more or less interchangeable. At length Jupiter, tired of the pyrotechnics, settles down in a puff of cumulus cloud, drawing as much of it over him as is necessary to blanket him from mortal view. This is the moment of transition to the final movement, and as the wood-winds of the bridge passage introduce a theme of musical serenity, so the thunderclouds roll away giving place, first, to bright intervals, then to a cloudless sky. The imagery of the prospect is now taken over by the sun itself, at first blindingly bright but gradually reduced to a level of light intensity in which it can be incorporated in the landscape. We begin to distinguish within its brilliance, like a watermark in a banknote, the sun god driving his team and chariot across the blazing heaven. The centaurs canter gently up the dipslope of an idyllic *cuesta* whose crisp horizon all but depicts the precipice on its further side. From this exalted vantage-point they stand and watch the deity renounce his incandescent power and assume the softened tones of a sentimental sunset.

The nursery-cum-fairy-tale mythology of Disney's interpretation of the Pastoral Symphony may delight, infuriate or merely bore, but if one had commissioned him to produce an illustrated companion to a treatise on prospect–refuge theory he could hardly have improved on *Fantasia*. I recently saw this film for the third or fourth time, and as I watched the black mantle of night drawn (literally) across the sky, narrowing what was left of its brightness to a sky dado and eventually eliminating it altogether, and saw the moon-goddess take her place of vigil over the sleeping landscape, I wondered how long it would be before I should see a more extreme demonstration of that symbolism which, we have inferred, imagination has derived and convention established from the primitive urge to see without being seen.

In fact the answer came in half an hour, or however long it takes to reach the concluding bars of Schubert's *Ave Maria*. After a spectacular 'inversion' scene, with a procession of lanterns creeping through the woods, there appears on the dark screen a narrow vertical slit of light. Gradually it widens, first into a forest vista and then into a panorama, revealing through the tree-top foliage, which gradually melts from the screen, a stark horizon of gently rolling hills silhouetted against a brightening sky. Above this floats a layer of fracto-stratus cloud, touched on the underside with a creamy glow, which creates the impression of yet another sky dado and emphasizes the presence of a hitherto unseen source of light far, far away. As the sun rises behind the skyline, throwing up radiant beams towards the ceiling of patchy clouds, a perfect balance is momentarily reached between the prospect of illuminating but disturbing solar energy and the refuge offered by the protective cover of the intervening hills. At the moment when the ascendant sun is about to burst over the horizon and strike savagely on the unshielded retina the picture fades and *Fantasia* comes to an end.

## Prospect and Refuge in Literature

> 'Of all those arts in which the wise excel,
> Nature's chief masterpiece is writing well.'
> JOHN SHEFFIELD, DUKE OF BUCKINGHAMSHIRE (*Essay on Poetry*, lines 1–2;
> Johnson and Chalmers, 1810, vol. X, p. 91)

We have already had occasion to turn to both poetry and prose for illustrations of the applicability of prospect–refuge theory to different kinds of landscape experience. Here a brief reference to some of the distinctive potentialities of the written word, as compared with those of other media, must suffice.

Verbal landscape description enjoys certain advantages shared by other media. In common with architecture, landscape design and the motion picture it is able to use the device (denied to the painter), of 'serial vision', inasmuch as the description of symbols can be successively employed whether or not they can all be seen from a single vantage-point. Reference back to several examples will quickly confirm this. We find it, for instance, in the passages from Wordsworth, Spenser and *The Flower and the Leaf* (see Ch. 5), quoted to illustrate the balance of symbolism in refuge-dominant landscapes. In each of these cases the author is able to add further refuge symbols without obscuring those which lie behind them, thereby circumventing the problem which so often confronts the painter (p. 203).

The purveyor of words, as opposed to those artists who work in more tangible media, is also given a particular advantage in achieving the device of reduplication, because most words can be so manipulated that they reinforce each other by drawing on vaguely defined but nevertheless powerful associations. It is an important part of the poet's craft to be able to exploit these associations in such a way that the potency of his phrases is greater than the sum of their component parts. Even a single word like 'refuge' conveys the idea of an implied relationship with the concept of 'hazard', and just as those artists working in other media must understand the potential of their material, so it is up to the writer in verse or in prose, who wishes to build his prospects and his refuges and to regulate the balance between them, to comprehend first of all the opportunities which the language affords and the limitations which it imposes on his techniques.

Among these limitations perhaps the most important is the more indirect relationship, in comparison with the visual arts, which his medium establishes between the observer and the environment. The workmanship of the architect, the landscape gardener, the painter, the photographer or the designer of stage scenery, is apprehended, like the natural environment, directly by the sense of sight. The writer has to translate this direct experience into a language code, from which the reader or listener must translate it back into a spatial experience. This limitation is not without its compensations. It is the very process of translation which allows the imagination to play such a powerful role in this particular kind of experience of landscape.

Having reminded ourselves of what Disney can do with his imagination in devising a landscape fantasy for the screen, let us therefore see what a word artist can do. Naturally the mind turns to Tolkien. Part of the secret of Tolkien's landscape description is that he pushes his imagery almost but not quite to the limits of credibility. His landscapes are drawn in terms which we know to be exaggerated but which we can still recognize as belonging to the symbolism of the real world. Just as the advocates of the picturesque relied on the use of highly potent symbols to arouse a more vigorous emotional response, so Tolkien confronts his little characters with environmental hazards recognizably similar to, but more formidable than, those which we have to face in ordinary life. To compensate, he furnishes them with refuges more secluded, safer and cosier than those of the real world, cuts out for them fantastic vistas through the forests, and projects vast panoramas to horizons more remote than any we have ever experienced. A few passages from *The Hobbit* will serve as examples.

Whatever the hazards to be encountered on the way, the adventure sets out from a super refuge, the description of which begins with the first word in the book:

'In a hole in the ground there lived a hobbit. Not a nasty, dirty, wet hole, filled with the ends of worms and an oozy smell, nor yet a dry, bare, sandy hole with nothing in it to sit down on or to eat: it was a hobbit-hole, and that means comfort'. (Tolkien, 1966 edn., p. 1)

Before the end of page one we have been presented with a word picture of the hobbit-hole, not only as a place of concealment and shelter, but as a storehouse of all the necessities for easy biological survival.

'No going upstairs for the hobbit: bedrooms, bathrooms, cellars, pantries (lots of these), wardrobes (he had whole rooms devoted to clothes), kitchens, dining-rooms, all were on the same floor, and indeed on the same passage'. (Tolkien, 1966 edn., p. 1)

Already the term 'hobbit-hole' has acquired a very high refuge value, so that, in later passages, where the symbolism of exposure, of prospect and/or hazard predominates, it can be used as a kind of shorthand reference to introduce the idea of refuge with no more equipment than ten letters and a hyphen.

'Long days after they had climbed out of the valley and left the Last Homely House miles behind, they were still going up and up and up. It was a hard path and a dangerous path, a crooked way and a lonely and a long. Now they could look back over the lands they had left, laid out behind them far below. Far, far away in the West, where things were blue and faint, Bilbo knew there lay his own country of safe and comfortable things, and his little hobbit-hole. He shivered. It was getting bitter cold up here, and the wind came shrill among the rocks'. (Tolkien, 1966 edn., p. 51)

The phrase 'his little hobbit-hole' is the antithesis of all the landscape symbolism of the mountain. It is introduced, not to tone down the imagery of exposure but rather to add to it. It is, after all, 'far, far away'. This technique of charging-up a symbol to a high level of potency has no exact counterpart in the other art forms to which we have referred, except the motion picture. The great advantage of the writer is that, since his landscape pictures have to be coded into words and then decoded by the reader into pictures, there are two opportunities for the enrichment of the landscape by the imagination.

## Common Themes and Intermedia Critisicm

> 'To the edge of the wood I am drawn, I am drawn . . .'
> SIDNEY LANIER (*The Marshes of Glynn*, line 37; Young, 1947, p. 15. See p. 148)

By way of comparing different media as vehicles for communicating the imagery and symbolism of prospect and refuge in landscape, let us briefly look at a common theme which we have already encountered: 'the edge-of-the-wood'. This phenomenon plays a very important role in animal ecology.

'The land manager or forester can take some positive steps to obtain a suitable environment for game species. The even-age philosophy of timber management calls for clear-cutting of areas. This is compatible with wildlife populations for three reasons. First, clear-cut areas provide browse for food and brush for cover. Second, the clear-cut area can provide the open areas that appear to be necessary for some wildlife species. Third, the valuable "edge effect" is created around the perimeter of the clear-cut block. The edge effect is described as the change in size and type of vegetation that takes place along dividing lines between open and timbered areas. Much of the wildlife can be found in this edge effect zone'. (Douglass, 1969, p. 301)

In the arts the 'edge-of-the-wood' is also a zone of special significance. In painting we have examined in some detail how Rubens handles the 'edge-of-the-wood' in his *Landscape with a Rainbow* (p. 165). We have seen also that it is a constantly recurring subject, not only in landscape painting *sensu stricto*, but as a background to portraiture (Figure 27) and the painting of the family group. If further evidence were needed it could be found, for instance, in Ogden and Ogden. In the following passage they are referring to changes in the painting of forest landscapes, particularly by the Dutch, from the middle of the seventeenth century.

'. . . There was a tendency to depict the edge of a forest rather than its interior. This tendency is exemplified in such pictures as Jacob van Ruisdael's "Forest Scene", "Entrance to the Forest", and "Skirts of a Forest", in the National Gallery, his "Edge of a Wood", at Dulwich Gallery, de Vlieger's etching "The Open Forest" . . . and Cornelis Decker's "Dutch Landscape", in the Metropolitan Museum of Art . . . Both of Jan Loten's landscapes "A Forest Scene" . . . and "The Edge of a Wood" . . . have extensive views at one side of each picture, and in each there is some contrast between prospect and forest'. (Ogden and Ogden, 1955, pp. 134–135)

The interface between woodland and open landscape (arboreal and carpeted surfaces in the terminology of our symbolism) is, however, equally important in landscape design, and it is interesting to see this zone of contact posing similar problems to Repton and to the landscape consultant to the Forestry Commission (Figures 36 and 37). It is even more interesting to see how closely their solutions to these problems compare. In both cases these landscape 'improvers' are confronted with uncompromising cases of what we may call 'prospect-*or*-refuge' landscapes, in which the balance is achieved, if at all, by the stark contrast between alternatives rather than by an integration of complementary components.

The solution in both cases lies in toning down the contrast by allowing the prospect-dominant 'voids' to spill over into the refuge-dominant 'masses' and vice versa. The common principle underlying both these problem cases is, I suggest, entirely consistent with the ideas discussed previously (p. 105) in connection with the interface between prospect and refuge, the penetrability of the latter and the device of the *coulisse*. The 'frayed edges' of woodland contrast

216

FIGURE 36. BAYHAM ABBEY, KENT

Drawings by Humphry Repton showing (above) the landscape as it was and (below) the proposed improvements. These drawings from the Red Book appeared in Dorothy Stroud (1962), p. 102, and are reproduced here by permission of Dorothy Stroud and *Country Life* with the stark, linear margins not only in geometrical terms. The 'edge-of-the-wood' need not present a choice between prospect and refuge—prospect outside, refuge inside. Given an appropriate blend of prospect and refuge symbols, it can be a zone of compromise in which the participant can achieve the advantages of good visibility and effective concealment at the same time.

In poetry we have already encountered a dramatic example of the 'edge-of-the-wood' in Lanier's *The Marshes of Glynn* (p. 148). It may be remembered that this poem, as well as using very strong prospect and refuge symbolism, also takes advantage of the device of serial vision, giving great emphasis to the moment of emergence. Compare this short passage from a modern poem:

'I climbed through woods in the hour-before-dawn dark
Evil air, a frost-making stillness,

Not a leaf, not a bird,—
A world cast in frost. I came out above the wood

Where my breath left tortuous statues in the iron light
But the valleys were draining the darkness

Till the moorline—blackening dregs of the brightening grey—
Halved the sky ahead. And I saw the horses . . .'
(From *The Horses*, in Hughes, 1967, p. 15)

Finally, let us look at a short prose passage from a twentieth-century novel. Again there is the serial vision, the experience of a gradual unfolding, achieved here in two stages. First the observer, the participant, emerges from the edge of the wood, just far enough to see the prospect before him. Secondly the prospect itself emerges from the partial concealment in which it is first perceived. Note the successive devices of reduplication, valley-plus-mist and valley-plus-trees, the importance of natural objects, particularly trees, as sign-symbols of a natural environment, and the overwhelming potency of the prospect imagery in the final cadence—falling ground, brightening light and rising towers. Imagine yourself to be standing on this hill as you read the passage slowly, like the awakening of the morning which it so poignantly describes, not forgetting to glance over your shoulder, as Lanier did in the marshes of Glynn, to assure yourself that the edge-of-the-wood is still there and can still afford you refuge.

'The ghostly trees dropped raindrops on his head and the undergrowth drenched him to the skin as he pushed his way through to the bridle path . . . He stumbled across it and came to a field that curved sharply over the brow of a hill. It was dotted over with low gorse bushes that he would have thought were crouching animals but for the faint scent that came from them. Here he felt himself to be high up on the roof of the world, with the quiet shapes of pines and beech trees looming up behind him, and in front of him, circling round the hill on which he stood, a valley filled with mist. Here he stopped to wait for the sunrise . . . The mist that had been as thick as sorrow became tenuous and

FIGURE 37. THE EDGE OF THE WOOD; GRESKINE FOREST, DUMFRIESSHIRE
The sketch below illustrates an improved design by Sylvia Crowe, landscape consultant to the Forestry Commission. The photograph and sketch appeared as Figures 7 and 7A in Sylvia Crowe, *Forestry in the Landscape* (1966) and are reproduced by permission of the Forestry Commission

frail. It had been grey like the rain but now it was opal-tinted. The green of the woods was in it, and the blue of the sky, and there was a hint of rose colour that told of the fires of the earth, of the sun and the warmth of daily living.

'The light grew yet stronger and showed Faithful that his valley was filled with trees and backed by low hills. He followed the curve of it with his eyes until they reached a certain spot to the right that the gypsies had told him of, where they stayed, his heart looking through them as though the eyes of lover saw his mistress.

'Gradually, with the same mysterious slowness with which night had changed to day, towers rose out of the mist, and he looked down from the heights of Shotover upon the city of Oxford' (Goudge, 1938, pp. 8–9).

# CHAPTER 8

# Fashion, Taste and Idiom

'. . . If Taste has no fixed principles, if the imagination is
not affected according to some invariable and certain laws,
our labour is like to be employed to very little purpose . . .'
EDMUND BURKE (Boulton, 1958, p. 12)

'Taste' is a subject which caused a good deal of difficulty in eighteenth-century aesthetics, partly, perhaps, because the word was not always used consistently and it could refer to the preference displayed either by an individual or by a group of individuals. We shall therefore use the terms *individual taste* and *collective taste* to keep these ideas separate. There is, however, a further distinction to be made, because 'taste', individual or collective, was often used to mean 'good taste', and this raised a further question: what was good about it? Did the goodness come from some absolute criterion or did 'good taste' mean simply 'approved taste', that is to say 'fashionable taste'?

This is a very important question in the context of our enquiries. It is a matter of common observation that different people at diverse times and places have shown clearly expressed preferences for all manner of types of landscape. This may seem to indicate that taste in this sense cannot be based on constant behavioural laws; however, prospect–refuge theory asserts that our enjoyment of landscape *is* based on such behavioural laws. We are therefore confronted with something of a paradox which we shall look at more closely in this chapter.

## Contrasting Styles in Landscape Design

There can be few examples of a change of fashion more striking than that which found expression in the landscape gardening of the eighteenth century and this subject would provide a good starting point for our enquiries. The rigid geometrical treatment typical of the work of André le Nôtre (p. 32) seems to be the very antithesis of the flowing irregularities of Kent and Brown, and any interpretation of these contrasting styles in terms of the abstract jargon of the eighteenth-century aestheticians inevitably leads to problems (Hussey, 1967, Ch. III). If one seeks a definition of beauty as 'regularity'. 'symmetry', 'order', 'proportion' or some such concept, it is not easy to understand how the eighteenth century could reject the formalism of the seventeenth and find aesthetic satisfaction in a landscape 'improved' by the substitution of all the opposite qualities. If, on the other hand, it is in these opposite qualities that beauty resides, how could an age which was aesthetically sensitive enough to revive the culture of Greece and Rome have been misled into believing the converse? We have already seen that certain eighteenth-century philosophers rejected the idea that beauty was to be sought in the intrinsic properties of allegedly beautiful objects (see Ch. 2), and it now becomes clear first, what an important step this was and, second, why they were so attracted to the idea of substituting other abstractions, such as 'the Sublime' and 'the Beautiful' which did not imply a monopoly of aesthetic excellence for one particular style. In 'the Picturesque' they developed an even more flexible concept which, in extolling the virtues of variation, found room to include both the Beautiful and the Sublime.

If we now introduce the symbolic framework of prospect–refuge theory, will it fare any better than the Beautiful, the Sublime and the Picturesque? Its expectations should, perhaps, be better, if we have correctly built it up from the observations of the behavioural scientists. If we discover that the great disparity of style represented in the work, of say, le Nôtre and Capability Brown reflects a fundamental difference in their capacity for exploiting the symbolism of hide-and-seek, then we should expect one to emerge as aesthetically successful, the other not. If, on the other hand, all that is involved in both cases is the employment of symbols, however different, to express a satisfying complement of prospect and refuge, then at least our findings should be compatible with our deriving pleasure from the contemplation of two styles which *prima facie* seem to have little in common.

The most striking characteristic of the style of le Nôtre is a prospect imagery which is strongly vistal and based predominantly on the avenue (Figure 5). In an extreme case, even within the plantations, the trees are set out like soldiers on parade, so that vistal effects are produced not only lengthways and crossways but also diagonally, as in an orchard, anticipating that practice for which the anti-conifer brigade reserves its supreme expressions of contempt. The device of reduplication is constantly applied to the symbolism of the prospect. In the great central avenue at Versailles the margins of the plantations line up with the more distant flanks of the lake or 'canal' which for regularity equal any lineal quayage in a modern port. The paths and rows of statues accentuate the effect of a direct visual channel symmetrically disposed about a central axis which is emphasized by the fountain. The admixture of large areas of aquatic and naked surfaces with the carpeted surfaces of the lawns further strengthens the direct prospect symbolism. The indirect prospect symbolism also tends to derive from the vista. Offsets are powerfully suggested where fountains or circular lily ponds punctuate the avenues. Panoramic views, on the other hand, are almost invariably closed (except in the sky); a long 'fetch' is allowed only in the vistas.

The refuge symbolism in a place like Versailles must necessarily rely principally on the large tract of plantation which can be thought of as a matrix of refuge into which the great vistas are cut. The avenue, however, on which the prospect symbolism so heavily depends, inevitably has the effect of weakening the efficiency of the refuge which it penetrates. Originally in fact this was its purpose; Hussey tells us: 'The functional origin of avenues was the ridings cut through forests, particularly around the chateaux in Northern France, in connection with hunting.' (Hussey, 1967, p. 15)

The carving-up of the forest matrix by these avenues leaves regular blocks of trees whose refuge value is further weakened when they are planted in rows, and a good deal of the responsibility for redressing the balance in favour of the refuge is left to the buildings, from the mansion down to the summerhouse or arbour. These buildings are generally placed at some key point in the system of intersecting vistas, so that the refuge symbol can be introduced in such a way as to complement the prospect symbolism most effectively without challenging its supremacy.

Even before the capitulation of the geometrical style in the face of the informality of Kent and Brown, there were other devices for combining prospect and refuge in very different ways. One of these was the 'maze'—a system of miniature vistas constructed out of opaque hedges so thick as inevitably to introduce an element of refuge in the whole design. The idea of hazard was also introduced in the most genteel manner imaginable. Suppose one could never find the way out!

Another device very popular in the seventeenth century was the 'wilderness', a tract of ground deliberately left in an untamed, or at most a semi-tamed condition in contrast to the extreme formalism of the park, from which, however, it was effectively separated. Here an entirely different arrangement of prospect and refuge symbols was possible, in which a strategic advantage could be sought in conditions where the sign-stimuli of the habitat more closely resembled those to be found in nature.

It was the introduction of some measure of this 'naturalistic' element into the park, hitherto subject to such strict geometrical rules, that characterized the work of the eighteenth-century landscape gardeners,[30] but though the new idiom was so radically different from that of the school of la Nôtre, it can be interpreted just as well in terms of the same basic concepts. The prospect symbolism tends to be much more panoramic, the panoramas being generally of the 'interrupted' kind. Where vistal effects are found they usually arise from the bounding of a view by visual obstructions which are not equidistant from the observer on either side. The vistas therefore tend to open or close as one passes. Undoubtedly this is one of the principal reasons why Brown was so devoted to the 'clump' which was the chief agent employed to achieve this effect. Other devices for introducing prospect symbolism were also freely exploited. We find, for instance, the horizontal vista, where the lower leaves of the trees have been grazed, accentuating the panoramic theme by its lateral development. We also find a clever use of the path and carriage drive to introduce token vistas in which the element of deflection is suggested by their curving form. In marked contrast with the vistas of le Nôtre these exercises in weak vistal development rarely employ reduplication (for instance by planting trees along the line of the road).

Le Nôtre and Brown both exploited the potentialities of water as open space, but whereas at Versailles it is the margins of the lake which chiefly catch the eye and play a role subservient to the creation, by reduplication, of an overwhelming vista, the irregular fringes of Brown's ornamental water have no such distracting office to perform. It is true that the water is important as a broad component of the panoramic motif, but it discharges this function less obtrusively. As a prospect symbol it is weaker in the sense of being less dramatic, yet it can be powerful in creating that sense of open space which is of the essence of the prospect.

Finally, in his prospect imagery Brown used his horizons in quite a different way. The tiny horizon between the poplars at Versailles (Figure 5) is one of the most dramatic in Europe, but it is virtually the only 'open' horizon anywhere in the vast design. Its supremacy is achieved in part by the elimination of all rivals. By contrast Brown leads the eye along as well as towards his horizons, introducing some variation between 'open' and arboreal surfaces, a technique which Repton was to develop considerably further. To summarize, Brown tended to spread his prospect imagery much more widely than le Nôtre, who put most of his eggs in the vistal basket.

Brown also had a very different way of handling his refuges. To begin with, his clumps, though often small, were more effective as screens, firstly because they were disposed irregularly within the design, secondly because they were of irregular shape, and thirdly because the individual trees were arranged irregularly within them. The serpentine 'belt' also was a very potent refuge symbol. It sealed off arboreally the prospect created within the park and although, measured statistically, Brown's belts often contained far fewer trees than, say, the great plantations at Versailles, they somehow arouse more of a sensation of enclosure. For one thing they are not intermittently punctured by vistas; for another their margins or 'fronts' tend to lie transverse to, rather than parallel with, the line of sight when viewed from the house or the more important viewpoints in the park.

It seems, then, that behind the outward disparity of these two styles there may lie a common philosophical concept. We have seen that the eighteenth-century philosophers were already expressing misgivings about seeking aesthetic explanations in such properties as order, symmetry, etc., which are basic to the one style and practically foreign to the other but that they were not very successful in postulating an alternative explanation which would accord with the observed facts. The suggestion now is that if we go back to the principles of prospect–refuge theory which underlie both styles, we can indeed find a formula which le Nôtre and Brown were able to interpret, each in his own way, without denying the hypothesis that aesthetic satisfaction in the contemplation of landscape is achieved when the observer is informed symbolically, spontaneously, and without the intervention of a rational process, that his environmental circumstances are favourable to the attainment of his immediate objective—to see without being seen. The style of le Nôtre laid greater emphasis on man's assertion of his emancipation from nature. The style of Brown rather symbolized the nostalgic backward glance at the world of nature from which that emancipation was sought; but it was still a far cry from the primeval environment where the prototypes were to be found from which, we have postulated, the whole system of landscape symbolism had been developed, and it was these prototypes which Uvedale Price and his fellow-thinkers sought to retrieve.

The imagery of 'The Picturesque' is more primitive, more direct, more 'natural', more dramatic and more extreme, but it can still be broken down into basically the same categories of prospect and refuge. In publishing his poem *The Landscape* (p. 35), Richard Payne Knight used a pair of etchings (here reproduced as Figures 38 and 39) made from drawings of the same park to illustrate the basic differences between the style he advocated and that followed by the established fashion of Capability Brown. In the Brown version the house is a smooth-faced Georgian building unencumbered by trees in its immediate precincts. The serpentine river is flanked by a wide expanse of grass into which are set small 'clumps' of trees; rather smaller, perhaps, than would be typical of Brown's practice. An ornate bridge of Chinese design spans the stream and beyond it a second bridge leads to a serpentine drive devoid of any bounding fence and unshaded by trees. To the right of the house the distant view is cut off by a 'belt'.

In the 'picturesque' version the house is of an entirely different architectural design, vastly more ornate and incorporating characteristics which hark back to Tudor and Jacobean styles. The bridge is a simple rustic affair and, although the distant 'belt' is not greatly altered, the isolated 'clumps' have merged together in an arrangement more suggestive of woodland than of parkland. To the arboreal vegetation is now added a component of bush, shrub and fern, and this more varied association has crept forward to encroach closely on the house and here and there on the river.

These two pictures, which bring out so eloquently the differences between the two styles, are well known and have been frequently cited, and sometimes reproduced in the literature on eighteenth-century landscape design (for instance, in Hipple, 1957, following p. 266, and Malins, 1966, as Plate XVIII). But what is the significance of their contrasting styles, in terms of prospect and refuge? The panoramic basis of the 'Brown' design is narrowed in the 'picturesque' version into a more vistal form which allows the refuge symbols to obtrude more effectively and introduces something of a *coulisse* effect. The massing of vegetation in the foreground converts an exposed, unprotected vantage-point into a little haven of seclusion from which the prospect may be observed. The bunching of trees around the house is an example of reduplication which begins to suggest an aristocratic version of the 'cottage-in-the-wood'. The architecture of the house introduces numerous devices for accentuating the penetrability of the building—the bulastrades, the terrace with flanking staircases linking exterior with interior, the three apertures underneath, the main entrance portal less ostentatiously forbidding than the unrelieved blank door of the 'Brown' version, the emphasis given to the idea of 'prospect-from-refuge' by the enlarged windows. It will be noted also that the chimneys have been reshaped. They are more like turrets than smoke-stacks. In short, the whole composition has moved in the direction of a more potent prospect–refuge symbolism.

No doubt there will be those who prefer the Brownian version, who find more satisfaction in the judicious grouping of trees in shaved lawns than in the irregularity, the rugosity, the contrived wilderness of the picturesque. If this is so; if

FIGURES 38 and 39. CONTRASTING STYLES OF GEORGIAN LANDSCAPE DESIGN
Top: A park landscaped in the style of Capability Brown. Bottom: The same park landscaped according to 'picturesque' principles. Both pictures, drawn by T. Hearne and etched by B. T. Pouncy, were published as illustrations to Richard Payne Knight's didactic poem, *The Landscape* (1794)

more, or even equal, aesthetic satisfaction is to be found in the landscape with the weaker prospect–refuge symbolism, does not this destroy the argument that such satisfaction derives from such symbolism? I think not. Any art can be killed by excess, and any individual can set his own range of tolerance, seeking satisfaction within its limits. Fortissimo is not necessarily more beautiful than pianissimo; colours which are more garish are not necessarily more pleasing than pastel shades; overacting is not synonymous with more moving drama; neither does the most adventurous oriental gourmet swallow his curry powder neat, nor the most high-class milliner pack the largest number of hats into his shop-window. Moreover, bearing in mind that the values and devices introduced by the picturesque, if pushed to their logical conclusion, would restore the landscape to that state of nature from which man has striven so hard to emancipate himself, the danger of excess is real enough.

All this suggests that we are dealing with differences which, however striking to the eye, are still contained within a common aesthetic concept and a common symbolic system. They are differences, not of fundamental principles, but of the idiom employed in the expression of those fundamental principles which underlie all experience of landscape. Within the continuum from the wholly natural to the wholly artificial and within the framework of symbolism which we earlier set up, there is ample room for André le Nôtre, for Capability Brown, for Sir Uvedale Price, and indeed for all the other innovators of fashion whom, if we had time, we should find in the nineteenth century and on to the present day. We should discover in England, for instance, that William Robinson applied the principles of prospect and refuge on a more limited scale to the disposition of trees, shrubs and open space not merely as a background to, but as an integral part of, the Victorian flower garden. We should find in Victorian architecture any amount of evidence that the period's preoccupation with aesthetically improving the design of buildings according to its own standards of taste and fashion found expression as much in the exaggeration of the symbols of prospect and refuge as in the revival of archaic styles. Spires and towers, porticos and verandahs: all bear this out. At the same time the Victorian revival of fashion in landscape features which restored, for instance, the avenue, albeit often in coniferous rather than deciduous form, indicates a continuing search for new variations of well-worn themes, all within the confines of a comprehensive symbolic system.

In the present practice of lansdcape design we should again find distinctive idioms rather than new principles. Twentieth-century urban parks, children's playgrounds, motorways, public cemeteries and industrial estates may strike us chiefly by the novelty of their appearance, but in so far as they are landscaped to make them conform to current aesthetic taste, I believe they can be fitted into the framework of prospect–refuge symbolism as logically and convincingly as the parks and pleasure grounds of earlier days.

Turning to the literature of modern landscape design, one finds at least a partial explanation of this. The theoreticians are clearly working within a system of conventions derived from the same basic aesthetic roots and these take us back to the same complementary processes of seeing and hiding which underlie the whole aesthetic experience of man in his environment. I have referred more than once to Brenda Colvin's work. *Land and Landscape* is an admirable introduction to the approach of the modern landscape architect, not least because it is lucidly written and makes practically no technological assumptions or demands on the layman. I doubt whether there is a single page in the book which does not furnish some example of landscape design consistent with the theories which we have considered in this book.

It will not have escaped the reader's attention that my references throughout have been very largely concerned with landscape as it has been seen through western eyes. A visit recently paid to the National Gallery of Canada quickly convinced me that Canadian landscape painting of the late nineteenth and twentieth centuries, while it portrays distinctive types of landscape, is no less susceptible to analysis in terms of the symbolism of prospect and refuge than are the classical paintings of Western Europe. This is, perhaps, to be expected, but what about the oriental experience of landscape? Surely we are dealing here not only with other kinds of physical landscape modified by peoples with different cultural traditions and distinctive architectural styles, but indeed with a whole philosophical outlook which, we are constantly told, has little in common with that of the West. It is one thing to find a means of reconciling the stylistic contrasts of André le Nôtre and Capability Brown, but where does the oriental garden fit in? In 1936 Tsuyoshi Tamura wrote a book, the whole purpose of which was to help western readers to understand the differences between the Japanese garden and its western counterpart. He is at great pains to stress their different symbolism and their different philosophic, religious and social antecedents.

'Lastly let us compare our gardens with those of the West. At first glance they exhibit a complexity of detail so crowded together that they may give an effect of cumbersomeness or even of gloomy disorder to an eye accustomed to the sunny openness of the Western garden.

'The crowded setting comes from the fact that our garden aims, in plain English, at the miniature representation of Nature's grand scenery, and so the close-set little objects naturally produce dusky shades. However, this is not the only cause of shadiness in our garden. Dusk is a feature of Japanese artistic taste, as is seen in other arts of ours such as India-pink painting or the setting for the tea ceremony. Fundamentally analysed, it comes from Zen Buddhist philosophy, where inward peace and enlightenment are sought in Nature's twilight profundity. It is a tendency of the mind quite opposite from the love of the colourful, the bright, the obvious in Nature.

'This difference between the Eastern and Western attitudes to Nature explains the fact that in the West, even in the English landscape art, to say nothing of formal gardening, the vista is made as open as possible, while in the Japanese garden the vista must be closed, so as to suggest depth of the earth and the invisible distance of heaven. This seems to be one of the most crucial points of difference in the Western and

Japanese landscape art, and is what makes our garden so strange to foreign taste.' (Tamura, 1936, pp. 11–12)

In spite of these differences of 'taste', however, it is not difficult to find an underlying unity of concept in prospect–refuge terms. The passage quoted above, for instance, is essentially saying that the Japanese garden lays more emphasis on refuge symbols ('dusky shades', 'twilight profundity') than its more prospect-dominant western counterpart ('sunny openness', 'as open as possible'). In the details of design we find in the Japanese garden an entirely different idiom, but reference to Figure 40 should quickly convince us that an *unfamiliar* arrangement of an *unfamiliar* vegetation, however much it symbolizes an *unfamiliar* religious philosophy, is certainly not grafted on to an *unfamiliar* basic composition. Here is the encircling fence to create a refuge. Here is the ornamental 'mount' to permit a prospect. Here is the token impediment hazard of a stream, here are the paths converging on the bridge by which the impediment is overcome. Even in this idiom, which is supposed to be fundamentally different from the Western landscape garden, there is much that we have encountered before. All the complexities of Christianity, the Renaissance and Zen Buddhism are based on different interpretations of a common basic relationship between man and his habitat, and it is at this radical, fundamental level that, in prospect–refuge theory, we have been looking for an explanation of the aesthetics of landscape.

FIGURE 40. JAPANESE GARDEN

A hill garden (*Gyo* style) as illustrated (Plate VI) in Tsuyoshi Tamura, *Art of the Landscape Garden in Japan* (1935). Reproduced by permission of the Japan Foundation

## The Superficial and the Fundamental

So deeply ingrained is our belief in the fundamental differences between contrasting styles and fashions that we may not find it easy to believe in the existence of a common aesthetic base. Even when an observer, familiar with European artistic tradition, finds in oriental paintings the same kind of prospect symbols, such as mountain peaks, high clouds, tree tops and, if not spires, then pagodas, and the same kind of refuge symbols, leafy boughs, verandahs and walled gardens, it is often the *details* of style, the idiom, which he chiefly notices. Of course, these expressions of cultural attitudes are extremely important, and we must recognize that loyalty to cultural, even political, ideas has often given shape to collective taste. Thus Van Zandt says:

'Denigration of the American landscape had practically become a tradition among the educated classes of Europe, and it also found support among some of the most sophisticated classes of the American population. European denigration was in part an inevitable by-product of the more general political opposition of the Old World to the "great experiment" of the new American society, but it was also a genuine expression of the prevailing European commitment to formal doctrines of aesthetic appreciation that left little room for an unqualified approval of the American landscape.' (Van Zandt, 1966, p. 190)

Particular fashions of technique or style in representing landscape may also have consequential implications for prospect and refuge. *Chiaroscuro*, for instance, the device of combining brightly illuminated surfaces with very dark shadows, though perhaps more commonly associated with portraiture and indoor scenes (p. 138), has the effect, when applied to landscape, of accentuating the contrast between the prospect values of the illuminated areas and the refuge values of the darkness.

The Impressionists, on the other hand, introduced a technique which, while accentuating the prospect symbolism, greatly weakened the refuges. Their principal concern was with the representation of light in new ways, following ideas prompted by nineteenth-century discoveries in the field of physics. The superficial brilliance of their surfaces, which reached its climax in the 'Pointillism' of the Neo-Impressionists, the use of at least moderately bright colours to depict even shaded areas, the denial of the existence of black as a colour to be found in nature, all these had the inevitable effect of suppressing the refuge symbols, as light of varying colour and intensity pervaded every corner of a canvas. In all paintings the balance can vary through a continuum from extreme prospect to extreme refuge, and all that one can say is that, in this style of painting, there is a tendency to move the balance towards the prospect-dominant end of that continuum in comparison with the more evenly balanced landscapes of the classical painters, and that this tendency would seem to result directly from the techniques which distinguish the Neo-Impressionist School.

In asserting that all landscape painting is susceptible of analysis according to the symbolism of prospect and refuge (in addition to analysis in many other ways) I am not suggesting that such symbolism always finds expression in similar images. We have to recognize that, just as periods, schools and individual artists have their own characteristic fashions for portraying, for instance, the human form, so there are widely differing styles in which landscape can be portrayed. Just as we can find the concept of 'hero' and 'villain' in Euripides, in the medieval morality play, in Shakespeare, in Victorian melodrama and in the 'cowboy western', albeit concealed behind very different images, so we can find prospect, refuge and hazard permeating the whole history of landscape painting and appearing through the imagery appropriate to every school and every style.

To illustrate the way in which a particular device can be represented in different forms characteristic of particular schools or periods, we may consider briefly the *coulisse* which, as we have seen, plays a contrapositive role in the prospect–refuge complement, because it always corresponds with an interface between the two kinds of symbol. In the 'Mannerist' school of the sixteenth century we find it pressed into service, sometimes to an absurd degree, in the series of promontories which are such a common feature of that style and period. A remarkable example of this is to be found in *Eurydice and the Serpents* (Figure 41) by Niccolo del Abbate. The symbolism of prospect and refuge throughout the picture is very strong. Mountains and crags, towers and spires, open spaces of grassland and water balance bushes, valleys, gorges, black shadows and cosily clustered buildings of all sorts. But the most conspicuous feature is the succession of headlands, the exact number of which may be disputed but undoubtedly reaches double figures. In the distance the right-hand margin is occupied by sea, into which the hill ridges of the left and centre project like fingers, the spaces between them suggesting 'offsets' into the wooded hills.

By contrast the French Rococo landscape painters employed the *coulisse* in a manner much more suggestive of the use from which the name is borrowed by the art critics, that is as scenery on the stage. 'Naturally enough', says Fry, 'the theatre, which was the very epitome of that fictitious life which he loved, had a special attraction for Watteau . . .' (1684–1721) (Fry, 1932, p. 57). His painting *La Perspective* (Figure 42), is perhaps an unfair illustration, because its title suggests a theme which cordially invites the use of this device, but it can be seen constantly dominating the composition in French 'woodland' painting throughout the eighteenth century, reaching its climax in the great arboreal fantasies of Fragonard. *The Swing* (Figure 43) is perhaps the best known though by no means the most extreme example of his reliance on the *coulisse* not merely, I suggest, to achieve perspective, but also to create that sense of cavernous refuges arranged, in this case, as 'offsets' to a central peep-hole vista. The *coulisse* always represents a particular kind of prospect–refuge interface, but it can appear in a wide variety of styles and fashions.

Individual taste may conform to the collective taste of the society concerned or it may deviate from it. Although all painters employ a mixture of prospect and refuge symbols, some seem to be habitually drawn towards one or the other. We have already noted (pp. 125 and 146) that Koninck prefers strong prospect

FIGURE 41. NICCOLO DEL ABBATE (c. 1512–1571): EURYDICE AND THE SERPENTS
An Italian 'Mannerist' painting of the sixteenth century. Reproduced by courtesy of the
Trustees, The National Gallery, London (No. 5283)

232

imagery with wide, sweeping panoramas, while Hobbema is more often attracted by refuge-dominant subjects (p. 123). Gombrich says, '. . . if you had analysed Hobbema you might have found out why he preferred to make capital out of Ruysdael's watermills rather than of Koninck's panoramas . . .' (Gombrich, 1963, p. 31)

FIGURE 42. ANTOINE WATTEAU (1684–1721): LA PERSPECTIVE
A vista with double *coulisses* arranged as in theatrical scenery. Reproduced by courtesy of the Museum of Fine Art, Boston, Massachusetts, Maria Antoinette Evans Fund (Accession No. 23.573)

There may well be personality characteristics deriving from heredity or experience or both which account for different preferences, just as there are people with claustrophobic tendencies. Hitler, for instance, seems to have had an exaggerated desire for refuge, which found expression in '. . . the underground bunker, in an East Prussian forest, known as the "Wolfsschanze"—the Wolfe's Lair'. This clearly went far beyond the demands of military defence:

> 'Hitler's own hut, with all windows facing north because he disliked the sun, was off in a corner apart from the others. Here in the middle of the forest of Gorlitz, where the trees grew so closely together it was rare for the sun to penetrate at all, Hitler spent most of the war.' (Elstob, 1971, p. 4)

FIGURE 43. JEAN HONORÉ FRAGONARD (1732–1806): THE SWING
A fantasy of cavernous, arboreal refuges, in which the *coulisse* is extended from its
usual function of flanking a vista to that of encircling a peephole. Reproduced by
permission of the Trustees of the Wallace Collection, London (No. 430)

Without going further into psychological explanations we can recognize
certain artists who regularly chose subjects which place them in the prospect-
dominant or refuge-dominant category, as we have seen in the case of Avercamp
(p. 148 and Figure 23) and van der Neer (p. 158 and Figure 25). Other artists
display a liking for particular subjects which, through constant repetition,

cause us to associate them with a particular form of symbolism. Cézanne, for instance, though he could use strong refuge symbols, was driven by his preoccupation with the Mont Sainte-Victoire to paint a series of landscapes dominated by this potent prospect symbol.

## The Origins of Taste

There have from time to time been vigorous arguments about the origins of taste whether it is the product of internal or external influences. The idea that taste is in some way an atavistic hangover from prehistoric times is by no means too improbable to have occurred to the art critics and historians. Kenneth Clark, for instance, constantly raises it. Of Altdorfer (c. 1480–1538) he says:

'Was there in his mind the unorthodox notion that our life began in some such wild surroundings and not in the Golden Age or the Garden of Eden? Although they would not have dared to formulate it, some of the more perceptive spirits of the time had already found that the story of Eden satisfied neither their imaginations nor their scientific curiosity. Some strange intuition of primeval slime seems to have impelled Grünewald. We are surprised to find that his two holy hermits are not accompanied by a dinosaur. And in Altdorfer's landscapes we have the same feeling that the world has been newly created.' (Clark, 1949, p. 39)

Later Clark hints at an even more direct link between an artist's individual idiom and some atavistic system of imagery and symbolism:

'As for particular images, we find in van Goch the enormous suns, the gnarled and hollow trees, the pierced and twisted rocks; and since he was completely oblivious of the earlier expressionists [Altdorfer, Grünewald, El Greco, etc.] and drew his inspiration from such utterly different sources as Millet and Horoshige, we may assume that these images are really part of the permanent furniture of the unconscious.' (Clark, 1949, p. 109)

These ideas, it will be quickly recognized, are very closely in line with the quotations taken earlier from Jellicoe's essays (p. 175) and from the writings of Dewey (p. 59). They support the view that taste is derived, however indirectly and however incomprehensibly, from some sensitivity in human nature which is communicated innately from generation to generation. They are highly consistent with habitat theory.

A contrary point of view may be found in Gombrich's interpretation of the origins of landscape painting, a point of view which at first sight seems much more difficult to reconcile with the ideas discussed in this book. According to Gombrich the painting of subjects frequently *preceded* their popularity in the public taste. He says:

'I believe that the idea of natural beauty as an inspiration of art . . . is, to say the least, a very dangerous oversimplification. Perhaps it even reverses the actual process by which man discovers the beauty of nature. We call a scenery "picturesque"—as Richard Payne Knight knew long ago—if it reminds us of paintings we have seen. And to the painter, in turn, nothing can become a "motif" except what he can assimilate into the vocabulary he has already learned . . . If Patinier, for instance, really embodied reminiscences of the Dinant scenery in his paintings, if Pieter Breughel really found the Alpine peaks inspiring, it was because the tradition of their art had provided them with a ready visual symbol for steep isolated rocks which made it possible for them to single out and appreciate these forms in nature.' (Gombrich, 1966, p. 117)

He goes on to recount the story of Cristoforo Sorte who, one night in 1541, witnessed a dramatic fire in Verona.

'Having reached the Ponte Nuovo he stopped for a while to admire the "marvellous effects of that fire because the places nearby and far away were at the same time illuminated by three different splendours." He describes in truly painterly terms the red glow of the flames, the reflection of the scene in the tremulous waters of the Adige and the effect of the moonlight on the billows of smoke which merged with the clouds. "And as I was a painter at that time I imitated it all in colours." Describing his procedure in great detail, Sorte adds that his observations may come in useful for painters who want to represent such night scenes as the Burning of Troy or the Sack of Corinth. May we not assume that the sight of the catastrophe he witnessed would not have struck him as "picturesque" if he had been unacquainted with this category of painting?

'Similarly, so it seems, the discovery of Alpine scenery does not precede but follows the spread of prints and paintings with mountain panoramas.' (Gombrich, 1966, p. 118)

On closer examination, even if we accept this interpretation (and the evidence is at best circumstantial) it is not really at all incompatible with habitat theory, as might at first be supposed. It is true that Gombrich is saying that we accept as beautiful what the painters have suggested is beautiful, but this merely raises the question of why they should make this suggestion in the first place if they did not feel some spontaneous response to it. One could as well argue that it was a *real* experience of the fire that awakened in Sorte some deep, atavistic sensitivity and led him to commend this 'inversion' as a suitable model for other painters to employ.

The whole argument becomes much more lucid if we recollect the grounds for believing that the mechanisms by which an animal establishes a relationship with its environment are made up of inborn and learned components (Chapter 3, see also Fletcher, 1968 edn.). The process by which the public acquires its preferences for particular kinds of visual experience can then be seen as a process of 'learning' from the painters, a process superimposed on a basic 'inborn' sensitivity to certain kinds of environmental phenomena which we have called 'prospects', 'hazards' and 'refuges'. Such a sensitivity is the common possession of painter and public alike. The painter first expresses it in a particular way. The public responds aesthetically to his expression and begins to look for similar expressions elsewhere, but the underlying sensitivity has been there all the time.

Seen in this light Gombrich's scepticism about an atavistic origin for taste seems less forbidding than when one encounters it in his cogent assertion:

> 'My sympathies are all with those who warn us against rash specula-
> tions about inborn reactions in man—whether they come from the
> racialist camp or that of Jung. The dignity of man, as Pico della
> Mirandola felt, lies precisely in his Protean capacity for change.'
> (Gombrich, 1960, p. 102)

However, if a capacity for change is compatible with the existence of inborn reactions in chaffinches and love-birds (pp. 59–61), why must we assume that it is *in*compatible in man? For it is only the assumption that it *is* incompatible which precludes a reconciliation between Gombrich's emphasis on taste as a derivative from the example of the painters and those broad hints at atavism thrown out by Clark, Jellicoe and any apologist for habitat theory.

**Taste as Preference**

The recognition of a dual origin of taste in inborn and learned components also helps to explain the changes of preference for environmental conditions which may be observed in the same individual, whether human or non-human, at different times. Carlos, our cat, displays clear evidence of well-defined prospect-seeking and refuge-seeking moods. When in the former he will risk injury, disgrace and even ejection from the house in order to reach the top of the sideboard or the highest shelf in the kitchen. When in the latter mood he will creep into the deepest recess of the darkest cupboard. Having attained either objective he will quickly settle down to sleep and one might think, therefore, that the environment was of little consequence. Yet if he is denied access to his chosen goal he will pace nervously round in ostentatious frustration. To try and fob him off by offering access to one destination when he is bent on attaining the other is a waste of time. I do not attempt to suggest any explanation of this behaviour; I merely offer it as evidence that, to Carlos, prospect and refuge are very real concepts, and that at different times he displays strong preferences for environments dominated by one or the other.

Whatever reservations we have to make about the links between animal and human psychology, we can find ample evidence for similar reactions in man. There are, of course, those people who have a more or less permanent predilection for open spaces or for cosy enclosures (Balint, 1955). But most of us have merely to examine our own attitudes to landscape to recognize how much our moods are liable to change. For most of us the pleasure of going for a walk is enhanced if the symbolism of prospect and refuge is not kept in constant balance but is allowed to vary, and even if we could calculate an optimum balance we should probably get bored with it almost as quickly as with a single, indefinitely sustained musical chord, however appealing it might be at first hearing.

In fact, the notion of an optimum balance between the symbolism of prospect and refuge is not only empirically insupportable; it is also theoretically invalid, because it implies that the environmental requirements of a creature are the same whatever the activity in which it is engaged, and all creatures, or almost all, have varying requirements at different times. Consider, for instance, a vixen rearing her cubs. If she is to be successful her paramount need is for refuge. There can be few refuges more complete than a fox's 'earth'. There comes a time, however, when she must seek food. Since she relies at least in part on her sense of vision, she now requires an environment in which the balance is very different. The attainment of a prospect is essential if she is to use that sense of vision successfully in finding her quarry, though a smattering of refuges here and there may enable her to approach closer to her prey before it runs away. Once the chase has begun refuges can be dispensed with, since they offer advantage only to the pursued. If, however, in the course of the chase the vixen is herself seen by the huntsman, or if she becomes aware that the hounds have picked up her scent, refuge objects again assume an importance, and yet another 'optimum' balance would result, a balance which could also be affected by her previous reconnaissance, or lack of reconnaissance, of the area concerned. Each situation, therefore, confronts the same individual creature with quite dissimilar requirements for prospect and refuge, and at different stages the vixen would profit from other associations and combinations of these complementary aids to survival. How far she is aware of this, recognizes it cognitively or emotionally and feels satisfaction or unease, it is no doubt dangerous to speculate, but it is a matter of common observation that she regulates her behaviour in relation to the balance of symbolism which affords improved opportunity for the achievement of her purpose at each stage.

If we go on to postulate that *Homo sapiens* possesses comparable inclinations to respond in alternative ways to his environment, then clearly we should expect the same individual to find gratification at various times in very different kinds of prospect–refuge equilibrium. If this holds good for the individual then it cannot apply any less to the behaviour of the species.

Are we, then, in a position to proceed to a definition of 'taste', which, it may be remembered, was a task we set ourselves in Chapter 1. I think we are. *Taste is an acquired preference for particular methods of satisfying inborn desires.* Here is a definition which can be employed to cover taste (individual or collective), in food, in clothing, in sexual practices, in all kinds of behaviour which display evidence of preferential choice, and it relegates that otherwise intractable argument about heredity and environment to the level of a demarcation dispute in which both protagonists have their legitimate rights and their inescapable limitations.

# CHAPTER 9

# The Aesthetic Potential of Places

'Consult the Genius of the Place in all . . .'
ALEXANDER POPE (*Moral Essays: Epistle to Lord Burlington*,
line 57; Bowles, 1806, vol. iii, p. 335)

If the aesthetic enjoyment of landscape is based on behavioural relationships between the observer and his visible environment, it is to be expected that places will vary in their capacity for stimulating aesthetic response, and that this variation will depend partly on the intrinsic properties of such places and partly on the behaviour mechanisms which govern these relationships. Having considered behaviour mechanisms, let us in this chapter look at places and see whether there are any grounds for believing that those which we think of as beautiful are favourably endowed in terms of the symbolism of prospect and refuge.

## The Components of Landscape

The most striking characteristics of places derive from the rocks which underlie them, the presence or absence of water and the form in which it occurs, the cover of vegetation, the climatic conditions and the intervention of man.

The rocks can contribute to the creation of prospect or refuge at very different scales. In the major mountain systems of the world we should expect to find very powerful symbols of prospect, refuge and hazard, deriving their strength from sheer size. If a pyramidal peak is symbolically suggestive of prospect, then Mount Everest and the Matterhorn cannot fail to convey that idea very forcefully. *Per contra* a great valley enclosed within a mountain system appears to the imagination as a huge refuge area, capable, by virtue of its magnitude, of swallowing the fugitive in a sanctuary as effective as it is vast.

At the medium scale we can distinguish structural features which again make for the provision of prospects and refuges but of more modest proportions. What they lose in magnitude (what the eighteenth-century philosophers would have called 'sublimity'), they gain in accessibility and in being more realistically proportionate to the actual experience of seeing the hiding in a plausible strategic situation. One of the simplest kinds of structure is that in which inclined strata of hard and soft rock produce a 'scarp-and-vale' type of landscape. The Palaeozoic succession of south-east Shropshire was one of the earliest features of this kind to be studied by the geologists, and it forms a suitable example because the strata are strongly differentiated, fairly thin and relatively steeply inclined (Earp and Hains, 1971). The Wenlock and Aymestry Limestone in particular produce parallel ridges, commonly less than a mile apart, rising some two or three hundred feet above the little vale of Hope Dale which separates them. To the north-west more irregularly placed escarpments of older rock give rise to similar ridges of high ground. There is therefore a natural succession of prospect-dominant *cuestas* and refuge-dominant vales which complement each other in producing the framework of a landscape which most visitors find attractive. In prospect–refuge terms it inherits a good balance from its geological structure.

Common variations occur when the strata are inclined, not in parallel straight lines, but concentrically around an area in which they are elevated into a 'dome' or depressed into a 'basin'. Although incomplete on the western side, a good example of a 'half-dome', (technically a 'pitching anticline'), is to be found in the same Wenlock–Aymestry succession at Bringewood Chase on the Shropshire–Herefordshire borders (Earp and Hains, 1971, Frontispiece and Plate VII). Here a group of little villages, Burrington, Aston, Elton and Leinthall Starkes, nestles within the protective horseshoe of the Wenlock Limestone escarpment above which the concentric Aymestry escarpment can be seen peeping here and there. A more complete dome can be found to the east of Harlech in North Wales, where the escarpments are much higher but more fragmented (Matley and Wilson, 1946). A general sense of protective enclosure can, however, be experienced within the Harlech Dome, particularly since it contains attractive patches of oakwood to reduplicate the refuge element. The high scarp-fragments which discharge this protective role are also highly charged with prospect symbolism.

The converse arrangement found in a structural basin also has powerful associations with the concept of prospect and refuge. Commonly, a structural basin forms a kind of central nest, around which the concentric rings of *outward* facing escarpments act as a series of protective walls. From the inside of the basin they tend, therefore, to be less conspicuous than the escarpments of a dome, but as one enters the system from outside, whether by surmounting the escarpments or by passing through gorges along river lines, one experiences the sense of entering a well-protected refuge area surrounded by elevated vantage-points. If the basin contains a town or city the refuge imagery is strengthened. London and Paris are both situated in basins with well-developed peripheral outward facing escarpments. The penetration of the steep face of the Chalk by the gaps at Goring (River Thames), or Dorking–Leatherhead (River Mole), produces an exaggerated impression of creeping into the refuge area of the London Basin by a low level route. A different sensation is afforded by those roads which cross the upper surfaces of the Chilterns or North Downs, where a climb over the surrounding skyline is followed by a *descent* into the refuge centre. The numerous dry gaps (so-called 'wind-gaps') provide an intermediate experience.

In the Paris Basin the Chalk is spread farther afield and the immediate approaches to the city are here dominated by the Tertiary rocks which overlie the Chalk. (Such rocks are also important in the London Basin where they produce attractive landscapes, for instance, in the Surrey commons, but they are much less conspicuous as escarpments.) The Paris Tertiaries are often covered with woodland and when one looks at an escarpment not merely as a vantage-point for a prospect but as a protective shell for a refuge, the crowning of the skyline by deciduous and coniferous trees adds strongly to the symbolism.

On an even smaller scale we can distinguish landscape features whose occurrence is still governed by geological conditions and by the physical processes operating on the rocks. For instance, chasms and ravines of all sorts figure prominently in landscape painting, not only of the Romantic period. Such features can frequently be attributed to similar origins. One common cause of the formation of ravines is the phenomenon known to geomorphologists as 'rejuvenation', consequent on a lowering of the level of the water-body into which a river drains. The process of excavation is thereby invigorated; the bed of the river is lowered and a gorge is formed. The influence of the structure of the rocks on this activity can often be observed where rapids or waterfalls mark the upward limit of the gorge. Many of the world's great waterfalls, such as Niagara (Figure 1) or the Victoria Falls, introduce stupendous hazard symbols at the point where the river forsakes the prospect symbolism of wide panoramas for the sequestered ravine. Here the prospect becomes vistal and acquires a full measure of refuge symbolism.

Not all ravines are formed in this way. In limestone country some have been attributed to the collapse of the roofs of caves as in the Carboniferous Limestone of Derbyshire. This district is generally dominated by prospect symbolism; its grazing pastures stretch away to wide exposed horizons, but within it are set some remarkably fine ravines and caves which, whatever their mode of origin, contribute towards the achievement of a balance of a particular and distinctive kind. It was the Carboniferous Limestone, incidentally, which formed so many of the sublime landscape features recorded by Gilpin and the eighteenth-century devotees of the picturesque.

There is not room here to record all the minor landforms which can be consistently associated with the experience of prospect and refuge. The natural rock arch is a feature greatly favoured by landscape painters, for instance by Leonardo da Vinci, Claude and Gaspar Dughet. It is not difficult to see why, as soon as one recognizes it as a dramatic example of 'inversion'. The usual arrangement under which refuges are set within prospects is here reversed, and a tiny peep-hole vista is achieved in the very heart of a cave.

Moraines have been defined as '(i) masses of boulder-clay and stones carried and deposited by a glacier; and (ii) the arrangement of this material to form a particular landform' (Monkhouse, 1965, p. 208). In flat country moraines of even modest elevation frequently provide viewpoints commanding prospects over the surrounding land, as in Koninck's panoramas. There are well-known paintings of Amersfoort by Cuyp (in the Wuppertal–Elberfeld Museum, Germany) and Salomon van Ruysdael (whereabouts unknown according to Stechow, 1966, Figure 59), in which the Amersfoort Moraine is used to provide such an elevated viewpoint.

Wind-borne deposits have certain properties which have a direct bearing on the balance of prospect and refuge. In sand dunes, hollows and hillocks occur irregularly in profusion and in close proximity. The result is strategically a 'close' type of country which many a child has found ideal as a setting for games of pursuit and escape. Together with the moraines, sand dunes provide the Dutch Polders with elevated viewpoints, and it is no accident that the panoramic views of Haarlem, that much painted Dutch city, are nearly all from the west, where the dune belt approaches within a few hundred yards of it.[31]

The occurrence of water in nature is again not haphazard, as we have already seen by a brief reference to waterfalls. Among the features of the English Lake District which so many poets found attractive were the lakes themselves. Geomorphologically they are very orthodox examples of glacial lakes (except where they have been artificially extended); but for our purposes they have another significance. At what we have called the medium scale the terrain of the Lake District derives a balance of prospect and refuge symbolism from its mountains and valleys. Most of the refuge symbols are predictably in the valleys, and the introduction of aquatic surfaces at these points has a profound effect in restoring balance to the composition. A typical lakeland view consists of an open prospect across the water in the foreground to an arboreal refuge in the middle distance surmounted by a carpeted, prospect-dominant surface, which leads the eye upward to a horizon.

Any physical process which affects the distribution of water surfaces can there-by influence the balance of prospect–refuge symbolism in a landscape. Among such processes those which induce changes in sea level are particularly im-portant, especially when they bring about the 'drowning' of river valleys to form estuaries of the *ria* type. The introduction of water into an existing valley has a profound effect on its balance of symbolism. By eliminating trees and other refuge symbols from the valley bottom it inevitably strengthens the prospect. If there are lateral valleys with intervening spurs or ridges, these are converted into promontories which, as we have seen, can take on the form and function of *coulisses*.

Vegetation can play a role equal with or even greater than that of the con-figuration of the land surface in establishing the mood of a landscape, and its distribution, although governed by quite different principles, is certainly not haphazard. Even at the level of generalization which one would find in a world distribution map of natural vegetation, one may surmise something about the capacity of different parts of the world to achieve an emphasis of a particular kind. Thus the desert, the steppe, the tundra and the ice-caps are prospect-oriented; the forest, deciduous or coniferous, is a refuge. The savannah and the Mediterranean *maquis* provide alternative variations on a composite theme, in which refuge symbols, either trees or shrubs or groups of the same, tend to be set in open grassland or scrub. If we had time to pursue this question further we could work out its implication for other categories of vegetation, the rain-forest, for instance, or the Everglades; or we could project the argument further afield to the intense prospect imagery of the surface of the Moon, where not only vegetational but also atmospheric impediments to visibility are non-existent.

The aesthetic potential of a place, then, is influenced (if 'determined' is too strong a word), by the shape of the land surface, the character of its vegetation, and even its climate, not merely because climate influences vegetation, but because the sky is an integral part of landscape and its visual properties are no less subject to the laws of nature than are those of the land. Reference has already been made to clarity and visibility in particular types of air mass (p. 146) and to the symbolism of cloud shapes (p. 112). Places vary considerably in their susceptibility to particular kinds of meteorological phenomena and therefore in the balance of symbolism likely to be encountered there.

All these components of landscape, rocks, water, vegetation and the appearance of the sky, may be modified by human intervention in varying degrees, even to the extent of replacement by a wholly artificial environment, but such modified features may still be characteristic of particular places. The conventional image of Holland, for instance, is one of reclaimed polders. Regional variations in building styles which at first sight may seem to be wholly the product of cultural fashion may, on closer examination, turn out to have some functional significance deriving from the physical environment. A good example may be found in house-types constructed in hot climates. Broadly speaking there are two principal ways in which a building can be constructed to keep cool without mechanical air-conditioning. In one type of building the walls are made thick and the windows small, so as to prevent the passage of heat by conduction and convection respectively. In the other direct sunshine is excluded by some kind of screen or canopy which does not, however, impede the movement of air underneath it. In the former category are to be found many of the older traditional houses in, for instance, the Mediterranean lands; in the latter the sort of houses we should think of as typical of Australia, California or much of the tropics. The distinction clearly has much to do with cultural tradition and may be affected by all sorts of considerations other than climate, such as the availability of building materials or the need for defence. The two types have a common objective, to keep down the temperature of the interior, but in achieving it by separate methods they present very different kinds of refuge imagery, the one efficient but forbidding, the other less like a fortification and visually much more penetrable.

Many features of the cultural landscape which we regard as typical of some particular region derive their character from the twin origins of cultural tradition and the physical environment. The Rhine castles, for instance, have made such an impact on the public mind that they may be said to symbolize the character of the whole river, though they are in fact confined to a comparatively short stretch of it. Their strategic situations were highly suitable for their function, which was to provide a refuge endowed with good visibility thanks to a surround of falling ground with, on the river side, a refuge-free aquatic surface, and vistal prospects of longer fetch up and down the valley. These genuine medieval structures prompted the construction of a later generation of *ersatz* fortifications, functionally irrelevant from the moment of their conception, but seeking by every extremity to offer more seclusion with a better view than their legitimate ancestors.

**The Evaluation of Landscape**

The notion, then, that modern man is emancipated from the tyranny of his environment is equally dubious whether applied to his economic or his aesthetic independence, and we have now seen how particular landscapes seem to have properties which favour the development of one kind of symbolism or another. This is what we mean by 'aesthetic potential'. It cannot be too strongly emphasized, however, that this is very different from the attribution of intrinsic aesthetic qualities to particular elements in the landscape. If a landscape component appears 'beautiful' its beauty, according to our hypothesis, is not an inalienable quality of itself; it derives from the contribution which it seems, *actually or symbolically*, to be capable of making to our chances of biological survival in the environment of which both we and it form a part. If a mountain is beautiful, its beauty is not to be sought in its mass, its outline or its mineralogical composition, but in its relationship to other landscape components: a relationship which invariably suggests a superior capacity for extending the field of vision, because mountains always rise above the surrounding land. If a forest is beautiful, this is not because of some quality, 'beauty', which resides in it, but because, in his strategic relationship with the environment, a creature, including man, *feels* that he needs a place where he can hide, and this need is supplied among the trees and in the shadow of their foliage. While it is possible, therefore, to recognize certain potential connections between different landscape components (whether landforms, water-bodies, vegetation associations, meteorological phenomena or indeed man-made features), and the opportunity to see and/or to hide, it is only in the total environmental context that we can assess the aesthetic qualities of a *particular* place, a *particular* view, a *particular* landscape.

Qualitative assessments of this kind are common enough. A good example will be found in any geographical textbook which seeks to describe the contrasting landscapes of *campagne* and *bocage* in Northern France. Gottmann's account will serve as well as any. It begins with a typical piece of campagne:

> 'The plain around is flat, dry, covered with fields, almost treeless; such is the case throughout most of Beauce. The same scenery extends westward north of the Seine to the sea-board; to the traveller on the railroad between Rouen and le Havre, the plain of the Pays de Caux may appear as a well-cultivated desert: he sees fields with small clusters of trees, but no habitation. The farms of this original section of the plain are hidden behind screens of trees, often of a very picturesque Norman style, with low thatched buildings scattered across a grassy yard.
>
> 'In this western direction, Normandy begins not far from Paris. This prosperous country consists of alternated *campagnes* of loam over limestone and depressions where, on clayey soil, the land is checkered with live hedges planted with trees; this latter landscape is called *bocage* and covers large stretches in the west of the country. The

bocage is a green scenery which looks from afar like woodland, and one must enter inside to understand its organization with the fields and meadows it enclosed. The trees and bushes supply some wood, charcoal, and stable litter, but they occupy considerable space and make circulation difficult; their main use is to enclose the area in which the cattle is left alone to graze, thus saving manpower and keeping the cattle from wandering on the neighbor's land. The hedges are therefore linked to an economy centered on cattle raising and grasslands, with rather little mechanization. In their advance through Normandy after the landings in 1944, American forces found progress complicated by the hedges; once in a while even tanks had difficulties in overcoming the barriers devised to stop a bull'. (Gottmann, 1951, p. 265)

The campagne then is essentially a prospect-dominant terrain, based on panoramic views except, perhaps, where straight, tree-lined roads locally introduce a vistal theme. Its refuges tend to be highly concentrated in little clusters of woodland and, much more important, in the farms and villages. The relative absence of hedges and hedgerow timber permits extensive views over the generally rolling plain. By contrast the bocage is a type of landscape in which refuge plays a much more important part. The high incidence of impediment hazards, so pointedly described by Gottmann, would be aesthetically very different if all the fences were of wire mesh. As it is, the banks, stone walls, hedges and hedgerow timber provide a cover which more than compensates for the interference with a strategically desirable freedom of movement.

In heavily populated, developed countries it has become a matter of urgent necessity, for planning purposes, to be able to identify aesthetically satisfying landscapes and, if necessary, to rank them in order of merit. In Britain this need became acute just about the time when geographers, planners and others had come to believe that they could measure anything quantitatively and that, if they could not, it was not worth considering. I am entirely behind the search for more refined methods of analysing landscapes, but early attempts to do this statistically in the aesthetic field do not fill me with confidence.

Two papers published in Britain in the late 'sixties may be taken to illustrate the problem. K. D. Fines and David Linton both struggle with it manfully, but both introduce so much subjective assessment into the preparation of their material that its subsequent processing by 'objective' methods never carries conviction (see Fines, 1968 and 1969, and Brancher, 1969). Fines, for instance, in explaining his system for quantifying aesthetic values in landscape, says:

'A value of 24·0 is taken to represent the highest that can be obtained on a world scale by a spectacular view which is not enhanced by transient atmospheric phenomena: for instance, some views of the Himalayan peaks from the foothills attain this value under average conditions but exceed it when the mountains are set against one of the spectacular sunsets that follow the monsoon. A value of 18·0 is taken to represent the highest that can be obtained by a view in Great Britain, such as some of the views of the Cuillins from across Loch Coruisk on the Isle of Skye. A value of 12·0 is taken to represent the highest that can be obtained by a view in Lowland Britain, such as the prospect from Newlands Corner near Guildford over the Lower Greensand hills of Surrey and West Sussex.' (Fines, 1968, pp. 43–44)

The most that can be offered by way of an explanation of these values is that they were compiled by reference to a 'representative group of forty-five persons' (thirty-five of whom subsequently had their opinions rejected). It is true that Fines prefaces the exercise by some discussion of the psychological basis. 'Five emotions, in particular, can enhance or diminish the response to intrinsic landscape beauty' (Fines, 1968, p. 42), he says, and goes on to list these as 'sentiment', 'fear', 'curiosity', 'surprise' and 'veneration'. But there is no argument whatever by which these can be linked *theoretically* to the empirical rankings of landscapes on the basis of expressed preference.

Linton's technique is even more subjective. If we have to rely on anyone to distinguish between 'mountains', 'bold hills', 'hill country', 'plateau uplands', 'low uplands' and 'lowlands', nobody could claim greater authority, but when he assigns points to each category (8, 6, 5, 3, 2 and 0 respectively) he begs fundamental questions which go much deeper than merely casting doubt on the uniformity of public opinion about the relative aesthetic values of these categories. Such doubt certainly is justified. One wonders, for instance, whether any admirer of the landscapes of Koninck could agree to the assertion that '. . . in general the scenic interest of lowlands derives from their human use, from their water features, or from the open views they give of the horizon sky at sunrise or sunset, and not from their surface form. They can thus be counted neutral and given a zero rating' (Linton, 1968, p. 227).

But variations of preference are mere details compared with the highly questionable assumption which underlies the whole procedure, that individual components of landscape, such as 'low uplands', can be said to have any intrinsic aesthetic values at all. It is precisely this concept of aesthetics which Dewey so decisively rejected and it is certainly at variance with the underlying assumption of prospect–refuge theory. Before anyone pursues these analytical methods further he must stop and ask himself whether he is analysing the right things.

Do these criticisms of Fines and Linton mean, then, that places do not differ in aesthetic potential or merely that the analytical methods so far tried have failed to identify and quantify them? Common experience tells us that most people would regard some places as being aesthetically better endowed than others, even if they do not understand why. The fact that I am astonished to find the eastern side of the Firth of Clyde marked on Linton's map of 'scenic resources' in the lowest category of all (minus 6), suggests that I must have a preconception of its aesthetic value, otherwise I should not be astonished.

It seems to me, then, that we must accept the existence of a wide variation in the aesthetic potential of particular places and recognize that differences between them have already affected investment decisions involving enormous sums of money (in *tourisme*, for instance) and must increasingly affect the way we plan the use of land. This being so we are desperately seeking more penetrating methods of understanding our scenic resources and more effective ways of evaluating them.[32] The temptation to press ahead with attempts at quantification is obvious. It is also highly commendable, academically as well as politically, to do so as soon as we possibly can; but we simply cannot go ahead with propriety until we understand much more about the mechanisms which induce us to experience satisfaction in one environmental situation and dissatisfaction in another. Only then can we be sure that we are measuring what matters. I make bold, therefore, to suggest that we are as likely at this stage to make progress towards the aesthetic evaluation of landscape by looking at places subjectively in terms of the hypotheses we have been considering, as by attaching numerical values to environmental objects whose function in the aesthetic process we do not properly understand.

## Case Studies

I shall conclude this chapter by briefly examining in terms of the symbolism of prospect and refuge a few places with which I have some personal acquaintance, which are generally regarded as aesthetically attractive, and which vary in scale and character. It must be understood, however, that the fundamental tenet of habitat theory (namely that the aesthetic experience of landscape arises from the exposure of the observer to a particular combination of environmental circumstances in their totality), places severe limits on the extent to which one can make valid generalizations about even quite small areas, let alone large ones, especially in a country with as much scenic variation as Britain, and this, I am sure, is another serious limitation in Linton's method of mapping landscape resources. Let us begin, then, with an example which illustrates this last point, and turn to a tiny fragment of highly 'picturesque' landscape which derives at least a part of its dramatic effect from the contrast between itself and the country in which it is set.

### (i) *Hawkstone Park, Salop*

Much of the plain of southern Shropshire is underlain by the Keuper marls of the Triassic system, which generally give rise to rather flat, or at most 'undulating' country. Among the marls, however, there occur, as well as deposits of salt and anhydrite, bands of sandstone which outcrop at several places in the form of little fragmentary escarpments. One such formed part of the estate at Hawkstone where, as early as 1784, Sir Rowland and his successor Sir Richard Hill had created a very remarkable landscape. Pevsner says:

'The grounds of Hawkstone are exceptionally happily situated for any improver who wanted his picturesqueness not gentle but rough, i.e., for the Later Georgian rather than the Mid-Georgian ideals of land-scape. The ridge of sandstone cliffs, falling precipitously away S.W. and S. of the house and being guarded by sudden isolated crags, could not be more dramatic. Moreover, when the improvements began, there was already a genuine ruined castle there, perched on its rock as no painter could have invented it more improbably . . . We have descriptions of the whole large and felicitous scheme as it originally was, including walks of ten miles, rocks compared with the ruins of Palmyra, the wax effigy of the ancestor of a neighbour in the grotto, a hermitage complete with a hermit "generally found in a sitting posture" with an hourglass, a skull, a book, and spectacles on his table, a vineyard laid out like a fortification with turrets, walls and bastions, an Elysian Hill, an Awful Precipice, a menagerie, a Gothic greenhouse the situation of which "would require the united efforts of Salvator Rosa, Claude, and Poussin to do it the smallest degree of justice" . . .' (Pevsner, 1958, p. 145).

Numerous additions, including the tunnel of the carriage drive, the obelisk and the citadel were added later.

It will be noted that this description not only captures the spirit of the 'picturesque' but also relies strongly on the imagery of prospect and refuge, '. . . falling precipitously . . . and being guarded by sudden isolated crags . . .'. Even in dereliction Hawkstone is a remarkable sight. Its paths are strangled by rhododendrons, its grotto, perched at the top of a precipice (Figure 44), has been converted into a genuine ruin, its carefully contrived steps and walk-ways have relapsed into the grasp of nature, but I know of no place in England where one could so vividly experience what I believe landscape meant to William Gilpin, Uvedale Price and Richard Payne Knight. Even with the detached Grotto Hill, the cliff itself is not more than a mile in length, and all around this little complex of scarp fragments extends the Keuper Marl plain, pleasant enough in its way but wholly unlike the landscape of cliffs and trees for which it provides an encircling panorama. On Linton's scale the plain would score very low marks, yet without it the potential of Hawkstone could not be half fulfilled. We are still far from conceiving a quantitative technique which can reduce the aesthetic properties of a landscape like this to terms which can meaningfully be measured.

(ii) *The lakes of Southern Ontario*

For our next case study let us turn to a very different environment where one could indeed make valid aesthetic generalizations, at least of a qualitative kind, about a much larger tract of country. An important geological boundary crosses southern Ontario from Georgian Bay to the St Lawrence a little below its exit from Lake Ontario (Figure 45). Between this boundary and the lake a wedge of country, tapering from about seventy miles in width at Toronto to zero near Gananoque, consists of Palaeozoic rocks, covered in places by glacial deposits and marine and lacustrine clays. The soils developed on these deposits provided the basis for agricultural settlement. It is also in this area, between Windsor in

248

the west and Ottawa and Cornwall in the east, that the principal urban development of the Province has taken place, especially in and around Toronto.

To the north of the geological boundary these rocks give way to the hard Precambrian rocks of the so-called 'Laurentian Shield', which stretch north around Hudson Bay to the Arctic. In terms of landscape the dividing line between the 'shield country' and the plains to the south has been somewhat blurred by the sands, gravels and other materials deposited by ice, so that the lakes extend

FIGURE 44. GROTTO HILL, HAWKSTONE, SHROPSHIRE
The ruined arch at the summit of the cliff marks the position of the grotto, which combined the primitive refuge symbolism of the cave with a vantage point commanding a wide panoramic view over the surrounding plain. It was this potency of the symbolism of prospect, refuge and hazard, occurring in combination, which so excited the devotees of the Picturesque. Photograph by the author

locally south of the boundary and pockets of fertile soil are found locally to the north, but these merely introduce minor modifications to a major contrast.

The juxtaposition of these two types of country, the one heavily populated (by Canadian standards) with urban communities, the other largely in a state of 'wilderness', gives rise to a remarkable development of the phenomenon of the weekend or vacation 'cottage'. A vast exodus of Torontonians on summer Fridays is followed by a mass southerly movement on Sunday nights. To say that this is a logical and predictable consequence of such a juxtaposition is reasonable enough, but if we press the question why people choose to put up with congested traffic conditions in order to reach this type of terrain we probably have to be content with some such explanation as that they want to 'enjoy the outdoor life', to 'see wild country' or simply to 'get away'.[33] An assessment of the potential of these recreation areas in terms of habitat theory, however, quickly reveals that their intrinsic properties are such as to enable people to establish a relationship with the environment wholly consistent with the gratification of those aesthetic needs which, we have inferred, derive from their basic survival mechanisms. It is true that this terrain scarcely begins to furnish a food supply. The tin can, the bottle, the cellophane pack and the Toronto supermarkets relieve the weekender of any anxiety on this account, and if he chooses to seek his food from the lake, he does so in the knowledge that failure to catch a fish does not imperil his

FIGURE 45. SOUTHERN ONTARIO AND NORTHERN NEW YORK STATE
Drawn by Anthony I. Key

chance of survival. He may, in short, pursue for their own sake all those activities which satisfy his desire to master his environment. He may explore, he may perfect the techniques of agile movement both in the forests and on, in, or even under the water. In particular he may take pleasure in the contemplation of his environment in so far as it possesses those visual attributes which suggest a favourable strategic situation. And by the time we have translated this situation into the symbolism of prospect and refuge, this 'shield country' emerges as very rich in both.

The prospect imagery is much influenced by water. The panoramic lake surface can be complemented by the vistal river line with the deflected vista playing a major role. The refuge imagery is almost everywhere dominated by the forest. Arboreal surfaces suggests a vast enveloping hiding-place within which primitive activities (however sophisticated by mechanization) can be enjoyed against a

250

background which provides enough assurance to enable danger to be tasted, within whatever limits one chooses to set, in such activities as water-skiing or shooting the rapids in a canoe. Into this landscape, too, the so-called 'cottages' can be inserted in such a way as to accentuate, rather than diminish, the sense that a potentially hazardous environment has been rendered benign enough to permit not only survival but comfortable living, without being made to yield up the outward symbols of its power. The cottages are nearly always placed under a canopy of trees, and frequently a few tree trunks stand between the cottage and the lake (Figure 46), which can be perceived from the windows through a light veil of foliage. Hobbema never achieved a feat of reduplication to surpass this Canadian version of the 'cottage-in-the-wood'.

FIGURE 46. COTTAGE IN THE WOOD, CANADIAN STYLE
Charleston Lake, Ontario (see Figure 45). Photograph by the author

(iii) *Highway 87, New York State*

My next case study deals not with an areal, but with a linear feature in the landscape—a section of highway singled out for recognition as the winner of the 'America's Most Scenic Highway Award, 1966–67'. It is a twenty-three mile stretch of Highway 87, the main route between New York City and Montreal, and lies roughly eighty to a hundred miles north of Albany in New York State (Figure 45).

The prospect is basically vistal within the seclusion of a forest endowed with a great variety of species of tree. The vistal effect is accentuated in those sections where the carriageways are separated by a forested central reservation. Here the route is narrower; the trees are closer; the vistal effect more dramatic. Deflected vistas play a very important part in arousing expectations which are quickly satisfied by the realization of the next stretch of the view, especially when one is travelling at speed. Every now and then the road rises above the level of the surrounding forest on one side or the other to expose a wide panorama, particularly to the east, where the broad, shallow valley is wholly forested, as far as can be seen, except when glimpses of water proclaim the presence of the river or a lake. To the west occasional views up valleys reveal the higher summits of the Adirondacks which rise high enough to arouse a keen sense of prospect beyond their horizons, even though they are clothed with forest. On this side also bare rock cliffs rise out of the forest, to be imitated in the immediate flanks of the highway by frequent rock cuttings. Just as the composition of the scene in terms of vista and panorama, rock and forest, western and eastern aspect, is constantly changing, so there is an alternating transition from the hiding-place of the forest to the look-out of the swelling hills.

All along the eastern edge of the Adirondacks the experience of the traveller on Highway 87 could be described in some such terms as these. Along a much shorter section, where the highway crosses between the drainage basin of the Hudson River, flowing south from Lake George to New York City, and that of the Richelieu River, flowing north from Lake Champlain to the St Lawrence, it is forced to climb out of the low-lying forest and over the broad, sweeping, though still forested surfaces of the watershed country. It is this necessity which is responsible for introducing the moments of panorama into an essentially refuge-dominant experience, and it is this stretch of highway that won the prize.

(iv) *Katoomba, New South Wales*

One of the most popular scenic areas in Australia is that part of the so-called Great Dividing Range which lies closest to Sydney and is known as the Blue Mountains. Within it the best known view is certainly that of the Three Sisters as seen from the Queen Elizabeth Lookout at Katoomba (Figure 47). Let us therefore subject this to analysis in terms of our symbolism.

The principal features of the landscape have been formed by river erosion acting on the nearly horizontal strata of the Hawkesbury Sandstone, which can be seen in the distance forming a cliff at the top of the valley slopes and also in the pinnacles in the foreground. The composition seems to fall into three main components, the distant plateau, the wide canyon and the sandstone pinnacles: almost corresponding to the classical trilogy of distance, middle-ground and foreground.

Each component displays properties of prospect and refuge symbolism, but in different proportions. The plateau is essentially prospect-dominant, an immense panoramic horizon seen against a weak false sky dado. (A true sky dado would further accentuate the prospect value.) On closer examination it can be seen to be arboreal, which introduces a weak suggestion of refuge, but the forest is so distant that, in the photograph at least, the eye requires a little support from the imagination.

The canyon is very different. The refuge symbolism normally associated with hollows and depressions is reduplicated by an almost complete cover of forest. The fringing sandstone cliffs form an impediment hazard which seals it off from the plateau, making it more difficult to penetrate. We have seen that an impenetrable appearance in buildings tends to diminish their refuge value. There, not only the person, but also the eye and even the imagination are rebuffed. Here the eye has already penetrated the forested basin very freely, thanks to a

FIGURE 47. THE THREE SISTERS, KATOOMBA, NEW SOUTH WALES
View from the Queen Elizabeth Lookout. Photograph by the author

fine vantage-point. The imagination can penetrate even further, because of the 'deflected vista' effect introduced into the panorama by the canyon. Wouldn't you like to know what really lies round that bend?

The Three Sisters in the foreground are again strong prospect symbols, like all pinnacles, though they derive a measure of refuge value from the nooks and crannies, accentuated in this light by the dense black shadows, and also from the light cover of eucalypts on the left. The strength of their prospect symbolism might be further accentuated if they were observed from a lower viewpoint, so that they cut the horizon and stood out against the sky, but one would then lose some of the strength of the hazard imagery contributed by the precipices when seen from a higher elevation.

Fitting the whole composition together, one can see that, while the breadth and distance of the view, assisted by the 'falling ground', ensure a prospect-dominant picture, each type of symbolism—prospect, hazard and refuge—is expressed with great power and through the agency of widely varying types of landscape feature at very different scales. It is this which produces such a dramatic expression of the sublime.


### (v) *Budapest*

For our last example let us, by way of contrast, take a city and rather than argue the relative merits of different contenders I will accept the authority of Margaret Shackleton and choose what she describes as '. . . probably the most beautiful inland city of Europe' (Shackleton, 1939 edn., p. 332), Budapest.

Budapest is not rich in medieval buildings. Its history of disturbance, occupation and destruction has seen to that, though it does contain some very interesting buildings of more recent date. Its attraction lies rather in its site and in the way in which this has been developed, and I doubt whether it would be possible to find another city of its size which illustrates better the operation of the symbolism of prospect and refuge at different scales.

At the largest scale there is the symbolism deriving from its hills, its valleys, its flat land and its river. Three hills approach close to the Danube on the Western side (Figure 48). To the north of the old city the Rókus-hegy rises gently from its banks. This is separated by the low ground of Moscow Square from the Várhegy, which rises more steeply and on which was built the fortified town of Buda. The most southerly, the Gellért-hegy, is also the steepest and most dramatic. On it is the Citadel. To the west of these hills the city spreads through a landscape of higher wooded hills and well-defined valleys. To the east there spreads out an uninterrupted panorama across the Danube over the low eastern bank of which the town of Pest has outgrown its partner and provided the modern city centre. At this scale elevated viewpoints and sheltered hollows (on the western side) endow the site with great potential in prospect–refuge terms. The hills are not only higher than those of, say, London and Paris, but they approach much nearer the river than Montmartre and Hampstead Heath. At this scale, too, from any of the bridges the Danube presents a majestic deflected vista in both directions.

On the next scale are the large artificial groupings of voids and masses which one finds within this landscape of hill and vale. As studies in the symbolism of prospect and refuge the two depressions between the three hills illustrate two entirely different kinds of development. The more north-westerly, Moscow Square, has little to embellish it in the way of grass or trees. It is not a square but an irregular triangle with the apex at the lower (eastern) end, and it rises away from the river to a staggered, interrupted base line from which, backed by tall buildings to give a sense of shelter, one can look out over falling ground towards the various streets leading out at the sides and the lower end. Of these the Mártírok útja forms the principal outlet from the apex of the triangle, curving away in a series of short deflected vistas, the last of which swings round on to the Margit Bridge. It is certainly not a conventionally beautiful square. Its buildings are mostly undistinguished and it is filled with trams, but even these escape through a hole in the ground in a primitively exciting way. As an

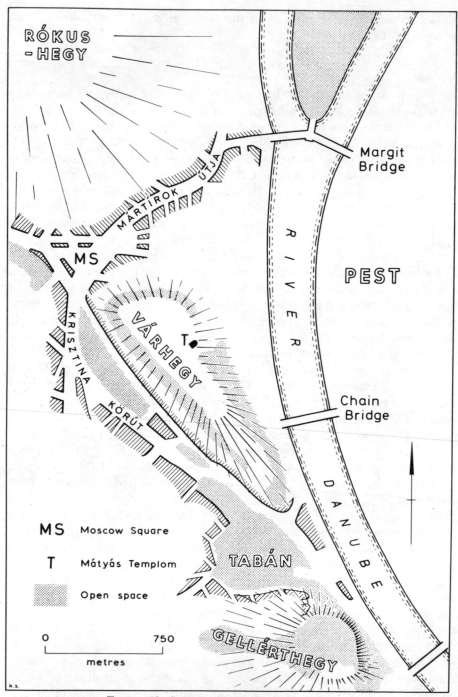

FIGURE 48. SKETCH MAP OF PART OF BUDAPEST
Drawn by Keith R. Scurr

amalgam of masses and voids Moscow Square is vastly more interesting than the sum of its architectural assets.

The more southerly depression, Tabán, between the Várhegy and the Gellért-hegy, is very different. It is a wide amphitheatre of grass and trees, laced and criss-crossed with roads, tramways (largely on independent tracks) and footpaths.

FIGURE 49. THE DUAL SYMBOLISM OF PROSPECT AND REFUGE, BUDAPEST
Drawn by Keith R. Scurr from a photograph by the author

Here one can savour the more open sensation of a prospect-dominant terrain, and if one moves away to the north-west in the direction of the Krisztina Körút and Moscow Square, one experiences a gradual closing in of the protective screens on either side, as in a funnel. On the left the grassy banks are terraced and surmounted by flats which cut a sharp architectural horizon. On the right the symbols of the larger scale again assert themselves; the. building frontage which rises directly from the street is overstepped by the more remote skyline of the castle hill (Várhegy), and it is principally this which protects the observer from exposure to the Danube and the wide-open skies of Pest.

On the smallest scale one can find excitement in the narrow streets and alleys of old Buda and in the irregular little flights of stairs which connect them with the surrounding lowlands on either side. Away from the river on the Buda side the hills bristle with poplars, those spire-like indirect prospect symbols which seem to rise everywhere above the 'cottage-in-the-wood' surface of roofs and foliage. But for my part I would choose the little group of walls and turrets which crown the steep brow overlooking the Danube on the eastern side of the Mátyás-templom (Figure 49). In these the Magyar vernacular has drawn out every ounce of the dual symbolism of prospect and refuge which, as we have seen, is latent in the very idea of the tower as an architectural form. In these, too, can be seen an expression of the perpetual conflict between the freedom of man to devise his own styles, his own fashions, his own forms of expression, and the limitations ultimately placed on him both by the character of the place in which he works and by the nature of his own behavioural reactions to it; the conflict, in other words, between the emancipation of imagination, of invention, of art, and the inescapable tyranny of what Pope, following Virgil, calls 'the Genius of the Place'.

# CHAPTER 10

# Stocktaking

What is it that we like about landscape, and why do we like it? This is where our questioning began, and we have now reached the point where we can review our position to see whether any significant progress has been achieved.

In the first two chapters, it will be remembered, we sketched out the main dimensions of the problem and selected some of the more important landmarks or milestones in the quest for a solution. If we have now reached a new view-point, do these milestones look any different when seen from that viewpoint? More fundamentally, does the problem itself seem to have yielded even a little under the pressures we have brought to bear on it? Have we anything to show for our exertions? At least the reader may now be in a position to understand more of the rationale which lay behind the selection of the 'milestones' in Chapter 2. Let us begin our stocktaking at the close of business with a quick backward glance.

The change of emphasis given by Shaftesbury to the word 'sublime' (p. 26) appears even more significant when seen in the light of habitat theory. The recognition that the pursuit of the source of aesthetic satisfaction might lead beyond its rhetorical expression and into the field of the direct experience of the physical universe anticipated the core of Dewey's philosophy by more than two centuries. It points the way towards a functional interpretation of landscape aesthetics in which involvement (Chapter 6) is a central theme, and it reverses the general emphasis habitually laid by the aestheticians on art rather than nature. It is a very important signpost.

We can now also see why, for our purposes, Burke is so much more significant than Hogarth. Hogarth was still arguing a case for believing that the origin of beauty lay in form. Certainly we have accepted that the 'line of beauty' can indeed occasion aesthetic satisfaction. We have found it, for instance, in the deflected vista, but we have postulated a functional rather than a morphological explanation for it. It is, of course, apprehended morphologically. It is the wavy line that we can see. But it is the expectation aroused by the deflection in the vista that causes aesthetic excitement, and that expectation is simply one phase in a comprehensive environmental experience.

Burke, on the other hand, has made a major breakthrough. Boulton says:

'The conclusion that Burke reaches—that taste operates by fixed principles in all men—illustrates the eighteenth-century inclination to discover immutable laws governing human life and activity. In the New-tonian tradition Burke looks for—and finds—immutable laws governing taste.' (Boulton, 1958, p. xxviii)

If to the Newtonian tradition Burke had been in a position to add the Darwinian and Freudian traditions, if, in short, he had had reason to look for 'immutable laws' not only in the physical but in the biological sciences, who is to say that we might not have had a scientifically based ethological interpretation of landscape aesthetics two hundred years ago? As it was, the whole exciting argument was allowed to degenerate into a quibble about the difference between a couple of abstract nouns, and this not unnaturally fails to carry conviction as a comprehensive aesthetic theory. But what we have postulated in this book about, for instance, the imagery and symbolism of the hazard, goes very little further than Burke went in his discussion of the sublime. The necessity to put oneself, if only in the imagination, at the mercy of the powers of nature, to experience that savouring of danger which Burke called 'pain', lies at the very heart of prospect–refuge theory and underlies the taste of the picturesque school which followed him.

In the evaluation of this school we can now see that many of the ideas which seemed paradoxical fall into a new perspective. The reference back to the seventeenth-century painters for a standard of excellence, the contemptuous attitude towards the style of Capability Brown, the exaggerated adulation of the wilderness and of a primitive antiquity—all can be seen as perfectly logical and, what is more, perfectly compatible with apparently irreconcilable views, provided we get down to that fundamental level where we are dealing with the inborn rather than the learned components of taste. One is no more obliged to say that, because one school of fashion is right, therefore all styles which do not conform to it are wrong, than to insist that one must like *either* tragedy *or* comedy but not both. Just as each of these can throw a different light on our experience of a social situation, so beetling cliffs and shaven lawns can each stimulate aesthetic sensitivity. The outstanding characteristics of the picturesque are to be found in the choice of symbols for which its apologists showed a preference. In general these symbols tend to be stronger than those of Capability Brown. The refuge symbolism, for instance, is more extreme—the vegetation denser and the shadows deeper—but what else could one expect if the hazard symbolism is also stronger?

Indeed, the whole Romantic Movement can be seen as an attempt to reconcile the dignity of man, supreme among God's creatures, with his continuing involvement in a natural order which he seeks to control but only within which he can find those sign-stimuli to which his inborn mechanisms still respond. When Alison says '. . . the qualities of matter are not to be considered as sublime or beautiful in themselves, but as being the signs or expressions of such qualities, as, by the constitution of our nature, are fitted to produce pleasing or interesting emotion' (p. 38) he is getting very near to habitat theory. His very phraseology recalls the language of those twentieth-century ethologists whom we quoted in Chapter 3, and his reference to 'the constitution of our nature' could well have come out of Dewey. When he says that aesthetic enjoyment arises from trains of ideas which must be connected by some linking principle, all he really needs in order to apply his philosophy to the interpretation of landscape is such a principle, which need not be any more complicated or sophisticated than 'seeing without being seen'.

Then what about the great American Myth and all that denigration of the wilderness which could not conjure up a respectable show of antiquities to give it an acceptable aesthetic basis? We can now see that ruins themselves are quite inessential. In the landscape of the romantics they were the clichés of a particular idiom. The symbol was glorified for itself rather than for what it symbolized. Even if we allow that the vestiges of past civilizations have a nostalgic role to play within the process by which we are emancipating ourselves from the tyranny of nature, as undoubtedly they have, the wilderness itself goes back still further in that evolutionary process. It is a more extreme example of antiquity than the Parthenon.

What the American romantics really discovered in their landscape was that fundamental refuge symbol, the primeval forest. If the Ancient Greeks had still been afraid of it, having barely emerged from its tyranny, the nineteenth-century Americans had come from a tradition which had already come to terms with it and found a place for it within its aesthetic philosophy. But forest by itself lacks balance in the sense in which we have now defined it; to achieve this it must have an element of prospect symbolism and where, in that interminable forest, can one find a decent view? There are, in fact, two common kinds of topographical situation in which the symbolism of the prospect is to be found within the forest. The first, usually with a vistal emphasis, is where the forest is interrupted by rivers. The second, characteristically in a more panoramic form, is where hills or mountains rise high enough to permit a view over its canopy; and the two topographical names which constantly recur in the literature of the American Ideal Landscape are those of the Hudson River and the Catskill Mountains.

In short, is the American Myth so uniquely American? (p. 55; cf. the allegedly unique character of the Japanese garden, p. 228). Or, if we listen more carefully to its chroniclers and their interpreters, do we merely hear the voice of a universally applicable prospect–refuge theory speaking with an American accent?

From the viewpoint we have now reached we may also find a new perspective in which to see the role of Ruskin. If he had been less preoccupied with the imperfections in the techniques of the seventeenth-century landscapists; if he had not allowed himself to be so outraged by the '. . . black round mass of impenetrable paint, diverging into feathers instead of leaves . . .' (p. 46), he might have devoted more attention to the development of a general theory of landscape aesthetics. It was suggested earlier (p. 47) that, when he writes of '. . . the physical conditions appointed for human existence' and '. . . the visible things which are dangerous or beneficial to men', he comes very near to enunciating such a theory, but that he never clearly explains how it can be made to relate meaningfully to the particular components of real landscapes. It is this next stage that we have now attempted to achieve, and if we have succeeded even to the smallest degree, our efforts may, I believe, give a new emphasis to many of Ruskin's prolific writings on landscape.

Perhaps the most fruitful backward glance is one which takes us no further than the nineteen thirties and what we may call 'the Dewey–Cornish Gap'. We saw that John Dewey and Vaughan Cornish were simultaneously exploring the fields of aesthetics and landscape respectively, but that neither could effectively break through into the language of the other (p. 52). Any vocabulary which would have enabled Dewey to express his aesthetic philosophy in terms of particular components of landscape could equally have provided Vaughan Cornish with a framework for fitting together his landscape word pictures into something like a philosophical system. I think a re-reading of the works of both these authors in the light of prospect–refuge theory confirms that they constitute, as it were, the approach viaducts to the bridge on either side. If our hypotheses do not yet provide the missing central span, it is my hope that they may enable us to prepare a rough sketch of what such a span may eventually look like.

I need scarcely dwell on the relevance of prospect–refuge theory to 'environmental perception studies' since, of all the fields of academic enquiry, this is the one into which our quest can most easily be fitted. It is here that we find a concern with the world, not as it is, but as it seems to be—a world, perhaps, of misapprehensions and distorted images but one which, in the phenomenon of spontaneous apprehension by a creature involved in surviving in it, is more real than reality.

Clearly we cannot again go through the whole of Chapter 2, re-examining every detail in the light of our hypotheses, much less through that vast repository of recorded human experience to be found in the gardens, libraries and art galleries of the world; but we can postulate some vindication of the view expressed in Chapter 1, that it is the fragmentation of this experience into discrete fields of academic enquiry which has proved a stumbling-block to the study of landscape aesthetics. Only when we refuse to be intimidated by the authority of the specialist or inhibited by the awareness of our own ignorance can we break through the diversity of disciplines and find the themes which transgress their boundaries.

This is all very well, I shall be told, but how does this prospect–refuge theory stand up to those two searching questions by which all theories must be assessed: 'Can it be substantiated, and is it of any use?' Let us take the second question first.

I have been at pains throughout to suggest that I do not wish to replace established methods of aesthetic analysis by a new system which at a stroke will render them all obsolete. The methodology of the art critic, for instance, has been evolved through long experience, and it would be an outrageous impertinence to suggest that the examination of landscape painting by the symbolism of prospect, refuge and hazard would be in all cases an 'improvement' on established techniques. But we have already seen that art critics *do* encounter difficulties arising from what I have called '. . . the absence, not only of a linguistic, but also of a conceptual bridge' (p. 22). We found in this connection that there is no difficulty in explaining a mother's grief at the death of her son. Although we did not say so, we assumed that her expected behaviour in wishing for his biological survival is a normal attribute of motherhood: a part of (in Alison's phrase) 'the constitution of her nature'. It belongs to that component of her behaviour-pattern which is inborn, though the method by which she expresses it may well be modified by learning. Re-phrasing the story of the *mater dolorosa* in this way contributes little if anything to our understanding of its poignancy. But once we cast a familiar and acceptable idea into this simple psychological formula we may find it much more helpful in extending our understanding of feeling into that area of experience which relates us, not to other people, but to the rest of our perceived environment, and it is here that the art critic's problem really lies. When we find that grief is occasioned by our inability to achieve the inborn desires proper to our species, as subsequently modified by our individual life experiences, whether these desires relate to the survival of our children or of ourselves, all that is needed to link the poignancy of the *mater dolorosa* with the poignancy of the sunrise and sunset is a symbolism which can relate both to an ethological explanation.

If we can look for only a limited usefulness for prospect–refuge theory in the interpretation of aesthetic phenomena within the several fields of the art critic, the historian of landscape design or any other specialist, its expectation of success must be greater in exploring those relationships which cross the boundaries of the established disciplines. Whereas in painting, for instance, I believe it *can* throw fresh light on the comparative study of different styles, schools and periods, it is when we seek to relate the particulars of landscape in painting to the *same yardstick* to which we have referred the landscapes of Wordsworth, Capability Brown and the indefatigable members of the Ramblers' Association that we may hope to discover a new meaning. This yardstick enables us to measure the superficial manifestations of particular periods, places or media of expression against a scale of criteria which is timeless. It allows us to express in terms of a common denominator not only landscapes but also attitudes of widely differing kinds. The afforestation, for instance, which so enrages the anti-conifer brigade and enraptures the coachloads of old-age pensioners (p. 4), can be seen to involve the replacement of a prospect dominant landscape with a particular kind of refuge symbol. The conifer itself is not visually unattractive. After all, an object which the Germans for centuries, and the English since they had a German Prince, have annually taken into their homes to become the centrepiece of their Christmas decorations, cannot be intrinsically unaesthetic. The way it is planted may certainly give offence, as it did to that most perceptive admirer of the English Lake District:

> 'The transformation of Ennerdale from a beautiful valley to a dense forest is now complete and is no cause for pride. Here trees are grown unnaturally and denied space and light so that the limbs wither and only a straight main stem develops. The aim is a thicket of living telegraph poles. This is battery forestry, and because trees have life and dignity it has all the objections of battery farming.' (Wainwright (n.d.) No. 217, *Great Borne and Starling Dodd*)

Or again, where conifers are planted in rows, they have all the artificiality of a

262

le Nôtre design without that glorification of the vista which more than compensates for the orchard arrangement. They can also create an environment so uniformly dark that the refuge effect is insufficiently relieved by prospect symbolism such as one might find in the glade of an oak forest. All these features can understandably upset the walker who penetrates the forest. The tourist in the coach is less likely to encounter them at close quarters and, seen from a distance, their principal effect is simply to strengthen the refuge symbolism by converting a carpeted into an arboreal surface. The objection that closely planted trees deny a prospect cannot be sustained when the forest is viewed from farther away. If, however, there is still a want of prospect symbolism this may be further supplied by the introduction of an aquatic surface, as at Thirlmere, Lake Vyrnwy and the Elan Valley (p. 4). In short, the apparently irreconcilable conflict between the protagonists in the afforestation debate begins to look less intractable when one looks at it in terms of the symbolism of prospect and refuge.

We are still left, however, with the question, 'Can our theory be substantiated?' and here again we must go right back to the beginning. We have looked at a good deal of circumstantial evidence and we have hinted at various ways in which the reader may pursue his own further enquiries in the light of his own experience, but is that sufficient to constitute a proof of the validity of our hypotheses?

It has never been my intention to prove anything, but rather to open up discussion. We have touched on so many disciplines and trespassed within so many fields that we must have left behind many unresolved questions. I will readily admit that this book has been a piece of advocacy rather than of judgment, and for the good reason that I have not the qualifications to judge. 'Proof', if it can be established at all, must be the product of a rigorous examination of the hypotheses within the context of those disciplines on which they impinge.

My self-imposed task is now completed; it has been to bring the argument to a level of plausibility at which scholars competent to pursue these further enquiries may conclude that there is enough *prima facie* evidence to warrant their attention. To conclude with a musical analogy, I should like to think of this book as a bridge passage played on a solo instrument, not very important, perhaps, in itself, but leading the imagination onwards into the next movement, in which the full orchestra must be involved. At that stage we may make some real progress in understanding what it is that we like about landscape and why we like it.

# APPENDIX A

# Notes

1. The importance of John Dewey is discussed in the next chapter.
2. Hamerton (1885) is an interesting example of an attempt to link the techniques of landscape painting with the study of a wide range of landscape components.
3. Gombrich (1966) is also important; see particularly his chapter on 'The Renaissance theory of art and the rise of landscape', pp. 107–121.
4. Ogden and Ogden (1955) is an example of a book which, while dealing predominantly with the history of painting, touches on other sources of evidence. As its title implies, however, it is limited to a very restricted field within the cultural history of artistic taste. About half of Friedländer's study (1949) is devoted to landscape.
5. James Hutton (1726–1797), the Scottish geologist, communicated his 'theory of the earth' to the Royal Society of Edinburgh in 1785.
6. Anthony Ashley Cooper, Third Earl of Shaftesbury (1671–1713). See especially his *Characteristics of Men, Manners, Opinions, Times* (1711). Some of the essays included in the *Characteristics* had been separately published somewhat earlier.
7. Kent was not the first to introduce these ideas: Bridgeman, for instance, to some extent anticipated him (Hussey, 1927, p. 28). But Kent can properly be credited with the leading role in establishing them as the basis of the accepted fashion.
8. As early as 1709, for instance, Shaftesbury had written: 'Your *Genius*, the *Genius* of the Place, and the GREAT GENIUS have at last prevail'd. I shall no longer resist the Passion in me for Things of a *natural* kind; where neither *Art*, nor the *Conceit* or *Caprice* of Man has spoil'd their *genuine Order*, by breaking in upon the *primitive State*. Even the rude *Rocks*, the mossy *Caverns*, the irregular unwrought *Grotto's*, and the broken *Falls* of Waters, with all the horrid Graces of the *Wilderness* it-self, as representing NATURE more, will be the more engaging, and appear with a Magnificence beyond the Mockery of princely Gardens.' *The Moralists* (first published 1709). See Shaftesbury (1749 edn.), vol. II, p. 255.
9. 'The fatal rock on which all professed improvers are likely to split is that of system; they become mannerists both from getting fond of what they have done before, and from the ease of repeating what they have so far practised; but to be reckoned a mannerist is at least as great a reproach to the improver as to the painter.' Price (1794), p. 255.
10. Alternatively called Gaspar(d) Poussin after his brother-in-law, Nicolas Poussin (1594–1665), with whom he is sometimes confused by writers on the picturesque.
11. The letter is published in Thomas Dick Lauder's edition of Price's essay *On The Picturesque* (1842), pp. 410–416.
12. Francis Hutcheson (1694–1747). His ideas on aesthetics are discussed particularly in his essays of 1725 and 1728.
13. It will be noted that Van Zandt is not using the word 'association' in quite the same sense as Alison.
14. Van Zandt (1966), pp. 153–154. Cf. Wilson O. Clough: 'At first the European mind tried desperately to link the lineaments of the new reality with past myths, or the myths with the reality; but in time the reality was sufficient to itself, and wonder was available within a real world.' Clough (1964), p. 5.

15. Published as Volumes III–VII in Cook and Wedderburn (1903–1912). For an account of the chronology of publication see the Introduction to Volume III (1903).
16. Boulding (1956). The concept of an 'image' is not necessarily limited to a purely visual phenomenon; it can be the product of the whole field of environmental experience. See Fitch (1970).
17. E.g. in *Christ Church Meadows* and *The Route of the M4*; Jellicoe (1966), vol. II, pp. 49–66 and 67–83.
18. 'A detailed knowledge of the geography of their home area will often mean the difference between life and death to a small mammal or bird as a predator swoops down.' Manning (1972 edn.), p. 190.
19. A number of the terms introduced in the following pages will be found illustrated in Figure 9. The reader is also referred to the glossary of terms (Appendix C).
20. Gombrich (1960) is much concerned with this subject. See particularly his Chapter VI, 'The Image in the Clouds'.
21. Hofstede de Groot (1908–1927) in Volume IV (1912) names over fifty paintings of watermills by Jacob van Ruisdael (1628/9–1682) and rather more by Hobbema (1638–1709). Seven paintings in each case contain more than one watermill.
22. J. M. W. Turner, *A Fire at Sea*. The National Gallery, No. 558. This unfinished painting was at the Tate Gallery between 1910 and 1956.
23. The dots (. . .) in these passages from Rölvaag do not represent omissions from the quotations; they are in the original translation.
24. Not all van der Neer's paintings were in this style; indeed his work included a number of winter scenes not unlike those of Avercamp, but it is for his evening and nocturnal landscapes that he is chiefly noted.
25. 'The Flower and the Leaf', published in Bell (1892 edition), vol. IV, pp. 351–352. The editor quotes the authority of W. W. Skeats for the assertion that this poem, at one time attributed to Chaucer, was apparently written by a woman probably about the middle of the fifteenth century (p. 348, fn.).
26. Perhaps the best known example is his *Charles I on Horseback* in the National Gallery, No. 1172.
27. Descriptions of the same place at different times also offer scope for contrasts in the balance of prospect–refuge symbolism. See, for instance, Goldsmith's *The Deserted Village* (1770).
28. 'He [Gaudí] finds in nature the rules and guidance that should define and govern the architectural elements. The roof like a mountain has ridges and slopes, the vaulting is like a natural cave of parabolic section. The more resistant parts of the soil form shelves projecting over the eroded sides . . .' Bergós (1954), quoted by Sweeney and Sert (1960), p. 133. See also Ridley (1965), who cites passages from Tolkien and other authors to illustrate the emotive association between buildings and the primitive natural environment, commenting on the fascination of grottoes and of buildings which seem to rise out of the solid rock.
29. Since writing this I have played my first round of golf after an interval of 35 years on a course much encumbered by gorse bushes. It is astonishing what foolish things one can write.
30. According to Hussey (1967, p. 27), '. . . the change from stag to fox hunting encouraged replacement of straight rides in the woodlands by expanses of turf interspersed with coverts. But Queen Anne still hunted the stag.'
31. Among many such paintings may be mentioned the Vermeer in the *Wallraf-Richartz* Museum, Köln, the view in the *Pinakothek*, Munich, attributed to the same artist, and the Jacob van Ruisdael in the *Kunsthaus*, Zürich, all reproduced in Stechow (1966).
32. In 1970 the Centre for Urban and Regional Research, University of Manchester,

was entrusted by the Countryside Commission for England and Wales with the preparation of a review of techniques of landscape evaluation. For an earlier review see Higgins (1967).

33. There is much discussion of this in the American 'wilderness' literature. See, for instance, Nash (1967) and Spectorsky (1955).

# *Grongar Hill* by John Dyer

Silent Nymph, with curious eye!
Who, the purple evening, lie
On the mountain's lonely van,
Beyond the noise of busy man,
Painting fair the form of things,
While the yellow linet sings;
Or the tuneful nightingale
Charms the forest with her tale;
Come with all thy various hues,
Come, and aid thy sister Muse;    10
Now while Phoebus riding high
Gives lustre to the land and sky!
Grongar Hill invites my song,
Draw the landskip bright and strong;
Grongar, in whose mossy cells
Sweetly-musing Quiet dwells;
Grongar, in whose silent shade,
For the modest Muses made,
So oft I have, the evening still,
At the fountain of a rill,    20
Sate upon a flow'ry bed,
With my hand beneath my head;
While stray'd my eyes o'er Towy's flood,
Over mead, and over wood,
From house to house, from hill to hill,
'Till Contemplation had her fill.
   About his chequer'd sides I wind,
And leave his brooks and meads behind,
And groves, and grottoes where I lay,
And vistoes shooting beams of day:    30
Wide and wider spreads the vale;
As circles on a smooth canal;
The mountains round, unhappy fate!
Sooner or later, of all height,
Withdraw their summits from the skies,
And lessen as the others rise;
Still the prospect wider spreads,
Adds a thousand woods and meads,
Still it widens, widens still,
And sinks the newly-risen hill.    40
   Now, I gain the mountain's brow,
What a landskip lies below!
No clouds, no vapours intervene,
But the gay, the open scene
Does the face of nature show,

In all the hues of heaven's bow!
And, swelling to embrace the light,
Spreads around beneath the sight.
   Old castles on the cliffs arise,
Proudly tow'ring in the skies!    50
Rushing from the woods, the spires
Seem from hence ascending fires!
Half his beams Apollo sheds
On the yellow mountain-heads!
Gilds the fleeces of the flocks;
And glitters on the broken rocks!
   Below me trees unnumber'd rise,
Beautiful in various dyes:
The gloomy pine, the poplar blue,
The yellow beech, the sable yew,    60
The slender fir, that taper grows,
The sturdy oak with broad-spread
   boughs.
And beyond the purple grove,
Haunt of Phyllis, queen of love!
Gaudy as the op'ning dawn,
Lies a long and level lawn
On which a dark hill, steep and high,
Holds and charms the wand'ring eye!
Deep are his feet in Towy's flood,
His sides are cloath'd with waving
   wood,    70
And ancient towers crown his brow,
That cast an aweful look below;
Whose ragged walls the ivy creeps,
And with her arms from falling keeps;
So both a safety from the wind
On mutual dependance find.
   'Tis now the raven's bleak abode;
'Tis now th'apartment of the toad;
And there the fox securely feeds;
And there the pois'nous adder breeds  80
Conceal'd in ruins, moss and weeds;
While, ever and anon, there falls
Huge heaps of hoary moulder'd walls.
Yet time has seen, that lifts the low,
And level lays the lofty brow,
Has seen this broken pile compleat,
Big with the vanity of state;
But transient is the smile of fate!

A little rule, a little sway,
A sun beam in a winter's day,    90
Is all the proud and mighty have
Between the cradle and the grave.
   And see the rivers how they run,
Thro' woods and meads, in shade and
   sun,
Sometimes swift, sometimes slow,
Wave succeeding wave, they go
A various journey to the deep,
Like human life to endless sleep!
Thus is nature's vesture wrought,
To instruct our wand'ring thought:   100
Thus she dresses green and gay,
To disperse our cares away.
   Ever charming, ever new,
When will the landskip tire the view!
The fountain's fall, the river's flow,
The woody vallies, warm and low;
The windy summit, wild and high,
Roughly rushing on the sky!
The pleasant seat, the ruin'd tow'r,
The naked rock, the shady bow'r;   110
The town and village, dome and farm,
Each give each a double charm,
As pearls upon an Æthiop's arm.
   See on the mountain's southern side,
Where the prospect opens wide,
Where the evening gilds the tide;
How close and small the hedges lie!
What streaks of meadows cross the eye!
A step methinks may pass the stream,
So little distant dangers seem;   120
So we mistake the future's face,
Ey'd thro' hope's deluding glass;
As yon summits soft and fair

Clad in colours of the air,
Which to those who journey near,
Barren, brown, and rough appear;
Still we tread the same coarse way,
The present's still a cloudy day.
   O may I with myself agree,
And never covet what I see;   130
Content me with an humble shade,
My passions tam'd, my wishes laid;
For while our wishes wildly roll,
We banish quiet from the soul;
'Tis thus the busy beat the air;
And misers gather wealth and care.
   Now, ev'n now, my joys run high,
As on the mountain-turf I lie;
While the wanton Zephyr sings,
And in the vale perfumes his wings;   140
While the waters murmur deep;
While the shepherd charms his sheep;
While the birds unbounded fly,
And with musick fill the sky,
Now, ev'n now, my joys run high.
   Be full, ye courts, be great who will;
Search for Peace with all your skill:
Open wide the lofty door,
Seek her on the marble floor,
In vain you search, she is not there;   150
In vain ye search the domes of care!
Grass and flowers Quiet treads,
On the meads, the mountain-heads,
Along with Pleasure, close ally'd,
Ever by each other's side:
And often by the murmuring rill,
Hears the thrush, while all is still,
Within the groves of Grongar Hill.

# APPENDIX C

# Glossary of Terms

(To which some particular shade of meaning is attached beyond that normally understood from general usage)

Accessibility. See Penetrability.

Animate hazard. An incident hazard in which the threat is posed by some animate agent.

Aquatic. (i) Of hazards; an inanimate incident (or impediment) hazard in which the threat is posed by water. (ii) Of surfaces or horizons; a surface or horizon of water, characteristically prospect-dominant.

Arboreal. (i) Of refuges; a term used to distinguish refuges on the basis of their substance or fabric. (ii) Of surfaces or horizons; a term used to denote cover by vegetation tall enough to afford refuge. 'Arboreal' generally implies refuge-orientation, but the tops of trees, particularly those of upright habit of growth, can act as prospect symbols.

Architectural. A term used of surfaces or horizons composed of artificial structures. Architectural surfaces and horizons may be further distinguished on the basis of components (e.g. walls, roofs, etc.) or materials (e.g. stone, timber, etc.).

Balance. The proportion in which different kinds of symbolism are combined in a landscape.

Canopy. An opaque covering above a horizontal vista, q.v.

Carpeted. An 'open' surface or horizon covered by vegetation (e.g. grass, heather, etc.) low enough not to impede visibility under normal conditions.

Closed. A term used of prospects in which a view is limited in distance by some intervening screen. A view of short 'fetch', q.v.

Cloud canopy. A canopy, formed by cloud, covering a sky dado, q.v.

Contraposition (Adj. Contrapositive). The juxtaposition of symbols of contrasting type; the opposite of reduplication.

Coulisse. Originally a theatrical term denoting scenery which projects from the wings on to the stage; applied in art criticism to any lateral projection from the flanks of a landscape, hence a particular form of interface between voids and masses. Highly significant as a zone of contact between prospect and refuge.

Deficiency hazard. A threat to comfort or survival resulting from some chronic deficiency (e.g. food) rather than from some incident.

Deflected vista. A form of secondary vista in which a deflection of the vistal axis terminates a direct prospect but suggests a continuation of the line of vision in the same general direction.

Direct prospect. A view as directly observed.

Dominance (Adj. Dominant). The prevailing influence of a particular kind of symbolism in a landscape, (e.g. 'prospect dominance', 'refuge dominant', etc.).

Exposure. A condition of refuge-deficiency in which the dominant symbolism is that of prospect and hazard combined.

Falling ground. A surface sloping downwards away from a vantage-point; a common prospect symbol.

False sky dado. A phenomenon similar to a sky dado (q.v.) in which, however, the bright layer near the horizon is caused by the diffusion of light by particles in the atmosphere impeding rather than facilitating the passage of light.

Fetch. The distance over which visibility can be achieved in a particular direction.

Fire hazard. One of the categories of inanimate incident hazard.

Habitat theory. The theory that aesthetic satisfaction experienced in the contemplation of landscape stems from the spontaneous perception of landscape features which, in their shapes, colours, spatial arrangements and other visible attributes, act as sign-stimuli indicative of environmental conditions favourable for survival, whether they are really favourable or not.

Hazard. An incident or condition prejudicial to the attainment of comfort, safety or survival.

Hide. A form of refuge which provides concealment from animate hazards. Cf. Shelter.

Horizon. A line, not necessarily horizontal, marking the limits within which an object or surface impedes visibility. A horizon is always conspicuous as a secondary vantage-point (q.v.); it differs from other secondary vantage-points in that its identity depends on its being observed from a particular primary vantage-point.

Horizontal vista. A view restricted by conspicuous bounding margins in a horizontal plane.

Human hazard. An animate hazard in which the threat is posed by a human agent.

Impediment hazard. An obstacle or condition which impedes the threatened party in securing an environmental advantage by restricting his freedom of movement (e.g. a wall, fence or river).

Inanimate hazard. An incident hazard in which the threat is posed by some inanimate instrument or by the onset of some condition not determined by any animate agent (e.g. a storm or earthquake).

Incident hazard. A hazard which seems to be occasioned by some incident rather than by some condition.

Indirect prospect. The imagined view from a secondary vantage-point, q.v.

Instability hazard. An inanimate incident hazard resulting from instability (e.g. a landslide).

Interface (Prospect–Refuge Interface). The zone of contact between those parts of the environment which are visible from a vantage-point and those which are not, or between prospect-dominant and refuge-dominant areas. See *Coulisse*.

Interrupted panorama. A panorama broken by obstacles insufficient to destroy the impression of a single landscape. Cf. Multiple vista.

Inversion. The association of one kind of symbolism with an object or situation normally associated with another; e.g. in nocturnal landscapes, when the usual symbolism of prospect in the sky (light) is replaced by that of refuge (darkness).

Involvement. Participation in any activity or experience which implies a functional, strategic or perceptual relationship between an observer and his environment.

Lateral vista. See Offset.

Locomotion hazard. An incident hazard resulting from movement by the threatened party, e.g. a fall.

Magnet (Adj. Magnetic). A part of the landscape which attracts the eye of the observer. The adjective 'magnetic' can be applied to a point, line, area, etc.

Meterological hazard. An inanimate incident hazard in which the threat is posed by some meterological phenomenon (e.g. wind, rain, snow, etc.).

Multiple vista. A view resulting from two or more breaches in an opaque screen, where the efficacy of the screen is sufficient to destroy the impression of a continuous panorama. Cf. Interrupted panorama.

Naked. A term applied to an open surface or horizon uncovered by vegetation (e.g. consisting of rock, sand, asphalt, etc.).

Nebulous. (i) Of apparent surfaces or horizons consisting of dust or water particles suspended in the atmosphere (e.g. fog, smoke, cloud, etc.). (ii) Of refuges formed by such substances.

Non-human hazard. An animate hazard in which the threat is posed by an animal other than a human.

Offset (lateral vista). An indirect prospect which results from an apparent breach in the confining flanks of a vista, suggesting the opportunity to achieve a prospect approximately at right angles to the vistal channel.

Open. A term used of surfaces or horizons relatively free from impediments to vision and therefore prospect-dominant. See 'Naked' and 'Carpeted'.

Panorama. A view in which breadth is a dominant characteristic.

Peephole. A view restricted in both horizontal and vertical planes, as in a window, rock arch, etc.

Penetrability (Accessibility). The property of the margin of a refuge which appears to offer easy access (e.g. by an opening, staircase, shaded edge, etc.).

Primary vantage-point. A place from which a direct prospect is observed.

Prospect. (i) A view. (ii) An environmental condition, situation, object or arrangement conducive to the attainment of a view.

Prospect–refuge theory. The theory that the ability to see without being seen is conducive to the exploitation of environmental conditions favourable to biological survival and is therefore a source of pleasure.

Reduplication. The use of two or more symbols of similar kind to reinforce each other (e.g. a cottage in a wood, both being refuge symbols).

Refuge. An environmental condition, situation, object or arrangement conducive to hiding or sheltering. See 'Hide' and 'Shelter'.

Secondary panorama, vista. An indirect prospect (q.v.) of panoramic or vistal form.

Secondary vantage-point. A place or object, usually elevated, which suggests a further extension of an observer's field of vision. See 'Indirect prospect'.

Shelter. A form of refuge which provides protection against inanimate hazards. Cf. 'Hide'.

Sky dado. A horizontal vista formed by a layer of bright, clear sky between a horizon and a cloud canopy, q.v.

Terrestrial. A term used of surfaces or horizons consisting of solid as opposed to fluid substances. Cf. 'carpeted' or 'arboreal' with 'aquatic' or 'nebulous' surfaces or horizons.

Texture. A property of a surface deriving from the material of which it is composed, chiefly apprehended by the manner in which it reflects light (e.g. 'naked', 'arboreal', 'aquatic', etc.).

Token symbols. Symbols introduced in a miniature or inconspicuous form to complement a dominant symbolism of a different kind.

Value. The capacity of an environmental situation, condition, object or arrangement to communicate a suggestion of prospect ('prospect value'), refuge ('refuge value') or hazard ('hazard value').

Vista (Adj. Vistal). A view restricted by conspicuous bounding margins, generally vertical or near-vertical; but cf. Horizontal vista, Sky dado.

# APPENDIX D
# List of Works Cited

Such a vast literature could be deemed relevant to the theme of this book that the preparation of a proper bibliography is out of the question. The following list of works of reference has been compiled by the application of a draconian but simple principle. It is this. If a work is mentioned in the text, the notes or the legend relating to any of the illustrative matter, it is included; otherwise, however relevant it may be to the experience of landscape, it is not.

ALISON, Archibald (1790) *Essays on the Nature and Principles of Taste* (3rd edn., 1812, consulted), Longmans, Edinburgh.
*Annals of Sporting and Fancy Gazette*, Sherwood, Jones, London.
APPLEYARD, D., LYNCH, K. and MYER, J. R. (1964) *The View from the Road*, M.I.T. Press, Cambridge, Mass.
AVEBURY, Lord (1902) *The Scenery of England and the Causes to Which it is Due*, Macmillan, London.
BALCHIN, W. G. V. (1954) *Cornwall: An Illustrated Essay on the History of the Landscape*, Hodder & Stoughton, London.
BALINT, Michael (1955) 'Friendly expanses—horrid empty spaces', *Int. J. Psychoanalysis*, **36**, pp. 225–241.
BALSTON, Thomas (1947) *John Martin (1789–1854): his Life and Works*, Duckworth, London.
BARBIER, C. P. (1963) *William Gilpin, his Drawings, Teaching, and Theory of the Picturesque*, Clarendon Press, Oxford.
BARTON, Stuart, *et. al.* (1972) *Monumental Follies*, Lyle Publications, Worthing.
BATTEN, H. Mortimer (1920) *Habits and Characteristics of British Wild Animals*, Chambers, London.
BEARDSLEY, Monroe C. (1966) *Aesthetics from Classical Greece to the Present: a Short History*, Macmillan, New York.
BELL, Robert (Ed.) (1892, rev. ed.) *The Poetical Works of Geoffrey Chaucer*, George Bell, London.
BERESFORD, M. W. and ST JOSEPH, J. K. S. (1958) *Medieval England: an Aerial Survey*, C.U.P., Cambridge.
BERGÓS, Joan (1954) *Gaudí l'home i l'obra*, Barcelona.
BERLYNE, D. E. (1971) *Aesthetics and psychobiology*, Appleton–Century–Crofts, New York.
BLUNDEN, Edmund (Ed.) (1929) *The Poems of William Collins*, Etchells & Macdonald, London.
BLUNT, Anthony (1967) *Nicolas Poussin*, Phaidon Press, New York and London.
BOULDING, Kenneth (1956) *The Image*, Univ. of Michigan Press, Ann Arbor, Michigan.
BOULTON, J. T. (Ed.) (1958) *Edmund Burke: a Philosophical Enquiry into the Origins of our Ideas on the Sublime and the Beautiful*, Routledge & Kegan Paul, London.
BOWLER, S. W. (1956 ed.) *Teach Yourself Photography*, English Univ. Press, London.
BOWLES, W. L. (1806) *The works of Alexander Pope, Esq.*, 10 vols., Strahan & Preston, London.
BRANCHER, D. M. (1969) 'Critique of K. D. Fines: landscape evaluation. A research project in East Sussex', *Reg. Studies*, **3**, pp. 91–92.

BRETT, R. L. (1951) *The Third Earl of Shaftesbury*, Hutchinson, London.
BROADBENT, Geoffrey (1973) *Design in Architecture*, Wiley, London.
BRONTË, Emily (1847) *Wuthering Heights*, Newby, London.
BROOKFIELD, H. C. (1969) 'On the environment perceived', *Prog. Geog.*, **1**, pp. 51–80.
● BRYAN, P. W. (1933) *Man's Adaptation of Nature: Studies of the Cultural Landscape*, Univ. of London Press, London.
BURKE, Edmund (1757), see Boulton, J. T.
CARROLL, Lewis (1865) *Alice in Wonderland* (1925 edn. consulted), Macmillan, London.
CECIL, Lord David (1934) 'Emily Brontë and *Wuthering Heights*' in *Early Victorian Novelists*, Constable, London.
CLARK, Kenneth (1949) *Landscape into Art*, Murray, London; (1964) *Ruskin Today*, Murray, London; (1969) *Civilization*, B.B.C. and Murray, London.
CLOUGH, Wilson O. (1964) *The Necessary Earth*, Univ. of Texas, Austin, Texas.
COLLINS, William. See Blunden, Edmund.
COLVIN, Brenda (1948) *Land and Landscape* (2nd ed., 1970, consulted), Murray, London.
COOK, E. T. and WEDDERBURN, Alexander (1903–1912), *The Works of Ruskin*, 39 vols., George Allen, London.
COOPER, Anthony Ashley. See Shaftesbury, Third Earl of.
CORNISH, Vaughan (1931) *The Poetic Impression of Natural Scenery*, Sifton Praed, London; (1932) *The Scenery of England*, C.P.R.E., London; (1935) *Scenery and the Sense of Sight*, C.U.P., Cambridge; (1943) *The Beauties of Scenery: a Geographical Survey*, Muller, London.
CRISP, Sir Frank (1924) *Medieval Gardens* (ed. C. C. Paterson), Bodley Head, London.
CROWE, Sylvia (1966) *Forestry in the Landscape*, H.M.S.O., (Forestry Commission Booklet 18), London.
CULLEN, Gordon (1961) *Townscape*, Architectural Press, London.
CUNLIFFE, Mitzi (1969) 'The eye and the mind's heart—the aesthetics of townscape', *J. Town Planning Inst.*, **55**, pp. 162–167.
DAVIES, Gordon L. (1966) 'Early British geomorphology, 1578–1705', *Geog. J.*, **132**, pp. 252–262.
DEWEY, John (1929) *Experience and Nature*, Allen & Unwin, London. (First published (1925) by Open Court Publishing Co., Chicago, etc. Lectures upon the Paul Carus Foundation, ser. 1); (1934) *Art as Experience* (1958 Capricorn edn. consulted), Allen & Unwin, London and New York.
DICKENS, Charles (1881 edn.) *The Works of Charles Dickens*, Chapman & Hall, London.
DILGER, William C. (1962) 'The behaviour of lovebirds', *Scient. Am.*, **206**, pp. 88–98.
DOUGLASS, Robert W. (1969) *Forest Recreation*, Pergamon, Oxford.
DOWNS, James F. (1966) *The Two Worlds of the Washo: an Indian Tribe of California and Nevada*, Holt, Rinehart & Winston, New York.
DOWNS, R. M. (1970) 'Geographical space perception', *Prog. Geog.*, **2**, pp. 65–108.
DYER, John (1761 edn.) *Poems by John Dyer*, Dodsley, London.
EARP, J. R. and HAINS, B. A. (1971) *British Regional Geology, The Welsh Borderland*, (3rd edn.), H.M.S.O., London.
EIBL-EIBESFELDT, I. (1970) *Ethology: the Biology of Behaviour*, Engl. trans. by Erich Klinghammer, Holt, Rinehart & Winston, New York.
ELSTOB, P. (1971) *Hitler's Last Offensive*, Secker & Warburg, London.
EMERSON, Ralph Waldo (1903, Century Edn.) *The Complete Works of Ralph Waldo Emerson*, 12 vols., Houghton Mifflin Co., Boston.
*Encyclopedia Britannica* (1969 edn.), Chicago.
*Environment & Behaviour* (1969 *et seq.*), Sage Publications, Beverly Hills, California.
FALKUS, Hugh. See Tinbergen, N.

FERGUSON, Denzel E. (1967) 'Sun-compass orientation in Anurans', in *Animal Orientation and Navigation* (ed. Robert M. Storm), Oregon State Univ., Corvallis, Oregon.

FINES, K. D. (1968) 'Landscape evaluation: a research project in East Sussex', *Reg. Studies*, **2**, pp. 41–55; (1969) 'Landscape evaluation—a research project in East Sussex: rejoinder to critique by D. M. Brancher', *Reg. Studies*, **3**, p. 219.

FITCH, J. M. (1970) 'Experiential Bases for Aesthetic Decision' in Proshansky *et al.* (1970), pp. 76–84.

FLETCHER, R. (1957) *Instinct in Man* (1968 edn. consulted), Unwin University Books, London.

FRAZER, Sir James G. (1890 and later editions to 1915), *The Golden Bough*, Macmillan, London.

FRIEDLÄNDER, Max J. (1949) *Landscape, Portrait, Still-Life* (trans. from the German by R. F. C. Hull), Cassirer, Oxford.

FRY, Roger (1932) *Characteristics of French Art*, Chatto & Windus, London.

GALERIE MOKUM (1970) *Fifty Years of Dutch Realistic Art*, (Dutch and English), Galerie Mokum, Amsterdam.

GEIKIE, Sir Archibald (1865) *The Scenery of Scotland, Viewed in Connection with its Physical Geology* (3rd edn., 1901, consulted), Macmillan, London.

GILBERT, Edmund W. (1965) *Vaughan Cornish and the Advancement of Knowledge Relating to the Beauty of Scenery in Town and Country*, Oxford Preservation Trust, Oxford.

GILBERT, Josiah (1885) *Landscape in Art before Claude and Salvator*, Murray, London.

GILBERT, W. S. (1876) *Fifty 'Bab' Ballads* (1887 edn. consulted), Routledge, London.

GILLEN, F. J. See Spencer, Baldwin.

GILPIN, Rev. William (1786) *Observations relative chiefly to Picturesque Beauty, made in the year 1772 on several parts of England; particularly the mountains and lakes of Cumberland and Westmoreland*, Blamire, London.

GLACKEN, Clarence J. (1967) *Traces on the Rhodian Shore*, Univ. of California, Berkeley, California.

GOLDSMITH, Oliver (1770) *The Deserted Village*, Facsimile reproduction (1970), The Scolar Press, Menston, Yorkshire.

GOMBRICH, E. H. (1960) *Art and Illusion*, Phaidon Press, London; (1963) *Meditations on a Hobby Horse*, Phaidon Press, London; (1966) *Norm and Form: Studies in the Art of the Renaissance*, Phaidon Press, London.

GOODEY, B. (1971) *Perception of the Environment: an Introduction to the Literature*, Univ. of Birmingham, Birmingham.

GOTTMANN, Jean (1951) *A Geography of Europe*, Harrap, London.

GOUDGE, Elizabeth (1938) *Towers in the Mist*, Duckworth, London.

GOUDIE, Andrew (1972) 'Vaughan Cornish, Geographer', *Inst. Brit. Geographers, Trans.* **55**, pp. 1–16.

GREENE, T. M. (1940) *The Arts and the Art of Criticism*, Princeton U.P., Princeton, New Jersey.

GRIMBLE, Augustus (1901) *Deer-stalking and the Deer Forests of Scotland*, Kegan Paul, London.

HADFIELD, Miles (1969) *A History of British Gardening*, Hamlyn Publishing Group, London. (A revised version of *Gardening in Britain*, 1960, Hutchinson, London.)

HAMERTON, P. G. (1885) *Landscape*, Seeley, London.

HENDY, Sir Philip (1960) *The National Gallery*, (4th edn., 1971, consulted), Thames & Hudson, London.

HEPBURN, Ronald W. (1968) 'Aesthetic appreciation in nature' in Osborn (1968), pp. 49–66.

HIGGINS, J. A. C. (1967) 'Landscape evaluation techniques' in Murray, A. C. (1967), pp. 24–30.

HINDE, Robert A. (1966) *Animal Behaviour: a Synthesis of Ethology and Comparative Psychology*, McGraw-Hill, New York.

HIPPLE, W. J. Jr. (1957) *The Beautiful, the Sublime and the Picturesque in Eighteenth-century British Aesthetic Theory*, Southern Illinois U.P., Carbondale, Illinois.

HOFSTEDE DE GROOT, Cornelis (1908–1927) *A Catalogue Raisonné of the Works of the most Eminent Dutch Painters of the Seventeenth Century*, 8 vols., Macmillan, London.

HOGARTH, William (1753) *The Analysis of Beauty*, Facsimile reprod., Scolar Press, Menston, Yorkshire.

HOSKINS, W. G. (1955) *The Making of the English Landscape*, Hodder & Stoughton, London.

HUGHES, Ted (1957) *The Hawk in the Rain*, Faber, London.

HUSSEY, Christopher (1927) *The Picturesque: Studies in a Point of View*, Putnam, London; (1967) *English Gardens and Landscapes, 1700–1750*, Country Life, London.

HUTCHESON, Francis (1725) *An Inquiry into the Original of our Ideas of Beauty and Virtue*, Darby, London; (1728) *An Essay on the Nature and Conduct of the Passions and Affections*, Knapton, London.

HUTCHINSON, Thomas (Ed.) (1895) *The Poetical Works of Wordsworth*, Frowde, London.

HYAMS, Edward (1971) *Capability Brown and Humphry Repton*, Dent, London.

*Hymns Ancient & Modern* (numerous editions), Clowes, London.

ISAACS, Susan (1933) *Social Development in Young Children*, Routledge, London.

ITTELSON, W. H. See Proshansky *et al.* (1970).

JACKSON, J. B. (1969) '1951–1968 Postscript', *Landscape*, **18**, No. 1, p. 1.

JACKSON, John (1908) *Virgil*, Clarendon, Oxford.

JELLICOE, G. A. (1960, 1966, 1970), *Studies in Landscape Design*, 3 vols., O.U.P., London.

JENNY, Hans (1968), 'The image of soil in landscape art, old and new', *Pontificiae Academiae Scientiarum Scripta Varia: Study week on organic matter and soil fertility*, North-Holland Publishing Co., Amsterdam and Wiley, New York, pp. 947–979.

JOHNS, Ewart (1965) *British Townscapes*, Arnold, London.

JOHNSON, Samuel and CHALMERS, Alexander (1810) *The works of the English poets from Chaucer to Cowper*, 21 vols., J. Johnson, &c., London.

JONES, H. L. (1917) *The geography of Strabo*, Heinemann, London.

JOURDAIN, Margaret (1948) *The Work of William Kent*, Country Life, London.

KATES, Robert (1966/7) 'The pursuit of beauty in the environment', *Landscape*, **16**, No. 2, pp. 21–25.

KIPLING, Rudyard (1902) *Just So Stories* (1930 illus. edn. consulted), Macmillan, London.

KITSON, Michael (1964) *J. M. W. Turner*, Blandford Press, London; (1969) *The Art of Claude Lorrain*, Arts Council, London.

KNIGHT, Richard Payne (1794) *The Landscape* (2nd edn., 1795, also consulted), Bulmer, London.

KRAUSE, Aurel (1885) *The Tlingit Indians, results of a trip to the northwest coast of America and the Bering Straits*, trans. by E. Gunther (1956), Univ. of Washington Press, Seattle.

KROEBER, Karl (1972) '*Tintern Abbey* and *The Cornfield*: Serendipity as a method of intermedia criticism'. *J. Aesthetics Art Crit.*, **XXXI**, pp. 67–77.

LACK, David (1933) 'Habitat selection in birds', *J. Animal Ecol.*, **2**, pp. 239–262.

LANDOW, George P. (1971) *The Aesthetic and Critical Theories of John Ruskin*, Princeton U.P., Princeton, New Jersey.

*Landscape* (1951–   ), Univ. of New Mexico, Santa Fe. See also Jackson (1969), Kates (1966/7), Ridley (1965), Searles (1961/2), Shepard (1961), Stea (1965) and Yi-Fu Tuan (1961 and 1966).

LANEGRAN, David A. (1972) 'The pioneer's view of the frontier as presented in the regional novel *Giants in the Earth*', *Int. Geog. 1972*, Univ. of Toronto Press, Toronto, pp. 350–352.

● LANGER, Susanne K. (1953) *Feeling and Form: a Theory of Art Developed from Philosophy in a New Key*, Routledge & Kegan Paul, London.

LANIER, Sidney. See Young, S. (1947).

LAUDER, Thomas Dick (Ed.) (1842) *Price's Essay on the Picturesque, with an Essay on the Origin of Taste*, Caldwell, Edinburgh. See also Price (1794).

LEE, Terence R. See Race (1972).

LEVI-STRAUSS, Claude (1966) *The Savage Mind*, Eng. trans. by Weidenfeld & Nicolson, London. (*La Pensée Sauvage*, Plon, Paris, 1962).

LINTON, David L. (1968) 'The assessment of scenery as a natural resource', *Scot. Geog. Mag.*, **84**, pp. 219–238.

LORENZ, Konrad Z. (1952) *King Solomon's Ring* (1964 edn. consulted), Methuen, London. (*Er redete mit dem Vieh, den Vögeln und den Fischen*, Borotha-Schoeler, Vienna, 1951).

LOUDON, J. C. (1822) *An Encyclopedia of Gardening* (new edition, 1859, consulted), Longman, London.

LOWENTHAL, D. (Ed.) (1967) *Environmental Perception and Behaviour*, Univ. of Chicago Press, Chicago.

LOWENTHAL, D. and PRINCE, H. C. (1964) 'The English Landscape', *Geog. Rev.*, **54**, pp. 309–346; (1965) 'English landscape tastes', *Geog. Rev.*, **55**, pp. 186–222.

LYNCH, K. See Appleyard, D. *et al.* (1964).

MACFADYEN, A. (1957) *Animal Ecology: Aims and Methods* (2nd edn., 1963, consulted), Pitman, London.

MALINS, Edward (1966) *English Landscaping and Literature, 1660–1840*, O.U.P., London.

MANNING, Aubrey (1967) *An Introduction to Animal Behaviour* (2nd edn., 1972, consulted), Arnold, London.

MARX, Leo (1964) *The Machine in the Garden: Technology and the Pastoral Ideal in America*, O.U.P., New York.

MATLEY, C. A. and WILSON, T. S. (1946) 'The Harlech Dome, north of the Barmouth estuary', *Quart. J. Geol. Soc.*, **102**, pp. 1–40.

MEITZEN, August (1895) *Siedelung und Agrarwesen der Westgermanen und Ostgermanen, der Kelten, Römer, Finnen und Slawen*, Berlin.

MELLY, George (1973) 'Obsession on the Plains', *The Observer*, 11th March.

MILTON, John, 'L'Allegro', *The Poetical Works of John Milton* (Ed. D. Masson) (1893), Macmillan, London.

MONKHOUSE, F. J. (1965) *A Dictionary of Geography*, Arnold, London.

MORRIS, Desmond (1967) *The Naked Ape*, Cape, London.

MORRIS, Johnny (1973) *Follow the Rhine*, Television broadcast script, BBC2, 28 June.

MUNRO, Thomas (1956) *Art Education: its Philosophy and Psychology*, Liberal Arts Press, New York.

MURRAY, A. C. (Ed.) (1967) *Symposium on Methods of Landscape Analysis*, Landscape Research Group, London.

MURRAY, Peter and MURRAY, Linda (1959) *A Dictionary of Art and Artists*, (1968 edn. consulted), Penguin, Harmondsworth, Middx.

MURRY, John Middleton (1928) *Poems of Anne, Countess of Winchilsea*, selected and with an introductory essay by John Middleton Murry, Cape, London.

MYER, J. R. See Appleyard, D. *et al.* (1964).

NASH, Roderick (1967) *Wilderness and the American Mind*, Yale U.P., New Haven, Connecticut.

NASR, Seyyed Hossein (1968) *The Encounter of Man and Nature: the Spiritual Crisis of Modern Man*, Allen & Unwin, London.

NOYES, Russell (1968) *Wordsworth and the Art of Landscape*, Indiana U.P., Bloomington, Indiana.

OGDEN, H. V. S. and OGDEN, M. S. (1955) *English Taste in Landscape in the Seventeenth Century*, Univ. of Michigan Press, Ann Arbor.

OSBORN, Harold (Ed.) (1968) *Aesthetics in the Modern World*, Thames & Hudson, London.

PATMORE, J. A. (1970) *Land and Leisure*, David & Charles, Newton Abbot.

PEVSNER, Nikolaus (1958) *Shropshire* (*The Buildings of England*), Penguin, Harmondsworth, Middlesex.

PICKFORD, R. W. (1972) *Psychology and Visual Aesthetics*, Hutchinson, London.

PITTY, Alistair F. (1971) *Introduction to Geomorphology*, Methuen, London.

PLAYFAIR, John (1802) *Illustrations of the Huttonian Theory of the Earth*, Edinburgh.

POPE, Alexander. See Bowles (1806).

PRICE, Uvedale (1794) *An Essay on the Picturesque, as Compared with the Sublime and the Beautiful; and on the Use of Studying Pictures, for the Purpose of Improving Real Landscape*, Robson, London. See also Lauder (1842).

PRINCE, Hugh (1971) 'Real, imagined and abstract worlds of the past', *Prog. Geog.*, **3**, pp. 1–86; See also Lowenthal and Prince (1964 and 1965).

PROSHANSKY, H. M., ITTELSON, W. H. and RIVLIN, L. G. (1970) *Environmental Psychology: Man and his Physical Setting*, Holt, Rinehart and Winston, New York.

RACE, Sally (1972) 'Report on "Psychological aspects of environmental problems" by Terence R. Lee', *Landscape Design*, No. 98 (May 1972), p. 15.

REPTON, Humphry (1803) *Observations on the Theory and Practice of Landscape Gardening*, Taylor, London.

RICARD, Mathieu (1969) *The Mystery of Animal Migration*, Engl. trans. by Peter J. Whitehead, Constable, London.

• RICHMOND, L. (1928) *The Art of Landscape Painting*, Pitman, London.

RIDLEY, Robert B. (1965) 'Architecture and a sense of wonder', *Landscape*, **15**, No. 1, pp. 20–24.

RIVLIN, L. G. See Proshansky *et al.* (1970).

RÖLVAAG, O. E. (1927) *Giants in the Earth*, trans. from the Norwegian version (1924–5) by Lincoln Colcord and the author, Harper & Bros., New York (A. L. Burt, 1929, edn. consulted).

RÖTHLISBERGER, Marcel (1961) *Claude Lorrain: the Paintings*, 2 vols., Zwemmer, London.

RUSKIN, John, *Modern Painters*. See Cook and Wedderburn (1903–1912), vols. III–VII; *Lectures on Landscape*. See Cook and Wedderburn (1903–1912), vol. XXII.

ST. JOSEPH, J. K. S. See Beresford and St. Joseph (1958).

SALVESON, Christopher (1965) *The Landscape of Memory*, Arnold, London.

SAUER, F. (1957) '*Die Sternenorientierung nachtlich ziehender Grasmücken*', *Z. Tierpsychologie*, **14**, pp. 29–70.

SCOTT, J. P. (1958) *Animal Behaviour*, Univ. of Chicago Press, Chicago.

SEARLES, Harold F. (1961/2) 'The role of nonhuman environment', *Landscape*, **11**, No. 2, pp. 31–34.

SERT, J. L. See Sweeney (1960).

SEYYED HOSSEIN NASR. See Nasr (1968).

SHACKLETON, Margaret (1934) *Europe: a Regional Geography* (3rd edn., 1939, consulted), Longmans Green, London.

SHAFTESBURY, The Third Earl of (Anthony Ashley Cooper) (1711) *Characteristics of Men, Manners, Opinions, Times*, 3 vols. (1749 edn. consulted).

SHARP, Thomas (1946) *The Anatomy of the Village*, Penguin, Harmondsworth, Middlesex.

SHEFFIELD, John, Duke of Buckinghamshire, 'Essay on poetry'. See Johnson and Chalmers (1810), vol. X, pp. 91–94.

SHEPARD, Paul, Jr. (1961) 'The cross valley syndrome', *Landscape*, **10**, No. 3, pp. 4–8.

SHEPPARD, June A. (1966) 'Vernacular buildings in England and Wales: a survey of recent work by architects, archaeologists and social historians', *Inst. Brit. Geographers, Trans. & Papers*, **40**, pp. 21–37.

SISSONS, J. B. (1967) *The Evolution of Scottish Scenery*, Oliver & Boyd, Edinburgh.

SITTE, Camillo (1965 edn.) 'Greenery within the city', printed as Appendix I in the translation by C. R. and C. C. Collins of *City Planning According to Artistic Principles* by Camillo Sitte (1889). Phaidon, London, and Random House, New York.

SPECTORSKY, A. C. (1955) *The Exurbanites*, Lippincott, Philadelphia.

SPENCER, Baldwin and GILLEN, F. J. (1899) *The Native Tribes of Central Australia*, Macmillan, London.

SPENSER, Edmund, *The Faery Queene* (1758 edn. consulted), Tonson, London.

STAMP, Sir L. Dudley (1946) *Britain's Structure and Scenery*, Collins, London.

STEA, David (1965) 'Space, territory and human movements', *Landscape*, **15**, No. 1, pp. 13–16.

STECHOW, Wolfgang (1966) *Dutch Landscape Painting of the Seventeenth Century*, Phaidon, London.

STEEL, R. W. (1967) 'Geography at the University of Liverpool', in Steel, R. W. and Lawton, R., *Liverpool Essays in Geography, a Jubilee Collection*, Longmans, London.

STOLNITZ, M. J. (1960) *Aesthetics and the Philosophy of Art Criticism: a Critical Introduction*, Houghton Mifflin, Boston.

STRABO. See Jones, H. L.

STROUD, Dorothy (1950) *Capability Brown*, Country Life, London; (1962) *Humphry Repton*, Country Life, London.

SWEENEY, J. J. and SERT, J. L. (1960) *Antoní Gaudí*, Architectural Press, London.

TAMURA, Tsuyoshi (1936) *Art of the Landscape Garden in Japan*, Kokusai Bunka Shinkokai, Tokyo.

TATARKIEWICZ, Wladyslaw (1972) 'The great theory of beauty and its decline', *J. Aesthet. Art Crit.*, **XXXI**, pp. 165–180.

THOMPSON, Colin (n.d.) *Guide to the National Gallery of Scotland*, Edinburgh.

THORPE, W. H. (1956) 'The language of birds', *Scient. Am.* (Oct. 1956), pp. 2–6.

TINBERGEN, N. (1951) *The Study of Instinct* (1969 edn. consulted), Clarendon, Oxford.

TINBERGEN, N. and FALKUS, H. (1970) *Signals for Survival*, Clarendon, Oxford.

TOLKIEN, J. R. R. (1937) *The Hobbit* (3rd edn., 1966, consulted), Allen & Unwin, London.

TRUEMAN, A. E. (1938) *The Scenery of England and Wales*, Gollancz, London. Later (1949) republished as Trueman, Sir Arthur, *Geology and Scenery in England and Wales*, Penguin, Harmondsworth, Middlesex.

VANCE, James E. (1972) 'California and the search for the Ideal', *Ann. Assoc. Am. Geographers*, **62**, pp. 185–210.

VAN ZANDT, Roland (1949) 'The Scotch School of aesthetic theory and the natural description of the Oregon Trail', *SW J.*, **IV**; (1966) *The Catskill Mountain House*, Rutgers U.P., New Brunswick, New Jersey.

VIRGIL, *The Eclogues*. See Jackson, John (1908).

WAINWRIGHT, A. (n.d.) *A Third Lakeland Sketchbook*, Marshall, Kentmere.

278

WALPOLE, Hugh (1911) *Mr. Perrin and Mr. Traill* (1919 edn. consulted), Macmillan, London.

WATSON, J. R. (1970) *Picturesque Landscape and English Romantic Poetry*, Hutchinson, London.

WEBB, Mary (1924) *Precious Bane*, (1928 edn. consulted), Cape, London.

WEDDERBURN, Alexander. See Cook and Wedderburn (1903–1912).

WESLING, Donald (1970) *Wordsworth and the Adequacy of Landscape*, Routledge & Kegan Paul, London.

WILSON, T. S. See Matley and Wilson (1946).

WINCHILSEA, Anne Finch, Countess of. See Murry (1928).

WOOD, L. J. (1970) 'Perception studies in geography', *Inst. Brit. Geographers, Trans. & Papers*, No. 50, pp. 129–142.

WORDSWORTH, Dorothy (1874, posth.) *Recollections of a tour made in Scotland, A.D. 1803* (Ed. J. C. Shairp), (3rd edn., 1894, consulted), Douglas, Edinburgh.

WORDSWORTH, William, *Elegaic stanzas, suggested by a picture of Peele Castle, in a storm, painted by Sir George Beaumont.* See Hutchinson (1895), pp. 578–579; *Nutting.* See Hutchinson (1895), pp. 185–186; *The Prelude.* See Hutchinson (1895), pp. 631–752; *Seven poems on the naming of places.* See Hutchinson (1895), pp. 146–152.

WRIGHT, J. K. (1947) '*Terrae incognitae*: the place of imagination in geography', *Ann. Assoc. Am. Geographers*, **37**, pp. 1–15.

YI-FU TUAN (1961) 'Topophilia: or sudden encounter with landscape', *Landscape*, **11**, No. 1, pp. 29–32; (1966) 'Man and nature', *Landscape*, **15**, No. 3, pp. 30–36; (1967) 'Attitudes towards environment: themes and approaches', in Lowenthal (1967), pp. 4–17.

YOUNG, Andrew (1967) *The new Poly-Olbion*, Hart-Davis, London.

YOUNG, Stark (1947) *Selected poems of Sidney Lanier*, Scribner, London and New York.

YOUNGHUSBAND, Sir Francis (1920) 'Natural beauty and geographic science', *Geog. J.*, **LVI**, pp. 1–13.

# Index

Certain words, such as 'aesthetics', 'landscape', etc., occur so frequently that the value of the index would be impaired if every mention were recorded. Only the more important references to such words or topics are given.